FREE APPROPRIATE PUBLIC EDUCATION

The Law and Children with Disabilities

Third Edition

H. Rutherford Turnbull III
The University of Kansas

LOVE PUBLISHING COMPANY
Denver, Colorado 80222

*To Jay, for whom these rights have meant
so much;
Amy and Kate, who teach and learn
from Jay;
Ann, our best teacher; and
Ruth W. Turnbull, gone but everlasting.*

Library of Congress Catalog Card Number 89-84214

Copyright © 1990 Love Publishing Company
Printed in the U.S.A.
ISBN 0-89108-211-5

CONTENTS

4 Testing, Classification, and Placement   81

8 Parent Participation and Shared Decision Making

III ENFORCING THE LAW

9 Case Law Techniques

PREFACE

The goal of American education is to value each child as equally an individual and entitled to equal opportunity of development of his own capacities, be they large or small in range. ... Each has needs of his own as significant to him as those of others are to them. The very fact of natural and psychological inequality is all the more reason for establishment by law of equality of opportunity, since otherwise the former becomes a means of oppression of the less gifted.

—*Thomas Dewey*

Dewey's sentiments have a familiar ring to those of us who have been working to establish the rights of children with disabilities to a free appropriate education. He admonishes us to value all individuals, whomever and whatever they are, recognize their needs and satisfy them, establish equal educational opportunity by law, and change a system that oppresses some because of their inequalities. How surprised Dewey would be to learn that his views have become so widely accepted!

This book tells the story of the initial rejection and ultimate acceptance of those ideas. It also shows how law adopts these ideas and enacts them as the idea of equal educational opportunities for children with disabilities. Its essential teaching is legal. Its essential message is moral: A person who is less able is not less worthy.

In the mid-1980s, the public schools—the governmental system that casts the widest net and exercises the greatest influence over us (next to the tax and revenue departments)—have finally begun to come to terms with educating all these children. How the nation's public schools have dealt with the challenge and opportunity of educating these children in the past, and how they must do so under present law, is this book's initial focus.

The book next analyzes in detail the six principles of special education law: (1) zero reject, or the right of every child to be included in a free appropriate publicly supported educational system; (2) nondiscriminatory classification, or the right to be fairly evaluated so that correct educational programs and placement can be achieved; (3) individualized and appropriate education, so that an education can be meaningful; (4) least restrictive placement, so the child may associate with nondisabled students to the maximum extent appropriate to his or her needs; (5) due process, so the child and child advocates may have an opportunity to challenge any aspect of education; and (6) parent participation, so the child's family may be involved in what happens in school.

Recognizing that these six principles generate widespread resistance, the last part of the book presents the most common objections to these principles. It also attempts to answer those objections on two major grounds: (1) the beliefs that support the principles, and (2) the system of values that undergird the principles.

Now, a word or two about the terminology used in this book. Federal special education laws use the terms *handicapped* and *handicapped children*—for example, the Education for The Handicapped Act and its important amendment, the Education for All Handicapped Children Act. I do not prefer that usage for two reasons. First, it emphasizes the characteristic of the child—namely, the disability—which society turns into a handicap by not accommodating to it, thereby relegating the child to secondary status as a student and person. Second, the collective noun form (the handicapped) implies that all children with disabilities are alike and not individuals.

I prefer "children with disabilities," with a substitution of "students" or "persons/people" for "children" and a substitution of "mental retardation" or "learning disabilities" (or other specific disability) for "disabilities" or "disabled" when the specific is preferable to the general. To resolve the problem of being consistent with federal laws and adhering to my own preferences, I sometimes use the federal term and sometimes my own. Undoubtedly, a change in federal terminology is desirable.

The first version of this book (written in 1978) focused on the new federal laws, the developments that led to them, and the implications of those laws for schools, students and parents, and institutions of higher education. Since then, the literature of special education has been flooded with research and commentary on implementation of the laws. Therefore, it does not seem appropriate to preserve the implementation focus of the first edition in the second version or in this one.

Moreover, since 1978 there have been significant developments in interpretation of the federal law. Literally hundreds of judgments have been entered concerning the meaning of "free appropriate public education." Since the first book emphasized developments leading up to the federal laws and the content of those laws, it seems particularly appropriate for subsequent editions to analyze and comment on the most important judgments and their effects.

For these two reasons only, this book is not co-authored by the original authors but is authored by only one of them, H.R. Turnbull. Ann Turnbull is a special educator whose contributions to the first book were principally with respect to implications of the law. Since that focus is not present in this or the previous edition, she is not shown as a co-author. Nonetheless, she has contributed to the development of this book in important professional and personal ways, and the present author—her colleague and husband—gratefully acknowledges all those contributions.

In addition, the author is extraordinarily appreciative of Dorothy Johanning and Judith A. Roesler, a law student who has been most helpful on technical matters. Both are exceptionally talented members of the staff of The University of Kansas. Through their professional skills and buoyant personalities, they have immensely aided in the production of this book. Finally, the many students at The University of Kansas who read and responded to the earlier book and helped sharpen it are entitled to—and hereby receive—my special thanks.

In the end, however, the greatest appreciation is owed to those pioneering parents and advocates who initiated the civil rights movement in education by challenging racial segregation; to the equally pioneering and risk-taking parents and professionals who started the revolution that we now call the right-to-education movement; to the members of Congress who brought the federal government into the lives of children with disabilities and their parents; and to the children who are disabled and who, through their disabilities, character, and sheer pluck, contribute so positively to the lives of their teachers, families, and friends.

H.R.T. III

SECTION I
Introduction to the Law

1
Introduction to the American Legal System

FEDERALISM

The law serves many purposes, among them ordering the public affairs of individuals and their governments and resolving disputes between them. These seemingly simple purposes are accomplished through an intricate network. To explain the workings of that network, we will use some familiar images.

Public law can be thought of in terms of three parallel ladders—descending rungs of parallel authority affecting the relationships between individuals and their governments and between various levels of government. At the top of the federal ladder is the United States Constitution; in the middle are laws enacted by Congress pursuant to constitutional authority; and on the bottom are regulations issued by federal agencies pursuant to congressional authority. Next to this ladder stands one representing the state governments, and it has similar rungs of parallel authority: state constitutions, state statutes, and state agency regulations. Finally, next to the state ladder is the local ladder with its three rungs: the charters of local governments, local ordinances, and local regulations.

The whole picture shows that the highest source of law in each "ladder" is the fundamental governing document: the federal Constitution, the state constitution, and the local charter. Federal, state, and local statutes are next in line, followed by federal, state, and local agency regulations:

Federal	*State*	*Local*
Constitution	Constitution	Charter
Statutes	Statutes	Ordinances
Regulations	Regulations	Regulations

This system of parallel governments (federal, state, and local) is known as the *federal system;* as a form of government, it is known as *federalism.*

Two major principles are involved in the form of government known as federalism. First, there is the sharing of responsibility and power between the federal, state, and local governments. As pointed out later in this chapter, the responsibility for and power over the education of children with disabilities is shared between those governments. Traditionally, local and state school boards (or other governing bodies) had the greatest responsiblity and power. Recently, however, responsibility and power have been allocated in greater part to the federal government. This shift is the result of the court cases that began with the desegregation cases in 1954, and it gathered force with two cases decided in 1972 (as pointed out later in this chapter and in chapter 2.) It also is the result of legislation—the Education of the Handicapped Act, which is reviewed in detail later in this book.

Second, there is the supremacy of federal constitutional and statutory law. Early in the history of this country, the Supreme Court, in *Marbury v. Madison,* made it clear that the Constitution of the United States and laws passed by Congress to implement the Constitution are the supreme law of the land. This means that state and local school boards must comply with federal law if, among other things, they receive federal funds (as they do when they educate children who have disabilities with money allocated to them under the Education of the Handicapped Act) or if their laws are in conflict with federal constitutional law or federal statutes. Clearly, the supremacy doctrine has permitted the federal role in the education of children with disabilities.

LAWMAKERS: WHO MAKES THE LAW?

For each source of law there is a lawmaker—a group of persons who make the law. For the federal Constitution and its amendments the initial lawmakers were the delegates to the constitutional convention and subsequently the legislatures of the various states that acted to ratify constitutional amendments (other than the first 10, the Bill of Rights, which was drafted by delegates themselves). The delegates were representatives of the franchised citizens of the states. Thus, the source of the federal Constitution was the citizenry of the United States. This is generally true, too, with respect to the constitutions of states and charters of local governments.

This is not true, however, of statutory law. In that case, the lawmaker is not the citizenry but, rather, its elected representatives serving in Congress or in state legislatures. The Congress and the legislatures may not enact laws that violate provisions of the federal Constitution or the constitution of the state in whose legislature they serve. All federal and state laws are subject to "testing" to determine if they are "constitutional" under the federal Constitution and the applicable state constitution because the federal Constitution provides that the Constitution shall be the supreme law of the land, protecting all citizens of the United States and regulating all state and local governments. Also, the fundamental law of each state is the local constitution, and no state law or state agency regulation has the effect of law unless authority for it can be found in the state constitution. There is, then, a lawmaker for each source of law, a fundamental law that has greater authority than any other, and a hierarchy of law in each of the three governments.

Although it may appear that all lawmakers are alike (that there are no basic differences between legislatures and legislators and regulations and regulators), there is a fundamental difference. Statutes are enacted by legislatures whose members are elected by the franchised citizens. Regulations are made by regulatory agencies whose staffs are not elected but, rather, are appointed by the legislatures or with the consent of the legislature or by the chief of the executive branch for which the person works. Agency regulations must be based on authority given to them by the legislatures. The regulators are both executives—persons who execute or carry out the legislature's statutes—and legislators—in the limited sense that they write regulations designed to carry out legislation.

We obviously have a complex system for enacting and carrying out law. This is especially true in the area of education for children with disabilities (called *handicapped children* in federal law). The system can be illustrated as follows:

1. *Constitutional law*
   Federal Constitution (especially Fifth and Fourteenth Amendments)
   State constitution (especially provisions about education)
   Local charter (especially provisions creating schools or school boards)
2. *Legislature (legislative body)*
   Congress (e.g., the Education of the Handicapped Act)
   State (e.g., equal educational opportunities legislation)
   Local (e.g., school board policies establishing programs for children)
3. *Regulations (executive agency)*
   Federal (Special Education Programs, Office of Special Education and Rehabilitative Services)
   State (e.g., Illinois Office of Education, Division for Exceptional Children; or North Carolina State Board of Education, Department of Public Instruction, Division of Exceptional Children)
   Local (e.g., director of pupil services or coordinator of special education)

CASE LAW AND THE COURTS

One important type of law and lawmaker has not yet been identified: case law (judicial decisions) and the courts. When the delegates to federal and state constitutional conventions wrote those constitutions, they created three branches of government—legislative, executive, and judicial. The function of the legislature is to make law, and the executive is to carry it out; the function of the judiciary is to resolve disputes between citizens or between a citizen and his or her government. Courts do this by applying law to a given set of facts and interpreting the meaning of the law in that factual context. It is their unique function to say what the Constitution or a federal statute or regulation means in a given case, to issue a decision setting forth the facts that underlie their interpretation, and to enter an order commanding the parties in the case (or other courts, if the case is on appeal) to take certain action.

Within the overall federal system are three parallel systems: trial courts, U.S. circuit courts of appeals, and the U.S. Supreme Court (the court of last resort). State and local systems also consist of trial courts, appellate (appeals) courts, and a court of last resort. It is a matter of great complexity why a case may be tried in one court, appealed or reviewed by another, and finally disposed of by yet another. We do not need to enter that thicket. A brief discussion of court jurisdictions will serve our purpose.

The terms used to describe trial and appellate courts vary from state to state and sometimes are different from the terms that describe the United States courts. This makes it difficult from time to time to understand precisely which court is deciding a case. For example, United States trial courts are called district courts, but trial courts in the state system are called circuit courts, district courts, or even supreme courts. Likewise, the United States appellate courts are called circuit courts or circuit courts of appeals, with the country divided into 11 circuits (regions) over which the appeals courts have jurisdiction. In some states the appeals courts consist of intermediate courts of appeals, together with courts of final appeals. Other states have no intermediate courts of appeals, only courts of final appeals. And states use different terms to describe the intermediate courts and courts of final appeals.

The U.S. Supreme Court is the court of last resort for all cases, whether from the state court system or from the federal courts, and its decisions are binding throughout the United States. The U.S. circuit courts of appeals have appellate power over cases decided in the trial courts in their circuits. Their decisions are binding throughout the circuit but may be only persuasive, not binding, in other circuits and in all district courts. The U.S. district courts are the trial courts in their respective districts; their decisions are generally binding in the district only (not throughout the appellate circuit in which they are located) and may be only persuasive, but not binding, on circuit courts and other district courts.

The state court systems are parallel to the United States court system. Each state has a court of final appeals or last resort, whose decisions are binding throughout the state. The diagram on the following page illustrates the relationships between the courts in a federal system.

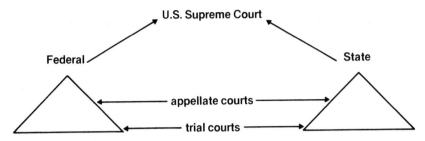

Note that decisions may be appealed to the U.S. Supreme Court from the U.S. circuit courts of appeals and from the court of final appeals (or last resort) of the states. Again, it is a matter of great complexity as to when a case may be taken to the U.S. Supreme Court. Several special education cases have gone to the U.S. Supreme Court (the *Rowley* and *Tatro* cases, discussed in chapter 5, and the *Smith* case, discussed in chapter 8) from the U.S. circuit courts of appeals. No special education cases have gone to the U.S. Supreme Court from the state courts of final appeals. But in the *Brown* case, discussed next, one case went to the U.S. Supreme Court from the Delaware court of final appeals.

BROWN v. BOARD OF EDUCATION

In the field of education law, the following diagram is well reflected by the original school desegregation case, *Brown v. Board of Education*. *Brown* * was not one case, but four that were consolidated and heard as one by the U.S. Supreme Court. Three of the cases were on appeal from federal district courts (the appeals went directly to the Supreme Court, bypassing the circuit courts of appeals, because, under the Federal Rules of Civil Procedure, a federal constitutional issue was an indispensable element of the case). One was on appeal from a state appellate court after having been heard first in a state trial court. Thus, *Brown* can be illustrated as follows:

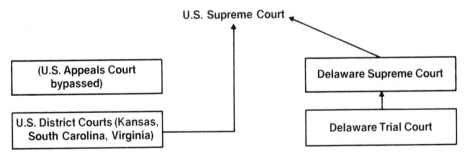

*Typically, cases are given a shortened name, usually the name of the appealing party, for easy reference in discussions. The name—in this case, *Brown*—is italicized to indicate the case, not the person being discussed.

Aside from the structural (functional) aspects of the case, *Brown* was a landmark because it had an impact on so many aspects of educational law and procedure:

1. *Brown* illustrates the principle that the federal Constitution, as interpreted by the U.S. Supreme Court, is the supreme law of the land, is binding on all federal, state, and local governments, and is the precedent that must be followed by all federal and state courts in subsequent similar cases.

2. *Brown* is a nearly perfect example of one of the major lessons of this book: All educational issues (such as the educational rights of handicapped students) are essentially political policy and social issues cast in the guise of constitutional litigation (should handicapped students be educated and, if so, how and by whom?) and, because they are presented in the garments of the law, ultimately are resolved by the courts.

3. *Brown* also demonstrates that the truly difficult educational issues are fought on various civil rights battlefields. Just as *Brown* was the first case on the battlefield of racial desegregation of schools, it was the seed that gave birth to other civil rights battles and to grounds for successful challenges to governmental discrimination against certain persons because of their unalterable personal characteristics (such as race and sex). *Brown* gave rise to the *right-to-education* cases, and they in turn helped establish other rights for handicapped persons. The point—so obvious, but so important—is that judicial resolution of educational issues on constitutional grounds becomes precedent for judicial resolution of related civil rights issues on similar constitutional grounds.

4. *Brown* gave immense comfort and support to civil rights activists, legitimizing their legal arguments and furnishing them with a powerful tool for persuading legislatures, particularly Congress, to enact antidiscrimination legislation. Case law frequently is the underpinning of legislation, and federal cases and legislation frequently precede state case law and legislation. Nowhere has this been more true than in establishing the rights of handicapped pupils to an education.

5. *Brown* caused a fundamental change in the federal system. As precedent for other federal school desegregation cases and as the legal foundation for federal school and other civil rights legislation, *Brown* heralded the entry of the federal government into public education in the United States. Thus, it made significant inroads into an area that had been reserved almost wholly by states and local governments as their province. Over the long run, its effect has been to shift the balance of the federal system heavily toward the side of the federal government. Right-to-education cases and legislation also have shown us that the areas of state and local autonomy in education are quickly diminishing. According to current interpretation, it is questionable if there is any such thing as a "purely local" concern in education. Are all educational concerns truly national, requiring national leadership in the form of case law precedents and legislation enacted at the federal level? This surely is the conclusion that has been reached in the right-to-education movement.

6. In *Brown* it was proven that although the U.S. Constitution never once refers to a public education, its principles of equal protection and due process under the Fifth and Fourteenth Amendments have a significant effect on public education. Nowhere is this fact clearer than in the right-to-education cases. This is significant because, as noted, the federal Constitution does not guarantee the right to an education. State constitutions do guarantee it. But if a state denies (as many had) an education to some students, usually those with disabilities, but provides it to others, the state violates the equal protection doctrine of the federal Constitution and, depending on the provisions of the state constitution, its own constitution as well. The essential point of *Brown,* however, is that the states were violating the *equal protection clause* of the federal Constitution. Chapter 3 discusses this point in detail.

7. *Brown* illustrates one kind of lawsuit—the *civil action*—that is typical of litigation between citizens and their governments. This type of suit is brought by a citizen who alleges that a government or a governmental official denied him or her rights or benefits to which the person is entitled under the law (constitution, statutes, or regulations). In this case, the plaintiff, Brown, sued the defendant, the Topeka Board of Education. In two of the consolidated cases, other citizens sued governmental officials who represented school agencies. A civil action is typical of the right-to-education cases. Criminal actions—in which the state prosecutes a person accused of a crime—are alien to education law.

8. *Brown* is almost ideal for teaching someone how to read a case and how cases are decided, particularly in the right-to-education area. If "handicapped" is substituted for "Negro" and "nonhandicapped" for "white" wherever those words appear in *Brown,* it is fairly easy to understand why *Brown* is important to education of the handicapped and how the Fourteenth Amendment became the constitutional basis for the rights of the handicapped to be educated. Appendix A gives excerpts from the U.S. Supreme Court opinion on *Brown.*

  a. What are the *controlling* (or *dispositive)* facts of the case? Blacks are denied admission to schools attended by whites under laws requiring or permitting segregation according to race, and racial segregation in public education is inherently damaging to the educational opportunities of black children.
  b. What are the *allegations?* The facts constitute a denial of equal protection of law as guaranteed by the Fourteenth Amendment because segregated public schools are not and cannot be made equal, and the "separate but equal" doctrine should be set aside.
  c. What are the *issues of law* the Court must resolve? The Court must determine whether the separate but equal doctrine applies to public education and whether segregation, under that doctrine, violates the equal protection clause.
  d. What is the Court's *holding* (answer to the issue)? Segregation solely on the basis of race in the public schools violates equal protection and denies minority (black) children an equal educational opportunity.
  e. What is the Court's *reasoning?* Equal educational opportunities are denied when, in light of (1) the importance of education, (2) the stigmatizing effects of racial segregation, and (3) the detrimental consequences of racial segregation on the education of those against whom segregation is practiced, a state segregates by race.
  f. What is the Court's *order?* The cases are to be argued again before the

Court, and the argument should focus on the nature of the remedy that the Court should order.

g. What is the *principle* of the case? State action in segregating the races in public education violates equal protection, and, by extension, any state-required or state-sanctioned racial segregation is unconstitutional. Ultimately, any state-required or state-sanctioned segregation solely because of a person's unalterable characteristic (race or handicap) is usually unconstitutional.

h. What are the *implications* of the case? They are massive, and will be discussed throughout this book.

i. What is the *public policy* in the case? State-created stigma or badges of inferiority based on race (or other characteristics, such as handicaps) are constitutionally intolerable because they mean that the state acts invidiously (i.e., discriminatorily, by denying equal opportunities) with respect to persons who have certain traits. In brief, invidious (discriminatory) action is unconstitutional.

j. Whose *interests* are at issue? The interests or *claims* of blacks to an equal educational opportunity are at issue.

k. Finally, what *functions* of government are at issue? At issue are the functions of education—namely, cultural assimilation, preparation for participation in the political process, and training so that economic opportunities might become available. Given the interests, the functions could not be parceled out or denied solely according to race.

Brown is worth an extended discussion here because it speaks directly to public schools, special education, and handicapped children. There are undeniable similarities between the *Brown* plaintiffs and children with disabilities: Both can prove they have been denied equal educational opportunities; both allege an unconstitutional denial and base their arguments on equal protection principles; both challenge separateness in education; both find comfort in the holding of *Brown* and the right-to-education cases concerning denials of equality; both are strengthened by the reasoning that relies on concepts of stigma and detrimental educational consequences; both successfully advance a public policy against invidious state action; both have similar interests in obtaining an education; and both lay claim to the functions of the schools to meaningfully educate all students.

2
Introduction to Law and Free Appropriate Public Education

EGALITARIANISM AND NORMALIZATION

A major legal development in this decade has been the extension of the principle of egalitarianism to people with disabilities. This principle says that all persons, however unequal they may be in terms of their abilities, should be treated equally by being granted equal opportunities. Many professionals, including educators, have argued for egalitarianism in the treatment of disabled citizens. Their arguments are couched in terms of *normalization* or *social role valorization,* a term given by Wolf Wolfensberger,[1] one of the originators of the normalization principle, to clarify the intent of normalization.

Normalization stands for the proposition that handicapped persons should live and be treated like nonhandicapped persons as much as possible and that their differences from nonhandicapped people can be reduced by minimizing the degree to which they are treated different from nonhandicapped people. Social role valorization means that people with disabilities should be given opportunities, including education or special education, to have socially valued roles. Those roles include being students (and thus being included in schools), associating in all aspects of life with people who do not have disabilities, and having real jobs for real pay. Like normalization, social role valorization seeks to minimize the differences between how people with disabilities are viewed and treated by those who do not have disabilities. One step in minimizing those differences is to acknowledge that handicapped persons do, in fact, have an equal right to an education.

With the foundation of a political ideology (egalitarianism) and a human-service ideology (normalization), it became feasible and desirable to extend those ideologies into the law and thereby to ensure that they had the force of law. This extension of ideologies—and their combination with a legal doctrine—occurred through the doctrine of equal protection and the refinements that began with *Brown*.

EQUAL PROTECTION: JUDICIAL PRECEDENTS

In the eyes of the law, egalitarianism invokes the concept of equal protection and gives rise to the argument that limiting the civil liberties of disabled students violates their constitutional rights to equal protection under the Fourteenth Amendment because there is no rational reason for imposing special burdens or limitations on them. This argument also asserts that the educational opportunities granted to nonhandicapped pupils are constitutionally required to be granted to handicapped pupils.

"Equal protection of the laws" is such a simple phrase, but it is by no means as simple to understand and apply as one might think. As chapter 3 shows, simplicity in interpretation and application is hardly the case when the educational rights of disabled students are involved. Long before those rights were affirmed under the doctrine of equal protection, however, other disadvantaged persons were successfully arguing that their rights had been infringed upon unconstitutionally. Establishment of their rights was the indispensable foundation for establishing the educational rights of students with disabilities.

The high-water marks made by the equal protection doctrine on the shore where the disadvantaged waited can be delineated by looking first to *Brown* (see chapter 1) and its progeny—the many cases that held that equal educational opportunities may not be predicated (granted or limited) upon race. Under the equal protection doctrine, a person's financial status also cannot be used as a basis for denying benefits to him or her. For example, the Supreme Court has held that the right to vote,[2] ensured access to court to settle disputes with others,[3] and entitlement to financial assistance from a state a person has the right to move into[4] are rights that may not be denied to those who cannot afford them. Equal protection, the Court said, requires that the poor be treated as though they were not poor; they must have free access to the franchise, to courts, and to interstate movement.

Other disadvantaging characteristics have been added to those of race and poverty. The fact that a person is illegitimate,[5] an alcoholic,[6] a narcotics user,[7] a convict,[8] or a female[9] has been held by the Court to be improper grounds upon which to base legislation if the result of the legislation is to discriminate against such persons but not against others in similar circumstances. Chapter 3 discusses more fully the equal protection doctrine and its application to people who are disabled.

The point here is to highlight a series of cases that indicate a strong egalitarian movement—a movement that, despite recent cases, furnished a solid foundation for extending the concepts of egalitarianism and equal protection to people with disabilities. This line of cases did more than provide precedents that were adapted and tailored to remedy unhappy conditions the public schools were imposing on disabled children. It also, and perhaps just as significantly, made law reformers realize that they should—and could successfully—move from other civil rights battlefields to the school grounds and work to extend the equal protection doctrine to children with disabilities.

THE HISTORY OF FEDERAL LEGISLATION: STATUTORY PRELUDES TO THE EHA

It takes more than a cursory review of constitutional developments to explain how handicapped children's rights to an education were established. To be sure, the case precedents were indispensable (as later chapters demonstrate), but a slowly evolving federal role that turned into a massive involvement in the education of disabled children was an equally indispensable ingredient.

The earliest federal role—creating special schools for the mentally ill, blind, and deaf between the 1820s and the 1870s—paralleled a similar movement at the state level, in which state schools for the handicapped were established as early as 1823. No further significant federal activity occurred until World Wars I and II spurred the government into vocational rehabilitation programs and aid for disabled veterans and other disabled persons. Public assistance programs were evidence of increasing federal concern for the handicapped. Application of the Social Security Act to blind, disabled, aged, and dependent persons, the grant of benefits under Medicare and Medicaid programs, the payment of Supplementary Security Income, and a host of programs under Title XX of the Social Security Act all give testimony to the federal government's concerns.[10]

The parent movement was typified by formation of the Association for Retarded Citizens of the United States (formerly the National Association for Retarded Children/Citizens) in the 1950s and its increasing clout on the federal and state scene in the 1960s. It was enhanced in the early 1960s when President John F. Kennedy and Vice President Hubert Humphrey used their influence to advance the interests of mentally retarded persons by establishing the President's Committee on Mental Retardation.

Congress first addressed the education of children with disabilities in 1966, when it amended the Elementary and Secondary Education Act of 1965 (P.L. 89-750) to establish a program of federal grants to the states that would assist them in initiating, expanding, and improving programs and projects for the education of handicapped children. In 1970 Congress repealed the 1966 law but established a grant program that had a similar purpose (P.L. 91-230). Both the 1966 and 1970 laws tried to stimulate the states to develop special education resources and personnel.

By 1974 Congress had become dissatisfied with the states' progress and was confronted with the courts' decisions in two pioneering special education cases, *Pennsylvania Association for Retarded Children (PARC) v. Commonwealth of Pennsylvania* and *Mills v. D.C. Board of Education* (both are discussed in full in chapter 3). Those cases ruled that handicapped children should be given access to public education. Accordingly, in

1974 Congress substantially increased federal aid to the states for special education and required them to adopt a goal of providing "full educational opportunities to all handicapped children" (P.L. 93-380). Congress also recognized that its 1974 law was an interim measure only and would have to be supplemented. Thus it was that Congress enacted the Education for All Handicapped Children Act (P.L. 94-142) in 1975.

The 1975 law was the most significant amendment of the Education of the Handicapped Act (EHA) to that time. But it has not been the only amendment. Congress amended the EHA in 1978 by P.L. 95-561, in 1983 by P.L. 98-199, in 1986 by P.L. 99-372, and again in 1986 by P.L. 99-457. The most important of these amendments are P.L. 99-372, the Handicapped Children's Protection Act, and P.L. 99-457, the Handicapped Infants and Toddlers Act.

In addition to the EHA, Congress had an effect upon special education in other ways. The Elementary and Secondary Education Act itself was the springboard for the EHA. The Vocational Education Amendments of 1968, the Economic Opportunities Act of 1972 (Headstart), the Rehabilitation Act of 1973, the Higher Education Amendments of 1972, and the Developmental Disabilities Assistance and Bill of Rights Act of 1974 not only contributed to the political feasibility of the 1975 amendments to the EHA (the Education for All Handicapped Children Act, P.L. 94-142) but also underscored the federal concern for people with disabilities.

School Practices

As a general rule, the nation's public schools were highly ingenious and very successful in denying educational opportunities, equal or otherwise, to disabled children. Their success was evidenced by data showing how many children were excluded: As reported in Section 1400(b) of EHA, Congress found that approximately one half of the nation's 8 million handicapped children were not receiving an appropriate education and about 1 million were receiving no education at all. The multitude of exclusionary practices that the courts found in violation of educational rights of the handicapped was also proof of the problem. Among these practices, two dominated: exclusion and classification.

Exclusion.   Exclusion occurs when children are denied education (denied access to all public educational programs or provided an inadequate education for their needs). *Total exclusion* may involve the school's refusing to admit a child or placing him or her on a long waiting list. Exclusion also occurs when programs are inadequate or unresponsive to students' needs, as when Spanish-speaking children are given an English curriculum and no special provision is made to accommodate the fact that they do not understand English. Another example of exclusion occurs when moderately retarded children are put in large regular classes and given little or no training or education. Practices such as these constitute *functional exclusion;* although the child has access to a program, the program is of such a nature that the child cannot substantially benefit from it and therefore receives few or none of the intended benefits of education.

The schools excluded school-aged handicapped persons individually and as a class.[11] They admitted some but not all students with the same disability.[12] They inadequately funded tuition-subsidy programs that would have enabled families to purchase appropriate education from alternative sources (such as private schools) when appropriate education was not available in the public schools.[13] When appropriate programs were not available, the schools placed handicapped pupils in special education programs that were inappropriate for them.[14] When faced with a shortage of special education programs, schools created waiting lists for admission to the few available programs, thus excluding many eligible pupils.[15]

Also, the schools created different admission policies for the handicapped.[16] They placed handicapped pupils in situations with virtually no programs of instruction available.[17] They excluded retarded children on the grounds that they created behavioral or disciplinary problems.[18] Finally, they limited the number of students that could be enrolled in special education programs by using incidence projections that bore little relation to the actual number of handicapped children in the school district[19] or by restricting state-level funding for hiring special education teachers by establishing artificial quotas such as one state-paid teacher for every 12 pupils in each special education class.[20]

Classification. Classification is at issue when children are misplaced or wrongly tracked.[21] Misclassification denies children the right to an equal educational opportunity because it results in their being denied schooling that will benefit them.

Past challenges to school placement criteria were often accusations of racial discrimination as much as they were complaints about denial of education. The objection was that the tests used to classify children were biased toward knowledge of English and familiarity with white middle-class culture. Accordingly, test scores resulted in minority children being placed in special education programs in far greater numbers than were other children. The result was a dual system of education based on race or cultural background.

Other Practices

A host of other practices, not easily categorized, also denied education to disabled students. State and local appropriations for special education were shamefully sparse. Institutionalized children often were denied even the barest programs of care and habilitation. The responsibility of state and local governments for educating handicapped children was fragmented, and competitive bureaucratic structures within the school or institutional agencies rarely undertook any cooperative efforts. The result was that meager resources (money and personnel) were diluted, gaps existed in service, services often overlapped, and accountability was nearly impossible.

Architectural barriers to physically handicapped students, the lack of adaptive materials and materials for vision, speech, and hearing impaired children, and the inability or unwillingness of school personnel to teach some handicapped children (emotionally disturbed, learning disabled, mentally retarded) likewise contributed to their exclusion. It was not unusual for teachers of handicapped students to be uncertified to teach them or to be the least skilled teachers in a school system. Teachers often were required to use the oldest, least adequate facilities, located far from the classrooms of nonhandicapped students. The separateness and devaluation of handicapped children were underscored by separate financing, administration, and organization of special education services.[22]

Once a child was placed in a special education program, the placement often became permanent. For the child it was a terminal assignment, and reconsideration or reevaluation was out of the ordinary. The assignment usually was carried out without parental participation and without opportunities for due process. Frequently, schools failed to identify the handicapped children in their districts; child census procedures were rare, and the school's target population was not known, planned for, or served.

Early intervention programs for handicapped children were the exception, not the rule. Placement in private programs was encouraged, because it relieved the school of any responsibility for serving children whose families were able or desperate enough to pay for private school opportunities. Local noncompliance with state law requiring education of handicapped children was rarely punished. Preschool, elementary, and secondary school programs—when they existed at all—were unequally available. Finally, the schools' longstanding discouragement of pupils ("don't call us—we'll call you") made many parents weary of trying to rectify wrongs, kept them in ignorance of their children's rights, and reinforced the unbalanced power relationships between the powerful schools and the less powerful parents.

Many readers may object to these generalized characterizations, possibly being able to point to specific circumstances in which some or all of these practices did not exist. But the generalizations have been true more often than not, and the practices have been the rule more than the exception. Some of the better studies of school practices substantiate the generalizations;[23] court decisions have set forth facts that support the generalizations;[24] and Congress itself has filed a broad-based indictment of the public schools based on findings of many of these practices.[25]

Reasons for the Practices

Schools have followed these practices for many reasons. Not only is the cost of educating or training a handicapped child normally higher than the cost of educating a nonhandicapped child, but manpower, money, and political clout for handicapped children are also limited when compared with the same resources for nonhandicapped children. Many educators have not considered handicapped pupils, particularly mentally retarded ones, educable in the traditional sense. The time-honored "reading-writing-arithmetic" philosophy has been a reason for exclusion. The fact that special education has been separated from the mainstream of education and that both special educators and educators in programs for nonhandicapped students have desired this separation has also tended to diminish educational opportunities for handicapped individuals.

As pointed out before, a handicapped child, once placed in a special education program, often has had little chance to return to a normal program. Placement in special education has tended to be permanent because there were no requirements for periodic re-evaluation and the schools understandably were reluctant to question their own decisions.

Special education has served as an important escape hatch, permitting schools to classify as handicapped those children they considered undesirable—the racial minorities, the disruptive, and the different. Behind this practice (indeed, underlying all of the discrimination) was the widely held attitude that governmental benefits, including education, should be parceled out to the most meritorious—a belief that equates merit with average intelligence or nonhandicapping conditions and asserts that the less able are less worthy.

The three ideologies or principles—egalitarianism (a political ideology), normalization (a human services ideology), and equal protection (a legal doctrine)—play important roles with respect to the reasons for the practices. First, they are based on a different value system. The new value system holds that although a person is less able, the person is not therefore less worthy. Second, they shape the legal and educational practices embodied in and required by the EHA. Third, they demonstrate that values are as effective as politics, economics, and science in shaping how people with disabilities are treated. Indeed, given the resistance to the education of all children with disabilities and their inclusion, to the maximum extent appropriate for them, in the regular school programs, these ideologies demonstrate that values prevail over other forces.

CHARACTERISTICS OF
COURT ORDERS AND LEGISLATION

None of the exclusionary or discriminatory practices has entirely escaped the long arm of the law, and each reason for the practices has been challenged in court or in state or federal legislation. As shown in greater detail in chapters 3 through 8, judicial remedies and recent legislation at the federal level have mounted a successful attack on these practices. For present introductory purposes, it will be sufficient to set out the major characteristics of state legislation:[26]

- zero reject (no handicapped child to be excluded) under so-called mandatory legislation (requiring education of all handicapped children);
- census of and planning for the education of handicapped students;
- enumeration of the ages during which handicapped children must be educated and, sometimes, of the ages during which they may obtain an education (early intervention or compensatory education);
- requirements that either a single agency be principally responsible for carrying out court or legislative requirements or that each agency responsible for some portion of a state's overall special education program cooperate in specified ways with the others;
- nondiscriminatory evaluation;
- individualization of programs;

- placement in the least restrictive (most "normal" or most "facilitating") educational program;
- procedural due process (opportunity to protest);
- general confidentiality of records subject to parent access to records;
- assignment of advocates (usually called agent surrogates) to represent handicapped children who have no known parents or guardians;
- provision of technical assistance and preservice and inservice training and retraining, and requirements of teacher certification or other competency criteria;
- appropriations earmarked for special education programs; and
- sanctions for noncompliance.

It would be premature to discuss how federal statutes respond directly to the manifold exclusionary and discriminatory practices, and thus mirror some aspects of judicial remedies and state legislation, but it is important to state that the acts do speak to each practice. At this point, it is convenient for us to introduce the EHA and Section 504 of the Rehabilitation Act.

THE EHA AND SECTION 504: ONCE OVER LIGHTLY

The Relationship of the Two Laws

The EHA provides federal funds to states and local education agencies if they agree to comply with certain conditions set out in the EHA and the regulations that implement the Act. Thus, the EHA is a federal grant program with conditions attached.

By contrast, Section 504 is federal antidiscrimination legislation. It prohibits any state or local government or any private organization that receives federal funds from discriminating against an "otherwise qualified handicapped person" solely on the basis of the person's handicap. It does not provide funds to state and local governments or private organizations and therefore is not a federal grant program with conditions attached (as is the EHA). Instead, it is civil rights legislation that reaches all recipients of federal funds and prohibits them from discriminating against handicapped people. In both its language and intent it is like other federal civil rights laws that prohibit discrimination by federal recipients on the basis of race or gender.

> References to sections of the EHA that are cited in the text in brackets [ ] are references to the Act itself, as passed by Congress. The Act has been codified at 20 United States Code, Sections 1401-1468. The Department of Education has issued regulations implementing the Act. They are codified in 34 Code of Federal Regulations, Part 300, and are cited in the text as, e.g., Sec. 308.

> The Rehabilitation Act, of which Section 504 is part, is codified at 29 United States Code, beginning at Section 706. Section 504 is codified at 29 U.S.C., Section 794. The Department of Health and Human Services has issued regulations implementing Section 504, which are codified at 30 Code of Federal Regulations, Part 104, and are cited in the text as, e.g., Sec. 104.2.

The State Plan

Any state desiring to receive EHA funds must apply for them by submitting an application from its state education agency (SEA) to the U.S. Secretary of Education. The application is called the *annual program plan*. The plan must be submitted when required by the Secretary of Education and must indicate how the state will comply with the EHA and its regulations.

Regardless of whether an SEA or LEA receives federal funds, it must comply with Section 504 and its regulations. The law prohibits any recipient of *any* federal financial assistance from discriminating against a handicapped person solely because of handicap. Because Section 504 is intended to prohibit the same discrimination in the education of handicapped children that the EHA prohibits, its regulations are consistent in concept and policy with the regulations under the EHA. They apply to any SEA, LEA, or any state or local agency that receives funds from the Department of Education. Thus, an SEA or LEA (local education agency) that does not receive EHA funds but receives other federal funds from the Department of Education or other federal agencies must comply with essentially the same regulations (under Section 504) as for funds under EHA.

EHA applies to more than SEAs or LEAs receiving EHA funds. Assume that an LEA chooses not to receive funds but that the SEA does. Is the LEA exempt from EHA? No—not entirely. If an LEA elects not to receive funds, it does not have to comply with requirements of the EHA; however, the SEA, as a recipient of funds, is required to ensure that the handicapped children residing in the LEA's jurisdiction are granted all of the rights and protections of the EHA. The EHA's requirement that the SEA must provide special education directly to children with disabilities when an LEA refuses to do so has been reaffirmed by the United States Supreme Court in *Honig v. Doe,* a 1988 decision. Moreover, if the LEA receives any other federal funds, it must, of course, comply with Section 504.

The SEAs and LEAs are not the only state and local agencies affected by the EHA. All state and local agencies (including LEAs) that furnish "special education" and "related services" to handicapped children, such as state departments of mental health, welfare, or corrections (hereafter called *public agencies*) are treated as though they were SEAs or LEAs. There are two reasons for this.

First, the EHA requires the SEA to assure the federal government that the Act is carried out statewide; it assigns the SEA the responsibility for general supervision of all educational programs for handicapped children in the state. Thus, requirements of the Act are binding on the state itself, not just on an agency or a department of the state.

Second, because the basic rights granted handicapped pupils under the EHA are also included in the regulations for Section 504, *any* recipient of federal funds has to comply with these provisions. Accordingly, the EHA provides that the regulations apply to each *state* (not just to an agency or department thereof) that receives EHA funds. The SEA submits an application for funds on behalf of the state as a whole. As a consequence, the Act and the regulations apply to all agencies and political subdivisions of the state involved in educating handicapped children.

The effect of the EHA and Section 504, then, is to assure that handicapped children receive a free appropriate education and are not discriminated against in or by any public agencies furnishing special education services. Together, the two laws cover all handicapped children without regard to where they live in the state (whether in the community or in an institution, for example) or which state or local agency serves them (whether a department of public education or a department of human resources, for example). There is no real escape from these Acts for state and local agencies dealing with handicapped children. The two Acts seal all the cracks in services and carry out policies of zero reject and nondiscrimination.

Handicapped Children: Definitions

For purposes of the EHA, handicapped children are those who are mentally retarded, hard of hearing, deaf, speech or language impaired, visually handicapped, seriously emotionally disturbed, orthopedically impaired or other health impaired (including autistic), deaf-blind, multi-handicapped, or who have specific learning disabilities. All must need special education and related services because of any one or more of these disabilities. (See Appendix E for the current definitions of these terms.)

Under Section 504, which prohibits discrimination against an otherwise qualified handicapped individual, and for the purposes of special education only, the term "handicapped person" means any person who has a physical or mental impairment that substantially limits one or more major life activities, has a record of such an impairment, or is regarded as having such an impairment.

"Physical or mental impairment" means (1) any physiological disorder or condition, cosmetic disfigurement, or anatomical loss affecting one or more of the following body systems: neurological, musculoskeletal, special sense organs, respiratory (including speech organs), cardiovascular, reproductive, digestive, genito-urinary, hermic and lymphatic, skin, and endocrine; or (2) any mental or psychological disorder, such as mental retardation, organic brain syndrome, emotional or mental illness (including addiction to alcohol or drugs), and specific learning disabilities.

"Major life activities" means functions such as caring for oneself, performing manual tasks, walking, seeing, hearing, speaking, breathing, learning, and working.

"Has a record of such an impairment" means the person has a history of or has been classified as having a mental or physical impairment that substantially limits one or more major life activities.

"Is regarded as having an impairment" means the person (1) has a physical or mental impairment that does not substantially limit major life activities but is treated by a recipient of federal funds as constituting such a limitation, (2) has a physical or mental impairment that substantially limits major life activities only as a result of the attitudes of others toward such impairment, or (3) has none of the impairments listed above but is treated by a recipient of federal funds as having such an impairment.

With respect to public preschool, elementary, secondary, or adult educational services conducted by public schools other than universities, a "qualified handicapped person" is someone who is (1) of an age at which nonhandicapped persons are provided such services, (2) of any age at which it is mandatory under state law to provide such services to handicapped persons, or (3) guaranteed a free appropriate public education under the EHA.

The Supreme Court clarified the meaning of "otherwise qualified handicapped person" in its 1979 decision, *Southeast Community College v. Davis* (see Appendix B). In that case, Frances Davis, who was hearing impaired and had a degenerative hearing disability, applied for admission to the college's nursing program. After being examined for her ability to hear, she was denied admission and sued to be admitted, claiming that she was discriminated against because she is a person with a disability, in violation of Section 504.

The Supreme Court ruled that she is not "otherwise qualified" and thus is not entitled to the protection of Section 504 and could not be discriminated against in violation of the law. The Court interpreted "otherwise qualified handicapped person" to mean one who is able to meet all of a program's requirements in spite of the handicap. Because Frances Davis could not meet all of the requirements of the curriculum in nursing, she was not "otherwise qualified." If she could have met them in spite of her handicap, even with some accommodations the college made for her, she would have been "otherwise qualified" and would have been the victim of discrimination.

The Court's decision is notable for reasons other than that it offers the first definition of "otherwise qualified." First, it makes clear that Section 504 is an antidiscrimination statute, one that requires some accommodations to be made by a recipient of federal aid; but it is not an affirmative action law that requires substantial accommodations, such as Title VI (race discrimination) or Title IX (sex discrimination) of the Civil Rights Act.

Second, it recognizes the need to balance the rights of a person with a disability (Frances Davis) against the rights of other people—namely, the patients who would be cared for by a nurse who may not be able to hear adequately, and the institutions of higher education, which have a claim to control their curriculum and make independent judgments concerning the suitability of a person for the curriculum. As chapter 3 points out, balancing the interest of people with disabilities against the interests of others is a matter that affects the interpretation of Section 504 and its application to the education of students with disabilities.

Other Differences Between the EHA and Section 504

The language of Section 504 provides that no recipient of federal funds shall discriminate against an otherwise qualified handicapped person solely on account of a handicap. The regulations for implementing this law make it clear that Section 504 applies to preschool, elementary, and secondary public education programs that receive *any* federal assistance from the Department of Education or other federal agency. They also make it clear that the schools must adopt a zero reject policy (chapter 3 discusses zero reject), provide a free appropriate public education to each handicapped person who is a legal resident of the recipient's jurisdiction regardless of the nature or severity of the handicap, conduct nondiscriminatory testing (see chapter 4), place handicapped children in the least restrictive environment (see chapter 6), and guarantee due process for handicapped children (see chapter 7). Thus, Section 504 and its implementing regulations accomplish largely the same results as the EHA with respect to prohibiting exclusion and discrimination against handicapped children.

Despite a similarity to the EHA, Section 504 and its regulations differ in several important respects:

1. Section 504 includes as handicapped those persons who are so defined by the EHA, but it also includes many others, such as persons addicted to the use of drugs and alcohol (not for employment discrimination purposes). The two laws take different approaches to the issue of who is handicapped. The EHA basically relies on a *categorical* approach and anticipates the continuation of categorical labeling of children. A child is "MR" or "LD" or "ED."

   Section 504, however, relies on both a categorical approach and an entirely different approach, best described as *functional*. Under that approach, a child is handicapped if he or she functions as though handicapped, or if a state or local government receiving any federal funds acts as if the child were handicapped. There is an impairment in major life activities, a record of an impairment, or the child is treated as having an impairment. Although Section 504 generally applies to handicapped persons without respect to their age, age *is* at issue when the person is a handicapped student, because the regulations define a handicapped student as one who, under state law or the EHA, is entitled to a public education (ages 3–21).

2. Section 504 prohibits discrimination not only in preschool, elementary, secondary, and adult public education, but also in the employment of handicapped persons and in social and health services. By contrast, the EHA addresses only preschool, elementary, secondary, and adult education. Both laws, however, speak to the problems of architectural barriers and access to facilities and, in a limited sense, to the employment of handicapped people by the public schools (see chapter 3).

3. Section 504 does not require individualized education programs for handicapped children; the EHA does. Both require appropriate education.

NOTES

1. Wolfensberger, "Social Role Valorization: A Proposed New Term for the Principle of Normalization," 21 *Mental Retardation* 224 (Dec. 1983).

2. Harper v. Virginia Board of Elections.

3. Boddie v. Connecticut.

4. Shapiro v. Thompson.

5. Weber v. Aetna Casualty and Surety Co.; Levy v. Louisiana.

6. Wisconsin v. Constantineau.

7. Robinson v. California.

8. Martarella v. Kelley.

9. Reed v. Reed.

10. LaVor, "Federal Legislation for Exceptional Persons: A History," in *Public Policy and the Education of Exceptional Children,* edited by Weintraub et al. (Reston, Va.: Council for Exceptional Children, 1976); and Boggs, "Federal Legislation Affecting the Mentally Retarded," in *Mental Retardation,* vol. III, edited by Wortis (New York: Grune & Stratton, 1971).

11. *See, e.g.,* Children's Defense Fund, "The Exclusion of Children with Special Needs," ch. 4 in *Children Out of School in America: A Report of The Children's Defense Fund, Washington Research Project, Inc.* (Washington, D.C.: The Fund, 1974); Mills v. D.C. Bd. of Ed.; PARC v. Commonwealth; Wolf v. Legislature of Utah; MARC v. Maryland; North Carolina ARC v. North Carolina; and Tidewater Ass'n. for Autistic Children v. Tidewater Bd. of Ed.

12. Mills; PARC; and Tidewater Ass'n. v. Tidewater Bd. of Ed.

13. PARC; MARC v. Maryland.

14. MARC v. Maryland.

15. Mills; LeBanks v. Spears; David P. v. State Dep't. of Ed.

16. PARC and Mills.

17. PARC; MARC v. Maryland.

18. Mills.

19. David P. v. Dep't. of Ed.

20. North Carolina's Department of Public Instruction allocated funds to local units, for use in hiring special education teachers, on the basis of 12 TMR handicapped children per classroom.

21. Hobson v. Hansen; Larry P. v. Riles.

22. Milofsky, "Why Special Education Isn't Special," 44 *Harvard Education Review* 437-58 (1974).

23. *Supra* n. 12.

24. *See infra,* chs. 3, 4, 5, 6, and 7.

25. P.L. 94-142, Sec. 1402(b).

26. Bolick, "State Statutory Law," in *Public Policy and the Education of Exceptional Children* (Reston, Va.: Council for Exceptional Children, 1976).

SECTION II
The Six Major Principles

3
Zero Reject

CONSTITUTIONAL FOUNDATIONS

The Fourteenth Amendment provides that no state may deny to any person within its jurisdiction equal protection of the laws. As indicated in chapters 1 and 2 and interpreted by the courts, this amendment has produced a remarkable series of judicial results that have effectively prevented government from denying governmental benefits to persons because of their unalterable and uncontrollable characteristics (such as age, gender, race, or disability) and in many cases require affirmative or other positive or remedial steps to redress the unequal treatment those people have experienced at the government's hand. Inequalities have existed in the opportunity to be educated, and handicapped children have been among the victims of educational discrimination. The Fourteenth Amendment has recently become the vehicle for redressing that inequality.

Brown as Precedent in Right-to-Education Cases

Judicial attacks on the many exclusionary practices of schools focused on the importance of education, its protected status under *Brown,* and its claim to favored treatment under the Fourteenth Amendment. In holding that racial segregation in public education violated the Fourteenth Amendment, *Brown* stressed the importance of education in terms that have been quoted or cited with approval in nearly every subsequent related case. "The importance of education to our democratic society" and the relationship of education to "the performance of our most basic public responsibilities" were the grounds on which the Court reached the conclusion that the opportunity of an education, "where the state has undertaken to provide it, is a right which must be made available to all on equal terms."

Representatives of disabled students, relying on *Brown,* have claimed that handicapped children have the same rights to education as nonhandicapped children. Their complaint has two major elements. First, they complained that there was differential treatment among and within the class of handicapped children—that is, some handicapped children were furnished education while others were not. They sought the remedy that all excluded handicapped children be given an education. Second, they complained that some handicapped children were not furnished an education while nonhandicapped children were. They sought the remedy that all children, including handicapped children, be included in the public education system.

The basic argument of *Brown* was that the equal protection doctrine protected a "class" of persons—in this instance, a racial minority. In applying the equal protection doctrine, the courts have asked whether a state's action in distributing benefits and burdens (such as educating some but not others) was based on a "classification" of persons with apparently equal characteristics, and whether that classification resulted in some members of the "class" being treated less equally than others. For example, in the school desegregation cases the class to be protected was all students, whether white or black. When a state treated black students differently by requiring them to attend segregated schools, the courts found that black students had been denied equal protection of the school laws on the basis of an unalterable and uncontrollable trait—their race.

In the right-to-education cases, the class is all students, whether handicapped or nonhandicapped. A state undertakes to provide a free public education system for its school-age citizens; when the state treats handicapped students differently by denying them an opportunity to attend school or by inappropriately assigning them to special education programs, the courts have found that handicapped children had been denied equal protection of school laws on the basis of their unalterable and unchosen trait—their handicap.

The Evolution of Equal Protection Analysis

Until the advent of the Warren era of the Supreme Court, the Court generally held that governmental action alleged to be discriminatory and in violation of the equal protection doctrine was not unconstitutional. When the traditional equal protection analysis applied in these cases failed to correct abuses of individual rights, the Warren Court applied a new equal protection analysis. The application the Court used depended principally on who the complaining party was, the nature of his or her interest or what right was being infringed upon, and the ability of the government to justify its action.

Under the new equal protection concept, if the case involved a "suspect classification" (such as a person being classifed by race) or a "fundamental interest" (such as the right to vote), the Court subjected the classification to "strict scrutiny" and required the state to show a "compelling interest."[1] The Court also required the state to prove that the distinction drawn by the law was necessary, not merely convenient, in order to achieve the government's purpose.

If no fundamental interest or suspect classification was involved, the Court resorted to the "rational basis" standard, asking only whether the ends or purposes sought were legitimate state purposes and whether there was a rational relationship between the ends or purposes and the particular classification. A state practice was much more likely to survive an equal protection attack under the rational-basis test than under the strict scrutiny test.

Even more recently, the Court has developed an "intermediate" or "middle-tier" approach to equal protection. In cases involving women and aliens (but not racial minorities) or in cases involving important personal interest (but not one that is "fundamental" in the sense that it is explicitly guaranteed by the Fourteenth Amendment or is necessarily implied by explicit guarantees, as is the right to privacy), the Court has given some protection to disadvantaged people, but not as much as it has given in the race segregation cases. Thus, a state must show an exceedingly important or special justification for a law that puts women or aliens at a disadvantage. This middle-tier approach has enabled the Court to strike down some laws that discriminate against people who have been traditionally excluded from the political process (and thus unable to correct the laws that single them out). But it also has not required the Court to create any new suspect classes (such as racial minorities) or to imply any new fundamental rights from the explicit guarantees of the Bill of Rights.

Understanding the basic equal protection analyses is necessary to appreciate how a claim of equal protection is generally made and resolved in right-to-education cases, despite the fact that recent right-to-education cases generally lack a clear or formal equal protection analysis. Until recently, the courts deciding those cases typically have cited the equal protection clause and added an accompanying reference to *Brown.* But they have failed to state that education is a fundamental interest and that the handicapped plaintiffs are a suspect class, and they usually have not specified which equal protection tests finally apply.[2]

Under a 1985 decision of the U.S. Supreme Court, involving a local ordinance that excluded group homes for people who are mentally retarded from a nonresidential zone, people who are retarded, and apparently all disabled people, were held not to fall into a suspect or quasi-suspect class and therefore are not entitled to special protection under the equal protection doctrine.[3] The impact of this decision, in *City of Cleburne v. Cleburne Living Center, Inc.,* is not entirely clear. On the one hand, the Court seems unwilling to give people with disabilities any special protection under the equal protection doctrine; it says it does not want to do so. Yet it also uses language and an approach indicating that it has special concerns for those people, and it reaches a result that strikes down the exclusionary zoning ordinance as blatantly discriminatory, thereby granting them some protection under the equal protection doctrine.

In addition, the Court seems to give great weight to legislative judgments, saying that they are presumed to be valid. But it also strikes down the particular legislative judgment—the exclusionary ordinance—on the ground that discrimination against people with mental retardation had no valid reason.

In sum, the Court seems to be saying one thing and doing another. On the face of the opinion, however, it appears that the Court will not give any special protection under the equal protection doctrine to people with disabilities. If this result holds over the period of years, *Cleburne* will have marked a clear retreat from an activist or liberal use of the equal protection clause—that is, away from the suspect class/fundamental interest or intermediate/middle-tier approach to protecting minority populations from majoritarian decisions.

PARC and *Mills*

Although *Brown* established the right to an equal educational opportunity based upon Fourteenth Amendment grounds, it was not until *Pennsylvania Association for Retarded Children (PARC) v. Commonwealth of Pennsylvania* and *Mills v. D.C. Board of Education* that *Brown* became meaningful for handicapped children. In both *PARC* and *Mills*, the courts relied on legal and educational authorities to support their finding that education was essential to enable a child to function in society and that *all* children can benefit from education. They applied the equal protection and due process guarantees of the Fifth and Fourteenth Amendments to furnish this important right to handicapped students. Neither court engaged in careful legal analysis; each was content to make the assertion of fundamental interest and strike down school policies denying education to handicapped children. *Mills*, citing *Brown* and *Hobson v. Hansen*, concluded:

> In *Hobson v. Hansen*, … Judge Wright found that denying poor public school children educational opportunities equal to that available to more affluent public school children was violating the Due Process Clause of the Fifth Amendment. *A fortiori*, defendants' conduct here, denying plaintiffs and their class not just an equal publicly supported education but all publicly supported education while providing such education to other children is violative of the Due Process Clause.

Subsequent cases closely followed the arguments made in *PARC* and *Mills*, and the form of the decision and the relief granted have been similar. *PARC* relied on the following findings (the so-called *PARC* syllogism):

> 1. Expert testimony in this action indicates that … all mentally retarded persons are capable of benefiting from a program of education and training; that the greatest number of retarded persons, given such education and training, are capable of achieving self-sufficiency and the remaining few, with such education and training, are capable of achieving some degree of self-care; that the earlier such education and training begins, the more thoroughly and the more efficiently a mentally retarded person will benefit from it; and, whether begun early or not, that a mentally retarded person can benefit at any point in his life and development from a program of education and training.
> 2. The Commonwealth of Pennsylvania has undertaken to provide a free public education to all of its children between the ages of six and twenty-one years, and further, has undertaken to provide education and training for all of its mentally retarded children.
> 3. Having undertaken to provide a free public education to all of its children, including its mentally retarded children, the Commonwealth of Pennsylvania may not deny any mentally retarded child access to a free program of education and training.

4. It is the Commonwealth's obligation to place each mentally retarded child in a free, public program of education and training appropriate to the child's capacity, within the context of the general educational policy that, among the alternative programs of education and training required by statute to be available, placement in a regular public school class is preferable to placement in a special public school class and placement in a special public school class is preferable to placement of any other program of education and training.

One important premise is absent from the court's findings: It is generally true that educators have the ability to educate and train the handicapped. Without both the ability of disabled children to learn and the ability of educators to help them learn, it would be a futile expenditure of public money to attempt to teach handicapped children in the public schools. Instead, it would be rational and arguably constitutional for the state to exclude them from school if they could not benefit from it and if there were no educators competent to teach them. It was significant that the defendants in *PARC* and *Mills* did not deny that they were under a duty to educate *all* children or that mentally retarded or other handicapped children could be educated.

From the point of view of the principle of zero reject, the changes ordered in *PARC* were comprehensive. The state was required to locate and identify all school-aged individuals excluded from public schools. State and local districts were required to place all retarded children in a "free public program of education and training appropriate to the child's capacity." In addition, the state's Department of Public Welfare, insofar as it was charged with arranging for the care, training, and supervision of a child committed to it, was also required to provide a program of education and training appropriate to the child's capacity.

Parents of retarded children were excused from liability under the compulsory school attendance statutes if, with the approval of the local school board and the secretary of education and upon a finding by an approved school psychologist, they chose to withdraw their child from school. But school districts were enjoined from using the withdrawal provisions as a means of excluding retarded children against the parents' wishes. The compulsory school attendance statutes were construed to mean that when a child is between 8 and 17 years of age, the parents must make sure that the child attends an educational or training program. And any school district that provided free preschooling to nonhandicapped children under the age of 6 was prohibited from denying such schooling to retarded children of the same age.

The state's tuition maintenance statute (granting funds for payment of tuition at private schools) was interpreted by *PARC* to mean that a mentally retarded child is entitled to its benefits if he or she attends a private school. Previously, the statute had been interpreted to apply only to children who were blind, deaf, cerebral palsied, brain damaged, or afflicted by muscular dystrophy. Statutory provisions for at-home instruction were construed to mean that such instruction must be made available to retarded children even though they may not be physically handicapped or suffering from a short-term disability as well.

Unlike *PARC, Mills* was not resolved by a consent decree but, rather, by judgment against the defendant school board. Also unlike *PARC,* the suit was brought on behalf of children who had disabilities other than mental retardation. Like *PARC,* however, *Mills* resulted in a court order stating that before any handicapped child eligible for a publicly supported education may be excluded from a regular school assignment, the child must be furnished adequate alternative educational services suited to his or her needs, including (if appropriate) special education or tuition grants. The District of Columbia school board was required to provide each handicapped school-aged child a free and suitable publicly supported education, regardless of the degree of mental, physical, or emotional disability. The school board was also enjoined from making disciplinary suspensions for any reason for longer than 2 days unless school authorities gave the child a hearing before suspension and continued the child's education while he or she was suspended.

School authorities were ordered to provide suitable education, within 30 days after the date of the order, to all handicapped children then known to them. Handicapped children who might later come to their attention were to be provided for within 50 days. The authorities also were required to advertise the availability of free public education for handicapped children, to identify previously excluded handicapped children and advise them of their rights under the court order, and to evaluate the educational needs of all handicapped children. Finally, they were required to file a proposal with the court for placing each handicapped child in a suitable educational program. The proposal was to include: compensatory educational services where required; a plan for identifying, notifying, evaluating, and placing the handicapped children; a report showing the expunction from or the correction of all official records of the plaintiffs' former expulsions, suspensions, or exclusions made in violation of due process requirements contained in the court order; and a plan for allowing the children's parents to attach to their records any clarifying or explanatory information.

Uses of Equal Protection for Zero Reject

The equal protection doctrine was put to many uses in the context of zero reject policy. It was used to prevent: (1) the total exclusion of all or some handicapped children in the schools, (2) the total exclusion of some handicapped children when others with the same handicap were included, and (3) the total exclusion of all persons with one kind of handicap (such as autism) when persons with different types of handicaps (such as physical disabilities) were included. In each of those instances, the class of persons entitled to equal protection was "students," not just *some* students.[4]

A fourth use of equal protection came into play when handicapped children were included in school programs on a different basis than nonhandicapped students. For example, it applied when handicapped children's parents were required to pay tuition for attending public schools but the parents of nonhandicapped children were not.[5] It also applied to handicapped children who were ruled medically ineligible to attend school (because they were nonambulatory or not toilet-trained) when nonhandicapped children were not screened out because of their medically related characteristics.[6] And it also operated for handicapped children who were denied free transportation to school when nonhandicapped students were given such service.[7]

The fifth way the equal protection doctrine has been applied in right-to-education cases is in establishing a new doctrine of equality—the equal access doctrine. *Brown* and other school desegregation cases interpreted the equal protection doctrine as requiring that black students be given *equal access to the same resources* as whites. Typically, the courts ruled that when a school system provides facilities to white children, exactly the same facilities (not an equivalent separate set of facilities) must be made available on the same terms to black children.

In right-to-education cases, the theory of equal protection is quite different and can be best understood in terms of claims for handicapped students to *differing* resources for *differing* objectives.[8] Under this approach, the right to education for handicapped students means that the schools must furnish *all* handicapped children equal opportunities to develop their own capabilities. Thus, schools are required to provide different programs and facilities for pupils with different needs, according to those needs. This "new access" doctrine was originally developed in *Mills, PARC,* and *LeBanks v. Spears,* all of which required not only that the handicapped plaintiffs be provided with public education but also that the education be "appropriate" to their capabilities or "suited to their needs." Recent cases, such as *Board v. Rowley* and *Irving Independent School District v. Tatro,* both decided by the U.S. Supreme Court, continue to adopt the new equal access approach. These cases are discussed at length in chapter 5.

Although the courts have developed the new access theory, they have been unwilling to abandon the earlier *Brown* theory of equal protection. For example, they have responded favorably to cases challenging the placement of disproportionate numbers of minority students in classes for the mentally retarded.[9] In a sense, the cases assert the traditional *Brown* doctrine that minority students be given "equal access to the same resources." In those cases, equal protection is being used in a sixth way to expand educational opportunity on the basis of discrimination because of race rather than handicap.

Whenever this sixth use of the *Brown* theory might be applied so that school systems would be able to restrict appropriate educational opportunity to handicapped students on the theory that they were furnishing equal access to the same resources, it tends not to be followed. For example, the plaintiffs in *Lau v. Nichols* argued that equal educational opportunities had been effectively denied to Chinese-speaking children because public school programs were taught only in English. They claimed that equal protection requires school programs to take into account the children's inability to understand English. The Ninth Circuit Court of Appeals responded with a *Brown*-type equal access theory of equal protection, saying that equal protection was not denied, because all children were given equal access to the standard, English-taught curriculum available to other students.

The U.S. Supreme Court reversed the decision. The Court's opinion closely paralleled the equal protection arguments made in the recent right-to-education cases, stating that some school practices have denied a meaningful opportunity for education. The

Court, however, decided the case solely on the basis of Section 601 of the 1964 Civil Rights Act (prohibiting racial discrimination in any federally assisted program) and did not touch on the equal protection issue.

The fact that the Supreme Court disposed of *Lau* on nonconstitutional grounds gave a clue to the nature of forthcoming litigation. It suggested that state or federal statutory grounds for a claim to appropriate education were more likely to be favorably received than a new access claim. Indeed, almost all of the post-*Lau* cases involving the EHA are decided on statutory grounds (under the EHA, Section 504, or other federal statutes). This point will become clear in subsequent chapters. But *Lau* by no means undercuts the new access theory. If anything, it strengthens it by acknowledging that students have a strong claim to appropriate and meaningful educational opportunities.

Early Interpretation of Appropriate Education. Early case law developments sought to litigate what the *Lau* decision avoided—the issues of *functional exclusion* and *appropriate* education. In *Lau,* the question was whether the plaintiffs were excluded from an equal educational opportunity because they could not learn in the regular school program because of their language handicap. One could have cast *Lau* in different terms without changing the nature of the case, and said that there were two legal issues: Does the equal protection doctrine come into play when functional exclusion is practiced (as when a seriously emotionally disturbed child who can hear is placed in a class with hearing impaired children and receives no additional attention)? And does the equal protection doctrine operate when determining what is an appropriate education? The answer to both questions was yes, because both raised the issue of exclusion of a handicapped child from a *meaningful* equal educational opportunity because of handicap, whereas nonhandicapped children were not excluded from such an opportunity.

For example, in *Allen v. McDonough,* a consent decree was entered in a case brought under Massachusetts law that challenged the failure of school officials to complete the required evaluation process of more than 1,000 handicapped students and raised the issue of consequent denial of placement in an adequate program. The case resulted in an order requiring that the children be provided with an "educational plan" and a periodic review of that plan, both to be furnished on an accelerated time schedule.

The plaintiffs in *Crowder v. Riles* claimed that their right to an appropriate education as guaranteed by the California constitution was denied when they were assigned to inappropriate public education programs because their parents could not afford to pay the tuition for private programs and because the state's tuition-grant funds were inadequate to cover the needs of all the handicapped children who did not have appropriate public programs available to them. The state court held that the state violated the plaintiffs' right to equal protection under the *state* constitution by failing to fund fully the tuition-grant program, and it ordered the state to pay all the tuition, transportation, and maintenance costs of private school placement when appropriate public school programs are not available. The court did not rule on the allegations that the EHA and Section 504 were violated. Thus, the holding is limited to state law grounds.

In *Fialkowski v. Shapp,* the handicapped plaintiffs, relying on the equal protection and due process clauses of the Fourteenth Amendment, claimed they had been denied their right to an appropriate education because they had no chance to benefit from the programs offered them in the Philadelphia schools. The federal district court held for the plaintiffs.

In *Frederick L. v. Thomas,* the federal district court held that failure of the Philadelphia schools to provide special programs and classes for learning disabled children (who were not physically excluded from attending school) violated the children's rights under state law. The court found that the children were "effectively excluded" because they were unable to learn unless they were given educational services appropriate to their needs.

The plaintiffs in *Rhode Island Society for Autistic Children, Inc. v. Rhode Island Board of Regents* alleged that although they were not actually excluded from an educational opportunity, they were *de facto* (in fact) excluded because the programs they had been assigned to were lacking in meaningful educational opportunities. In a settlement of the case before trial, the court approved the parties' stipulations designed to prevent misclassification and, hence, functional exclusion.

According to the early cases, then, appropriate education consisted of timely and sufficient evaluations, individual programs, and review of the programs *(Allen v. McDonough).* It also included claims for tuition subsidies for private or technical institute schooling when appropriate public programs did not exist *(Crowder v. Riles).* "Appropriate education" was a justiciable claim (one that could be resolved by a court) under the equal protection clause *(Fialkowski);* and included more than admission to programs, in addition requiring programs that were more likely to benefit the handicapped child *(Frederick L. v. Thomas* and *Rhode Island Society for Autistic Children).* All of these cases had a "new access" flavor and relied on the use of equal protection for meaningful education.

There was yet another set of appropriate education cases. These cases were brought on behalf of Spanish-speaking students allegedly misclassified as handicapped because they were tested in English rather than in Spanish, or who were arguably denied an appropriate (meaningful) education because their classes were not taught bilingually or in Spanish. Some of these cases challenged placing Spanish-speaking students in special education programs; others sought bilingual education in "regular" or mainstream programs along with enforcement of the Bilingual Education Act.[10] By and large, the plaintiffs in these cases were successful.

Early Cases on Free Education. There was, of course, more to zero reject and equal protection than functional exclusion and appropriate education. Zero reject and equal protection included the right to compensatory education when a handicapped student had been denied an equal educational opportunity during his or her school-age years.[11] At-home or other nonschool programs for children who were unable to attend school also were included.[12] The cases extended the right to education to handicapped children whose parents were forced to seek private school training because appropriate public programs were unavailable.[13]

The early cases (before 1975) raised the issues of *free* and *appropriate* education. Although *PARC* and *Mills* held that handicapped children were entitled to a free appropriate education regardless of the nature or severity of the child's handicap, it remained to refine the zero reject issue as it related to a free education.

In *Kruse v. Campbell,* learning disabled students in Fairfax County, Virginia, brought a suit that challenged the state's tuition-payment program on equal protection grounds and under Section 504. The Virginia program consisted of two basic components. First, when a handicapped child had to be enrolled in a private special education program because there were no appropriate public school programs, the state paid 75% of the cost of the private program (up to a maximum of $1,250 a year for nonresidential care or $5,000 a year for residential care), but the parents had to make up the difference between the state tuition subsidy and the actual cost. Although local school boards had the option of paying the difference, they usually did not. Second, the state's welfare department would pay the full cost of residential care only if the child's parents gave the department custody of the child, in which case the local board had no responsibility.

Partly because the state's program discriminated against the poor and partly because of the enforced custody requirement, a federal district court struck down the program and ordered the plaintiffs to file a new plan for tuition reimbursement. The grounds on which the court made its decision were the familiar Fourteenth Amendment ones (nondiscrimination against the poor), and its finding that "something is wrong" with the existing system clearly affirmed the plaintiffs' right to a free and appropriate education.

In a subsequent action in the case, the district court ruled that the state must furnish appropriate education to all poor handicapped students commensurate with the education available to more affluent handicapped children until appropriate public education was made available to them. The decision turned on wealth discrimination grounds and treated the poor handicapped students' rights to an education as equal to those of the more affluent. The court ordered the state to devise a plan for educating *all* of the handicapped children. Also, handicapped children who had been placed in the state's custody were to be returned to their parents or guardians within 60 days of the order. The U.S. Supreme Court reversed the federal district court and ordered the case to be retried on statutory grounds (EHA and Section 504) rather than on constitutional ones.

The decision in *Doe v. Laconia,* a federal court case decided under New Hampshire law, held that the state board of education's policy of spending funds allocated for supplemental tuition payments for *all* handicapped children on a priority basis (geared to the severity of the handicap and discriminatory to emotionally disturbed children) did not violate the equal protection doctrine. According to the court, the board's program had a "rational basis for giving those children with the severest handicap preferential treatment," and it was held that equal protection does not require the decision to be based on the parents' ability to pay.

None of these tuition cases was based on the EHA, which guarantees a free appropriate education to all handicapped children. They were instead based on the equal protection doctrine of the Fourteenth Amendment and could well be decided differently if brought under the EHA. Except as otherwise noted, none of the cases described in the preceding discussion of zero reject and equal protection were disposed of under federal statutes granting handicapped persons protection against discrimination by public school authorities.

FEDERAL LEGISLATION

Nothing is clearer in the EHA than the intent of Congress that no handicapped child be excluded from school by recipients of federal funds for education of the handicapped, and that all involved agencies follow a policy of zero reject. Finding (as the courts did) that both total and functional exclusion existed [Sec. 1400(b)(3) and (4)], and concluding that it was in the national interest to provide programs to meet the needs of handicapped children and thereby assure them equal protection of the law [Sec. 1400(b)(9)], Congress declared the purpose of the EHA to provide a free appropriate education to the handicapped [Sec. 1400(c)] and acted in numerous ways to implement the zero reject policy.

Free Appropriate Public Education (FAPE)
By the 1975 amendment (P.L. 94-142), Congress required the states to provide full educational opportunities to all handicapped children between the ages of 3 and 18 ("ages-certain" requirements) by September 1, 1978 ("dates-certain" requirements), and to all handicapped children between the ages of 3 and 21 by September 1, 1980.

There was, however, an exception. If a state law or practice or court order were inconsistent with the ages-certain and dates-certain requirements, the state was not required to follow those requirements. This provision recognized that the states themselves should have some autonomy to continue to educate certain age groups. In a very real sense, the exception paid deference to the tradition, engrained in some states' laws, of state and local autonomy over education. But the exception also was a political necessity: The EHA probably would not have passed or it would have been substantially weaker with such a provision in it.

The 1975 amendments (P.L. 94-142) do, however, require all states to make a free appropriate education available to all children with disabilities ages 6 through 17 if the state does not have a mandatory education law for children in that age range.

Early Intervention and Special Education
Subsequent amendments of the EHA expanded the age coverage. Under the 1983 amendments (P.L. 98-199, codified at 20 U.S.C. Sec. 1419), Congress emphasized the need for more early education. It authorized incentive grants to states for special education and related services to handicapped children from birth to 3 years of age. It also expanded

the early childhood state implementation grant program enabling states to receive grants to plan, develop, or implement a comprehensive system of services for children with disabilities from birth to 5 years.

By P.L. 99-457 (adding a new Part H to the Education of the Handicapped Act), enacted in 1986, Congress extended the federal role in education of very young children. It did this by two separate additions to Part H: Title I (birth through age 2) and Title II (ages 3 through 5). (Title I is new law and is codified at 20 U.S.C. Sec. 1471 and following; its regulations are codified in 34 Code of Federal Regulations, Part 303. Title II amends previous law and is codified at 20 U.S.C. Sec. 1412 and following.)

As members of Congress made clear when they were introducing P.L. 99-457, the legislation is a "pro-family" bill. Thus, the focus of P.L. 99-457's Part H—infants and toddlers—is on the person with a disability and the person's family. This is very different from the other major provisions of EHA—namely, those in Part B that provide for the free appropriate public education of children with disabilities—because Part B focuses on the person and then on the parent, not the family.

Moreover, Part H is motivated by concerns that are broader than those that persuaded Congress to enact Part B. For one thing, it is perfectly clear from the legislative history that Congress has been convinced that early intervention services are cost-effective. Similar evidence was simply not available when Congress enacted P.L. 94-142 and Part B.

In addition, Part H sets four goals that are different and more comprehensive than Part B, which deals only with free appropriate public education as a goal. The Part H goals are: to develop the capacities of infants and toddlers; to reduce the costs of special education; to minimize the likelihood that people with disabilities will be institutionalized; and to enhance families' capacities for working with their children. Although human development and family/parent-child interaction are subsumed as goals of Part B, they are explicit goals of Part H. Moreover, the goals of preventing institutionalization and reducing special education costs are distinct to Part H. With these observations in mind, it is now appropriate to describe Part H.

With respect to Title I (birth through age 2), it provided separate funding for the education of handicapped infants and toddlers. Those infants and toddlers who qualify for the services must need early intervention because they either (a) experience developmental delays or (b) have diagnosed physical or mental conditions with a high probability of causing developmental delays. In addition, each state has the option of serving infants and toddlers who are "at-risk" for developmental delays. Developmental delays must be in the following areas of development: cognitive, physical, language and speech, psychosocial, or self-help. The states may otherwise define "developmental delay" but must include delays in those areas of development.

Under Part H, early intervention services are those that are designed to meet the infant's needs in any one or more of certain areas of development (physical, cognitive, language and speech, psychosocial, and self-help), comply with state standards, include at least 10 different types of intervention, and are provided by qualified personnel. Also, early intervention services are those that are designed to meet the family's needs related to enhancing the child's development in the stated areas, are selected in collaboration with the parents, are provided under public supervision by qualified personnel, are provided in conformity with an individualized family service plan (IFSP), and are free unless the state establishes a sliding fee scale of payment.

The 10 different types of intervention include family training, counseling, and home visits; special instruction; speech pathology and audiology; occupational therapy; physical therapy; psychological services; case management services; medical services only for diagnosis and evaluation; early identification, screening, and assessment services; and health services necessary to help the infant or toddler benefit from the other intervention services.

The regulations make it clear that professionals have new or expanded roles and responsibilities with respect to families. They are expected to consult and train parents, participate in the assessment of a family and the development of the IFSP, provide case management services, provide psychological and social work services, and offer special instruction to the child and information to the parents about special instruction. The regulations also say that the list of services is not exhaustive; other services, such as respite and other family support services, may be provided. In addition, parent-to-parent support personnel, not just professionals or paraprofessionals, may provide those services. Finally, services to families also may include family training, counseling, and home visits. In short, the regulations not only expand what professionals must offer but also who may offer it.

The personnel authorized to provide these services include those who have qualified as special educators, speech-language pathologists, audiologists, occupational therapists, physicians, physical therapists, psychologists, social workers, nurses, and nutritionists.

Each state that has not yet mandated early intervention or preschool special education as a matter of its own law has the option to participate in Part H (infants and toddlers, birth through age 2) and in the early childhood programs for children from ages 3 through 5. As of March, 1989, each state had elected the option of participating in Part H.

It is important to contrast the broad eligibility provisions of Part H with Part B (ages 3-21). Under Part H, those infants and toddlers who have or may experience developmental delays or are at-risk for such delays are entitled to receive services. Each state may determine which children are "at-risk." The federal law does not define those children.

But, under Part B, only those children and youth who have disabilities that cause a need for special education are entitled to the law's benefits. This means, for example, that a student who has AIDS but who experiences no adverse effect in education because of the disability is not entitled to the EHA. Very few students are in this category, but there are some.

The zero-reject rule has a somewhat different meaning for infants and toddlers. Not until the fifth year of a state's participation in Part H is the state required to have in place a program that serves all age-eligible, disability-eligible infants and toddlers. Because all states have chosen to participate in Part H (as of March, 1989), this means that 1991 is the target year for full compliance. Thus, during the first 4 years of a state's participation, some eligible infants and toddlers may not receive any direct services. Once the state is in its fifth year, all such infants and toddlers must receive the services. (Note that each state may drop out of Part H after a planning, start-up period. This means that some states may later decide not to serve infants/toddlers.)

Moreover, although Part B provides for services free of charge to parents, Part H allows the state and local agencies to establish a system of payments for early intervention services, including a schedule of sliding fees. Some services must be free; they include child-find, evaluation and assessment, case management, and certain administrative and coordinative functions. If state law, however, provides for free early intervention services, the state law prevails and a state may not use the federal law as permission to charge fees.

Note that the IFSP must contain a statement of the services that are "necessary" to meet the child's and family's needs. This is a different standard than in Part B, which provides instead for an "appropriate" education.

Title II of P.L. 99-457 relates to children ages 3 through 5 and essentially broadens the previous law relating to them, as enacted by the 1983 and 1975 amendments to EHA. The 1983 amendment relating to children aged 3 through 5 authorized incentive grants to states for special education and related services for those children—but only for those children, not their families, and only on behalf of children who traditionally qualify as handicapped under the EHA. The 1983 amendments also expanded the early childhood state implementation grant to enable states to plan and implement comprehensive systems of services for children birth through age 5.

The significance of the 1986 amendments, particularly as represented by Title I (birth –2), is set out later in this chapter. As noted there, the 1986 amendments represent a major departure from the traditional federal role and an overwhelming reaffirmation of the more recent, activist federal role.

Transition Out of School

Also under the 1983 amendments, Congress paid special attention to a new problem—the transition from school to adulthood (also called "aging out"). First, it gave the Secretary of Education (who acts in special education matters through the Assistant Secretary, Office of Special Education and Rehabilitative Services (OSERS), acting principally through the Office of Special Education Programs (OSEP), authority to enter into contracts with SEAs to develop and operate and to disseminate information concerning specially designed programs of post-secondary education [Sec. 1424(a)]. Second, it provided for secondary education and transitional services for handicapped youth [Sec. 1425]. Third, it authorized the creation of a national clearinghouse on post-secondary education for the purpose of providing information about available services and programs in post-secondary education [Sec. 1433]. Finally, it authorized SEAs to make transition services available to deaf-blind children upon their becoming 22 years old [Sec. 1422].

The decision to emphasize transition and post-secondary educational programs under the EHA is consistent with Congress' later decision in 1986 to amend the Rehabilitation Act to create a program of supported employment for people with severe disabilities. Supported work substantially changes the notion of vocational rehabilitation services. Traditionally, those services were targeted for people with mild to moderate disabilities, and who, with short-term interventions (basically, evaluation and training), could return to work and not require much, if any, further vocational rehabilitation services. Under the supported work program, however, vocational rehabilitation services were focused on people with severe disabilities who, with ongoing or continuous vocational rehabilitation services (as contrasted with short-term services), could work with support from a nondisabled worker or "job coach," in competitive employment.

The 1986 amendments to the Rehabilitation Act, creating supported employment programs, did not do away with the traditional vocational rehabilitation programs. Instead, they added new programs. And they were consistent with the 1983 amendments to the EHA, creating transition and post-secondary programs, in that they recognized the need for special education to concentrate on the future of students who first benefited from the EHA and who were leaving special education ("aging out" or "transitioning") and entering the world of work and adult services. By combining the EHA's focus on transition with the Rehabilitation Act's focus on supported employment, Congress attempted to ensure that special education would have lasting benefits for all students, especially those with severe disabilities.

Coverage: LEAs, IEUs, Residential Facilities, and Private Schools

Congress applied the full-service goal to public elementary and secondary LEAs and IEUs (intermediate educational units) [Sec. 1412], private schools [Sec. 1412 and 1413], and publicly operated residential facilities that provide elementary or secondary education [Sec. 1412]. By providing for such extensive coverage, Congress obviously intended to prevent "service gaps" or "cracks." It attempted to reach all handicapped children without regard to the nature of the educational system by which they are, might, or should be served. As noted in chapter 2, Congress was able to affect the LEAs, IEUs, and state residential facilities by requiring compliance with the requirements of the EHA as a condition for receiving funds and by applying Section 504 to them.

There are other reasons—besides closing the gaps or cracks—behind the coverage requirements. First, students with disabilities are citizens of the state; if the state receives federal funds, they should benefit, wherever they are served or live within the state. Otherwise, they are not treated as full citizens of the state. This concept of treatment of full citizens also has a strong equal protection flavor, because it ensures equal treatment of comparable citizens (those with disabilities). Second, it allows advocates for children with disabilities to concentrate their efforts on a single state agency and state program—the SEA (state education agency) and the state school system, with its component local school district. (This desire for accountability is also part of the "single-agency responsibility" provisions described later in this section.)

Placement by Public Agencies.   Congress distinguished between two types of private school placement. One type concerns children referred to or placed in private schools by public agencies. Each state's annual program plan contains policies and procedures to assure that, to the extent consistent with the number and location of handicapped children in the state who are in private elementary and secondary schools, the plan will provide for their participation in the state program by furnishing them special education and related services [Sec. 1413].

There are additional requirements for children placed in private schools by public agencies. They must (1) be provided with special education and related services (2) in conformance with an individualized education program (3) at no cost to their parents if the public agency refers them to such schools or facilities as a means of carrying out requirements of the EHA [Sec. 1413]. Moreover, when the agency makes such a placement or referral, the state must have determined previously that the private school or facility meets the standards set by the state and that the child retains all rights under the EHA [Sec. 1413].

Placement by Parents. A second type of private school placement is one made by the child's parents. As a general rule, if a free appropriate public education is available to a child in a public agency but the parent chooses to place him or her in a private school, the agency is not required to pay for the education. The agency must, however, make services available to the child, as described previously, if he or she attends the private school. If the agency and the parents disagree about whether an appropriate program for the child is available or whether the agency is financially responsible for the private school fees, either may initiate a due process hearing. (Exceptions to the general rule about unilateral placement are discussed in chapter 7.)

Clearly, Congress intended for zero reject to apply to handicapped children placed in private schools by their parents or by school authorities. Congress keeps pressure on the public sector to remain responsible for them, thus attempting to answer its findings that, "because of the lack of adequate services within the public school system, families are often forced to find services outside the public school system, often at great distance from their residence and at their own expense" [Sec. 1400(b)(6)].

Finally, the Secretary of Education may bypass SEAs in providing special education to children attending private schools in states where there is a state constitutional prohibition against public-private sharing of educational services [Sec. 1413].

Rationale. The reasons for applying the Act to private schools are easy to understand. If an LEA places a child in a private school as its way of discharging its duties to the child under the EHA, the child's rights to a free appropriate education should follow him or her to the private placement because the child is a citizen of the state and entitled to benefit from the EHA in the same manner as any other citizen of the state; the place of education is irrelevant to the child's rights. Moreover, the LEA is not allowed to divest itself of its duties to the child by making a private school placement when it cannot discharge those duties by educating the child itself. Finally, because LEAs are not always able to provide an appropriate education to every handicapped child and enter into contracts with private schools to educate some of the children, the children in the private schools become the beneficiaries of the contract between the LEA and the private school. In that capacity, the children retain the rights they have with the LEA, and the LEA should not be able to deprive them of their rights by contract.

Direct Services by SEA

The EHA [Sec. 1414(d)] provides that an SEA must use the federal funds otherwise available to an LEA to provide services directly to children with disabilities whenever it determines that an LEA is unable or unwilling to do so or to be consolidated with another LEA, or has students who can be served best in a state or regional center. The purpose of the direct services provision is to ensure that all eligible students in a state receive a free appropriate public education; it is another one of the "gap-closing" provisions of the law.

Although use of the direct services provision was before the Supreme Court in *Honig v. Doe,* a 1988 decision, the Court did not rule on it and instead left standing the court of appeals decision that ordered the SEA (California) to provide services directly to two students who had been suspended illegally from an LEA (San Francisco).

A similar result—court-ordered direct services—was reached in *Doe v. Rockingham County School Board,* when a child had been suspended and received no hearing on his suspension and no services during the suspension, which was for 29 days. The irreparable detriment (which the student experienced during the 29 days) and the LEA's refusal to make a hearing available were decisive facts. Similarly, when an LEA has failed to comply with a decision by a hearing officer (see chapter 7 for a discussion of hearing officers and due process protections) for 18 months and when the SEA's withholding of funds from the SEA has not produced LEA compliance with the decision for still another 18 months, an SEA may be compelled to provide services directly, under the holding in *Wilson v. McDonald.* These cases suggest that advocates will succeed in seeking direct services if there is a long period of time of interrupted education, bad faith on the LEA's part (refusal to convene a hearing), or illegal action (suspending in violation of the EHA).

Child Census

Each SEA and LEA must conduct an annual program to identify, locate, and evaluate all handicapped children residing in their respective jurisdictions, regardless of the severity of their handicaps [Secs. 1412 and 1414]. Congress recognized that a zero reject policy would be meaningless without a child identification program. It also realized that identification of handicapped children was a necessary prerequisite to planning, programming, and appropriating for them to attend school.

In light of past school practices that excluded the most severely handicapped children, it is significant that Congress specified that the programs must identify *all* children, "regardless of the severity of their handicap" (emphasis added). The requirement of a child census is consistent with Congress' findings that many handicapped children are totally excluded from schools and are denied "a successful educational experience because their handicaps are undetected" [Sec. 1400(b)(4) and (5)].

The purposes of the child census are to ensure that no children are denied a free appropriate education because they have not been found or located, to ensure cooperation between the educational agencies and others (such as health, mental health, developmental disabilities, social services, corrections, and even private agencies), and to enable the

SEA and LEA to appropriate funds, plan and deliver programs, and be held accountable to all children with disabilities.

Service Priorities

Realizing that many excluded handicapped children are the most seriously handicapped and that they usually do not receive an appropriate education, Congress required recipients to use federal aid for two service priorities [Sec. 1412 and Sec. 300.320-.324]. First in line are handicapped children receiving no education ("first priority" children). Next are children with the most severe handicaps within each disability who are not receiving an adequate education ("second priority" children).

The policy was designed to overcome the total exclusion of some children [Sec. 1400 (b)(4)] and the inadequate education or functional exclusion of others [Sec. 1400(b)(3) and (5)] as a method of implementing a zero reject policy [Sec. 1400(c)]. Apparently, Congress intended to make sure that funds would be distributed across the whole spectrum of handicapping conditions and prevent them from being spent wholly on one class of severely impaired children (e.g., the seriously emotionally disturbed). There is a strong equal protection flavor in this approach.

In addition, Congress has emphasized transition services for deaf-blind children [Sec. 1422]. Congress obviously recognized that service priority requirements should have special attention when severely disabled youth are "aging out" of school and "aging in" with respect to adult services—i.e., when they are in "transition."

The purpose of the service priorities is to ensure that the children who are most likely not to be served because of the severe nature of their disabilities are, in fact, given a claim on federal funds so that they may be served. Considering that the schools historically had excluded students (total exclusion) or served only those with mild to moderate disabilities (partial exclusion), it makes sense for the EHA to require federal funds to be spent first on unserved and then on harder-to-serve students.

Naturally, the service priorities have a strong equal protection flavor to them, and they clearly support the principle of zero reject. But they also raise the issue of competing equities—namely, to what extent some students (those with mild to moderate disabilities) should be disadvantaged (by having lower claims to federal dollars) in order to provide an advantage to other students (those with the most severe disabilities). Of course, the issue of competing equities is not new. All policy decisions, whether by Congress or by state legislatures, and all legal decisions by courts (resolving the complaints of some people against others), involve the balancing of competing claims.

Finally, the service priorities illustrate a familiar approach by Congress—which is often to prefer to fund programs for persons with severe disabilities if a choice must be made between funding programs for all people with disabilities or only those with severe disabilities. This approach exists, for example, in the Developmental Disabilities Assistance and Bill of Rights Act, in the 1986 amendments to the Rehabilitation Act (creating the supported work initiative), and in various programs under the Social Security Act (such as Medicaid and Medicare). This approach attacks a problem (here, the need to provide an appropriate education to all students with a disability) from the bottom (a "bottom-up" approach) rather than from the top (a "creaming" approach). The bottom-up approach focuses funds on those with the greatest disabilities; the creaming approach focuses funds on those who are the easiest to serve because they have the mildest disabilities.

Appropriate Education and Functional Exclusion

Congress answered the problem of functional exclusion by requiring SEAs and LEAs to provide an *appropriate* education to handicapped children [Sec. 1400(c) and Sec. 1412(1)]. It defined appropriateness in two ways.

First, appropriate is defined generally in terms of the procedure schools must use in dealing with handicapped children: (1) The child must be furnished with an individualized education program, (2) must be evaluated on a nondiscriminatory basis, (3) is entitled to a due process hearing if the appropriateness of his or her education is in doubt; (4) the parents are entitled to be included in the development of their child's individualized education program; (5) the child is entitled to appropriately and adequately trained teachers, (6) has the right of access to his or her school records, (7) is entitled to a barrier-free school environment, (8) may be included in preschool programs; and (9) the child's representatives (parents or others) are entitled to participate in and be given notice of school actions affecting special education programs and the child's own education. Although separately provided for by the EHA, as a whole these requirements are intended to answer the problem of functional exclusion and to assure an appropriate education.

Second, Section 300.4 and Section 300.300-.307 of the regulations defined *free appropriate education* to mean special education and related services that (1) are provided at public expense, under public supervision and direction, and without charge; (2) meet the standards of the SEA, including requirements of the EHA; (3) include preschool, elementary, and secondary school education in the state involved; and (4) are provided in conformity with the child's individualized education program.

Chapter 5 discusses the details of appropriate education. The point here is that the EHA and Section 504 both attempt to prevent functional exclusion by requiring that the handicapped child be given an education appropriate to his or her conditions and needs.

Hiring People with Disabilities

Congress pushed the zero reject principle a step farther than the courts did by requiring that a child's education be meaningful after he or she leaves school. SEAs and LEAs were charged with making positive efforts to hire and promote qualified disabled persons in programs receiving EHA funds [Sec. 1405]. Thus, an SEA or LEA must take affirmative action on employment of the handicapped in EHA programs (such as hiring a blind teacher to teach handicapped children or promoting an orthopedically impaired person to supervise special education programs funded under the EHA). Of course, the emphasis on transition in the 1983 amendments reflects Congress' concern with employment.

All of the education and training the schools provide is meaningless to students unless they have a realistic opportunity to make later use of it. Zero reject in special education should not be an empty promise. Equal protection should be meaningful to its intended beneficiaries. And, of course, economic benefits will accrue to the public if handicapped individuals are hired. The employment provisions in Section 1405 dovetail with Sections 503 and 504 of the Rehabilitation Act [29 U.S.C. Sec. 706(7) and Sec. 794] to prohibit discrimination in employment.

Comprehensive System of Personnel Development
To provide a sufficient number of adequately trained teachers and related-services personnel to educate all students appropriately, and to ensure that regular education faculty members in the schools are trained to accommodate students with disabilities in their programs (in the least restrictive environment), the EHA requires SEAs and LEAs to have programs for personnel development (Sec. 1412 and 1431 through 1435). Without sufficient adequately trained personnel, the zero reject principle (as well as principles relating to appropriate education and least restrictive environments) could not be implemented.

Single-Agency Responsibility
Congress sought to make the zero reject principle effective by providing for one, and *only one,* point of responsibility and accountability. It required a *single* state agency, the SEA, to be responsible for assuring HEW that requirements of EHA are carried out. In addition, all educational programs for handicapped children within the state, including programs administered by *another* state or local agency (such as social services, mental health, mental retardation, human resources, public health, corrections, or juvenile services), were placed under the *general* supervision of persons responsible for educational programs for handicapped in the SEA, must be monitored by the SEA, and must meet the SEA's educational standards [Sec. 1412(6)].

To buttress the single-agency device for zero reject, Congress enabled the SEA to preempt LEA programs [Sec. 1414(d)] and to require LEAs to consolidate their services [Sec. 1414(c)]. Section 1414(b) provides for a complaint procedure for local and state agencies. There is no doubt that these provisions were designed to close the service gaps and prevent the buck-passing and responsibility-shuffling that resulted in some handicapped children not being included in educational programs in the past.

As the states attempted to implement the EHA with the limited federal and state dollars (the EHA never has been funded by Congress at the full limit it authorizes—see chapter 10 for a description of the authorization of federal funds), they found that they were facing huge expenses. Not only did they increase their own appropriations, but so did LEAs. And still funds were not sufficient, particularly for people with severe disabilities.

A major funding stream, however, existed outside of the EHA: the Medicaid and Medicare programs created by the Social Security Act. Those programs provided federal funds to pay for some of the medical or medically related expenses of people with severe disabilities who usually are required to be poor to qualify for the medical assistance funds.

To tap into the Medicaid and Medicare funding streams, some states created programs that combined the special education personnel and funds under the EHA with the medical personnel and funds under the Medicaid and Medicare programs. By taking this approach, they could ensure enough funds in the aggregate to pay for the education and related services (such as physical therapy, occupational therapy, medical evaluations) required to provide an appropriate education to students with severe disabilities. In short, they sought to prevent either total exclusion or functional exclusion, either of which would violate the zero reject principle.

The federal agency that administers Medicaid—the Health Care Financing Agency, Department of Health and Human Services—refused to reimburse Massachusetts for Medicaid dollars that it had spent in the jointly administered EHA-Medicaid program of education for students with severe disabilities who lived in a Medicaid-approved facility (an intermediate care facility for the mentally retarded—ICF/MR). Massachusetts sued the federal government for reimbursement, and the Supreme Court, in *Bowen v. Massachusetts*, approved the use of the Medicaid funds for joint education of ICF/MR residents.

Shortly after that decision was rendered in 1988, Congress enacted The Medicare Catastrophic Coverage Act of 1988. This law prohibits Medicaid agencies from refusing to pay for medical services covered under a state's Medicaid or Medicare plans that are provided to children with disabilities, as long as the services are included in the students' individualized education programs (IEPs are discussed in chapter 5).

Under the 1988 amendments, Section 1903 of the Social Security Act (42 U.S. Code; Sec. 1396b) was changed by the addition of a new paragraph. That paragraph provides that nothing in the Medicare title of the Social Security Act shall be construed as prohibiting or restricting payment for medical assistance for covered services furnished to a handicapped child because those services are included in the child's IEP or are furnished to an infant or toddler as part of the IFSP.

The Congressional committee that sponsored this amendment has added clarifying language. The committee reported that the amendment clarifies that the federal Medicaid matching funds are available for the cost of health services, covered under a state's Medicaid plan, that are furnished to a child with a disability or to an infant or toddler under the IEP or IFSP even though those services are included in the IEP or IFSP. The committee added that, although the SEAs are financially responsible for educational services, the state Medicaid agencies, in the case of Medicaid-eligible handicapped children, remain responsible for the "related services" identified in the child's IEP or IFSP if they are covered under the state's Medicaid plan. These services can include speech pathology and audiology, psychological services, physical and occupational therapy, and medical counseling and services for diagnostic and evaluation purposes.

The effect of the *Bowen* case and the Medicaid Catastrophic Coverage Act is that a new funding stream for related services will exist for states that decide to combine educational programs (funded under the EHA) with medical programs (funded under the Social Security Act's Medicaid or Medicare programs). This will relieve the pressure on the state's educational dollars but increase the pressure on its health-care dollars. In the case of students who have medical complications or are primarily in health-care delivery systems (such as those in ICFs/MR or in early childhood programs administered by departments of health), the prospects are good that they will receive jointly operated services. This will have the ultimate effect of ensuring no violation of the zero reject rule by their total or functional exclusion from special education.

Use of Private Insurance; Free Education

One way in which the schools traditionally excluded students with disabilities was by charging them fees for services. The fees often were very high (because the services were expensive or because they were set high to discourage the students' enrollment). Therefore, the EHA implements the zero reject rule by providing that education must be furnished free to the students and their parents. If an LEA charges any fees to any students, it may charge students with disabilities, too; uniformly assessed fees are permissible. But expenses for transportation may not be billed; parents who have insurance policies that reimburse for medically related services may not be required to make a claim on their insurers if the services are provided to comply with the EHA[14]; and states may not charge for the living expenses for students whom they place in public or private residential programs to comply with the EHA.[15]

Architectural Barriers

Physical barriers can cause some handicapped children to be excluded from school (whether they are mobility impaired or not—e.g., blind or in wheelchairs; some children with mental retardation also have physical disabilities). Therefore, Congress has authorized the Secretary of Education to make grants to and enter into cooperative arrangements with SEAs to remove architectural barriers [Sec. 1406].

Section 504

Regulations implementing Section 504 make it clear that Section 504 applies to preschool, elementary, and secondary public education programs receiving any federal assistance. They also make it clear, especially in Section 104.33(a), that a zero reject policy is required by the schools. Section 104.32 requires the schools to undertake a child identification program. Section 104.33(b) requires them to provide an appropriate education to each handicapped person who is a legal resident of the recipient's jurisdiction, regardless of the nature or severity of the person's handicap. Section 104.33(c) ensures that the program will be without cost to the child's family.

As pointed out in chapter 2, Section 504 and its implementing regulations differ in important respects from the EHA. There are other differences related to the principle of zero reject.

Section 504 applies to public schools not only as providers of educational services [Subpart D of the regulations] but also as providers of health, welfare, and social services [Subpart F], and as employers [Subpart B]. It applies to school facilities as well, requiring them to be accessible to handicapped persons [Subpart C]; the EHA authorizes grants of federal funds to SEAs and LEAs to enable them to comply with federal architectural barriers legislation [Sec. 1406]. Under the Section 504 regulations, as of 1977 all new school construction had to be barrier-free [Sec. 104.23] and all other programs had to be made accessible within 3 years [Sec. 104.22].

Section 104.22 of the regulations provides that SEAs or LEAs do not have to make each existing school accessible to students with disabilities if programs for them are "on the whole" accessible. Schools may redesign equipment, reassign classes or other services from nonaccessible to accessible buildings, make aids available to students, or provide services at other sites, including the students' homes. Each building in a school district need not be completely accessible, but the district may not make only one facility or part of a facility accessible if the result is to segregate students with disabilities from their nondisabled peers. In choosing between alternative acceptable methods of accessibility, an LEA or SEA must give priority to those that offer programs in the most integrated settings appropriate for the students with disabilities (see chapter 6 for a discussion of the principle of integration and least restrictive environments).

Subpart D also sets forth requirements for nondiscrimination in preschool, elementary, secondary, and adult education programs, including secondary vocational education programs. "Adult education" refers to educational programs and activities for adults operated by elementary and secondary schools. The provisions of Subpart D apply to both public and private state and local education agencies that are federally assisted.

The basic requirements of Section 504's regulations, which parallel the cases and the EHA, are that handicapped persons, regardless of the nature or severity of their handicap, must be furnished a free appropriate public education, and educational agencies must undertake to identify and locate all unserved handicapped children. These requirements are designed to ensure that no child is excluded from school on the basis of a handicap. Thus, a funding recipient that operates a public school system must either educate handicapped children in its regular program or provide them with an appropriate alternative education at public expense.

CASE LAW

It was entirely predictable when the EHA was enacted that its efforts to prevent the absolute exclusion of handicapped children from a free appropriate education would not be entirely successful. By the same token, it was predictable that courts would be called upon to interpret the EHA and its regulations in cases in which school districts attempted to exclude handicapped children completely or subject them to conditions that the EHA was intended to correct. Yet, the scope of the courts' involvement is surprising, and the issues they have been obliged to resolve are manifold and sophisticated.

Expulsion

The most pressing issue early on was whether school districts may expel handicapped children or whether the EHA prevents them from doing so because expulsion is a denial of any special education. The courts seemed to speak with a unanimous voice: The EHA prevents a school district from expelling a handicapped child if the behavior that triggered the expulsion proceedings is related to the child's handicap. Instead of expelling the student, a school agency may change his or her placement from a less to a more restrictive one—but only after notifying the parents and giving them an opportunity to protest through due process proceedings, and only after reevaluating the child and preparing a new IEP for him or her. Short-term suspension is allowed. So too is expulsion when the child's behavior is not causally related to the handicap.

This result was confirmed by the Supreme Court in *Honig v. Doe,* a 1988 decision that followed the language of the EHA and the line of reasoning established earlier by lower courts. In *Honig,* the Court ruled that the "stay-put" provisions of the EHA (see chapter 6—the stay-put provisions prohibit an LEA from moving a student from the current placement during the time of a dispute before a hearing officer or court concerning the student's rights under the EHA) prohibit school authorities from unilaterally excluding disabled children from the classroom or appropriate programs because of dangerous or disruptive conduct that grows out of their disabilities, at least while the dispute is under way. The Court found that the EHA is clear and unequivocal in its language that the student must "stay put." Moreover, it found that Congress intended to prevent school authorities from making unilateral changes of placement.

Of course, if parents and school authorities agree on a change while a dispute is being contested, the student's placement may be changed. The effect of this part of the Court's decision was to affirm the stay-put rule and prevent unilateral expulsions if the behavior grows out of the student's disability.

Yet the Court did not leave the LEA defenseless. It said that school authorities may use normal, nonplacement changing procedures (including temporary suspensions of up to 10 days) if a student poses an immediate threat to the safety of others. It also said that the EHA [Sec. 1415(e)(2)] allows school authorities to file a lawsuit for "appropriate" relief if the parents and the school authorities cannot agree on an interim placement. In such a suit for relief, the EHA creates a presumption in favor of the student's present placement. But the presumption can be overcome if the student's present placement and behavior are substantially likely to result in an injury to self or to others.

The effect of the *Honig* decision is difficult to predict, especially so soon after it was rendered. Some effects seem likely, however. First, the case may encourage schools to seek injunctive relief—an order that the student's placement be changed, even during hearings on the dispute. Before the *Honig* decision it was not entirely clear whether LEAs could do this. Now that it is clear, they may well go to court for relief. Second, given the 10-day rule (no suspensions for more than 10 days), the case may prevent not just a

simple expulsion of more than 10 days but also "serial" or "tacking-on" expulsions of
fewer than 10 days that, in the aggregate, amount to more than 10 days.

Third, the case may have the effect of encouraging schools to find ways to intervene
to prevent student dangerousness other than expelling a student. By putting pressure on
schools to intervene during the stay-put period, the case may create both good and bad
results, depending on the type of intervention. For example, some school authorities may
seek to prevent dangerous conduct by positive interventions such as increased rewards for
good behavior. Or they may resort to aversive or negative interventions such as corporal
punishment, physical restraint, in-school suspensions by means of time out, or the use
of noxious substances. Special educators, behavioral and other psychologists, lawyers, eth-
icists, and families are engaged in heated debate concerning the use of these aversive interventions. As of September, 1988, it was not settled law that aversive interventions—
particularly when used to prevent dangerous behavior—are illegal. There are strong arguments that they are or should be illegal, but no court had prohibited them under the
EHA and one federal district court has held that time-out does not violate the EHA.

Finally, the *Honig* case may encourage school authorities to prosecute students for
dangerous behavior. There has been no doubt but that LEAs resort to the criminal process
to handle disruptive or dangerous students and may try to do so again, when faced with
Honig's confirmation of the stay-put rule and the difficulty and expense of seeking an injunction to get the student's placement changed. Whether the courts would see that use
of the criminal process is an attempt to escape the stay-put rule, and thus a violation of
the EHA, is unknown.

Honig dealt only with use of the stay-put provision and expulsion of students with
disabilities. It did not address the expulsion issue in its broader sense—whether any expulsion is permissible under the EHA. As noted, a long line of cases does establish the
following rule: Students with disabilities may not be expelled if the cause of their behavior
is their disability.

S-1 v. Turlington was the leading case on expulsion. Seven retarded students were expelled from high school early in the 1977-78 school year and for the entire 1978-79 school
year because of alleged misconduct; two other handicapped children, not under expulsion
orders, contended thay had not been properly evaluated and placed. All sought due process hearings, alleging that their retardation was the cause of their disorderliness and that
the EHA prohibits their expulsion, even for disciplinary reasons. The schools refused to
give them any hearings, contending that the students lost their right to a free appropriate
public education and hearing opportunities under the EHA when they were expelled because of their misconduct; that their misconduct was not related to their handicap; that
only if they had been classified as "seriously emotionally disturbed" would their conduct
have related to their expulsion; and that disciplinary procedures are independent of and
should not be limited by the EHA.

The court rejected the schools' argument that disciplinary procedures are totally independent of and may supersede the rights granted under the EHA. It stated that only specialists, not school boards, are competent to determine the relationship between behavior
and handicap. And it agreed with the holding of *Stuart v. Nappi* that expulsion is a change

in placement within the meaning of the EHA. Cases reaching the same result include *Doe v. Koger, Stanley v. School Administration Unit, Adams Central School District v. Deist,* and *Kaelin v. Grubbs,* holding that expulsion is a change of placement; a student may be suspended temporarily without using EHA procedures and may be expelled if no causal relationship exists between the student's behavior and the disability and if the school follows EHA procedures.

Stuart v. Nappi, first of the expulsion cases, held that a school may not expel a handicapped child, only change the placement pursuant to parent notice and IEP conference provisions of the EHA, if the disability is causally related to the behavior for which the school seeks to expel the student. Similarly, *Blue v. New Haven Board of Education* cast doubt on the legality of suspensions that are for more than 10 days and found that homebound instruction or private school placement violates the least restrictive educational placement rule. Also see *Howard S. v. Friendswood Independent School District* for a similar result.

But short-term removal seems permissible, according to *City of Peoria Board of Education v. Illinois State Board of Education,* which held that a 5-day suspension of a handicapped child is not an expulsion, a change of placement, or a termination of services under the EHA. Likewise, in *Mrs. A.J. v. Special School District No. 1,* the federal district court held that a student who had not been formally classified as handicapped but who was simply suspected of being handicapped was not entitled to additional hearing procedures (in addition to those provided all students under Minnesota law) before being suspended for 15 days. In a footnote, the court said that the temporary disciplinary measure of suspension does not change or alter a student's educational placement and therefore apparently is not prohibited by the EHA, citing *Stuart v. Nappi.*

As of February 1989, there had been no court decisions indicating when *causality* exists. So far, the courts have only specified the procedures that must be followed and the nature of the standard (i.e., there must be causality before expulsion is allowed). It is likely that causality will be difficult to disprove (i.e., there will be a presumption that causality exists) in cases involving seriously emotionally disturbed children, learning disabled children, and mildly handicapped children. This is so because in those cases the definition of the disability or a fair view of its characteristics will tend to support a finding of causality. In other cases, however, the nature of the disability most likely will not justify a presumption in fact that there is causality. Motor, hearing, speech, or vision impairments, for example, do not usually give rise to maladaptive or other troublesome behavior.

Educability

Another important issue involves the expense of residential placement for a handicapped child for whom residential or private school education is appropriate. In seeking to avoid the full expense of residential placement, school districts generally have been unsuccessful. But in challenging their duty to pay, school districts have raised a troublesome issue: Are any children totally ineducable and therefore not entitled to protection of the EHA? Until 1988, the courts were reluctant to hold that there is a child who cannot learn anything and therefore is not protected by the Act. But *Levine v. New Jersey* and *Matthews v. Campbell* first put the question up for debate.

In *Levine v. New Jersey*, the parents of severely retarded children challenged New Jersey's practice of charging parents for residential care provided for their children. The New Jersey Supreme Court held that the state constitutional mandate for a free public education does not apply to mentally disabled children who are so severely impaired that they are unable to absorb or benefit from education. The court also found that the residential care such children require for day-to-day well-being does not qualify as education. The court based its interpretation on a finding that the "thorough and efficient" education clause of the state constitution was intended to provide children with an education that will prepare them to function politically, economically, and socially in a democratic society. Because profoundly impaired children will never be able to exercise that franchise and vote intelligently, they are not included within the constitutional guarantee of education.

This interpretation of "education" casts doubt on the purposes of special education, which are not always and for all students to make them capable enough to vote. More than that, it suggests that some children do not qualify for special education under federal or state law because they cannot attain the competence to vote. Such children could be regarded as ineducable in the important sense of not qualifying for special education benefits under the law.

A 1988 decision by a federal district court in New Hampshire, in *Timothy W. v. Rochester School District,* reached the conclusion—for the first time on the merits of a case—that a child is unable to benefit from special education and therefore has no right to be included in schooling or to any of the benefits of the EHA.

In *Timothy W.,* the court reviewed conflicting testimony concerning a 13-year-old boy. According to the testimony accepted by the court, he is blind and deaf, has cerebral palsy, is spastic and subject to frequent convulsions, lacks carotid tissue, is profoundly retarded, has no communication skills, operates "at the brainstem level," has acquired the highest degree of reflex behavior (some ability to respond to external stimuli—light and noise) but has made no progress in about a year. Further, he seems to be regressing, has not achieved a level of response to stimuli beyond his original baseline (first measured response), engages in only passive and nonvolitional activities, must have his hands and feet completely manipulated in order to move them, and, for these reasons, is "not capable of benefiting from special education" at the present.

Given these facts, the legal issue for the court was whether the student is entitled to benefits and rights under the EHA. The court engaged in curious reasoning to reach the result that he is not. Although it quoted the EHA's purpose [Sec. 1400—to assure that *all* handicapped children have a free appropriate public education] and the eligibility requirements for the states' receipt of federal funds [Sec. 1414(a)—to ensure that "all handicapped children residing in the state, regardless of the severity of their handicap, and who are in need of special education and related services" are identified and evaluated for special education], it nonetheless disregarded the clear and absolute language of the EHA and instead relied on the Supreme Court's decision in *Board v. Rowley.*

The district court stated that the Supreme Court said that the EHA's purpose is to promote the education of children who (according to the district court) "otherwise would be glossed over in the scheme of public education, as a result of their inability to attend 'regular classroom' instruction due to the nature of their handicap." The district court quoted a footnote in *Rowley* relating to the effect of the *PARC* and *Mills* cases on Congress' intent: According to the Supreme Court's footnote, *PARC* holds that the school systems are to provide "access to a free public program of education and training appropriate to (the student's) learning capabilities." The district court also cited with approval the Supreme Court's *Rowley* language that the term *free appropriate public education* means "educational instruction specially designed to meet the unique needs of the handicapped child, supported by such services as are necessary to permit the child to 'benefit' from the instruction."

On the basis of these statements in *Rowley*—which seem to some to deal only with the standards for the type of services to be provided and not to be justifications for the exclusion of any child—the district court said:

> It logically follows that a handicapped child who cannot "benefit" from special education, or who does not have learning capacity (*Mills,* 334 F. Supp. at 1258), was not intended to receive education under the (EHA). Surely, Congress would not legislate futility.

Holding that in "rare" cases a child is not able to benefit, the district court interpreted the EHA as allowing the exclusion of some children. But it did require that the child be subjected to "continuous, but periodic evaluations, intended to identify any development which illustrates a capability to benefit from special education."

In holding that a certain child is ineducable, the court attacked the underlying premise of *PARC.* In *PARC,* the federal district court found that all children are educable and that there is therefore no reason to exclude any of them from an educational system. If, however, it appears that some children are not educable, there would be no reason to include them in an educational system; the system would be asked to do that which it cannot do (by definition, the children are not able to benefit from the system's efforts), and no purpose would be served in including them in the system. Indeed, their inclusion would cause an unjustifiable expense to the education system. Public policy would justify their exclusion from that system, then, on two grounds: (1) The system cannot benefit them, and (2) the expenditure of funds cannot be defended.

The Court of Appeals reversed the district court in *Timothy W.* and held that the Education for All Handicapped Children Act was enacted to ensure that all children with disabilities are provided an appropriate public education; indeed, "not only are severely handicapped children not excluded from the Act, but the most severely handicapped are actually given priority under the Act." In short, the Court of Appeals affirmed the zero reject principle of the Act. Moreover, there is no prerequisite in the Act that the student be able to benefit; instead, the Act speaks about the state's responsibility to the child.

As the court noted, "The language of the Act in its entirety makes clear that a 'zero-reject' policy is at the core of the Act, and that no child, regardless of the severity of his or her handicap, is to ever again be subjected to the deplorable state of affairs which existed at the time of the Act's passage, in which millions of handicapped children received inadequate education or none at all. In summary, the Act mandates an appropriate public education for all handicapped children, regardless of the level of achievement that such children might attain."

The court cited the congressional history to support its contention that the Act is intended to benefit all handicapped children, "without exception," and that an "educational benefit was neither guaranteed nor required as a prerequisite for a child to receive such an education."

Moreover, the court noted that Congress has amended the Act four times since it was enacted in 1975 and that Congress not only has "repeatedly reaffirmed the original intent of the Act—to educate all handicapped children, regardless of the severity of their handicap, and to give priority attention to the most severely handicapped—but it has in fact expanded the provisions covering the most severely handicapped."

Next, the court noted that Congress relied on the *PARC* and *Mills* cases when enacting the Act; both cases establish a zero reject principle. Moreover, "the courts have continued to embrace the principle that all handicapped children are entitled to a public education, and have consistently interpreted the Act as embodying this principle." It noted that the trial court's reliance on *dicta* in several cases involving educability was "misfounded," since those cases did not hold that the Act permits a school to exclude a child whom it regards as ineducable.

And, the court observed, the courts have construed "education" in a very broad way, so that the trial court's conclusion that "education must be measured by the acquirement of traditional 'cognitive skills' has no bases whatsover in the 14 years of case law since the passage of the Act. All other courts have consistently held that education under the Act encompasses a wide spectrum of training, and that for the severely handicapped it may include the most elemental of life skills."

Accordingly, the court found that the district court had misconstrued the *Rowley* decision. That decision, the court held, focused on the level of services and the quality of programs that a state must provide, not the criteria for access to those programs. The Supreme Court's use of "benefit" in *Rowley* was a "substantive limitation placed on the state's choice of an educational program; it was not a license for the state to exclude certain handicapped children." And the Supreme Court even explicitly acknowledged the Congressional intent to ensure public edcuation to all handicapped children without regard to the level of achievement that they might attain, since the Supreme Court said that the Act's intent was to open the doors and not guarantee any particular level of education once they are open.

Finally, the Court of Appeals relied on the *Honig* case, in which the Supreme Court ruled that school districts may not exclude dangerous children from schooling altogether.

The *Honig* decision from the Supreme Court relied on the language and legislative history of the Act, and the Court of Appeals did likewise in *Timothy W.* to reach the result that the school must provide special education to the student.

In language that is destined to be litigated again and again, the Court of Appeals also seems to have established a duty on schools to use state-of-art procedures for educating children with severe handicaps:

> The law explicitly recognizes that education for the severely handicapped is to be broadly defined, to include not only traditional academic skills, but also basic functional life skills, and that educational methodologies in these areas are not static, but are constantly evolving and improving. It is the school district's responsibility to avail itself of these new approaches in providing an education program geared to each child's individual needs. The only question for the school district to determine, in conjunction with the child's parents, is what constitutes an appropriate individualized education program (IEP) for the handicapped child.

The problems with concluding that some children are not educable are manifold. First, no conclusive research data, to date, justify that conclusion; indeed, there is strong debate on both sides of the educability issue. A conclusion that some children are not educable, then, seems scientifically debatable. Second, there is the problem of where to draw the line. Once a child is found not educable, the tendency may be to open up the class of ineducable children so as to include some children who are simply difficult or expensive to educate but who can be educated or benefit from training. Third, the special education profession would be relieved of the pressure to find ways to educate the more profoundly disabled children. Lacking an incentive to find ways to train them, the profession may not try to find any ways. A result might be that development of new knowledge that could benefit some children would be stifled.

Notice that the debate about educability and the problems with expulsion are related. Both seek to define who is handicapped for the purpose of special education. If a school may expel a child who is receiving special education because the child's behavior was not caused by the disability, it is no longer responsible for the child. In a very real sense—i.e., in the sense of being entitled to special education—the child is not "handicapped." Likewise, if a school may find as a matter of fact that a certain child (or group of children) is ineducable, it too may argue that it is no longer responsible for the child (or group), since the EHA is intended to benefit only those who are capable of learning. Again, children who are incapable of learning are not "handicapped" in the sense of being entitled to special education. Thus, some educators and school systems are attempting to limit the meaning of *handicapped* by excluding children who violate certain rules and children who are ineducable and by creating disincentives to classification as "handicapped."

Another, similar effort is underway to limit the meaning of *handicap* by making it more difficult to classify certain "borderline" children as entitled to special education under federal law. The effort to tighten up on classification takes several forms. Some states are redefining *learning disabled* and *mildly retarded*. Likewise, some are creating new procedural hurdles that schools and parents must leap before a child may be classified (e.g., "preassessment" before the child is referred for EHA nondiscriminatory evaluation).

Students with AIDS

As the nation faced the grim prospects that AIDS would become a wider-spread disease, the schools faced three issues: first, whether students with AIDS are entitled to special education as "handicapped" or to the protection of the nondiscrimination statute (Sec. 504); second, whether to exclude students with AIDS; and, third, if not, where to educate them. Not all of the answers to these questions were available as of March 1989, but some are.

As you consider these issues, recall that in chapter 2 you encountered the argument that all educational issues are basically social policy issues. You faced that argument in the discussion of *Brown,* the school desegregation case, and you met it again in this chapter in discussions of how the courts wrestled with the problems of expulsion/ suspension and educability. Now you see it again in the ways in which the AIDS issue is answered in the context of special education and nondiscrimination law.

The First Issue: Is a Person with AIDS "Handicapped"?   The first question was whether students with AIDS are entitled to special education under EHA as "handicapped" or to nondiscrimination in education under Section 504 (see chapter 2 for a discussion of Section 504). The Supreme Court seems to have answered that question, with the result that students with AIDS are entitled to EHA and Section 504 protection.

In *Board v. Arline,* a 1987 decision, the Court ruled that a person with a contagious disease (tuberculosis) is handicapped under the meaning of Section 504. The Court relied on the intent of Congress to cover people with contagious diseases under the protection of Section 504, the regulations issued by the Department of Health and Human Services to implement Section 504, expert testimony that Arline (a public school teacher) has a significant physical impairment and a record of such an impairment (having been hospitalized for TB treatment), and the clear intent of Section 504 to prohibit discrimination based on the effects that Arline's handicap may have on others (such as the effects generated by fear alone). It held, accordingly, that Arline is handicapped, but it did not hold that she is "otherwise qualified" to be a teacher. That issue remained unsettled by the case and is being retried by the lower courts.

The disability community, school authorities, and public authorities generally had looked to the *Arline* case to settle, once and for all, whether a person with AIDS is handicapped under Section 504, and therefore entitled not only to protection from discrimination but also to special education under the EHA if the disability causes the student to need special education. Knowing that the *Arline* case was to be the harbinger of law involving AIDS-affected people, the Court said in a footnote, "This case does not present, and therefore we do not reach, the questions whether a carrier of a contagious disease such as AIDS could be considered to have a physical impairment, or whether such a person could be considered, solely on the basis of contagiousness, a handicapped person as defined by (Sec. 504)."

Notwithstanding this disclaimer, many people have concluded that the *Arline* case does compel the result that some, if not all, people with AIDS are protected under Section 504 and, if they are students, under the EHA. This conclusion rests on the nature of AIDS and on the similarities between TB and AIDS—disease coupled with contagiousness.

The Nature and Effects of AIDS. AIDS is caused by a retrovirus now commonly called the human immunodeficiency virus (HIV). Physicians (to whose expert judgment the courts must defer, as long as that judgment is reasonable and professionally defensible, said the Supreme Court in *Arline, Davis,* and *Youngberg v. Romeo*) use three categories to classify the nature and effect of HIV infection.

1. An infected person is diagnosed as having full-blown AIDS if he or she manifests one of the "opportunistic infections" listed by the National Centers for Disease Control. These infections signal that the retrovirus has seriously damaged the person's immunological capability.
2. Another person may manifest lesser symptoms collectively referred to as AIDS-related complex (ARC), ranging from swollen lymph nodes and simple fever or lethargy to more serious neurological disorders.
3. Still another person, typical of the vast majority of people who have been infected with the virus, is not presently ill with AIDS or ARC and is asymptomatic. In such a person, the virus cannot be routinely isolated, but the fact that it is present can be inferred from the presence of antibodies stimulated by the virus. Prevailing medical opinion is that these "seropositive" people have been infected with the virus at one time, are presumed to have the virus dormant in their systems, and certainly are presumed to be able to transmit the virus to others.

The modes of transmission are limited and, by and large, include sexual intimacy involving the exchange of bodily fluids, transmission of blood via shared needles among intravenous drug users, or transmission of blood that is contaminated (as by way of blood infusions after surgery). The overwhelming evidence is that the AIDS virus is not transmitted by casual contacts.

Section 504 and AIDS. It is beyond doubt that people with full-blown AIDS and with ARC are handicapped for the purposes of Section 504. Whether a carrier (a seropositive person) also is "handicapped" under Section 504 was not addressed by the Supreme Court in *Arline.* Indeed, the Court's footnote, quoted previously, is precise proof that the Court avoided deciding about the application of Section 504 to seropositive people.

Section 504 defines a person to be handicapped who has a mental or physical disability that substantially limits one or more of the person's major life activities, has a record of that impairment, or is regarded as having that impairment. Clearly, people with full-blown AIDS, ARC, and seropositive diagnoses are covered by Section 504 as having a disability or as being regarded as having such a disability. Whether those who are sero-positive also are covered as having a record of such a disability is not as clear. But a person with full-blown AIDS or ARC clearly is covered under that standard; the person has a record of a disability.

Many lower courts have concluded that people who test seropositive and are carriers are covered by Section 504. (The American Bar Association's publication, *Legal, Medical, and Governmental Perspectives on AIDS as a Disability, 1987,* catalogues and analyzes those decisions.) The same result seems to apply in the few cases involving AIDS-affected students and the EHA.

The Second Issue: May an AIDS-Affected Person be Excluded?

The Courts and AIDS. The New Jersey Supreme Court, in *Board of Education of City of Plainfield v. Cooperman,* decided in 1987, approved regulations of the state Commissioners of Education and Health that determine when children with AIDS may be excluded from public schools. The regulations provide that students with full-blown AIDS, ARC, or seropositive diagnoses will be admitted into regular school unless they are not toilet-trained, are unable to control their drooling, or are unusually physically aggressive toward other students. A panel of medical experts must review all decisions in which an LEA decides to exclude a child from school on the basis of AIDS. The LEA bears the burden of proving that the child meets the criteria for exclusion. There must be a full hearing before the LEA and medical panel, with a right to appeal to the State Commissioner of Education.

Other courts have followed the principles approved by the New Jersey Supreme Court. That is, there is a presumption in favor of inclusion and against exclusion (a principle of zero reject), medical judgment is controlling as long as it is reasonable, and individualized determinations—on each student's case, not all of the "AIDS kids" as a group—must be made.

New York City school authorities adopted a policy that children with AIDS would not be automatically excluded from schools but, rather, reviewed on a case-by-case basis to determine if their health and development would permit them to attend school in an "unrestricted setting." A panel of medical experts was charged with making those determinations.

When a child who was diagnosed as having or suspected as having AIDS and who had remained well for several years was allowed by the medical panel and school commissioner to enter a neighborhood school, the local school board sued to overturn the commissioner's decision. The state court, in *District 27 Community School Board (Application of) v. Board of Education of New York City,* ruled that the child should be admitted and that the student is protected by Section 504. Because the student did not need special education, however, the court did not have to decide whether the EHA applied.

The case-by-case, individualized decision making that characterizes the New Jersey and New York approaches is followed in other states as well. For example, a federal district court in Oklahoma overturned the SEA's attempt to implement a regulation that no child with AIDS, and certainly not any individual child whose rights to attend school have been determined to be valid by the LEA, may be permitted in the state's schools.[16]

EHA and AIDS. The rights of the child to special education do not automatically arise upon the finding that the child has AIDS. That was the decision in the New York case and in an Illinois case as well.[17] Both courts made it clear that the student with AIDS, although protected by Section 504, does not automatically qualify for special education and EHA protection. Unless the student's condition requires special education [Sec. 1401(a)] or adversely affects his or her educational performance, the child does not meet the standard for being a "health-impaired" child [Sec. 300.5(b) of the regulations] and the child is not entitled to EHA rights. To meet these standards, the Illinois court held, there must be evidence of limited strength, vitality, or alertness because of chronic or acute health problems; these limited conditions must adversely affect the student's educational performance; and the child must require special education or related services.

The Third Issue: Where Must an AIDS-Affected Student be Educated?
Once a student meets the test of needing special education or related services, the issue shifts from whether the child qualifies under the EHA to what services the child is entitled to under the EHA. This issue has been answered only twice, and neither time fully.

Thomas v. Atascadero USD, a 1987 decision of a federal court in California, prohibited the LEA from excluding a student with AIDS who has bitten a classmate unless he has received an opportunity to protest his exclusion. The case did not determine that the student is handicapped under the EHA but, rather, that he is handicapped under Section 504. Because there was no evidence that he poses a "significant risk of harm to his kindergarten classmates or teachers" and because the LEA failed to meet its burden to show that he is not "otherwise qualified" to attend a regular-school kindergarten class, the court ordered that he be retained in that class.

Although the decision did not involve an interpretation of the EHA, it may be followed by courts applying the EHA. This is because the regulations and burden of proof under Section 504 are substantially the same as under the EHA. Thus, placement in the regular class, unless there is proof of dangerousness, is presumed to be correct.

But where the student's behavior or condition is or can be dangerous to others, an LEA is permitted to exclude the student from the otherwise appropriate placement. A federal district court, in *Martinez v. School Board of Hillsborough County, Florida,* held that a student who is incontinent and has been observed drooling and sucking her thumb continually, and who has a diagnosis of "trainable mental retardation," should not be allowed to be in the TMR classroom. This is because those behaviors increase the risk of AIDS transmittal by the exchange of bodily fluids from the student to others. Instead, the student should be provided homebound instruction. Permanent and total exclusion is not allowed.

Conclusion and Rationale. The AIDS cases to date clearly demonstrate that there must be individualized determinations (not a "meat-ax" approach that covers all students or persons affected by an AIDS condition); there must be a basis in the public health interests for exclusion (there must be a close connection between the child's condition and behavior, on the one hand, and the safety of students and teachers, on the other); and the exclusion must rest on defensible and reasonable medical testimony. This result obtains for several reasons:

1. People with AIDS are considered to be handicapped under Section 504 and may be considered handicapped under the EHA if the disability causes them to need special education or related services.
2. The zero-reject principle and the equal protection doctrine prohibit discrimination and exclusion, as long as the person is found to be handicapped under Section 504 or the EHA.
3. The doctrine of the least restrictive alternative/environment (see chapter 6) creates a presumption that those with AIDS should be educated in the regular programs. The presumption may be overcome when dangerousness to others is demonstrated, but the LEA has the burden of proof in seeking to overcome the presumption.
4. The due process clause of the Fourteenth Amendment (see chapter 7) requires not only individualized determinations but also opportunities for the student to protest any planned exclusion; and the regulations implementing Section 504, as well as the EHA and its regulations, codify the principle of due process and procedural protections.
5. The public's fear—"fear itself"—does not justify exclusion of the student any more than fear justified an exclusionary zoning ordinance that prohibited group homes for people with mental retardation *(City of Cleburne v. Cleburne Living Center, Inc.)* or permitted a person who is not dangerous to himself or others to be incarcerated in a mental hospital involuntarily *(O'Connor v. Donaldson)*.
6. Education is an especially valuable public service, and access to it should not be denied except for the most serious of reasons *(Brown v. Board of Education* and *Plyer v. Doe)*.
7. Exclusion, coupled with identification of the student as having an AIDS condition, creates special stigma and can, in the words of the Supreme Court in *Plyer v. Doe,* cause "lifetime hardships on a discrete class of children not accountable for their disabling status."
8. Homebound or hospital-based special education is an appropriate alternative to total exclusion for the student whose dangerousness has been proved and for whom the presumption of inclusion in regular programs or in nonspecial classes has been overcome.

Section 504's Requirements: Reasonableness, Cost, and Burden of Proof

Only one state—New Mexico—refused to accept federal funds under the EHA. But handicapped children in that state sued the state for its failure to provide them an appropriate education, and they won. Instead of relying on the EHA, however, they relied on Section 504 of the Rehabilitation Act, which (among other things) prevents any state that receives federal educational funds from discriminating against handicapped children by denying them an appropriate education. (Because Section 504 was a "winner" in *New Mexico As-*

sociation for Retarded Citizens (ARC) v. New Mexico, it has come into play in a host of other cases; see chapters 9 and 10 of this book.)

The question that the Section 504 cases raise, however, is whether a handicapped child must prove that the state or a school district *intended* to discriminate or only that the school district action had a discriminatory *effect.* The courts are divided on this matter.

In *New Mexico ARC v. New Mexico,* the federal district (trial) court held that a state that receives federal funds for special education must comply with Section 504 of the Rehabilitation Act (nondiscrimination on account of handicap) even if it does not receive EHA funds. It also held that handicapped children need not prove that the state intended to discriminate against them to win their Section 504 case; a discriminatory effect suffices. (Note that *Anderson v. Thompson, Akers v. Bolton,* and *Lora v. Board of Education,* however, required proof of an intent to discriminate, rejecting the easier standard of effect alone.)

On appeal by the state, the Tenth Circuit Court of Appeals reversed and remanded the decision of the trial court. The appeals court agreed with the trial court that the handicapped children did not have to prove that the state intended to discriminate against them, only that discrimination occurred. But it also found that *Southeast Community College v. Davis* requires under Section 504 that the state must accommodate handicapped people only up to a certain limit. Unlike the EHA, Section 504 does not require affirmative action by the state, only nondiscrimination. And nondiscrimination is limited; accommodation is required only when it does not generate undue financial or administrative hardship on the state. Because the trial court did not frame its relief under the "reasonable accommodation" standard of *Davis,* the appeals court remanded the case, requiring the trial court to change its order (relief), analyzing its requirements in terms of its costs and its effectiveness.

Certain aspects of the *New Mexico ARC* case are occupying the courts' attention. One has to do with the *reasonableness* of the accommodation that a school district must make, under Section 504, for a child with a disability. The others have to do with *cost* and *burden of proof* that the plaintiffs must carry out to be successful.

Reasonableness. With respect to the reasonableness issue, the U.S. Supreme Court has made it clear in *Davis* that Section 504 is a nondiscrimination statute, not an affirmative action one—i.e., it addresses discrimination and prohibits it so that people with disabilities will have opportunities comparable to the opportunities of people without disabilities. In this respect, it differs from an affirmative action statute, which typically requires special accommodations, over and above those made under equal opportunity approaches, for people with disabilities.

Thus, in *Davis,* the Supreme Court held that the community college was not required to make substantial modifications in its nursing curriculum to accommodate as a student a licensed practical nurse who sought admission to the nursing program and who was severely hearing impaired. The Court noted that such extraordinary modifications would change the character of the school's curriculum in such a way that patient safety and academic standards might be seriously jeopardized. It also stated that the modifications would change the character of Section 504 from one of nondiscrimination to one of special opportunity or affirmative action. It did make it clear, however, that Section 504 does require some, but not all, accommodations for persons with disabilities and that the cost of the modifications is a legitimate factor for courts to consider in deciding whether and how many accommodations are required.

Taking *Davis* as their lead, several courts have applied it to students with disabilities who have sought various types of accommodations under Section 504, as applied to their public school education. Thus, *Troutman v. School District of Greenville County* held that an appropriate education can be provided at a "satellite" school, not a neighborhood school (where the expense would be considerable and possibly beyond what *Davis* requires). In *Troutman,* the cost was a factor in the court's decision about reasonableness of the accommodation required.

Cost. By the same token, in *William S. v. Gill,* where an issue was whether the school district is required to send a child to a private residential program whose costs greatly exceed those of a public school program that has not benefited the student, the court noted that the district has no responsibility for residential programs that represent a new service not available to nondisabled students, as distinguished from a modification of existing services available to nondisabled students. The court cited *Davis* for the proposition that the district is not required to fund such programs, their cost apparently being a factor in the decision as to whether they are required by Section 504: "Sec. 504 does not obligate a school system to finance a private placement *under any circumstances."* The court cited *Colin K. v. Schmidt, Turillo v. Tyson,* and *Kruelle v. New Castle County School District* for authority.

Similarly, *Pinkerton v. Moye* held that the EHA does not require unreasonable accommodations. The court said that Congress intended a balancing test between cost and the claims of handicapped children (to self-contained classes for emotionally disturbed children in the local programs). And in *Roncker v. Walters,* the district court stated *in dicta:* "Cost is a proper factor to consider since spending on one handicapped child deprives other handicapped children. ... Cost is no defense, however, if the school district has failed to provide a proper continuum of alternative placements for handicapped children. The provision of such alternative placements benefits all handicapped children."

Other cases have different views of cost. In *Jose P. v. Ambach,* the district court rejected the state's argument that the "affirmative action" it ordered in an earlier phase of the case (granting a class action, appointing a master, and ordering broad-based relief involving classification and programming in learning disabilities) was warranted, despite *Davis.* Finding that handicapped children are "otherwise qualified" under Section 504 and have never been considered "unqualified" to receive an education, the court held that the children have a right to an appropriate public education and, thus, the extensive modifications that might be "substantial" in other contexts may be wholly reasonable efforts to educate the children in this context.

Likewise, *Hawaii Department of Education v. Catherine D.* rejected a *Davis*-based challenge to the relief sought for the children, and *Department of Education v. Katherine*

Dorr held that private school placement and tuition reimbursement were due to parents of a cystic fibroic child where the child's mother could perform the cleaning and reinsertion of the child's tracheotomy tube more conveniently at the private school than at a public one and the expense of having that service done by the child's mother was lower than having it done by school employees. The case involved a choice between homebound placement, proposed by the school, and private school placement, sought by the parents.

In *Georgia ARC v. McDaniel,* another case that clearly confronts *Davis,* the Eleventh Circuit Court of Appeals held that certain handicapped children are entitled to an education beyond the state-prescribed 180 days. The limitation is contrary to the obligations of states and local school districts, under EHA and Section 504, to provide individualized education. In that case, the state asserted that a 12-month program is not required under *Davis,* it being too great an accommodation and too great a cost to the schools. The court of appeals distinguished *Davis* on two grounds. First, unlike the plaintiff in *Davis,* the mentally retarded children in the Georgia case could benefit from the special accommodations they sought (extended-year programming). Second, the year-round programming did not amount to a change in the scope of services provided by the schools, as the change in the nursing programs would have in *Davis.*

It thus appears that in the *Davis*-type situation the amount of the accommodation ordered will be contextually determined—which is as the Supreme Court indicated it should be in *Davis.* Not all accommodations, however costly, will be excused, although some will.

Burden of Proof.   The other aspect of *New Mexico ARC* that affects the education of children with disabilities has to do with the burden of proof that plaintiffs must carry. Both the district court and the court of appeals in *New Mexico ARC* found that the plaintiffs were not required to prove intentional discrimination against them, only the fact that discrimination existed. As noted, however, there were cases requiring proof of intent to discriminate.

Conrail.   The *New Mexico ARC* result (intent does not have to be proved) is now put into jeopardy by the U.S. Supreme Court's 1984 decision in *Conrail (Consolidated Rail Corporation) v. Darone.* In that case, the Supreme Court held that a person who claims intentional discrimination, on the basis of a disability, has the right to bring a lawsuit under Section 504 to recover monetary damages (back pay). The Court did not address whether the lawsuit based on nonintentional discrimination (as in *New Mexico ARC*) could be brought. Although prior case law suggests that such suits can be brought, the issue may be somewhat in doubt because *Conrail* dealt only with intentional discrimination.

Conrail did, however, clarify some issues that have plagued the lower courts faced with Section 504 cases. First, it made clear that a private right of action exists for an individual who claims discrimination based on a handicap; the person may sue directly in court, after exhausting administrative remedies, to correct the discrimination. *Davis* had caused some doubt about whether a private right of action exists under Section 504, and *Conrail* settled the matter. The right of action *does* exist.

Second, *Conrail* makes it clear that certain types of monetary damages are available under Section 504. Some cases (e.g., *Camenisch v. University of Texas*) had awarded non-monetary relief but concluded that congressionally authorized relief did not include monetary relief (and thereby suggested that such relief was not available under Section 504). Other cases (e.g., *Miener v. Missouri*) had granted non-monetary relief (injunction against certain type of school district behavior) but refused to grant monetary relief. Thus, *Conrail* seems to settle the matter: In certain types of cases (alleged intentional discrimination and award of back pay for employment that was illegally denied), monetary relief is available.

It remains to be seen whether the *Conrail* result will extend beyond those circumstances to nonintentional discrimination and to cases in which monetary damages other than back pay or other employment-related benefits are sought. Opinion is divided. Some courts hold that damages are not available under either Section 504 or under EHA (and its component, P.L. 94-142). Other courts hold that damages are available under Section 504 in education discrimination cases that are coupled with EHA complaints.

Conrail also puts to rest a conflict that had existed among the federal courts of appeals. Some courts had ruled that a person who alleges discrimination on the basis of handicap must be affected by a program whose primary objective is employment; they limited employment discrimination cases under Section 504 to only those situations in which the primary objective of the federal aid received by the employer was to provide employment opportunities. The leading case was *Trageser v. Libbie Rehabilitation Center*. Other courts had ruled that a suit for discrimination may be brought by a person affected by any program that received federal assistance. These courts rejected the "primary objective" test (the objective being employment) on the bases of congressional intent and the broadly remedial nature of Section 504.

In *Conrail*, the Supreme Court, with all of the justices agreeing, concluded that the language, legislative history, administrative agency interpretation, and purpose of Section 504 are not limited to the primary objective test but are broadly remedial. Thus, any program that receives federal assistance, whether its purpose is to provide employment or not, is covered by Section 504 and must comply with its provisions and implementing regulations.

Finally, *Conrail* did not decide the meaning of "program or activity" in the context of Section 504's prohibition of discrimination on the basis of handicap against any otherwise qualified person in any federally assisted program or activity. The Court's own decisions in *Grove City College v. Bell* and *North Haven Board of Education v. Bell*, both of which interpreted Title IX of the Civil Rights Act (prohibiting discrimination based on gender), seemed to leave open the precise meaning of *program* and *activity*. *Conrail* seems to suggest that the phrase means not just the particular activity that the federal government assists but the entire operation of the recipient. Such an expansive interpretation would benefit children with disabilities (as well as other people with disabilities), since it would give them rights to sue against discriminatory practices by the recipient of federal assistance even though the disabled persons were participating in an activity of the recipient that did not, itself, receive federal assistance. That conclusion is premature and speculative at this time and must be affirmed or rejected by the Court in later litigation.

Compensatory Education

Compensatory education cases continue to favor handicapped children. In the early cases, the trend was firmly established. For example, *Capello v. D.C. Board of Education* ordered education to age 21 of a handicapped child to whom the school district was slow in providing an appropriate education. A subsequent order in the case required the child's education in a residential school, at school district expense. A case that concurs is *North v. D.C. Board of Education.* Similarly, *Campbell v. Talladega County Board of Education* awarded 2 years' compensatory education beyond the child's 21st birthday because of a school district delay in giving the child an appropriate education. And *Bennett v. D.C. Board of Education* awarded compensatory education under the EHA, basing the decision on the fact that children's rights cannot be safeguarded, retrospectively, by the procedural safeguards in the Act or by injunctive relief. But the court denied compensatory education under Section 504 because that statute applies only prospectively. Likewise, *Adams Central School District v. Deist* awarded compensatory education for a student who was illegally expelled from two schools and who was denied any education for 18 months.

Finally, *Allen v. McDonough* ordered compensatory education for 2,300 students whose EHA rights were violated in 1979-80. But in a case distinguishable on the facts, *Rettig v. Kent City School District* denied compensatory services and held that a multi-handicapped child who was excluded from school in 1971, before enactment of the EHA, was not denied equal protection or due process because the school's system of classification (to admit only mildly handicapped children) had been found constitutional in *Cayahoga County ARC v. Essex;* also, any claims he might have had were extinguished when his parents enrolled him in a private school.

There were some contrary results. The main case is *Timms v. Metropolitan School District of Wabash County,* which denied compensatory services to a student who was given only 1½ hours' instruction per week but later was given 5 hours of services daily by the schools on a voluntary basis (after the parents had instituted a lawsuit to obtain longer-day services). Relying on *Anderson v. Thompson,* the court found that compensatory education was contrary to congressional intent.

The more recent cases continue to award compensatory education. *Max M. v. Thompson* upheld a student's right to compensatory education beyond the 21st birthday, noting that if the school could avoid compensatory education beyond age 21, there would be an incentive to deny any services to the child. The same court also rejected the doctrine of *Anderson v. Thompson* that compensatory education can be ordered only if a school district acts in bad faith.

The Supreme Court itself laid to rest the notion that no compensatory education could ever be ordered, by holding, in the *Burlington v. Department of Education* case, that compensatory education is the equivalent of a tuition reimbursement that itself may be ordered if an LEA defaults in its obligation to a student. Other cases approving compensatory education are *Miener v. Missouri* and *Helms v. Independent School District No. 3 of Broken Arrow.*

Participation in Sports

The cases reach contradictory results in deciding whether handicapped children are entitled to the protection of Section 504 when seeking to engage in contact sports. Factual differences most likely explain the results in these cases. In one case in which a student won a court decision requiring a school district to allow him to compete, the evidence was persuasive that contact sports posed no unusual risk of injury and the student and his parents were willing to assume a risk of injury.

Kampmeier v. Nyquist held that Section 504 does not entitle a student to participate in contact sports. But *Poole v. South Plainfield Board of Education* ruled that the student may participate in contact sports, under Section 504, if he and his parents knew of the risks and decided in a rational way to participate. Likewise, *Grube v. Bethlehem Area School District* found a violation of Section 504. A high school student was excluded from the football team on which he had played for 3 years. His only physical problem was the absence of one kidney. The exclusion was ordered despite expert medical opinion that the risk of injury was slim and there was no medical reason for nonparticipation. The court found that the exclusion violated Section 504, particularly when the student's participation would require no substantial adjustments to the program and would not lower the standards of the team as a whole.

Qualification for Services

In addition to the cases involving students with AIDS and the cases on educability, several other cases have decided who is "handicapped." It is clear from them that a child will not be afforded the protection of the EHA unless and until the child has been formally classified as handicapped and found to be in need of special education services, all according to procedures and standards of the EHA. Thus, *Johnpoll v. Elias* held that unless and until a child is classified under the EHA as handicapped, that child is not entitled to the Act's protection (here, a change in placement).

Akers v. Bolton held that not all school-aged children with epilepsy are entitled to special education services as a matter of course because not all (only some, as individually determined) are handicapped in the sense of needing special education. And when children are improperly classified (children not mentally retarded although placed in MR programs, without testing or parental consent), they are entitled to the protection of Section 504, which protects children "regarded" as disabled *(Carter v. Orleans Parish Public Schools).*

Wolff v. South Colonie Central School District held that a student with congenital limb deformities (legs approximately 1 foot in length, deformed hand on natural limb, and prosthetic arm) was not "otherwise qualified" under Section 504 to participate in an out-of-country tour (in Spain) that required much ascending and descending of stairs, extensive walking tours, crossing congested streets, and so forth. The tour also was found dangerous to her safety.

The issue of qualification for services also surfaces when the question is whether a child is too old or too young to claim the benefits of EHA. In a case involving the "coverage" provisions of the EHA (all handicapped students receive the benefits of the Act without regard to the governmental agency that has custody or jurisdiction over them), *Green v. Johnson* held that inmates in prison who are not yet 22 years old have a right to special education under the EHA.

VanderMalle v. Ambach held that a 21-year-old person still qualified for services under the EHA notwithstanding the fact that he was an adult under state law. And in *Helms v. Broken Arrow,* the court held that a school may not exclude a disabled child who reaches the age of 19 but has completed 12 years of school. The EHA mandates that states do not have to provide special education to children ages 18 to 21 if (as of September 1, 1980) that requirement would be inconsistent with state law or practice. That means the state may not apply different standards for handicapped children that will deprive them of educational opportunities enjoyed by nonhandicapped children. In Oklahoma, nonhandicapped children may attend school until they are 21. Accordingly, under the EHA, handicapped children may do so, too, even if they have already completed 12 years of schooling.

But once 19 years old, a person may be prohibited from interscholastic wrestling, as are all 19-year-olds under state policy, even though disabled, protected by Section 504, and receiving special education *(Cavallaro v. Ambach)*. Such a student experiences the same age limitations as nondisabled students and therefore does not suffer discrimination.

State and federal special education does not, in this case, apply to children under age 6. Thus, a child who is 4½ is not entitled to the benefits of such laws (see *Stewart v. Salem School District*).

Minimum Competency Testing

Recent national concerns about the quality of education have prompted states to take steps to measure how well their schools are teaching their students. One step is the minimum competency test (MCT). The test, sometimes administered during the student's primary and middle school years and almost always during the last year or two of high school, determines whether a student has mastered the minimum competencies for functioning in an adult world.

A legal issue is whether the MCT may be given to handicapped children and whether students' failure of the test may be the basis for schools to withhold their graduation or other diplomas or certificates. As a rule, courts have allowed states to administer the tests as long as they do so in ways that accommodate students' disabilities (e.g., longer time to take a test if a child is learning disabled or the assistance of an aide if a child is communication impaired) and as long as the states give adequate notice to all students, including those who are handicapped, that they will be required to take the tests.

Thus, the federal district court in *Brookhart v. Illinois State Board of Education* held that the administration of state-required minimum competency tests to handicapped children and the withholding of graduation diplomas from handicapped children who fail the test does not violate Section 504 or the EHA as long as the manner of administration of the tests accommodates students with physical handicaps. Students who fail the test are not denied due process of law (see chapter 7) because they have not been educated in the test's subject matter where lack of exposure to subject matter results from a determination, in preparing their IEPs, that exposure is inappropriate in view of their handicapping conditions. But notice of the test is required under due process.

On appeal of *Brookhart,* the court of appeals held that: (1) denying a diploma to special education students who fail the MCT does not deny their right to a free appropriate education under the EHA, (2) use of the MCT does not violate the nondiscriminatory evaluation requirement of the EHA when the MCT is one of three requirements for graduation, (3) denial of a diploma does not violate Section 504 because a handicapped student is not "qualified" for graduation in spite of a handicap, and (4) adequate notice of the MCT and graduation requirements must be given lest a substantive due process violation occur (because students have a liberty interest in the diploma). The court of appeals reversed the district court on the grounds of a violation of procedural due process, which requires notice and adequate time to prepare for the new diploma requirement.

A similar result was reached in *Board of Education v. Ambach,* wherein the failure of handicapped students to pass the MCT and denial of the diploma for that reason did not violate Section 504 because the children were not "otherwise qualified." The EHA does not prevent the denial of a diploma to a child who has received an appropriate education according to the child's IEP. And the New York Court of Appeals (the highest appeals court in the state) has upheld a state law requirement that all students, including those with disabilities, must pass an MCT before they are entitled to high school diplomas. The case is *Board of Education of the Northport-East Northport Union Free School District v. Ambach.*

Children's Residence

Some parents of handicapped children have "gone shopping" for appropriate programs and, in the process, raised questions about the legal residence of the child and the identity of the school district responsible for the child's education. As a rule, the courts have not been sympathetic to the parents.

A good illustration is *Connelly v. Gibbs,* in which the court found that when the parents and child have their principal residence in one school district and a secondary residence in another, the second district is not required to educate the child. The plaintiffs were unable to show any reason other than education of their handicapped child for establishing a second residence. Likewise, in *Fairfield Board of Education v. Connecticut Department of Education,* a state appeals court held that a town board of education was not liable for the costs of placing a handicapped child at a residential center. The child's natural parents, who had moved to Vermont, had transferred guardianship to another couple to maintain the child's placement. The transfer of guardianship was termed a "sham."

EFFECTS OF THE ZERO REJECT RULE

Having reviewed developments that led to adoption of the zero reject rule by the courts and later by Congress, and having examined provisions of the EHA and their interpretation by the courts, it is now appropriate to discuss briefly the major effects of the zero reject principle.

New Definitions for Equality

The debt that handicapped children owe to the civil rights movement is enormous. Without doubt, *Brown* (the first school desegregation case) is the most important case ever decided by any court insofar as the education of handicapped children is concerned. At the very least, it established the doctrine of equal educational opportunity, attacked the dual system of education and law that had relegated blacks, handicapped children, and other minority children to second-class status, and laid a foundation in the Constitution's Fourteenth Amendment (the equal protection clause) for *PARC, Mills,* and the other early special education cases.

The early cases and the EHA began to fulfill the promise of the *Brown* case—that no schools or other government agencies lawfully may establish the second-class citizenship of any children. Extension of the civil rights movement from one discrete minority (blacks) to another (handicapped children and adults) was the fulfillment of the Supreme Court's principle of equality under the eyes of the law.

Right-to-education cases following *Brown* deliberately and creatively expanded *Brown's* equal opportunities doctrine by establishing that the exclusion of handicapped children from any opportunities to learn—much less from any reasonably beneficial opportunities—is unconstitutional under the equal protection clause. More than that, those cases established a new equal access (or equal opportunity) doctrine. They articulated the proposition that handicapped children require different types of opportunities—namely, access to different types of resources for different purposes—in order to have opportunities for education that are equal to those of nondisabled children.

This notion of equality is different from the customary one. The usual meaning of equality is (per *Brown*) equal access to the same resources for the same purposes. The new meaning, in disabilities law, is *access to different resources for different purposes,* by disabled ("different") children. There is an important reason that equality means something different for handicapped children than it does for nonhandicapped children and, thus, one major reason that the new equal access doctrine was worthy of being recognized and legitimized by the courts. The major reason is that *the child's disability is a distinction that justifies a different approach.*

The fact is best illustrated by examining the cases of three different handicapped children. One child is mobility impaired; his spina bifida condition has crippled his legs. He seeks to follow a college preparatory curriculum in his local high school. For purposes of that curriculum only, it is entirely consistent with the doctrine of equal opportunity to admit him into classrooms with nondisabled students and to make no adjustments in his education. In *most* classrooms (a biology or chemistry lab, or a physical education class may require adjustments) equal opportunity for him consists of being treated *exactly equally.*

A second child is hearing impaired but is not so disabled that she needs an interpreter. She uses a hearing aid, which the school must assure is in working order. She is placed in the front of the room. The teacher distributes outlines of the course, frequently writes on the chalkboard, and directly faces the class, thus enabling the child to be instructed both verbally and with written materials. For this child, some accommodations are required in order to provide equal educational opportunity. The new equal access doctrine now is in play, and equality consists of *equal treatment plus accommodations.*

A third child is severely mentally retarded and has cerebral palsy, resulting in speech and mobility impairments. Clearly, neither "exactly equal" nor "equal-plus" treatment would provide an opportunity to benefit from instruction. In this case, special and different accommodations are required—typically, education by specially trained teachers, a curriculum that is substantially different from that offered to nondisabled children, and perhaps extra services (the "related services" of the EHA—see chapter 5). In this child's case, equal educational opportunity consists of *different (but favorable) treatment.*

Thus, one important effect of the early zero reject cases and Congress' enactment of a zero reject rule was to redefine the doctrine of *equal educational opportunity* as it applies to handicapped children and to establish different meanings of *equality* as it applies to disabled and nondisabled people. These fundamental redefinitions—based on the fact of the disability, which is the distinction that makes a difference—remain apparent in the zero reject cases that have followed enactment of the EHA and are based on interpretations of it.

In some of the recent cases, however, there is a small but discernible trend away from the absolute rule of zero reject. The cases having to do with expulsion require a "but-for" or causal relationship between the disability and the behavior if the child is not to be excluded; absent that connection, the child who has a disability may be excluded. The cases involving children with AIDS entitle the child to the protection of EHA only if the disability of AIDS requires special education services; if the condition does not require them, the EHA does not apply, even though the child clearly is handicapped under Section 504. Finally, the trial court decision involving educability reaches a similar conclusion: A child may be handicapped but still not qualify for EHA protection.

These cases indicate more than that the zero reject principle has exceptions. They indicate, as well, that there may be a new "class" of children who are not entitled, under the equal protection doctrine, to the same rights—in this case, a free apppropriate public education—as others who have or do not have disabilities. This incursion into the equal protection doctrine does not affect the meaning of equality (as described) for children who are covered under the EHA. But it does create a new class of children—those who are not entitled to the EHA under the terms of the Act itself or perhaps under the equal protection doctrine.

The equal protection doctrine requires equal treatment of people who are equally or comparably situated. In the desegregation movement, it meant that blacks and whites are to be treated alike, because both are members of the class known as students. In the right-to-education movement, it meant that children with disabilities must have the right to schooling, as do children without disabilities, because both are also members of the class known as students.

But the few cases that create exceptions to the zero reject principle arguably create a new class: children who cannot be special education students, either because they cannot be educated (the educability case), because their behavior is not protected under the same laws that apply to other students who are disabled (the expulsion cases), or because they may be disabled but not entitled to EHA services (the AIDS cases).

It may be too harsh and too early a judgment to say that exceptions to the zero reject rule are being created and that a new class of people is being created, incrementally, with the result that there may be now an exception to the equal protection rule. But the lesson taught by those cases may prove to be equal to that judgment, particularly if other courts follow these precedents or begin to carve out still other exceptions to the zero reject principle.

In considering whether a new class is being created for equal protection purposes, one must bear in mind that Congress has the power to clarify its intent to create a nonexception zero reject approach. Indeed, the addition of students who are deaf-blind and multihandicapped to the list of those who qualify for the EHA should have been a signal to the New Hampshire district court in *Timothy W.* that the zero reject rule bodes no exceptions.

One also must remember that the cases themselves have not been decided on constitutional grounds but only as interpretations of the EHA itself. A challenge to these judicially created exceptions may be made, based on the equal protection doctrine, and that challenge might be successful. The result, then, would be that the worst-case scenario described above (redefinition of the "class" and creation of exceptions to the zero reject rule) would not come to pass.

Precedent Setting by Early Cases
The early cases were precedent setting in still other ways (besides redefining equal educational opportunity). They clearly led to enactment of the EHA. They also established the six principles of law—zero reject, nondiscriminatory evaluation, appropriate and individualized education, placement in the least restrictive environment, procedural due process, and parent participation—that comprised the foundation of the EHA. And, of course, they were precedent for other cases involving educational discrimination and disabled children. Moreover, those cases represented a massive judicial response to patterns and practices of gross education discrimination against handicapped children. They resulted in court-ordered remedies that directed systemic, institutional reform, nothing less.

Change of Locus of Control of Education
By attacking patterns of conduct that went to the very heart of education—exclusion from educational opportunity and improper educational assessment and placement—the early cases and, later, the Congress and the courts that interpreted the EHA graphically demonstrated that schools and their officials are not immune from judicial examination. Each case has brought the conduct of schools—traditionally a matter of state and local control—under significant judicial oversight. Frequently that oversight was by federal judges, supervising the actions of state and local elected or appointed officials.

For example, *Brown* established federal control over *where* students were to be educated. But *PARC, Mills,* and the other early cases established federal control over *which* students are to be educated ("All children can learn...all children shall be educated") and the *terms* on which they are to be educated (the new equal access doctrine). When it enacted the EHA, Congress simply validated the courts' rulings.

Like *Brown,* the special education cases and the EHA together have had an enormous impact on state and local education budgets. They caused state and local legislators and school administrators to redirect the flow of funds within education so as to benefit handicapped children. They also caused those same officials to seek new money for the education of handicapped children. And, because the EHA itself authorized Congress to spend money to help the states implement the EHA, the cases, once they were enacted into the EHA, caused a massive shift in federal educational aid.

Cost-Effective Education
A related but somewhat tangential effect of the zero reject doctrine has been economic in nature. There always have been—and probably always will be—people who argue that it is not a wise expenditure of public money to fund the education of handicapped children. Indeed, the *Davis* case and some cases involving the education of disabled children explicitly relieve educational agencies of some of the especially high costs of accommodating handicapped children or adults in educational systems.

These arguments and cases notwithstanding, early childhood education for handicapped children clearly is cost-effective. And, as the data developed and experiences in post-secondary programs of special education graduates are recorded, it has become clear that special education at the elementary, middle school, and secondary levels is cost-effective. Special education is regarded as cost-effective because it reduces the number of persons classified as handicapped, prevents or reduces grade retention, makes it possible for some disabled people to acquire skills that make them less dependent on others, and enables some to become wage earners.

The fiscal contribution of zero reject and the equality doctrine is important not only for disabled persons but also for the larger public. More than that, the nay-sayers of equality have been answered with doctrine and dollars. The response is, indeed, powerful.

Parent Participation

The zero reject rule has had an impressive effect on still other people. It has revolutionized the relationship of parents and school officials. By providing for nondiscriminatory evaluation, individualized appropriate education, and procedural due process, the rule has created a new doctrine (or, arguably, resurrected an old one): parent participation in the education of handicapped children. In doing so, it legitimized *parent advocacy*—parents' assertion of the rights of their disabled children against the educational system (i.e., to gain access to it, to be admitted to it) and within the system (i.e., to be given an appropriate, useful education once admitted).

Family Services and Relationship to Other Federal Policy

The 1986 amendments, creating the Part H program for infants and toddlers (P.L. 99-457), extend the notion of parent participation in several significant ways. First, they recognize that parents not only have the right to participate in their children's educational process, but they also are highly influential in their children's development, particularly in the very early years (birth to age 5). That is why the amendments provide for development of an individualized family service plan (IFSP): to ensure that parents are involved in their children's development and education.

Second, the amendments recognize the inextricable link between the child with a disability and other members of the family. Whatever happens to the child with a disability affects the child's family and its members, albeit in different ways—some positive and some negative. By acknowledging this reality and providing for an IFSP, the 1986 amendments recognize that families themselves are systems and that any intervention in the life of one member has effects on the others and on the system as a whole. The family-system approach to special education and other interventions[18] takes a holistic view of the family and of the effect of a disability and disability-related interventions. The IFSP does this, too, by providing for multidisciplinary, interagency, family-focused assessments and interventions.

Third, the 1986 amendments reject the notion—once prevalent under the medical model or the behavioral model of remediating a disability—that a disability is caused by and therefore is able to be ameliorated by one, and only one, discipline. By calling for multidisciplinary interventions and providing for interagency approaches to service delivery, the amendments recognize that a disability can have medical, behavioral, psychological-psychiatric, or environmental (socioeconomic) origins; accordingly, a disability can require a combination of approaches and interventions.

Fourth, the amendments relax the criteria by which a child is classified as handicapped. For example, they use the criteria of developmental delay or probability of developmental delay. By contrast, the EHA requires not only a confirmed diagnosis of a disability but also a clear need for special education because of that disability (see the previous discussion of AIDS cases, which illustrate this point). Similarly, the amendments permit states to serve at-risk children. By relaxing the criteria, the amendments not only may substantially enlarge the number of children served, but they also may assure that the larger numbers either (a) are diverted from special education because their disability or potential disability has been remediated to the point that they do not need special education, or (b) are given a head-start in school, in special education or not.

Fifth, either of these effects would be consistent with the purpose of the amendments. Those purposes are to (a) enhance children's development or minimize potential developmental delays, (b) reduce the educational costs related to disability, (c) minimize the likelihood that children with disabilities will be institutionalized and maximize the likelihood of their living independently, and (d) enhance families' capacities to meet their children's needs.

Sixth, the very purposes of the amendments and the means by which they are carried out—the child's IEP and the family's IFSP—signal that the government (federal, state, and local) not only will enter the private lives of families but that it should do so. If a litmus test of policy in the 1980s has been whether and to what extent government has a legitimate role in the private sector and the lives of families as symbolic of the private sector (and surely the debates around abortion, Pledges of Allegiance and school prayer, intervention in decisions about treatment of newborns with disabilities, and the extent to which childcare will be federally subsidized reflect that debate), the 1986 amendments proclaim, loudly and clearly: Government is here to stay, even in your family life.

Finally, the 1986 amendments also clearly demonstrate that Congress has adopted a largely consistent policy affecting people with disabilities and their families. That policy includes, among other things, incentives for community-based, family-based living; for integration of disabled and nondisabled people; for family support; for the policy of avoiding institutionalization; and for the policy of independence, as represented not just in a person's ability to do things without help or with only the amount of help necessary to the task, but also in the person's and the family's ability to participate in decisions that affect its daily life. Other federal legislation (principally the Developmental Disabilities Assistance and Bill of Rights Act, the Rehabilitation Act, and the Social Security Act, in its Medicare and Medicaid programs) declares these purposes.[19] Now, it is beyond argument that the EHA and particularly its most recent restatement (Part H) make the policy abundantly clear.

So it is that the rationale for the zero reject principle is expressed in Part H: to establish equal protection of comparably situated citizens (those with or at risk of a disability); to ensure that exclusion in school, which is a cause of exclusion in other life-activities, is replaced by a practice of inclusion in school as a means for inclusion in other life-activities; to educate early and well and thereby, one hopes, avoid a lifetime of dependency caused by disability and the failure to ameliorate it; to respond to the horrible economic and human costs associated with a disability; and to establish an equality—an equity—between those with and those without a disability.

New Growth Industry

The early cases—especially once they were enacted into the EHA and Congress began to channel money to the states, colleges, and universities for teacher education and research—had a dramatic impact on personnel preparation. Together, the courts and Congress created a new growth industry in America: special education. Not only did they give tremendous impetus to that discipline, but they also affected the education of regular education teachers by requiring them to be competent to teach disabled children in the mainstream (in least restrictive or more integrated settings).

Expanded Practices and Individualization

In short, the cases and the EHA have pushed hard at the limits of public educational systems. They have demonstrated the plasticity of the system. They have shown that seemingly intransigent systems can change (albeit slowly—never underestimate the power of inertia), that there is a (sometimes fragile) consensus about the inherent rightness of special education of special children, and that the limits of educational systems are a great deal more expansive than they sometimes appear. The early cases, coupled with the EHA, thus have had the effect of both commanding and enabling change, of requiring and facilitating expansion of the educational system so that it can provide equal educational opportunities to handicapped children.

One of the most significant changes in school practices has been in the methods of instruction. By addressing functional exclusion as an aspect of pure exclusion, the zero reject principle has individualized educational services for handicapped children. More than that, it has caused educators to extend the individualization practice to gifted and talented children (and states to enact special education laws that grant to such children substantially the same rights as are granted to handicapped children). It also has caused educators and policy makers to be particularly aware of the deficits in educating slow learners (children who are not formally classified as handicapped under the EHA but who still require special education attention). The mega-politics of the zero reject doctrine, then, have been to extend to others the benefits (individualized education) that handicapped children have as a matter of right.

The Integration Impetus

On still another level, the legal cases and the EHA have begun to integrate disabled children into the mainstream of American life. The courts and the Congress both asserted the value of integration in requiring that, to the maximum extent appropriate, disabled and nondisabled children should be educated together.

The integration principle also has had an important effect on state mental retardation centers, psychiatric hospitals for children, and schools for deaf or blind children. The children in those institutions have been given an opportunity to be deinstitutionalized. They have been given a right to education in the public school system, with the result that, in many cases, they have not been placed in the institutions to begin with, have been discharged from institutions, or have been kept in the institutions but given more adequate and effective educational services there or in cooperating local school districts.

The integration principle in education was developing at the same time that the institutions—psychiatric hospitals and mental retardation facilities—were experiencing a reduction in the number of children admitted. This reduction had at least several related and important causes. First, state legislatures were tightening up the procedures by which people could be committed to the state institutions. They were requiring much more due process, thereby discouraging commitment. Similarly, legislatures were enacting stricter criteria for commitment, requiring that the usual standard of "dangerousness" be met more obviously.

Second, the U.S. Supreme Court ruled in *Addington v. Texas* and in *Parham v. J.R.* that states must prove dangerousness by fairly strict procedures and that states must provide for neutral review of admission decisions when children are candidates for institutionalization. Both cases had the effect of putting real or perceived clamps on the ease of institutionalization. Third, the states were developing more community-based treatment programs for children and using institutional placements less and less.

The cumulative effect of these three developments was to accelerate the integration impetus. In conjunction with the EHA provisions for zero reject, least restrictive placement, and service priorities that favored previously unserved and severely disabled children, these developments significantly changed the character of the public schools.

Lifetime Service

The court cases and the EHA also have forced health, mental health, social services/welfare, and education systems to begin serious efforts, separately or in cooperation, to provide community-based services. These include child-find, educational placement, cost-sharing, facility-sharing, and family support services. These efforts represent the first long-range efforts, on a large scale, to secure community integration and at-home placement of handicapped children. They also represent the beginnings of a lifetime service system for disabled people.

Given the early childhood initiative, the requirement for related services, and the "transition" or "aging out" initiatives, the EHA set into motion a linkage between schools and other agencies, in which the schools are the primary service providers during a disabled person's school years and other agencies are secondary providers but thereafter take over the principal-provider role. Accordingly, the change wrought in schools also effected a change in adult service systems (which are regulated by Section 504, just as the schools are).

"Defective" Newborns

At the same time that *Brown* and the zero reject rule were applied to handicapped students, there developed an awareness within the public and especially among the professions dealing with disabled people that gross discrimination has been and is being practiced against newborns who have birth defects. The practice of withholding medically appropriate treatment from "defective" newborns now is the center of a major policy and legal debate. The policy issue is whether the withholding of treatment (or other practices that jeopardize the child's life) should be condoned by families, physicians, and the public. The legal issues, on the other hand, center on the constitutional rights of newborns, the enforcement of child abuse and neglect laws, the application of nondiscrimination laws (particularly Section 504) to their treatment, and the tolerable zones of privacy that families and physicians may establish to fend off external review of their treatment/nontreatment decisions.

In a very real sense, the constitutional doctrines of *Brown* and the special law cases are applicable by analogy to the Baby Doe cases (so-called because of the name given to unidentified newborns in lawsuits involving their treatment). If equality before the law means anything, it means that "defective"newborns are entitled to appropriate medical treatment. And if that treatment is given and is life-saving, the medical and other inventions must be forthcoming: A society that compels a life to be saved is one that also must compel services to the person. Thus, special education is involved in the Baby Doe cases in two ways—first, by extension of the equal treatment doctrines; and second, by providing early childhood education.

Personal Growth

At the same time that the cases and the EHA have commanded and enabled schools and other governmental systems to change their ways of operation and their definitions of equality, they have enabled people to change and to overcome tremendous personal limitations. Students who once were regarded as subtrainable or ineducable have begun to acquire learned skills. Parents who once were regarded as the permanent custodians of their children (even into their children's adulthood) have been given massive help from the educational and other systems of government. Parents who once were regarded as trouble-making radicals because they advocated for their children have been given the green light to participate in their children's education. Nondisabled students, who would have been excluded from education with disabled students (who would have borne the brunt of the exclusion by being denied any education), have had an opportunity to learn about their handicapped peers, to develop accepting attitudes toward them, to regard them as valuable, and to develop ways of thinking about disabled people that will carry into their adult lives.

New Norms and Pluralism

The "norms" of children in school have changed in important ways. As of the 1982 school year, the schools included 10.76% handicapped children. Between 1976, when the first child-count was conducted under the EHA, and the 1982 school year, nearly 600,000 new handicapped children were enrolled in the nation's schools. The norm now is not nearly so "nondisabled." The presence of handicapped children in school has changed the complexion of the schools. In a very real sense, their presence has augmented the cultural diversity and pluralism of the schools.

This enrichment undoubtedly will have important effects on the lives of adults. A result of the integration impetus is greater diversity in society. And professionals who once regarded some children as unworthy of an education or unable to benefit from training are now engaged in educating and training those same children. Not only have systems changed, but so too have people. On the whole, the change has been much for the better.

NOTES

1. *E.g.*, Frontiero v. Richardson, Graham v. Richardson, Levy v. Louisiana, and Loving v. Virginia, to the effect that, respectively, race, alienage, illegitimacy, and race (again) are suspect classifications.

2. *E.g.*, Mills and MARC v. Maryland.

3. City of Cleburne, Texas v. Cleburne Living Center, Inc.

4. For other zero reject cases not discussed elsewhere in this chapter, *see*, for example, Association for Mentally Ill Children v. Greenblatt; Beauchamp v. Jones; Brandt v. Nevada; California ARC v. Riles; and North Carolina ARC v. North Carolina.

5. For other tuition cases not discussed elsewhere in this chapter, *see*, for example, Crowder v. Riles; Davis v. Wynne; and State of Wisconsin ex rel. Warren v. Nussbaum.

6. Reid v. Bd. of Ed. of City of New York.

7. Davis v. Wynne.

8. Weintraub and Abeson, "Appropriate Education for All Handicapped Children," 23 *Syracuse Law Review* 1037, 1056 (1972).

9. See ch. 4 for more complete discussion of issues of racial discrimination in special education.

10. *See, e.g.*, Rios v. Read; Hernandez v. Porter; Guadalupe Org., Inc. v. Tempe Elem. School Dist.; Ruiz v. State Bd. of Ed.; and Bilingual Education Act, 20 U.S.C. 880b-880b-13.

11. Mills; LeBanks v. Spears.

12. MARC v. Maryland; Reid v. Bd. of Ed.

13. PARC; Mills; and MARC v. Maryland.

14. Seals v. Loftis.

15. Parks v. Parkovic; Jenkins v. Florida.

16. Parents of Child v. Coker.

17. Doe v. Belleville Public Schools Dist. No. 118.

18. Turnbull, Turnbull, Summers, Brotherson, and Benson, *Families, Professionals, and Exceptionality: A Special Partnership* (Columbus, OH: Charles E. Merrill, 1986).

19. Turnbull and Barber, "Future Policy Issues in Mental Retardation," in *The Future of Mental Retardation,* edited by Meyen (Reston, VA: Council for Exceptional Children, 1984); Turnbull, "Legal and Policy Issues in Community Programs," in *Community Services: Here to Stay,* edited by Krauss, Seltzer, and Janicki (Baltimore: Paul Brookes, 1987); and Turnbull, "Law and the Mentally Retarded Citizen: American Responses to the Declarations of Rights of the United Nations and International League of Societies for the Mentally Handicapped: Where We've Been, Are, and Are Heading," 30 *Syracuse Law Review,* 1093-1142 (1979).

4
Testing, Classification, and Placement

CONSTITUTIONAL FOUNDATIONS

Constitutional arguments against certain types of educational evaluations and the resulting classifications of children turn on the Fifth and Fourteenth Amendments. Both provide that a person shall not be deprived of life, liberty, or property without due process of law. Denying an education is arguably tantamount to denying an opportunity to develop the ability to acquire property.[1] Classifying children as handicapped when they are not, or classifying them inaccurately with respect to their handicaps, can result not only in denying them their rights to an educational opportunity[2] (not to mention their rights to an appropriate education) but also in unjustifiably stigmatizing them. It follows, then, that substantive due process has been violated when a pupil is misclassified on the basis of invalid criteria and thus placed in an inappropriate "track" in school.[3]

The Fourteenth Amendment is involved in still another way. By requiring that states treat citizens equally (the equal protection clause), the Fourteenth Amendment has become the traditional bulwark against state-imposed racial discrimination. Inasmuch as special education classes (particularly for the mildly handicapped) have been filled with a disproportionate number of minority students (racial minorities—principally blacks—and cultural minorities—principally Latin Americans), there is at least an arguable claim of discrimination based on race or cultural background. The following discussion will show how the substantive due process rights under the Fifth and Fourteenth Amendments and the equal protection rights under the Fourteenth Amendment came into play in school testing and classification before the EHA was effective, as amended by P.L. 94-142.

Pre-EHA Criticisms of Testing

The alleged violations have involved the use of IQ or aptitude tests. These tests supposedly are objective and allegedly do not depend on irrelevant variables such as teacher prejudice or social class, but they nevertheless have been subject to criticism, particularly when test results are the primary basis for assigning a disproportionate number of minority pupils—black or non-English speaking—to special education programs for educable mentally retarded (EMR) or trainable mentally retarded (TMR) children. Reestablishment of racially dual systems of education is threatened by such assignments, but the constitutional doctrine of equal protection under the Fourteenth Amendment comes into play to prohibit segregation by race in any school program, including special education.

One basis for criticizing the tests has been that they have been used to determine the intelligence of children unfamiliar with the language or with the white middle-class culture that underlies the test questions.[4] In short, it has been argued that tests based on a white middle-class socioeconomic group should not be used with persons not of that group because the tests put them at an initial disadvantage and may lead to their mistakenly being classified as handicapped. There have been other criticisms of the tests or the ways in which they are administered or used. In some cases, they have not been administered in the child's native language (e.g., Spanish).[5] Or they have not measured adaptive behavior—a child's ability to cope and get along in his or her *own* cultural environment.[6]

Misclassification resulting from inappropriate testing arguably imposes on students the stigma of being retarded or different; it can isolate them from normal school experiences and cause them to be rejected by students and adults alike; sometimes it sets up stereotyped expectations of behavior and can lead to self-fulfilling prophecy—all of this to the student's irreparable harm.[7] Often the label is permanent and cannot be escaped, outgrown, or rebutted.

Moreover, the label can limit (or increase) the resources available to the child, since public and private agencies tend to serve only persons identified as belonging within their categorical clientele. Misclassified children might be placed in special education programs whether they need it or not, or they might be placed in inappropriate special education programs or be inappropriately institutionalized. Being placed in a special education program does not necessarily ensure that the child will receive training that will be effective in overcoming the disadvantages of being classified as handicapped. Assignment to a special education program can become permanent, despite an original intention to make it temporary.[8]

Testing alone is not sufficient for developing an accurate picture of a child's abilities and handicaps, but it has often been treated as if it were. In some cases,[9] a single test has been used as the sole criterion for classification and placement. Testing results, when not supplemented by other evaluation techniques (e.g., medical information, parent conferences), are particularly subject to misinterpretation. Parent conferences to determine adaptive behavior have been rare, and parent participation in classification decisions has been negligible. Procedural due process concerning evaluation and periodic review of the placements has been the exception, not the rule.[10] Misclassification tells a child that he or she is deficient; the injury to self-esteem is incalculable.

Pre-EHA Court-Ordered Remedies

Given these criticisms of the nature, administration, and use of classification and testing procedures, it is not surprising that recent judicial response, based on substantive due process (Fifth Amendment) and equal protection (of racial or cultural minorities under the equal protection doctrine of the Fourteenth Amendment), has been massive. The key word is *recent* because only since 1972 have the courts become embroiled in classification issues. Their traditional posture had been to find that mere classification does not of itself deprive a group of equal protection[11] and that there is no constitutional prohibition against assigning individual students to particular schools on a basis of intelligence, achievement or other aptitudes upon a uniformly administered program.[12] Because of the criticisms of testing—criticisms centering on the permanent and stigmatizing consequences of being labeled as mentally retarded and on the racial differentiation that results from testing—courts in the early and mid-1970s began to make inroads on the testing practices and procedures of schools.

Accepting the argument that intelligence tests bear little relationship to the intelligence they are supposed to measure when there is language or cultural unfamiliarity, some courts have held that IQ tests may no longer be used to place children in ability tracks.[13] They have forbidden schools to use biased (unvalidated) tests that do not properly account for the cultural background and experiences of the children being tested.[14] They have enjoined school authorities from placing minority students in classes for the educable mentally retarded on the basis of IQ tests if using the tests brings about racial imbalance in the composition of such classes. They also have ordered the dismantling of EMR classes in which Chicanos were overrepresented.[15] They have given the schools the burden of proving that a test is a valid measure of intelligence and does not discriminate because of race or culture if the test is the primary basis for classifications that are resulting in racial imbalance.[16] In addition, they have ordered that pupils be tested or retested in their primary language or be given bilingual instruction.[17] By ordering these remedies, the courts have made it clear that they have adopted as fact the presumption that statistical imbalance (racial imbalance) would not occur unless there is some sort of discrimination based on race.[18]

The courts have ordered that factors such as socioeconomic background, social adaptation, and adaptive ability be considered in making an evaluation for appropriate placement.[19] Use of the IQ test alone was found to violate substantive due process, since the basis for the school's action—the IQ score—was not reasonably related to the purpose for which it was used— namely, to determine a pupil's ability and what would be a "suitable" or "appropriate" education for him or her.

Just as the criteria must be related to what they are supposed to measure (that is, that they not be arbitrary), the standard for evaluation may not be arbitrarily applied. Thus, when white and minority students with similar abilities are assigned to remedial classes and classes for the educable mentally retarded, it is discriminatory to put the white students in the remedial classes and the minority students into the classes for the retarded.

Accordingly, schools have been prohibited from having a disproportionate number of minority students in classes for the educable mentally retarded[20] and must justify their reliance on tests that have resulted in an imbalance.[21] And schools were required to furnish handicapped children with intensive training to help them attain their peers' skill levels. Finally, the courts have ordered compensatory education for adults who were improperly classified, thus being denied an equal educational opportunity as children.[22]

Why Testing Is Required

It is obvious that testing, classification, and placement in special education programs must be continued, for several reasons. The schools must be able to identify and evaluate handicapped children in order to (1) plan, program, and appropriate funds for them, (2) provide appropriate services for them, (3) comply with federal and state laws requiring that handicapped children be counted and served, (4) evaluate their own efforts to educate children, and (5) serve their bureaucratic interests in maintaining and expanding their own services.

Classification can assist in measuring the results of special education efforts.[23] Classification also can create educational opportunity for the handicapped, supply a common denominator to create and stimulate activities of volunteer or professional interest groups, assist in the enactment of legislation to aid individuals in a specific category, provide structure to governmental programs, and serve as a basis for financial appropriation decisions.[24] Classification is useful for determining incidence and prevalence data, which is helpful in planning how many professionals will be needed for a wide variety of services and assuring accountability in programs and services. Some of the reasons students perform poorly on standardized tests—such as slow work habits, emotional insecurity, low motivation, lack of interest, and culturally related conditions—also account for their below-average performance in school. Thus, testing can provide an early warning of probable or possible future problems.

Nevertheless, classification remains a powerful political tool,[25] capable of regulating people, degrading them, denying them access to educational opportunity, excluding them as "undesirables," and, in the case of minority persons, forcing dominant cultural values and mores on them.

The label of "handicapped" also often has the effect of excluding a person so labeled from an appropriate education and, in some instances, from any education at all. The label itself emphasizes the handicap and underscores the differences between "them" (the handicapped) and "us" (the nonhandicapped). It creates not only a dual system of services but also a dual system of law—law for "them" and law for "us."

For all of these reasons, it is important to establish procedures to protect children from improper testing, misclassification, and inappropriate placement. That is the principal thrust of current federal legislation. Federal legislation seeks to minimize labeling and to ensure that labels, when necessary, accurately describe the handicaps and become useful devices for appropriately serving handicapped children.

FEDERAL LEGISLATION

A school's failure to detect handicaps can prevent children from receiving an appropriate education [Sec. 1400(b)(5)]. Misuse of classification data can result in discrimination, and erroneous classification represents a major obstacle to a child's receiving an appropriate education.[26] Recognizing these problems, Congress sought to accomplish *nondiscriminatory evaluation*. Its effort is broad-based and multifaceted.

Nondiscriminatory Evaluation Procedures

Congress required that three strategies be followed to assure nondiscriminatory evaluation. The SEAs and LEAs must establish procedures to assure that testing and examination materials and procedures used for evaluating and placing handicapped children will be selected and administered so as not to be racially or culturally discriminatory [Secs. 1412(5)(C) and 1414(a)(7)]. Next, each SEA and LEA must provide and administer such materials or procedures in the child's native language or mode of communication unless it is clearly not feasible to do so [Secs. 1412(5)(C) and 1414(a)(7)]. The term *nondiscriminatory testing* applies to evaluation materials and procedures used with all handicapped children, as the regulations make clear [Sec. 300.530-.534].

In response to the requirement for racially and culturally nondiscriminatory testing and evaluation, Section 300.532 requires that:

(a) Tests and other evaluation materials
    (1) Are provided and administered in the child's native language or other mode of communication, unless it is clearly not feasible to do so;
    (2) Have been validated for the specific purpose for which they are used;
    (3) Are administered by trained personnel in conformance with instructions from the producer;

(b) Tests and other evaluation materials include those tailored to access specific areas of educational need and not merely those which are designed to provide a single general intelligence quotient;

(c) Tests are selected and administered so as best to insure that when a test is administered to a child with impaired sensory, manual or speaking skills, the test results accurately reflect the child's aptitude or achievement level or whatever other factor the test purports to measure, rather than reflecting the child's impaired sensory, manual, or speaking skills (except where those skills are the factors which the test purports to measure);

(d) No single procedure is used as the sole criterion for determining an appropriate educational program for a child and placement;

(e) The evaluation is made by a multidisciplinary team or group of persons, including at least one teacher or other specialist with knowledge in the area of suspected disability;

(f) The child is assessed in all areas related to the suspected disability, including, where appropriate, health, vision, hearing, social and emotional status, general intelligence, academic performance, communicative status, and motor abilities.

Section 300.531 requires that before a child is initially placed in a special education program, a complete and individual evaluation of his or her educational needs must be conducted in accordance with Section 300.532. Section .533 regulates placement procedures and the use of evaluation results. Public agencies must:

> (1) Draw upon information from a variety of sources, including aptitude and achievement tests, teacher recommendations, physical condition, social or cultural background, and adaptive behavior;
>
> (2) Insure that information obtained from all of these sources is documented and carefully considered;
>
> (3) Insure that the placement decision is made by a group of persons, including persons knowledgeable about the child, the meaning of the evaluation data, and the placement options; and
>
> (4) Insure that the placement decision is made in conformity with the least restrictive environment rules in Secs. 300.550-.554.

Reevaluation must occur at least every 3 years or more often if "conditions warrant" or the child's parent or teacher requests it [Sec. 300.534].

The regulations require parental consent for a preplacement evaluation only. In the event the parents withhold consent, a due process hearing may be held at the school's request. Federal law does not require parental consent for subsequent evaluations [Sec. 300.504 (b) (1) and (2)].

The cases follow the EHA's commands, almost without exception. There may be no placement until the child is evaluated according to the nondiscriminatory evaluation requirements. If those requirements are not met, the child's individualized education program (IEP—see chapter 5) may be rejected.[27]

This general rule—that there may be no program or placement in special education until evaluation occurs according to the nondiscriminatory evaluation requirements—also is the command of *Honig* (the "stay-put" case involving suspension) and of the long line of cases that followed *Turlington* (the suspension-exclusion cases). Both *Honig* and *Turlington* require nondiscriminatory evaluation before a school may suspend or expel (except for suspension for a period of less than 10 days). As chapter 7 (due process) points out, a change of the child's placement in the sense of movement from one school to another does not trigger the nondiscriminatory evaluation requirement; only a change of program, which can occur simultaneously with a change of placement, does.

By the same token, it is well settled that the administration of standardized tests to an entire group of students does not constitute an individualized assessment that must comply with the nondiscriminatory evaluation requirements. Thus, a school may administer the Iowa or California achievement tests or minimum-competency tests to a student with a disability and not have to comply with the nondiscriminatory evaluation requirements. Those tests are not administered for the purpose of evaluating the child for special education services.

Ceiling

Congress placed a ceiling on the number of children a state may count for the purpose of receiving federal funds under the EHA [Sec.1411(a)(5)(A)(i) and (ii)]. The limit is 12% of the number of all children aged 5 through 17. The ceiling reflects Congress' concern that recipients might have counted children who were not in fact handicapped, in order to receive more federal funds. More than 12% of the school population may be classified as handicapped, but federal funding will be available only for up to 12%.

Part H—Infants and Toddlers

The requirements for nondiscriminatory evaluation of infants and toddlers are set out in its regulations, not in the statute. In a nutshell, these regulations require that tests be given in the parent's native language or other mode of communication, that they not be racially or culturally discriminatory, that no single procedure be used, and that qualified personnel administer the tests. Evaluation is for the purpose of determining a child's eligibility for Part H; assessment is for the purpose of identifying the child's needs, the family's strengths and needs, and the services needed to meet the child's and family's needs.

There are special rules for evaluation and assessment of the child and of the family. Generally, with respect to the child's evaluation and assessment, appropriate personnel must administer nondiscriminatory procedures and use *informed clinical opinion*. With respect to the family's assessment, the purpose is to determine the family's strengths and needs related to enhancing the child's development; thus, the family assessment must be voluntary on the family's part, and it must be based on information provided by the family through a personal interview and incorporate the family's description of its strengths and needs with respect to the enhancing the child's development.

As a general rule, child and family evaluation and assessment must be completed within 45 days after the state lead agency is notified of the family's application for service.

As pointed out in chapter 3, the 1986 amendments to the EHA created a new program—Part H, early intervention services for handicapped infants and toddlers. Part H requires that the instruments and procedures for evaluating those children be "appropriate." It also provides that the children and their parents shall have certain procedural protections, including rights to a hearing on the child's evaluation.

Does the requirement of nondiscriminatory evaluation also apply to the infants and toddlers? Yes. There are two reasons why this is so, despite the fact that Part H makes no explicit provision incorporating the nondiscriminatory requirements of Part B of the EHA.

First, Part H itself is part of the EHA and, for that reason, the provisions of the EHA generally apply to infants and toddlers. Second, Section 504 and its regulations (which require nondiscriminatory evaluation) also apply to the programs that administer Part H. Those programs therefore must use nondiscriminatory evaluation methods.

"Learning Disability" Narrowly Defined

Congress carefully defined "children with specific learning disabilities" [Sec. 1401(15)] so that children who do not satisfy the definition will not be classified as handicapped. In addition, the Department of Education has adopted regulations that specifically regulate the procedure for evaluating students to determine if they are learning disabled. The EHA and regulations set up specific requirements for evaluation of children thought to have specific learning disabilities. First, the general requirements of nondiscriminatory evaluation (Sec. 300.530-.534) must be followed. These are the same requirements that apply to all children thought to be disabled. Additional evaluations must be made if the child is thought to have a specific learning disability.

Second, the evaluation team must consist of either the child's regular education teacher, a regular education teacher if the child is not then in regular education, or an early education specialist if the child is younger than school age. In addition to one of those people, the evaluation team must include at least one person qualified to conduct an individual diagnostic examination (school psychologist, speech-language pathologist, or remedial reading teacher).

Third, the regulations allow the evaluation team to determine that the child has a specific learning disability if:

> (1) The child does not achieve commensurate with his or her age and ability levels in one or more of the areas listed ..., when provided with learning experiences appropriate for the child's age and ability levels; and
> (2) The team finds that a child has a severe discrepancy between achievement and intellectual ability in one or more of the following areas:
> (i) Oral expression;
> (ii) Listening comprehension;
> (iii) Written expression;
> (iv) Basic reading skill;
> (v) Reading comprehension;
> (vi) Mathematics calculation; or
> (vii) Mathematic reasoning.

The team may not identify a child as having a specific learning disability if the severe discrepancy between ability and achievement is primarily the result of:

> (1) A visual, hearing, or motor handicap;
> (2) Mental retardation;
> (3) Emotional disturbance; or
> (4) Environmental, cultural, or economic disadvantage.

The purposes of the regular and special evaluations in the area of specific learning disability are several. First, they seek to reduce the number of children classified as having a learning disability. They do this by erecting additional procedural hurdles to that classification.

Second, by seeking to limit the number of children so classified, they seek to hold down the costs of special education. Congress and the states realize that a very large number of children could be classified as learning disabled; after all, a large number of children simply do not perform well but do not have obvious other disabilities—and they are candidates for classification as having a learning disability. If all students were classified as having that disability, the costs of educating them appropriately would be enormous.

Third, the regular and additional evaluation requirements recognize that there is a stigma attached to having any disability. Accordingly, they seek to prevent that classification to prevent stigmatization of the child.

Yet the regular and special evaluation requirements for learning disability convey a strange message. It is that it is worse to have the stigma of sensory, physical, mental, or emotional disability than to have the stigma of learning disability. This message is inherent in the definition of learning disability: Children with a specific learning disability do not include those who have learning problems that are primarily the result of sensory (visual or hearing), physical (motor), mental (mental retardation), or emotional (emotional disturbance) disabilities [Sec. 1401(15) and Sec. 300.541].

Another message is inherent in the definitions of specific learning disability, and it is essentially culturally, racially, and socioeconomically biased. The Act [Sec. 1401(15)] and regulations (Sec. 300.541) make it clear that a child may not be classified as having a specific learning disability if the child's learning problems are primarily the result of environmental, cultural, or economic disadvantage. In the views of some, this limitation gives the message that specific learning disabilities are those that are primarily of white middle-class or upper-class children.

Service Priorities

Congress also established the service priorities. (See chapter 3 for a discussion of the priorities.) Like the ceiling, the service priorities are intended to stop an LEA from miscategorizing children as handicapped in order to increase the amount of federal funds it may receive. Serving the *first-priority* (previously excluded) and *second-priority* (most severely handicapped not receiving an appropriate education) children makes it unlikely that the LEAs will soon have federal funds free to spend on handicapped children who do not fall in either category. There is little risk that LEAs will unnecessarily classify children as handicapped, since many of them are still a long way from satisfying the needs of the first- and second-priority children.

Recoupment

Congress required the SEAs to adopt procedures for recouping funds from LEAs in order to furnish services for children who were erroneously classified and thus were not eligible for federal funds (Sec. 1416(a)(5)). This requirement is intended to prevent misclassification. The desire for federal funding, after all, does make it tempting to count a child as handicapped.

Accounting

Congress provided that SEAs and LEAs must report and account for the receipt and expenditure of EHA money. It granted the Secretary of Education the power to audit those agencies and check the accuracy of their data with regard to the number of handicapped children the state is actually educating [Secs. 1412 and 1416]. The Secretary's power to trace federal dollars is intended to help enforce the service priorities and thereby prevent misclassification.

Due Process Hearing

Congress granted procedural safeguards—essentially a due process hearing right—to children who have been identified, evaluated, and placed in programs for the handicapped [Sec. 1415]. These safeguards protect against misclassification by furnishing a forum for investigating whether a misclassification has occurred. (See chapter 7 for further discussion of due process.)

Sanctions

Congress provided that federal funds be withheld from any SEA that is alleged to be or found to be in violation of provisions of the EHA [Sec. 1416].These sanctions contain an element of overkill not evident in the other enforcement measures described in the preceding paragraphs. For that reason, the other measures should be used before invoking the sanction of withholding. The withholding sanction has an undoubtedly counterproductive element: It can penalize the handicapped (by cutting off federal dollars) in the name of aiding them.

Section 504

Like the EHA regulations, the regulations of Section 504 acknowledge that failure to provide handicapped students with an appropriate education is usually the result of misclassification or incorrect placement. Accordingly, Section 104.35(a) requires an evaluation of any person who needs or is believed to need special education or related services because of a handicap. The evaluation must be completed before a school takes any action (including denial or placement) with respect to *initial* placement in a regular or special education program or any subsequent significant change in placement. But a full reevaluation is not obligatory every time a lesser adjustment in the child's placement is made.

Section 104.35(b) and (c) sets out procedures to ensure that children are not misclassified, unnecessarily labeled as handicapped, or incorrectly placed because of inappropriate selection, administration, or interpretation of evaluation materials. Section 104.35(b) requires schools to establish standards and procedures for evaluation and placement to ensure that tests and other evaluation materials are validated for the specific purpose for which they are used and are administered by trained personnel in conformance with the instructions of their producer. Tests and other evaluation materials are to include those tailored to assess specific areas of educational need and not merely those designed to provide a single general intelligence quotient.

In addition, tests are to be selected and administered to students with impaired sensory, manual, or speaking skills, so that the test results accurately reflect the student's aptitude or achievement level—or whatever other factor the test purports to measure—rather than the student's impaired skills, except when those skills are the factors that the test seeks to measure. Section 300.35(b) drives home the point that tests should not be misinterpreted, that undue reliance on general intelligence tests is undesirable, and that tests should be administered in such a way that their results will not be distorted because of the student's handicap.

Section 104.35(c) requires schools, when evaluating and placing students, to draw upon information from a variety of sources, including aptitude and achievement tests, teacher recommendations, physical conditions, social or cultural background, and adaptive behavior. Schools must establish procedures to ensure that information obtained from all such sources is documented and carefully considered; and the placement decision is to be made by a *group* of people, including those knowledgeable about the child. The meaning of the evaluation data and the placement options must be made clear to all concerned, and placement decisions are to conform with the doctrine of least restrictive (most integrated) setting.

Section 104.35(d) requires periodic (though not necessarily annual) reevaluation. It makes clear that reevaluation procedures consistent with the EHA (which allows reevaluation at 3-year intervals unless more frequent reevaluations are requested) are a means of meeting the requirement of reevaluation.

Section 104.36 requires schools to provide for due process in evaluation procedures. This includes notice, right of access to records, impartial hearing, right to counsel, and appeal procedures. Chapter 7 discusses due process in detail.

CASE LAW

As noted, a vital and hotly debated issue (in special education as well as in legal circles) is whether standardized intelligence tests discriminate against students from economically deprived or racial minority backgrounds by placing them in classes for mentally retarded or learning disabled children. The early decision in *Larry P. v. Riles* seemed to signal the death knell of these tests. But a later case, *PASE,* validates use of the tests when evaluation is accomplished by additional means and seems to mute the tune that *Larry P.* sang.

Larry P
Larry P. may be poor precedent for special education in light of *PASE* and, considering that it was, as much as anything, a race discrimination case that put the court in the un-

enviable position of choosing among three possible explanations for the over-representation of minority children in special education: (1) the tests and their invalidity, (2) the "gene pool" argument that minority children are inherently less intelligent than non-minority children, and (3) the socioeconomic explanation of low performance on standardized tests. Given that the court in *Larry P.* found minority over-representation in special education, the tests were the most likely candidates for the court: The court could hold them invalid and impose a remedy (no more testing, under most conditions), but it would have been at a loss to impose a remedy that spoke to the politically charged gene pool or socioeconomic arguments.

In *PASE,* however, the court did not face these choices as dramatically as in *Larry P.* and took care to consider the tests' validity. Far more than *Larry P., PASE* is a special education decision that, in light of requirements of the EHA for multifaceted, multidisciplinary evaluation, commands special educators' adherence.

Larry P. v. Riles held that schools no longer may use standardized but unvalidated IQ tests for the purpose of identifying and placing black children into segregated special education classes for educable mentally retarded (EMR) children. The district court ruled that schools using such tests violate Title VI of the Civil Rights Act of 1964, Section 504 of the Rehabilitation Act of 1973, the EHA, and the equal protection clause of the Fourteenth Amendment to the federal Constitution. The violation occurs because the tests are racially and culturally biased, have a discriminatory impact on black children, have not been validated for the purpose of essentially permanent placements into "educationally dead-end, isolated, and stigmatizing classes for the so-called educable mentally retarded," evidence the schools' discriminatory intent (in violation of equal protection), and cannot be justified under the "compelling interest" standard applicable to racial discrimination cases.

The district court found that the Stanford-Binet, Wechsler, and Leiter IQ tests discriminate against blacks on several grounds: They measure achievement, not ability; they rest on the "plausible but unproven assumption that intelligence is distributed in the population in accordance with a normal statistical curve" and thus are "artificial tools to rank individuals according to certain skills, not to diagnose a medical condition (the presence of retardation)"; and they "necessarily" lead to placement of more blacks than whites in EMR classes. The court rejected two explanations for the disproportionate enrollment: the *genetic* argument ("natural selection has resulted in black persons having a 'gene pool' that dooms them as a group to less intelligence") and the *socioeconomic* argument (poverty and inferior home and neighborhood environments explain why more blacks than whites are EMR). Instead, it explained the difference in IQ test scores by the *cultural bias* argument that IQ tests measure intelligence as manifested by white, middle-class children and therefore are racially and culturally biased against blacks.

The district court converted its 1972 temporary injunction into a permanent one and (1) enjoined the state from using any standardized IQ tests for identifying EMR children or placing them into EMR classes without prior court approval, which will be granted only if the defendants, by statistical evidence, can show that the tests are not racially or culturally discriminatory, will not be administered in a discriminatory manner, and have been validated for the determination of EMR status or placement in EMR classes; (2) required the state superintendent and board to compile statistics enabling them to monitor and eliminate disproportionate placement of blacks into EMR classes and required local school boards to prepare and adopt plans to correct the imbalance; and (3) required the state superintendent and board to direct each local school to reevaluate nondiscriminatorily every black student already identified as EMR.

On appeal, the Ninth Circuit affirmed the district court's conclusions and remedies. Specifically, it rejected the state's argument that tests that are valid predictors of future performance can be used even if they have a discriminatory impact. The court of appeals stated that assignment of children to classes for EMR students means that they are denied an academic education and therefore experience a discriminatory impact because of the tests. In addition, the court of appeals found that the state could not sustain the burden of showing that the tests predict specifically that black elementary school children who score in the EMR range (IQ of 70 or below) are mentally retarded and incapable of learning in the regular school curriculum. In fact, the state had not sought to validate the tests to adjust for non-innate differences between blacks and whites (as it had adjusted tests to accommodate for innate differences between boys and girls); the reason the state had not adjusted for such differences is that it had assumed blacks have a lower level of intelligence. Finally, the state did not use other measures or criteria—such as the child's educational history, adaptive behavior, social and cultural background, or health history—for determining special education placement.

In language that suggests that discriminatory intent does not have to be proven, the court of appeals noted that improper placement in EMR classes has a demonstrable and negative impact, putting children into dead-end classes that do not teach academic skills but do stigmatize them, and that no nondiscriminatory factors, only the tests, are the cause of the adverse impact. Accordingly, it upheld the district court's remedy of suspending the use of the tests and requiring school districts with disproportionate racial balance in special education to devise 3-year remedial plans and to report racial disparities to the district court.

PASE

By contrast, *PASE V. Hannon* upheld the same tests that *Larry P.* had held unlawful as racially discriminatory. Although *PASE* found that some items in the tests were discriminatory, it upheld the tests as generally nondiscriminatory. More important, it found that the tests were not the *sole* basis for classification and that the school district therefore was complying with the EHA, which requires multifaceted testing. The minimal discrimination in tests and the adherence to classification safeguards were the decisive factors in this carefully reasoned opinion. To understand that *PASE* is an exceptionally appealing case, at least as it compares with *Larry P.*, it will be useful to examine the court's reasoning.

The Gene Pool Argument.   With respect to the gene pool argument, the court recognized that since "the early days of standard intelligence tests, around the time of World War I, blacks as a group score about one standard deviation—15 points—lower than whites" on the tests. There is, however, "considerable disagreement" about the causes of that result.

Noting that the "genetic view never did take account of the fact that many blacks scored above the white mean," that "northern blacks scored higher on the average than southern blacks," that blacks who moved north "often experienced an increase in their IQ scores," and that black infants adopted by white families tended to achieve IQ scores in later years that correlated "highly" with the scores of the natural children of the adoptive parents, the court concluded that IQ tests measure something that is changeable rather than fixed for all time, something that can be increased and improved. It also noted that the parties to the case—both the students and the school officials—agreed on that much. Moreover, it stated that "there is no evidence to support a hypothesis that blacks have less innate mental capacities than whites." Accordingly, the court rejected the gene pool argument as an explanation for the disproportionate representation of blacks in special education.

Racial/Cultural Bias Arguments.   The court also rejected the argument that the disproportion is caused by blacks' use of non-standard English: "The evidence does not establish how the use of non-standard English would interfere with performance on the Wechsler and Stanford-Binet tests. ...What is unclear is how the use of such non-standard English would handicap a child either in understanding the test items or in responding to them." In addition, a child's response in non-standard English "should not affect a child's score on the (test) item, since the examiners are specifically instructed by the test manuals to disregard the form of the answer as long as the substance is correct."

In addition, the plaintiffs made no effort to show that any of the 96 words challenged as racially biased are peculiar to the culture of whites but not blacks. The vocabulary words are of "ordinary, common usage." Accordingly, the court also discounted the argument that the tests are "Anglocentric" rather than "Afrocentric" and therefore necessarily biased against blacks. Blacks' lack of exposure to white culture and the fact of a separate co-existing black culture, said the court, "has not been connected to the specific issue in this case," which was "whether the (three tests—WISC-R, WISC (Wechsler), and Stanford-Binet) are culturally biased against black children, so that it is unfair to use these tests in the determination of whether a black child is mentally retarded."

In determining that the tests are culturally neutral, the court examined carefully all items of the three tests, particularly the ones that the plaintiffs alleged were culturally biased. It found—after 35 pages of its opinion—that only eight items on the WISC-R and WISC are "either racially biased or so subject to suspicion of bias that they should not be used," and only one item on the Stanford-Binet falls into the same category.

As to the WISC-R and WISC, the suspect items are:

1. What is the color of rubies?
2. What does C.O.D. mean?
3. Why is it better to pay bills by check than by cash?
4. What would you do if you were sent to buy a loaf of bread and the grocer said that he did not have any more?
5. What does a stomach do?
6. Why is it generally better to give money to an organized charity than to a street beggar?
7. What are you supposed to do if you find someone's wallet or pocket book in a store?
8. What is the thing to do if a boy (girl) much smaller than yourself starts to fight with you?

On the Stanford-Binet, the only item that the court found to be biased or racially suspect was on the "aesthetic comparison" test, in which 4½-year-old children are asked to identify which of two similarly colored persons is "prettier."

Having found that only nine of 488 items on the three tests are racially biased or racially suspect, the court turned its attention to interpretation of the tests. It found that the importance of an individual item is lessened by the fact that "the child continues with the sub-test (in which the item appears) until he has a certain number of consecutive misses." In addition, as far as some items of the tests are concerned, they occur at a level of difficulty that children in their early school years (when EMR placement generally is made) are not expected to reach the item or answer it correctly. The tests thus are not interpreted in a way that indicates racial bias but, rather, in a way that reflects racially-free educational assessment. In the Stanford-Binet, the consequences of racial bias are "negligible" since only one item of 104 is biased or racially suspect.

Moreover, the IQ score is "not the sole determinant" of whether a child is classified as EMR; "clinical judgment plays a large role in the interpretation of IQ test results." Indeed, "the examiner who knows the milieu of the child can correct for cultural bias by asking the questions in a sensitive and intelligent way." Finally, "the likelihood of a black child being placed in an EMH [emotionally mentally handicapped] class without at least one black professional having participated in the evaluation is very slight." The court thus concluded that "the possibility of the few biased items on these tests causing an EMH placement that would not otherwise occur is practically nonexistent."

The Socioeconomic Argument. The court addressed the socioeconomic explanation for special education placement by acknowledging that, "(E)arly intellectual stimulation is essential. ... Lack of opportunity for cognitive development is ... often due to factors associated with economic poverty in the home." Moreover, it was "uncontradicted that most of the children in the EMH classes do in fact come from the poverty pockets" of Chicago. "This tends to suggest that what is involved is not simply race but something associated with poverty."

The court then addressed the assessment process, finding that it involves several levels of investigation (IQ testing, observation in the classroom, screening conferences by educators, individualized examinations by professionals, multidisciplinary staff conferences, and a potential veto of special education placement by the psychologist who has evaluated the child). In that process, the court observed, any "hypnotic effect" of an IQ score is substantially mitigated. Indeed, later reevaluation of the children involved in the case indicated that they were not mentally retarded and had normal intelligence but "suffer from learning disabilities which make it difficult for them to perform well in certain kinds of learning situations."

***Comparison with* Larry P.**   Finally, the court addressed *Larry P.*, noting that, while the court there "largely" devoted its lengthy and scholarly opinion to the question of legal consequences resulting from a finding of racial bias in the tests, it engaged in "relatively little analysis of the threshold question of whether test bias in fact exists" and even noted that the cultural bias of the tests "is hardly disputed." Indeed, the *Larry P.* court made reference to specific test items on only one page and, then, only with respect to one item. Its inferences of bias from the one item, in a case that "hardly disputed" the cultural bias of the tests, were unpersuasive, lacking a more detailed examination of the test items.

Ability Grouping

Just as the first school classification case, *Hobson v. Hansen,* raised the issue of ability grouping and the disproportionate effect it has on racial minorities, so another, more recent case has charged that ability grouping is illegal because of its effects on minorities. In *Georgia State Conference of Branches of NAACP v. Georgia,* the use of ability or achievement grouping was challenged on the basis that the disproportionate racial impact violates the equal protection clause of the Fourteenth Amendment, Title VI of the Civil Rights Act (prohibiting discrimination on the basis of race), Section 504 (prohibiting discrimination on the basis of disability), and the EHA.

The federal court of appeals found, however, that ability or achievement grouping violates none of those laws. The court ruled that ability or achievement grouping is a sound education practice that provides the benefit of significant educational and academic progress. It also noted that the plaintiff (NAACP) had failed to show the existence of equally beneficial education practices that would result in less racial disproportionality.

Larry P., PASE, and Ability Grouping Cases—Effects

Fundamentally, *Larry P.* and *PASE* were school desegregation cases that took the form of a challenge to special educational practices. *Georgia NAACP* was a school desegregation case that took the form of a challenge to a regular education practice that had special education impacts.

On their surface, *Larry P.* and *PASE* clearly sought to prevent the schools from classifying students as handicapped and providing them with special education. Both cases challenged the use of IQ tests; those tests are the integral—some would argue, the principal—means for classifying students as handicapped. If the tests could be held invalid because they discriminate against minority students, and if their use were prohibited because of their invalidity, a major tool for classification would be outlawed.

One result of prohibiting use of IQ tests would be that schools would have to find other means for classifying students as handicapped. But another, and probably more fundamental, result would occur: The principal means by which minority students are classified into special education would be illegal. Classification of minority students into special education would be more difficult because the primary means for classification would not be legal. In turn, the number of minority students placed into special education would decrease. Finally, the number of minority students retained in regular education would increase, so that the schools—that is, the regular education programs—would be more racially integrated.

Thus, *Larry P.* and *PASE* clearly were cases that sought racial desegregation of the schools; this was their basic purpose. Their secondary purpose was to reduce the number of minority students who—already having the factor of their race as a potential stigma— would be placed into special education and thereby acquire an additional stigma—that of being "handicapped." Likewise, the *Georgia NAACP* case sought to prevent the use of tracking systems that had racially disproportionate results: more minority students being placed into lower or "special" tracks than whites, as a proportion of their representation in the school population as a whole.

Whatever one might think of the results of the cases—and it seems clear that the court's reasoning and use of evidence in *Larry P.* is not as persuasive as in *PASE*—it is clear that several policy issues are being fought out and resolved. First, the issue of means of classification is being challenged. In *Larry P.* and *PASE,* the means were the IQ tests; in *Georgia NAACP,* the means were ability or achievement tracking systems.

Second, the means are challenged to prevent minorities from being classified as handicapped and having to bear a double stigma of racial minority-ship and disability. (This observation assumes that, for some, the stigma of racial minority-ship is a reality. It does not condone that result: Race should not be stigmatizing. But it accepts as a fact that, for some people, both black and white, it may be. It also accepts as a fact that disability is stigmatizing. Again, it does not condone that fact.)

Third, the challenge seeks not simply to affect special education. At its heart, it seeks to reform the process of re-segregation of regular education. It acknowledges that school desegregation by race is an elusive goal. It admits that the goal is imperfectly realized. And, to more fully realize the goal, it attacks the means by which segregation by race, allegedly under the guise of classification by disability, occurs.

Fourth, the challenge is less than fully successful. Although *Larry P.* outlawed the use of IQ tests, *PASE* did not, and *Georgia NAACP* sustained the use of ability or achievement grouping.

Do the results make good law? In *PASE* and *Georgia NAACP* the results seem defensible on the basis of the legal analysis. In *Larry P.,* the results are defensible but not as carefully reasoned. Do the results make good social policy? That is a question that the reader must answer. What is clear, however, is that the social policy of desegregation and the social policy of fairness in classification so that appropriate education can be provided (if necessary, in special education) may seem to be in conflict with each other.

What is also clear is that the issue of educational policy is only the surface issue. These cases—and indeed the entire history of special education and especially its recent history and the EHA—essentially are social policy issues. The issue underlying them is this: What is the role of a government agency (the schools) and of the law in addressing the segregation of people by race and disability? Posed another way, the issue is this: What kind of society shall the schools and the law seek? Shall it be one that is more integrated than segregated? And posed still another way, the issue is this: How shall "we" (whether we are black or white, nondisabled or disabled) be with "them?" How shall people *be* with others, or shall they have the liberty not to *be* in the presence (and in the schools) with others who are different?

Other Cases

As noted earlier, classification concerns also affect the learning disabilities programs, not just MR programs. Thus, in *Riley v. Ambach,* New York's Commissioner of Education was enjoined from defining a learning disabled child as one who exhibits a discrepancy of 50% or more achievement (based on intellectual ability) and actual achievement. The court criticized the state's regulation for determining a learning disability on grounds that the standard is too inflexible, tends to under-identify LD children, and is not sufficiently individualized. The standard (50% discrepancy) was the same one previously adopted by the U.S. Office of Education but later rejected by it. On appeal, the decision was reversed, not on the merits of the lower court's decision but because the plaintiffs failed to exhaust their administrative remedies.

Another federal district court later approved a settlement in a class action that challenged the procedures in New York state regarding evaluation, classification, and placement of disabled children. The classification procedures were somewhat at issue in *Riley.* The settlement was approved in *J.G. v. Board of Education of Rochester City School District.*

With respect to parental consent for evaluation, the court in *Rettig v. Kent City School District* held that the school district is not required by the EHA to obtain parental consent for testing a student with standardized tests when the test results are not used for evaluation, an appropriate education, or placement, but only to comply with funding legislation. This result was unchanged by the Sixth Circuit Court of Appeals, affirming in part and reversing in part. And when a school tests a handicapped child as part of its reassessment (to assure an appropriate education, as required by the EHA), it does not have to obtain parental consent to the reevaluation (*Carroll v. Capalbo*).

OBSERVATIONS ABOUT CLASSIFICATION

As the early cases on nondiscriminatory evaluation recognized, as Congress acknowledged in the EHA, and as various critics have pointed out, classification of a person as disabled can have important educational and adult-life consequences. At the worst, it can relegate the person to second-class citizenship and, as such, subject the individual to a *dual system* of law. That dual system allows some of us (the nondisabled) to treat others (the disabled) as less worthy than us because of their disabilities.

It may be helpful to show how a dual system occurs by discussing the "classification system" and its consequences at law. It is appropriate to start by describing society's perceptions of disabled people, because those perceptions too often are reflected in law; next, to discusss who classifies; then, to show how society uses professionals to classify and why professionals play pivotal roles. This is followed by a discussion of the legal effects of and responses to classification.

But, first, it is important to recall that special education is not a new invention. It originated, according to Sarason and Doris (and as fully documented by them in their definitive text *Educational Handicap, Public Policy, and Social History),*[29] as a response to the inability of the schools to accommodate to the wave of immigration that began in the middle of the 19th Century. As Irish, Italian, German, Russian, and other immigrants came to the United States, they were classified as "special" and segregated in their education from well established Americans. (The fact that this classification had religious undertones and was done by native language, country of origin, or ethnicity should not pass unnoticed.)

For Sarason and Doris, classification of the new immigrants was a prelude to classification of other students who are different, in a different time. The separation of blacks, Chicanos, and Hispanics from other students during the remainder of the 19th century and into the 20th century has its origin in the 18th century. And yet its reasons are the same, according to Sarason and Doris: Classification occurs to (1) preserve the social status quo and prevent disruption of the social structure, (2) put distance between people so that those who are different (read: subject to a negative stigma) are not in the presence of others, and (3) altruistically justify some ameliorative (read: special education) interventions.

Sarason and Doris direct their attention to a single disability—mental retardation—arguing that classification of a person as having mental retardation reflects social policy—that the disability itself is a social invention. To make this point, they argue that disability—unlike genetic make-up—is not a characteristic inherent in a person. Rather, disability is a consequence of how a person functions within a social context. It is a transactional phenomenon—something that results from the way a person relates to and transacts social relations with others.

If the person functions differently from others, the person is said to be disabled. And thus the person is said to be at fault; the disability is part and parcel of the person (it is inherent in the person). That being the case, special interventions—special education, for example—are warranted; the disability reflects a "broken" aspect of the person, and the person must be "repaired" or "fixed." Similarly, separation of those who are "different" or "broken" from those who are not "different" becomes justifiable. Those with disabilities need certain interventions that the others do not. The "abnormal" and the "normal" are not just different but should be maintained as different. The consequence of this "pathology focus," Sarason and Doris show, is that special education is justified. The person with a disability is provided something that is intended to change the person.

What that focus fails to acknowledge, however, is that changing the person is only one part of the solution to the "misfit" of the person in society—only one way of accommodating to the fact of difference. The other part of the solution is, of course, to change the society itself. Accommodation, after all, should be a two-way street.

The EHA and Section 504 attempt to make mutual accommodations. They acknowledge that certain special intervention is warranted; the EHA provides rights to special education. They also acknowledge that special adjustments in society are required, too; the EHA's principles of zero reject and presumptions of integration (the doctrine of the least restrictive environment) and Section 504's prohibition of discrimination solely on the basis of disability requires adjustments by society to the person.

Given that mutual accommodations must be made and that the EHA and Section 504 attempt to ensure those accommodations, the issue remains: How shall the law respond to the fact of classification? To answer that question, it is appropriate to make additional observations about classification and then to document the law's response.

Perceptions and the Bias in Classification

Consider the disabled person. The characteristic of the person on which intervention usually is predicated is "disabled," not "person." Disabled people are seen to be qualitatively different from other people in this important and debilitating sense: They are "deviant." For example, the retarded newborn is commonly called a "defective child." Because the defect is seen to inhere in the child itself rather than in the society into which the child is born,[29] it must be "treated" in the sense of being subjected to diagnosis, prescription, regimen, and "cure." The treatment is rendered by many "helping" professionals, not just physicians. But this kind of treatment frequently strips the disabled person of social being.[30]

Disabled persons then can be regarded as "perpetual patients" for whom a cure can never be found. They are defined by what they are *not*, not by what they are or may become. Regarded as "sick" (i.e., disabled) and not responsible for their own condition, they are obliged to "fulfill permanently the role obligations of the good patient." In this role, they learn to be helpless and inferior, to accept professionals' control over their lives.[31] Infrequent rebellion against professional dominance is itself treated as a symptom of sickness; and the person's parents or family also become "patients."[32]

The obedience of the person and family to professional dominance reinforces the original perception that the person is incapable and possibly incurable. "Treatment" of this sort essentially reflects the prevailing social mores.[33] Classifying a person as disabled enables "us" to use a convenient concept—one ostensibly rooted in science—to do unto others what we would abhor being done to us, all in the name of altruism. Incorrectly seeing disabled persons as sick and not responsible for their condition,[34] "we" can easily conclude, as "the law" traditionally did, that they are not responsible (competent) and must be dealt with in unusual ways.[35]

Thus, able-bodied and mentally competent people come to regard the disabled person's incapacity as a kind of failure of the person. Given that the person is a failure, there is a reduced duty, if any, of the professions and of society as a whole to act on the person's behalf. "We" are off the hook for any responsibility to "them."[36] "We" have, ultimately, no responsibility for their exclusion from normalcy and, with relatively clean conscience and legal impunity, we can assign them to lower echelons of life, to second-class citizenship at law.

Who Classifies

Every society needs its "operatives"—professionals who will do society's bidding by bringing their expertise to bear on difficult situations and resolving those difficulties through the use of special training, talents, and status.

Physicians. It is ironic in the extreme that physicans are agents for dealing with physically or mentally disabled people—ironic because, while they have great ability to help these people, they also have great ability to injure them. Thus, physicians' curative abilities (to prevent a disability, intervene early so that its effects are minimized, and be a sustaining force throughout a person's life) make them important resources for saying who is disabled. They do this through developmental testing of newborns, infants, and children. Since disabled children need treatment, the disability is the physician's province. Given the need of society and its lawgivers for professional operatives, it is little wonder that physicians also have become one of the law's group of agents for deciding what to do about disabilities. Exactly how the law has allowed them to discharge their agentry will be discussed later.

Educators. Educators are another of society's classifiers. Schools label more children as disabled than does any other governmental or social entity.[37] This classification has massive consequences—both positive and negative—for children, especially when the disability is questionable or mild. Educational classification as disabled can, among other things, determine the nature or effectiveness of the child's curriculum,[38] the characteristics of his or her peers, and thereby the child's tendency to learn from peer interactions,[39] the extent of teacher demands and the type of teacher expectations of the child,[40] his or her self-image, the nature of educational resources made available, the child's mobility within or even out of special education, the nature of disciplinary proceedings, and the child's potential for higher educational opportunities, especially those of a vocational nature.

Some disabled children are spotted and classified well before they enter the public school system; their disabilities are such that they are unmistakably handicapped. Others, however, become known to us only when schools tell us they are different, special, exceptional, or otherwise regarded as atypical,[41] as not being easily subjected to the mass education of the masses. The reasons for and techniques of educational classification, and the procedures for challenging them, are not relevant here. The fact that schools classify children as disabled who frequently "become" nondisabled when they have exited from public education's jurisdiction should, however, give us pause.

Other Professionals and Agencies.   Educators and physicians are not the only professional sorters, though they are the principal ones.[42] Any profession having contact, however tangential, with different people classifies, notwithstanding its limited competence to do so. Social workers, psychologists, and rehabilitation specialists classify. Institutions of higher education, particularly vocational, technical, and community colleges, do their own classification. Law enforcement and criminal justice agencies classify. Courts accept classification arguments in order to assess whether, and, if so, to what extent, persons are criminally or civilly liable for their actions or failures to act. The armed forces classify. Nearly every agency of government classifies. None comes to mind that does not.

Professional Organizations.   Professional organizations classify. The American Association on Mental Deficiency classifies by changing its definition of mental retardation (the lower the cut-off point of mentally sub-average, the more people are "cured" and classified by exclusion from being mentally retarded) and creating and altering its adaptive behavior scales. The American Psychiatric Association classifies when it changes the standards and definitions in its *Diagnostic Standards Manual.* Learning disabilities societies classify by defining a specific learning disability to exclude some types of children.

Families.   Finally, families classify. It is not so much that families say that their child, brother or sister, or relative is disabled; others do that for them. It is more that they classify by determining how they will react to what others say. The decision to risk keeping a child in one's own home or securing placement in an institution, or to try a mainstream education instead of a more specialized one, is in the first (and sometimes the last) place a family decision. Among other things, it reflects a decision to classify a person more or less into or out of a disabled status. The option is less likely to be available if the person is severely or profoundly disabled than mildly retarded. For that reason, it is all the more important that the decision be made carefully.

Everyone.   Everyone classifies. We all make choices to associate or not with certain other people. Human beings are discriminating in the neutral sense of the word: We make discriminations about ourselves and others. We also are discriminating in a different sense: We discriminate for invidious as well as altruistic purposes. We let defective newborns die because their existence horrifies us, but we say we do it because we are concerned about the quality of their and others' lives. Classification is not inherently wrong, merely natural.

How We Classify

By Resort to Science. There is some magical quality in the concept of *science.* Call something scientific and it becomes less assailable. There is a presumption that science and its products are researched, reliable, validated, evaluated, and unbiased. But what we do—our policies—are not always based on good science, on defensible science. It is little wonder, then, that our policies are not always good.

The medical model's fallibility is well known.[43] After all, science taught that retarded people were a menace, so the eugenics movement spawned legalized compulsory institutionalization and sterilization.[44] Science teaches that intelligence can be measured, so classification as learning disabled or mentally retarded and categorization into special education receive the blessings of the law. It is no great matter that the basis for scientific facts is open to doubt as long as it is not clearly erroneous. There is far less debate about the fallibility of medical assessment for developmental delay (whether physical or mental); yet decisions by physicians, other service providers, and families, made on the basis of relatively acceptable assessment techniques, can still be highly debatable.

The case of Phillip Becker proves the point. There was no doubt about the fact that he was a young boy with Down syndrome and a heart defect that could be corrected surgically, with little risk to his life, as a means of substantially prolonging his life. Yet his family decided to refuse to authorize the surgery and, up to a point, so did the courts of California, because of debatable medical decision making.[45] Thus, we classify by using relatively fallible or infallible science or by acting in someone's interests on the basis of what that science tells us.

By Social Vulnerability. Classification is affected by other scientific means, and by nonscientific ones as well. Educators, for example, identify students as handicapped who make life difficult for them. Boys are more subject to special education classification than are girls, aggressive students more than acquiescent ones, racial and ethnic minority students more than white students.[46] The "science" of these classifications is highly doubtful. Instead, some students' differential vulnerability to special education classification appears to be a factor of cultural, social, or economic differentness.

By Legal Proceedings. Likewise, classification as disabled occurs in a host of legal proceedings, often without a sufficient "scientific" basis. For example, if persons are aggressive, unable to care for themselves, or, because of mental disability, "in need of treatment," society's caretakers—family, mental health, public health, or social services agencies—may choose to intervene by involuntarily committing them, adjudicating them to be incompetent so the third-party consent to treatment or placement can be obtained, securing temporary social service custody for treatment of neglect or abuse, or obtaining criminal prosecution for alleged violation of a crime.

Any of those four responses is legally sanctioned and may be effective as a way of intervening appropriately. So, too, is doing nothing; inaction is a form of action. Whatever the choice—whether to intervene and, if so, how—classification results. In Alan Stone's typology,[47] the classified person becomes mad, sad, or bad—mad if committed involuntarily, sad if referred to special education, social services, mental retardation, or developmental disabilities agencies, or bad if convicted of a crime. The classifier, of course, is good.

By Reason of Serendipity.   There is, moreover, no clear reason why a particular intervention prevails. So much depends on serendipity. Is the school's staff overloaded with disabled students? Is the state psychiatric hospital full? Are there enough beds in an MR center? What agency does the family of the person have the most contact with? Are private or third-party funds available to pay for services? Is the person an "interesting case" for the professional staff? How effectively does a lawyer represent the parties? Have political or social influences been brought to bear on the agencies or courts? Have community resources been tried unsuccessfully? These are some of the factors—all of them far removed from the allegedly precise scientific basis for classification that is supposed to be obtained in special education or mental health intervention, for example—that affect whether a person is classified and, if so, how, why, and with what effect.

Why We Classify

It may be impossible to avoid classification. We are, after all, discriminating, choosy, selective, and exclusive in almost every facet of our lives, whether the issue be so trivial as the choice of food at a carry-out restaurant or so momentous as the choice of a mate. In addition to our natural restrictions (age, gender, race, and ability), we restrict ourselves voluntarily,[48] such as by the jobs we choose. And in most cases the law recognizes our rights to be selective in the important matters of speech, religion, and personhood, as well as in less significant matters such as the types of clothes we wear ("symbolic speech").

Yet our natural instincts and legal rights to be selective, to classify ourselves and others, are not unbridled. Our rights of free speech do not extend to some aspects of pornography. Some consensual conduct is regulated and, of course, so is nonconsensual conduct (crimes against persons or property).

One reason for regulation is that the effects of absolute liberty for anyone are unacceptable to someone. Thus, the possession of pornography may be protected but its sale or distribution are not. Another reason is that the reasons for governmental classification must be examined; the due process and equal protection clauses of the federal Constitution forbid invidious, irrational, indefensible classifications (such as those made on the basis of race or, in some instances, disability, as discussed in chapter 3). It is legally relevant, therefore, to inquire into why people classify others as disabled.

Altruism. Sometimes classification is done for the most altruistic of purposes. When someone is classified as disabled, it enables him or her to be the recipient of services that the classifier (schools), and sometimes the classified, thinks will be helpful (special education). Classification also may prevent the person from being subject to disadvantaging conditions; segregation of students by disability has been thought by some to protect them from nondisabled students and the ordinary conditions of regular schools.

There are, however, negative results of classification that is motivated by social beneficience. Lionel Trilling[49] has made the point that people who are the objects of our pity become the objects of our coercion, and Kai Erickson[50] has highlighted the paradox that deviance—differentness on account of disability—is nourished by the agencies that were designed to inhibit it, in proportion to society's ability to control it. Thus, the conditions of education, including special education, have been disadvantageous to children in some instances. Sarason and Doris[51] have cast doubt on the motives and efficacy of special education systems. Blatt[52] documented the horrible conditions to which disabled people have been subjected in institutions originally predicated on a medical model. And Gleidman and Roth[53] have produced strong evidence of the shortcomings of the medical model in a host of "helping" professions.

Negative Reactions. We also classify for reasons having to do with our instinctive negative reaction to disabilities. After all, the grossly macrocephalic child may not be easily or immediately lovable. Fecal smearers can be unpleasant to live or work with. Some severely emotionally disturbed children are aggressive, and some profoundly disabled people are slow to show affection. Many aspects of disabilities, such as severe self-injurious behavior, are not only especially intractable, but deeply disturbing to families and caretakers alike. Thus, when the decision is made to place a child in special education, to institutionalize a child or, more seriously, to withhold medical treatment of a "defective" newborn, it seems inevitable that our instincts for being with pleasant, attractive, able, and promising people are at work.

By the same token, our ability to "succeed" with a disabled person—if we are a physician, to "cure," or an educator, to "teach"—is threatened by some handicapped people. Surely the emotional reactions of parents are not the only ones operating in a classification decision. Physicians report on the terribly difficult task of telling parents that their child is mentally retarded.[54] To place a child in an institution—to put him or her out of sight and sometimes out of mind—is partly a human condition. And the human condition is an imperfect one.

Riddance Motive. We also classify because we sometimes actively and admittedly wish to rid ourselves of the disabled person. The decision to abort a "defective" fetus, while constitutionally protected, may reflect the mother's wish to avoid life with a handicapped child. Decisions to withhold life-sustaining medical treatment or to institutionalize a child may reflect similar reactions of parents to not be handicapped by reason of having a disabled child.

Parents are not alone in their reaction to disabilities. Educators who refer a child to a special education program, community agency social workers who counsel for institutionalization, and institutional psychologists who recommend deinstitutionalization all may be motivated by a desire to rid themselves of a "problem" person.[55]

Agency Self-Interest.   Another motive that explains classification is more related to agency interests than to personal interests. Educators and others test and thereby engage in classification decisions to absolve themselves of moral responsibility for decisions about what happens to disabled people, taking refuge in science. By resorting to science, they also gain credibility with parents.

Finally, agencies serve school interests in categorization and program efficiency. A well organized school system has to have categories of children so that programs can be planned, financed, operated, and perpetuated.[56] By the same token, social services, health, and mental health agencies sometimes classify a person as disabled or as having a certain degree of disability (mild to profound) for self-serving purposes. They may want to include or exclude a person from a service category because it will increase their head count (number of people served) and thereby their budget or constituency base, or decrease it and thereby enable them to serve someone else. Resource allocation is a powerful motive.

Dual Diagnosis.   One familiar but subtle issue in classification is that of double diagnosis. Some mentally retarded people display symptoms of emotional disturbance. And some mentally ill people (or people whose behavior can be characterized as a mental illness) may be mentally retarded. How should the person be classified—as mentally retarded or as mentally ill? Or can a person be classified as both mentally retarded and mentally ill? The same choice of classification applies to mental retardation and learning disabilities or to learning disabilities and emotional disturbance.

The choice of diagnosis is important. It may determine whether the person receives a label as MR or ED, whether he or she receives one type of special education service or another, whether confinement in a mental retardation center or a psychiatric hospital could occur, whether the person will be placed in one type of community-based residential or service system or another, and so on.

Many times, service agencies are required by their regulations or operating procedures to classify a person as having a single disability. As a result, they report a single diagnosis even though a double diagnosis would be professionally feasible. The regulations or agency procedures may be valid in the sense that they seek to channel into the agency's service streams only those who can benefit by the services provided or who can be served effectively by agency personnel. But they also may have untoward consequences. They may prevent a person from obtaining services for a coexisting disability and, in the long run, make intervention less than maximally useful.

Agency regulations or procedures also may have the consequence of locking a person into the primary system and preventing him or her from transferring out of it and into another (or into none) when the system has outlived its usefulness or has become dysfunctional and harmful to the person.

The choice of diagnosis, therefore, is a critical one when there may be a choice to make a dual diagnosis. Special attention to the motivation of the classifier and to the effect of classification is warranted in these difficult cases. Since professionals cannot help but take into account parental or family wishes (e.g., the learning disabilities classification seems to be far less stigmatizing to families and client than the mental retardation classification), the motives of parents and family also are of concern.

Desire to Dominate.   Finally, classification occurs because the classifier seeks to subject the person to a position of powerlessness. An intelligence test given in English to a Spanish-speaking student may, but is not likely to, test accurately the student's potential to be successful in school or in his or her inherent or acquired skills. Persuasive arguments have been made that classification, especially by public schools, is a means for subjecting ethnic or racial minorities to a second-class status, thereby perpetuating the political, economic, or social dominance of non-minority people.[57]

LEGAL RESPONSES TO CLASSIFICATION

How We Classify
Legal efforts to rescue disabled citizens from second-class citizenship through classification have addressed both the techniques for classification and action founded on the classification. They require both procedural safeguards and substantive protection.

Fair, Individualized Assessment.   As an illustration of the techniques (procedures), the EHA requires a multidisciplinary, multifaceted, nonbiased evaluation of a child before classification and before provision of special education. The evaluation prohibits sole reliance on "scientific" assessment measures, such as IQ tests, and provides instead that "soft" data, such as teacher observations, may be used to evaluate and then classify someone as disabled.

The requirement of a fair evaluation as a prerequisite to classification also is a requirement of individualization. Due process mandates nothing less.[58] If a person is not assessed individually when the result of that assessment could be a benefit (e.g., special education if needed) or a special burden (e.g., assignment to special education if the child is *not* handicapped), the child's constitutional rights to due process—enjoyment of life, liberty, and property—may be violated. In this regard, the law has erected substantive protection.

Thus, legal requirements for fair assessments reflect constitutional concerns and traditional combinations of procedural and substantive safeguards. They also evidence an attempt to prevent people from being relegated to second-class citizenship. In addition, they reflect sound professional practice, assuring that service providers will deal appropriately with people whom they are trained to serve. This result inures to the benefit of the person and the provider alike.

Major Legal Restraints on Consequences of Classification. It is not legally sufficient that the techniques of classification be regulated. The use that one makes of the techniques is an important concern as well. The techniques may be entirely acceptable, but invidious classification and treatment of people could still obtain unless their uses were scrutinized. For example, simply being disabled is not a reason for being placed in special education; the person must need special instruction because of the disability (not in spite of it). Thus, the law limits the scientific basis for classification by a rigorous insistence that the techniques and effects of classification be mutually compatible. This approach is reflected in the cases involving students with AIDS (see chapter 3).

Just as the law seeks to minimize the potential for bias or error in educational or other scientific classifications, so it seeks to eliminate the "whimsy" factors in other classifying actions. It does so by four principal techniques: (1) It insists on knowable and measurable standards; (2) it requires procedural safeguards; (3) it sometimes provides affected parties access to professionals' records; and (4) it enables affected persons or their representatives to participate in decisions ordinarily made by professionals.

Standards. For example, a person may not be classified as handicapped under the EHA unless the person has one or more of the disabilities listed in the definition (see chapter 2) and "by reason thereof require(s) special education and related services" [Sec. 1400]. Similarly, a handicapped child does not qualify for a related service unless it is "required to assist (the child) to benefit from special education" [Sec. 1400]. In both cases, classification (as handicapped or as qualifying for related services) has a "but-for" element; the causal relationship between the service and the classification must exist.

Procedures. Procedural safeguards also tend to minimize the risk of error. Thus, under the EHA the disabled student's parents are entitled to notice of the action that the school proposes to take, a hearing before an impartial tryer of fact and law, an opportunity to present and rebut evidence, and the right to appeal from the initial decision (see chapter 7).

Access to Records. A third technique is to grant affected persons or their representatives access to the professional records concerning them or service systems that may be brought to bear on them. Thus, the EHA allows a student's parents to see the school records or records of school system special education programs. Some states also have enacted statutes that allow disabled people or their representatives access to social work, health, or mental health records.

Court and quasi-judicial proceedings or records (such as the impartial hearing guaranteed under the EHA) normally can be accessed by disabled people or their representatives. And some courts have taken the innovative step of requiring service professionals to divulge their records or make known certain information to the affected person or interested others.

Participatory Decision Making. Finally, the EHA and federal law governing vocational rehabilitation provide for the participation of disabled persons or their representatives with professionals in planning the goals and methods of professional services. Chapter 5 offers further discussion on this subject.

Why We Classify

As already noted, the law's response to the reasons we classify a person as disabled or as having a certain degree of disability is to insist on knowable and precise standards (e.g., for mental retardation, sub-average intelligence, and inability in adaptive behavior), procedural safeguards (notice, hearing, counsel, and appeal), access to records, and student-parent participation in decision making.

Eligibility. More than that, the law has created eligibility standards (e.g., if a person is disabled, he or she becomes entitled to special education) and accompanying funding streams (federal special education funds may be spent only on handicapped students or for administrative costs associated with their education). Sometimes the law selects certain kinds of disabled people for special benefits (and thereby denies others of those same benefits). For example, funds of the EHA are earmarked for the more disabled person, not the mildly handicapped person. This type of "bottom up" legislation—attacking the problems of disability at their more severe level and working upward to the least disabled person—contrasts with the "creaming" legislation or executive-administrative action that furnishes services to the mildly disabled person in preference over the severely disabled one (e.g., deinstitutionalization by transfer to group home affects mildly mentally retarded people more often than severely mentally retarded ones).

Prohibiting Discrimination. Another legal response is to prohibit governmental agencies or recipients of governmental aid from discriminating against otherwise qualified people solely because of their handicaps (Section 504). For example, it is a violation of federal law for a school system to exclude handicapped children solely because they are handicapped (see chapter 3).

Effect and Motive. The law entitles an advocate to inquire into both the effects of classification and the intent of the classifier (see chapter 3). If a discriminatory (invidious) effect can be found (e.g., the child may not attend school because he or she is handicapped and disruptive), the classifier's intent may be irrelevant. But if the classifier also has an invidious intent and seeks to discriminate against the person solely because he or she is mentally retarded, the law will provide a remedy. Fear alone—fear of a person with a disability—does not justify segregation. That rule of law is well settled by the United States Supreme Court in *O'Connor v. Donaldson, City of Cleburne v. Cleburne Living Center,* and *Board v. Arline.*

Advocacy.   To challenge the discriminatory effect or intent of classification, a disabled person must have an advocate. For example, the EHA requires state education agencies to appoint *surrogate parents* for disabled children who have no parents or are wards of the state. Recent federal law (the Developmental Disabilities Act of 1975) also has established a "protection and advocacy" system to enable disabled people to challenge unwarranted classification. Under this law, states that receive federal funds for use in serving disabled people must create a system to advocate for them against state and local governmental agencies. Federally financed P & A offices have been extensively involved in special education lawsuits involving retarded children's classification and education. Another federal effort to provide advocates for disabled people has been by way of funding the Legal Services Corporation, which in turn allocates its money for local legal services for handicapped and other disadvantaged citizens.

Personal Liability.   A similar legal response has been the court's use of a provision of the Civil Rights Act of 1971 that holds a state or local official liable for depriving someone of his or her rights under the federal Constitution or federal statutes. If, for example, a public school agency expels all handicapped children from school without cause, thereby violating the children's right to equal protection, a court may require the official to pay damages to the children (see chapters 9 and 10).

Least Restrictive Alternative.   In its many responses to classification, the law recently has taken the posture that the government itself is the victimizer and the disabled person is the victim. The issue is how to govern the government, recognizing that government becomes involved in classification because it offers services (education) and responds in a variety of ways (by excluding an otherwise qualified person from services, by subjecting a person to improper or unconstitutional treatment in a service system, or by treating a nondisabled person as disabled) to a complex set of explanations for classification.

A major principle of constitutional law—the doctrine of the least restrictive (least drastic) alternative—has become a useful device for curbing governments that harm citizens (see chapter 6). The doctrine forbids a government from acting in a way that restricts a person's liberty any more than necessary to accomplish its legitimate purposes. If a government has a defensible reason for restricting someone and may accomplish that restriction in either of two ways—one that infringes individual liberty to a greater extent and another to a lesser extent—it must choose the lesser of the two ways.

For example, sometimes it is legitimate to place people in institutions against their will because they are dangerous to themselves or others. But the nature of confinement may not be excessive. Thus, under the doctrine of least restriction, courts have reformed the conditions in institutions by requiring programs of education and training for children in institutions and by preventing institutional placement when community-based education would be as effective to serve the state's purposes. (Chapter 6 discusses the doctrine of least restrictive environment in detail.)

Substitute Consent.   Courts have even been able to address one of the most debilitating aspects of classification as mentally disabled—the loss of legal capacity to act for one's self. As a general rule of law, a person may not legally consent or withhold consent to educational, health, or mental health services if he or she is not mentally competent; mental capacity is an indispensible element of consent.[59] Moreover, children generally are presumed to be incompetent to act for themselves, especially in regard to special education services. And some handicapped children have no parents alive or available and are wards of the state.

Thus, it has been necessary for legislatures and courts to provide for the appointment of a legal guardian for incompetent children and to authorize the guardian to consent to services on their behalf. In addition, the EHA requires states to appoint surrogate parents for parentless children (see chapter 7).

Who Should Make Policy?   As chapters 5 and 6 indicate, Congress (in the EHA) and the courts (in appropriate education and least restrictive cases) rely heavily on professionals to say who is handicapped and needs special education. Certainly the court in *PASE v. Hannon* indicated that professional judgment—in establishing, administering, and interpreting intelligence tests and other measures of "handicapped"—plays a powerful role in resolving important legal issues (e.g., about special education and racial segregation).

By contrast, the court in *Larry P. v. Riles* did not give much weight to the professionals' views concerning intelligence testing and classification. But *Larry P.* was an exception to the normal judicial response to disability-classification issues—which has been to defer to professional judgment. The courts usually rely mightily on the perceived expertise of professionals, although professionals' expertise is certainly unexceptional in informing anyone what to do about social policy and "different" people.

By turning to the professionals to help determine who is disabled enough to be treated differently, Congress and courts can avoid coming to grips directly with the social, political, and moral dilemmas posed by disability. Thus, decisions about institutionalization are characterized as "medical" just as other types of decisions are called "educational" or otherwise dignified by being seen as "professional." The consequence is that the true nature of the decisions—what shall be done about disabilities, disabled people, and schools—is answered by letting professionals decide.

Classification, Professionals, and Policy.   By the fiction that disabled people really are different and should be treated differently, largely by "professionals," the "law" has avoided the ultimate questions: Who should decide who should care for disabled people, where, how, at whose expense, and why? Even more fundamentally, who is different enough to be treated differently? And who has the sagacity to tell us the answer? These are the issues of classification.

The answer to the first and last questions has been: the professionals. Once policy makers know that professionals can give the answers, they tend to seek answers to other questions from them. (Is this psychological examination valid for the purpose it is used? Is the student's program appropriate?) Thus it is that our responsibility (or lack of it) for "other" people, for disabled people, is made manifest to us: Do as the professionals say.

Dual Systems.   By avoiding some of the hard policy questions and by allowing disabled people to be devalued, the law can do an injustice not only to them but to itself. It condones a double standard, a dual system (see chapter 6). But when courts and legislatures insist on substantive and procedural changes in dealing with disabled people, the law not only reshapes itself but, it is hoped, our culture itself.

EFFECTS OF THE NONDISCRIMINATORY EVALUATION RULE

The requirements for nondiscriminatory evaluation have had multiple benefits and drawbacks. But they also have raised several important concerns.

Major Effects

Standard Intelligence Tests.   First, the requirements for nondiscriminatory evaluation, as interpreted by the courts, clearly have both outlawed and legitimized standard intelligence tests and their use in classifying students. The *Larry P.* and *PASE* cases cannot be read consistently with each other insofar as intelligence tests are concerned. For more than a decade now, the California federal district court has taken an unchanging stand against the use of tests except under the most stringent conditions. On the other hand, the Illinois federal district court has found the tests to be culturally fair and has allowed their continued use, in conjunction with other measures for classifying students. One unanswered question, then, concerns the future use of such tests, under law.

Additional Measures for Classification.   The limitation that other measures for classification also must be used is an important one and reflects another significant contribution of the requirements for nondiscriminatory evaluation. The requirements for multifaceted and multidisciplinary evaluation have created more equitable and more elaborate procedures for classification. In a sense, they have recognized that intelligence testing has a hypnotic effect, and they have tried to mitigate that effect by requiring that other procedures be brought to bear in classification.

Investments in Time. Of course, in creating these more equitable and elaborate procedures, the requirements have caused educators and their colleagues to spend a great deal more time in evaluation and classification. The benefit of this new investment is a more thorough, comprehensive picture of the student and, as a consequence, a greater ability to identify a student's strengths and build on them and a greater ability to identify a student's weaknesses and remediate them. The drawback of this new investment is that some school districts have long waiting lists of students to be evaluated and, some would say, increased frustration among educators, their colleagues, and parents concerning the delay between referral, evaluation, and service.

Careful Documentation. A fourth effect of the nondiscriminatory evaluation requirements is that educators, their colleagues, and parents have more carefully documented the child's abilities and disabilities and relevant educational decisions. The benefits of careful documentation are to establish more data-based and objective foundations, created by all affected persons, for educational decisions. Although subjective evaluation is still valid because the law recognizes the usefulness of teacher observation and professionals still recognize the legitimate role of clinical experience, this type of evaluation is less likely to prevail, especially as it is made by a single person.

The drawback of the new requirements is the increased emphasis on paper compliance—on meeting the letter of the law. It may be that in their quest to comply precisely with the procedures, educators, their colleagues, and parents have recorded the "trees" (the disparate parts of the child) but not the "forest." They may have failed to take a holistic view of the child, seeing only parts, particularly those that are problematic or pathological.

Who Is Disabled and the Distribution of Disabilities. Fifth, and finally, the new requirements clearly have impacted policy makers' concerns about who is disabled and about their distribution of disabilities.

Behaviorally Disordered/Emotionally Disturbed. For example, Congress in 1984 required the Secretary of Education to review and evaluate the term *behaviorally disordered* and to submit a report of that review and evaluation within 6 months after the effective date of the amendment (P.L. 98-199). The report recommended against any change. There are several reasons for the result:

1. A change in definition or terminology probably would cause an increase in the number of students eligible for services. For example, the change in definition might include students who are "socially maladjusted."
2. A change would increase the number of students referred for evaluation. This is so because the change would decrease the stigma, thus reducing a barrier to referral.

3. A change would not affect the settings in which students are educated. Absent an effect on settings, there is no substantial benefit to students.
4. Although the stigma perceived by parents and teachers may be reduced if the special education label is abandoned, there would be no change among nondisabled students' attitudes, because they judge their disabled peers by behavior, not labels.
5. A change would not affect professional training, and thus not produce any benefit there.

Learning Disabled.   Another example of policy makers' and educators' concerns about who is handicapped and the distribution of disabilities involves the classification of students as learning disabled. On the one hand, the category has been extraordinarily useful and popular. It is a way to classify a child who has problems with academics but is not mentally retarded or seriously emotionally disturbed. In addition, it is a relatively stigma-free classification. It certainly does not carry as much opprobrium and devaluation from the norm as mental retardation or serious emotional disturbance. Therefore, it has been acceptable to middle-class educators and parents.

But the rapid and large growth of the category (between 1976-1977 and 1985-1986 the LD population increased by 119%) has posed some problems.[60] Educators and policy makers are concerned about the definition of *learning disability.* They are worried about over-classification—placing too many children into the LD category because of its relatively low stigma and relatively high acceptability. They also are concerned because of the alleged lack of truly reliable conceptualizations of the term and the absence of highly dependable systems for classifying and educating students as learning disabled. And they are concerned about the increased cost of educating so many children who may not be truly disabled or are marginally handicapped.

Mildly Mentally Retarded.   In addition, the variable definition of *mild mental retardation* has posed similar problems. In 1973, the American Association on Mental Retardation, the nation's oldest and largest professional organization concerned exclusively with mental retardation, reduced the IQ cut-off for classification as mentally retarded from 85 to 70. In 1979, the Council for Exceptional Children began to press for a modification of the cut-off at 70. And in 1983, the AAMR, on its own, defined "mild" mental retardation as having a cut-off at 70 but being particularly subject to clinical judgment and experience of the evaluators. Indeed, the AAMR recognizes a "zone of uncertainty" of between 62 and 78 IQ.[61]

New Concerns

Clinical Judgments.   There is reason to believe that clinical judgments are not the only or even the major bases for classification of some minority children into special education. A study commissioned in 1979 by the Office of Special Education, U.S. Department of Education,[62] examined school practices for referring, assessing, and placing children in special education. The study attempted to determine whether those procedures were resulting in the erroneous classification of children.

Several findings are notable. One is that elementary-aged minority children were referred for special assistance (of any kind) at a rate proportionate to their incidence in the school-aged population. But secondary-aged minority students were referred at a higher rate than their incidence in the school-aged population. This result suggests that age is a critical variable.

A second finding is that school diagnosticians and teachers rated academic functioning to be the most important factor in determining disability classification and placement for both minority and non-minority students. They rated nonacademic factors as less important for both minority and non-minority children, but as somewhat more important for minority children. This finding suggests that adaptive behavior, aggression, or hallmarks of minority culture were at play in assessment.

A third finding was that approximately twice as many minority students as non-minority students were designated as "probably mentally retarded." But those students were not subsequently placed in special education programs in these larger percentages. Indeed, the greatest percentage (24%) of minority students was placed in educational programs for learning disabled. By comparison, only 21% of non-minority children was so classified. In addition, only about 4% of minority children was placed in programs for mentally retarded children; a similar percentage was placed in programs for seriously emotionally disturbed children. Thus, assessment and placement do not match perfectly.

Stigma.   Several other conclusions are fairly inferrable from known effects of the nondiscriminatory evaluation requirements. First, the stigma of mental retardation or serious emotional disturbance is powerful, and it acts to prevent classification in those categories. Second, clinical judgments are subverted by other judgments about how minority children should be classified and educated. Third, there are countervailing concerns about special education as a "dumping ground" for minority children. These concerns address the potential for using special education classification and placement as a disguise for resegregating the nation's schools by race. Finally, there is reason to believe that the science of classification is not precise, at least not at the edges between nondisabled and disabled. This inference is supported by the various redefinitions or attempts to redefine certain types of disabilities, particularly mild mental retardation, learning disabilities, and serious emotional disturbance.

Research and Practice.   The fuzziness concerning who is disabled and the nature of the disabilities may reflect poorly on past special education practices, which have been predicated on the purported ability to measure and classify with precision. Moreover, the fuzziness justifies new questions about the validity of prior special education research (and practices based on it), which was conducted on ostensibly "known" disabled children—those whose classification was thought to be reliable and undoubted.

Other Influences.   In addition, the ambiguity about classification and the reports concerning classification practices suggest that a student's age, race, socioeconomic status, or gender may influence classification practices as much as any test results. Further, the preferences of educators and parents, as well as their educational philosophies and objectives, may be influential.

Slow Learners/Under-Achievers.   Finally, classification procedures and practices raise fundamental questions concerning the education of slow learners. On the one hand, children who are under-achievers may be disabled. On the other hand, they may not—they may just be below "average" but still not classifiable as disabled. If they are disabled, they arguably have the right to be classified as such and given the benefits of special education. On the other hand, if a child is not disabled and in no way can be classified into special education but is still an under-achiever or slow learner, there is an obvious need to provide the child with an appropriate education. Should that help come from special education?

Sharing Techniques and Resources.   It is important for special education to share its techniques with regular education. Individualization and the related-service provisions are powerful tools for helping a child. But sharing techniques is not the same as sharing funds, personnel, and other resources. If the definition of handicapped is expanded to include under-achievers and slow learners, there will be new claims on federal, state, and local resources, particularly on funds and personnel.

With every new claim, there will be at least two responses. First, the special education profession and the parents of disabled children will seek to increase appropriations for special education. This will be problematic given the success, or lack thereof, of any education program in commanding new resources, and the current fiscal conditions of federal, state, and local governments. If the claims are successful, it is fair to assume that there will be an augmentation of resources sufficient to accommodate the new class of disabled children. If they are not successful, there will be a second response: to restructure the resources presently available to the traditional disabled children so as to provide some resources both to children whose classification and claim to special education is and always has been certain, and to children in the new class. That result is patently unacceptable to both slow learners and disabled children.

In sum, results of the nondiscriminatory evaluation rule have been generally positive. With respect to some school issues, however, it is still troubling and still unresolved.

NOTES

1. Brown v. Bd. of Ed.
2. Larry P. v. Riles.
3. *Id.*

4. Larry P. v. Riles; Mattie T. v. Holladay; and Hobson v. Hansen.

5. Guadalupe Org., Inc. v. Tempe Elem. School Dist.; Diana v. State Bd. of Ed.; and Hernandez v. Porter.

6. LeBanks v. Spears; Larry P. v. Riles.

7. Larry P. v. Riles; Hobson v. Hansen.

8. Hernandez v. Porter; Diana v. State Bd. of Ed.; and Guadalupe Org. v. Tempe.

9. Larry P. v. Riles.

10. LeBanks v. Spears.

11. Carrington v. Rash.

12. Stell v. Savannah-Chatham County Bd. of Ed.; Miller v. School Dist. No. 2, Clarendon County.

13. Hobson v. Hansen.

14. Larry P. v. Riles; Diana v. State Bd. of Ed.; and Mattie T. v. Holladay.

15. Larry P. v. Riles; Diana v. State Bd. of Ed.

16. *Id.*

17. Diana v. State Bd. of Ed.; Guadalupe Org. v. Tempe; and Lau v. Nichols.

18. Larry P. v. Riles.

19. LeBanks v. Spears.

20. Larry P. v. Riles; *cf.* Carmichael v. Craven, on use of intelligence tests to screen jurors.

21. Larry P. v. Riles.

22. LeBanks v. Spears; Mills v. D.C. Bd. of Ed.; and Hernandez v. Porter.

23. Hobbs (Ed.), *Issues in the Classification of Children* (2 vols.) (San Francisco: Jossey-Bass, 1975, p. 100).

24. *Ibid.,* at p. 101.

25. *Id.*

26. U.S. Senate, Report No. 94-168, *Education for All Handicapped Children Act,* June 2, 1975, pp. 26-29.

27. Bonadonna v. Cooperman.

28. Sarason and Doris, *Educational Handicap, Public Policy, and Social History: A Broadened Perspective on Mental Retardation* (New York: Free Press, 1979).

29. *Ibid.*

30. Gleidman and Roth, *The Unexpected Minority: Handicapped Children in America* (New York: Harcourt Brace Jovanovich, 1980).

31. *Id.*

32. Turnbull and Turnbull, *Parents Speak Out: Then and Now* (Columbus, Oh.: Charles E. Merrill, 1985).

33. Sarason and Doris, *supra* n. 28.

34. Gleidman and Roth, *supra* n. 30; Sarason and Doris, *supra* n. 28.

35. Morse, "Crazy Behavior," 51 *Southern California Law Review* 528 (1978).

36. Gleidman and Roth, *supra* n. 30.

37. Sorgen, "The Classification Process and Its Consequences," in *The Mentally Retarded Citizen and the Law,* edited by Kindred et al. (New York: Free Press, 1976).

38. *Id.*

39. Sorgen, *supra* n. 37; Gleidman and Roth, *supra* n. 30.

40. Kirp, "Schools as Sorters," 121 *Pennsylvania Law Review* 705 (1973); and Kirp, Buss, and Kuriloff, "Legal Reform of Special Education: Empirical Studies and Procedural Proposals," 62 *California Law Review* 40 (1974).

41. Hobbs (Ed.), *The Futures of Children* (San Francisco: Jossey-Bass, 1975).

42. Gleidman and Roth, *supra* n. 30; and Sarason and Doris, *supra* n. 28.

43. Gleidman and Roth, *supra* n. 30; Sarason and Doris, *supra* n. 28; Blatt and Kaplan, *Christmas in Purgatory* (Boston: Allyn and Bacon, 1966); Blatt, *Souls in Extremis* (Boston: Allyn and Bacon, 1973); and Blatt, McNally, and Ozolins, *The Family Papers* (Boston: Longman Press, 1979).

44. Wald, "Basic Personal and Civil Rights," in *The Mentally Retarded Citizen and the Law*, edited by Kindred et al. (New York: Free Press, 1976).

45. *In re* Phillip B.

46. Office of Civil Rights, U.S. Department of Education, 1987; Kirp, *supra* n. 40; Mercer, *Labeling the Mentally Retarded* (Berkeley: University of California Press, 1973); Larry P. v. Riles; and Hobbs, *supra* n. 23.

47. Stone, *Mental Health and Law: A System in Transition* (Washington, D.C.: National Institute of Mental Health, 1976).

48. Turnbull (Ed.), *The Least Restrictive Alternative: Principles and Practice* (Washington, D.C.: American Association on Mental Deficiency, 1981).

49. Trilling, quoted in Rothman, "Convenience and Conscience," *The Asylum and Its Alternatives in Progressive America* (Boston: Little, Brown, 1980).

50. Erickson, *Wayward Puritans: A Study in the Sociology of Deviance* (New York: John Wiley and Sons, 1966).

51. Sarason and Doris, *supra* n. 28.

52. Blatt, *supra* n. 43.

53. Gleidman and Roth, *supra* n. 30

54. Sarason and Doris, *supra* n. 28.

55. Hobbs, *supra* n. 41.

56. Sorgen, *supra* n. 37; Kirp, *supra* n. 40.

57. Hobbs, *supra* n. 41; Mercer, *supra* n. 46; and Larry P. v. Riles.

58. Turnbull et al. (Eds.), *The Consent Handbook* (Washington, D.C.: American Association on Mental Deficiency, 1978).

59. Turnbull, *supra* n. 48.

60. U.S. Dep't. of Education, *Sixth Annual Report to Congress* (Washington, D.C.: Government Printing Office, 1984).

61. Grossman, *Classification in Mental Retardation* (Washington, D.C.: American Association on Mental Deficiency, 1983).

62. U.S. Dep't. of Education, *supra* n. 60.

5
Individualized and Appropriate Education

CONSTITUTIONAL FOUNDATIONS

In its findings of facts in the EHA, Congress zeroed in on individualized education, characterizing it in terms of "appropriate" education and stating in Sec. 1400(b) (2) and (3) that:

—the special educational needs of handicapped children are not being fully met; and
—more than half of the handicapped children in the United States do not receive appropriate educational services and are thus denied full equality of opportunity.

These claims are well grounded on the constitutional principles of substantive due process under the Fifth and Fourteenth Amendments and on equal protection under the Fourteenth. The common element of substantive due process and equal protection, in the context of individualized or appropriate education, is *exclusion*. Total exclusion from any type of educational opportunity arguably violates both constitutional principles (see chapter 3 on zero reject). Functional exclusion from a meaningful educational opportunity likewise arguably violates both principles, since education that lacks meaning or significance for the pupil is tantamount to no education at all.

Pre-EHA Case Law
The courts early on realized the importance of *substantive due process* for opportunity. *Maryland Association for Retarded Children (MARC) v. Maryland,* for example, took the position that if all handicapped children are to be furnished an education, the purpose of that education must be redefined, since many of them are inherently unable to master even a modified regular academic program. The goal of their education must be to develop their capabilities to the highest possible level of achievement for each child. *Mills* required

a handicapped child's education to be "suited to [his or her] needs," and *PARC* ordered that it be "appropriate to [his or her] learning capacities." *MARC, Mills,* and *PARC* addressed the substantive due process aspects of appropriate education (a meaningful education in order to prevent functional exclusion). *Lau v. Nichols* skirted the issue but arguably gave comfort to it (see chapter 3).

Equal protection is the other constitutional foundation for claims to an appropriate education for handicapped children. A federal district court thus ruled that learning disabled children make a viable claim under the equal protection principles that they are victims of unconstitutional discrimination when they are not given instruction specially suited to their needs although nonhandicapped and mentally retarded children are being provided an *appropriate* free public education. The discrimination exists in learning disabled children being treated different from nonhandicapped or mentally retarded children.[1] Another federal court denied a state's motion to dismiss a case alleging that multiply handicapped persons were denied equal protection because the nature of the educational programs offered to the plaintiffs was such that no chance existed that the programs would be of benefit to them.[2] Both cases relied on equal protection concepts to argue discrimination in the provision of meaningful (i.e., appropriate or suitable) education.

Pre-EHA Court Remedies

None of the courts in the early cases defined "appropriate" or "suitable." At the most, they discussed the special educational opportunities that should be made available. *Mills* and *LeBanks* required compensatory or adult education to overcome the effects of prior exclusion. Although early intervention (preschool training) for handicapped children has not been ordered by the courts, legislatures often find, as a matter of state policy, that early education is desirable.[3] Congress made similar determinations in the EHA.

Zero reject policy did not mean that all children must be placed in regular classrooms within the public school system. "Suitable education" included homebound instruction for physically handicapped children who were unable to attend school. In some instances, however, homebound or in-hospital instruction was held permissible only if the pupil was physically unable to attend school.[4] A child who could not benefit from a program of instruction within the public school system could be assigned to the state department that oversaw state institutions, but he or she was nevertheless entitled to an appropriate program of education and training.[5] *Mills, PARC,* and *MARC* all ordered that tuition grants be made available if suitable education must be obtained from a private school or institution. These cases also noted, however, that a state has not discharged its duty to provide education if it refers a child to a private facility where he or she is only placed on a waiting list. (See chapter 3 for a fuller discussion of the tuition cases.)

Clearly, alternatives to regular classroom education were recognized as sometimes being the most appropriate form of education for a child. Some courts, however, stated that regular classroom instruction (with auxiliary services if necessary) is preferable to separate special classes, which in turn are preferable to homebound instruction.[6] This preference for mainstream placement is based on the belief that children with special problems benefit from contact with nonhandicapped children and suffer less from the stigma of difference attached to children who are separated from the regular program.

FEDERAL LEGISLATION

Individualized Education

In the cases, the requirement that a handicapped child's education be appropriate or suitable to his or her needs is simply a requirement that it be individually appropriate or suitable. In the language of the EHA, the requirement of an appropriate education boils down to a requirement that the education be individualized to redress problems found by the Congress [Sec. 1400(b)(2) and (3)].

The IEP

The policy of providing an appropriate education [Sec. 1400(c)] is achieved principally by the device of the individualized education program (IEP) [Sec. 1401(19)]:

> The term "individualized education program" means a written statement for each handicapped child developed in any meeting by a representative of the local education agency or an intermediate educational unit who shall be qualified to provide, or supervise the provision of, specially designed instruction to meet the unique needs of handicapped children, the teacher, the parents or guardian of such child, and whenever appropriate, such child, which statement shall include (A) a statement of the present levels of education performance of such child, (B) a statement of annual goals, including short-term instructional objectives, (C) a statement of the specific educational services to be provided to such child, and the extent to which such child will be able to participate in regular educational programs, (D) the projected date for initiation and anticipated duration of such services, and (E) appropriate objective criteria and evaluation procedures and schedules for determining, on at least an annual basis, whether instructional objectives are being achieved.

The SEA and the public agency must assume responsibility for implementing a child's IEP in a private or parochial school. This responsibility includes initiating a meeting to develop an IEP before the child is placed in the private or parochial school and ensuring that a representative of the school attends the meeting or that other methods, such as individual or conference telephone calls, are used to ensure participation.

Meetings must be held to review or revise the IEP after a child is placed in a private or parochial program. A representative of the public agency must be involved in any decisions made at these meetings and must agree to proposed IEP changes. The public agency also is responsible for ensuring that an IEP is developed and reviewed for each child placed in a private or parochial school by the agency [Sec. 300.341, .347, and .348].

Each LEA must establish, or revise, if appropriate, an IEP for each handicapped child at the beginning of each school year. The provisions must be reviewed and, if appropriate, revised at regular intervals, but not less than annually [Sec. 1414(a)(5) and Sec. 300.343]. Similarly, each SEA is required to assure the U.S. Department of Education, Office of Special Education and Rehabilitative Services, through its Special Education Program unit, that each LEA will maintain records of the IEP for each handicapped child and that the program will be established, reviewed, and revised as required in Section 1414 (a)(5) [Sec. 1412(4)].

The state plan must contain procedures for the SEA to evaluate—at least annually—the effectiveness of LEA programs in meeting the educational needs of handicapped children. The evaluation is to include an evaluation of IEPs [Sec. 1413(a)(11)]. If a child is placed in a private program by the SEA or an LEA, he or she is still entitled to an IEP in the private school [Sec. 1413(a)(4)(B)(i) and (ii) and Secs. 300.341(b), .347, and .348].

Sec. 300.346 requires the IEP to include the following elements:

(a) A statement of the child's present levels of educational performance;

(b) A statement of annual goals, including short term instructional objectives;

(c) A statement of the specific special education and related services to be provided to the child, and the extent to which the child will be able to participate in regular educational programs;

(d) The projected dates for initiation of services and the anticipated duration of the services; and

(e) Appropriate objective criteria and evaluation procedures and schedules for determining, on at least an annual basis, whether the short term instructional objectives are being achieved.

The regulations make it clear that the IEP is not a legally binding contract and that no agency, teacher, or other person may be held accountable if the child does not achieve the projected progress based on the annual goals and objectives [Sec. 300.349]. This section does not prevent parents from using due process procedures for problems related to the IEP, the agencies, or the teachers.

Developing an IEP.   The following people must be involved in developing the IEP: a representative of the public agency (other than the child's teacher) who is qualified to provide or supervise the child's special education, the teacher, one or both of the child's parents, the student, when appropriate, and other individuals at the discretion of the parents or agency. When a child is first evaluated, an IEP committee member must be a member of the team that evaluates him or her, or the public agency representative, the teacher, or some other person attending the IEP meeting who is knowledgeable about the evaluation procedures used and is able to interpret the results. Either the agency representative or the teacher should be "qualified" in the area of the child's suspected disability [Sec. 300.344].

Since parent participation in the child's education, and particularly in planning the IEP, is a high priority under the EHA, public agencies are to take specified steps to ensure that one, or both, of the child's parents has a chance to attend the IEP conference. These steps include advance notice of the meeting, mutually convenient scheduling of the meeting, and arranging for interpreters for deaf or non-English speaking parents. If the parent(s) cannot attend the meeting, they may still participate through individual or conference telephone calls. The agency may have an IEP meeting without parent participation only when it can document that it unsuccessfully attempted to have the parents participate. The documentation should include detailed records of telephone calls, copies of letters to and from the parents, and the results of visits to the parents' homes or places of work. The agency must give the parents a copy of the IEP if they ask for it [Sec. 300.345].

Timing of the IEP. An IEP for each child must be established, or revised if appropriate, by the beginning of each school year. Exactly when must the conference be held? The regulations specify that the planning conferences for a handicapped child who is already receiving special education and related services must be conducted early enough to ensure that the child's IEP is developed (or revised) by the beginning of the next school year. To meet this provision, a local education agency may conduct the meeting at the end of the school year or during the summer [Sec. 300.343]. If a handicapped child is not receiving special education, an IEP committee meeting must be held within 30 days of the determination that the child needs special education and related services [Sec. 300.343(c)].

Rationale for the IEP. The IEP is justified on many grounds:

1. The IEP is, of course, a method for assessing the child and, based on the nondiscriminatory evaluation, for prescribing an appropriate program, with related services, and an appropriate placement in the least restrictive environment (thereby overcoming objections based on substantive due process or equal protection—claims of functional exclusion or discrimination).
2. The IEP enables the teacher and other educators to better help the child develop his or her potential (not *maximum* potential). It is one of the most important elements of the child's success in school.
3. It enables the school and the parents to monitor the child's progress in school, measure development, identify areas of weakness, and concentrate on remediating those weaknesses.
4. It recognizes that each child is unique and should be treated in light of his or her own needs.
5. It is a safeguard not only for the child but also for the parents, inasmuch as they are legitimately concerned about misclassification, inappropriate placements, and inadequate programs.
6. The requirement of parental involvement not only recognizes parents' legitimate concerns to have their child protected against potential wrongs, but also strengthens the child's educational program by linking the parents' views of his or her needs and their needs with the school's and parents' ability to train the child. Parents have a wealth of information about their child that can enhance the child's schoolroom training and be carried over into the child's family life if it is shared with school personnel and

incorporated in the IEP. The "6-hour handicapped child" (one who is seen as hand-icapped only when at school) is too familiar, but parental involvement in the IEP has the potential of relegating this child to history. Quite simply, what happens to the child in school is relevant to his or her home life, and vice versa.

7. The IEP is a technique for sharing decisions and decision-making powers among school personnel and parents. It is another step along the line toward achieving participatory democracy in public education.

8. It is also a powerful device for assuring accountability. It makes the schools accountable to the child for what they do, by requiring an assessment of achievement; a statement of goals, services, and timetables; and procedures and criteria for determining if the goals are being met. It makes schools accountable to the parent as a taxpayer and as a participant in developing the individualized program. Parent involvement in curriculum decisions also promotes accountability on the part of the parents. As an outgrowth of IEP development, parents may come to assume specific responsibility for teaching or reinforcing particular skills and concepts at home.

9. By securing parent participation, the IEP also helps forestall the possibility of a due process protest and hearing under Section 1415. It is not a device of cooption, although some may see it that way. Rather, it is a positive force that assures parent/school decision sharing, contributing to a collaborative relationship instead of an adversarial confrontation between parent and school personnel.

10. IEPs are, of course, necessary to accomplish the zero reject principles; they tend to assure that no handicapped child is overlooked once identified as handicapped. They enable school authorities to plan services for handicapped children and to provide those services. In addition, they furnish a basis for OSERS evaluation of school programs at the federal level. They are a way to focus the capacity of a school system on the child. Like procedural due process, the IEP is child-centered, not system-centered.

11. IEPs reflect the best current thinking of special educators.

12. Finally, the policy of the IEP—individualization—is reflected in the EHA and in other federal laws affecting handicapped students or adults: the Rehabilitation Act and the Developmental Disabilities Assistance and Bill of Rights Act. These require individualized programs for handicapped persons.

Other Statutory Provisions for Appropriate Education

Although the IEP is the principal means in the EHA for assuring an appropriate education, it is not the only one.

1. Procedures to assure nondiscriminatory testing serve as safeguards against inappropriate placement and resultant inappropriate education [Sec. 1412(1)].

2. The requirement of placement in the least restrictive appropriate program also protects against inappropriate placement and unsuitable programs [Sec. 1412(5)]. It advances the concept of appropriate education by ensuring appropriate placement.

3. The rights of parents to see and comment on LEA records enables them to hold the school accountable for providing an appropriate education [Sec. 1414(a)(4) and Sec. 1415(b)(1)(A)].
4. The due process hearing is yet another method for accountability and compliance with the requirements of appropriate education [Sec. 1415].
5. The infants-toddlers and the early childhood incentive grants are intended to make elementary education, especially in the least restrictive setting, appropriate for the child upon attaining elementary-school age.
6. The exclusion (not more than 12% of a state's children aged 5 through 17 may be counted as handicapped for the purpose of receiving federal funds under the Act) is also a device for appropriate education. It tends to prevent overcategorization and miscategorization of children as handicapped, thereby preventing inappropriate identification, evaluation, placement, and unsuitable programs [Sec. 1411].
7. State education agencies must develop and implement a "comprehensive system of personnel development"; a means for disseminating to school personnel "significant information derived from educational research, demonstration, and similar projects" [Sec. 1413]; and, where appropriate, "promising educational practices and materials development through such projects" [Sec. 1413]. These requirements are intended to improve the schools so that they can provide appropriate education to handicapped children. SEA evaluation, particularly for IEP compliance, also will help LEAs provide appropriate programs [Secs. 1418 and 1413].

Determining What is Appropriate

There are few statutory definitions of "appropriate education" in the EHA. One of them derives from an understanding of the EHA as a whole. That definition seeks to define appropriate education by a *process*. The definition of appropriate education looks first to the child and second to the means by which an appropriate education is to be provided. It is child-centered and process-oriented, not system-centered or result-oriented; it takes account of educational "inputs," not educational "outputs."

For example, assume a 9-year-old child is moderately mentally retarded and school personnel (and the parents) are concerned about what kind of education, what kind of placement, is appropriate. How do they answer this question? They do it by: (1) making a nondiscriminatory evaluation; (2) developing an individualized education program; (3) attempting to place the child in the least restrictive appropriate program; (4) throughout this process, seeing that the parents have access to the child's school records; and (5) if the parents wish to protest the placement or any other action related to the child's right to a free appropriate education, calling a due process hearing. The Act's technique for defining "appropriate," then, is to require that a *process* be followed, in the belief that a fair process will produce an acceptable result—an appropriate education.

The regulations also define free appropriate education for special education and related services in terms of standards and conformity with IEPs [Sec. 300.4]. Thus, there are two techniques for determining what is appropriate. Specifically, Section 300.4 of the regulations defines free appropriate public education as one that (1) is provided at public expense, under public direction and supervision, without charge; (2) meets the standards of the SEA; (3) includes preschool, elementary school, and secondary school education; and (4) is provided in conformity with IEP requirements of the EHA and its regulations.

Part H

Part H (infants and toddlers) requires a basically similar approach to individualization and appropriateness. We will describe the regulations in this chapter and discuss the major differences that affect professional practice in chapter 10. The major difference is that Part H requires an individualized family service plan (IFSP), not an IEP.

The regulations implementing Part H are very specific about the IFSP and, because they are so new, deserve extended discussion here. The IFSP must:

- be developed by the family and appropriate qualified providers of early intervention services;
- be based on the multidisciplinary evaluation and assessment of the child and the assessment of the family;
- include the services that are necessary to enhance the child's development and the family's capacity to meet the child's special needs.

In addition, specific content of the IFSP must include:

- a statement of the child's present levels of physical, cognitive, language-speech, psychosocial, and self-help development;
- professionally acceptable objective criteria as a basis;
- a statement of major outcomes for the child and family and the criteria, procedures, and timelines used to determine the degree of progress and whether modifications or revisions of outcomes or services are necessary;
- a statement of specific early intervention services necessary to meet the child's and family's unique needs, including
  - the frequency, intensity, location, and method of delivering services;
  - the payment arrangements, if any;
  - to the extent appropriate, a statement of medical and other services that the child needs but that are not required to be provided under Part H;
  - if necessary, a statement of the steps to be taken to secure those services through public or private resources;
- a statement of the projected dates for beginning the services and of how long the services will be provided;
- the name of the case manager assigned to the family;

- a statement of steps to be taken to support the child's transition from early intervention services to preschool or other services, including discussions with and training of the child's parents regarding future placements and other matters relating to the child's transition.

There is an important note added to the regulations on the IFSP. It reminds you that family members play a variety of roles in enhancing the child's development. It also says that it is important that the degree to which the family's needs are addressed in the IFSP should be determined collaboratively with the full agreement and participation of the child's parents.

The participants in the initial and each annual IFSP meeting must include:

- the child's parent or parents;
- other family members as requested by the parent(s), if it is feasible to include them;
- the case manager;
- a person(s) directly involved in conducting the child and family evaluations and assessments;
- as appropriate, persons who will provide services to the child or family.

If a required person is not available to attend the meeting, other means for participation must be used, such as telephone conference calls, attendance by a knowledgeable representative, or making pertinent records available at the meeting.

The initial meeting for developing the IFSP must be within 45 days after the child or family is referred to the state's lead agency. Thereafter, periodic review is available in two ways: (1) every 6 months, the IFSP must be reviewed for progress and appropriate revision, by a meeting or other means agreeable to the parties; and (2) annually, a meeting must be held to evaluate the IFSP and review it as appropriate.

The meetings must be at times and places convenient to the family. The family's native language or other mode of communication must be used. And the meetings must be scheduled so that the families have enough time to plan to attend.

There are special rules for providing services before the evaluation and assessment of the child and family are complete. Services may begin prior to evaluation and assessment if the parents agree; an interim IFSP is developed (naming the case manager and demonstrating that the services are needed immediately by the child and family); and the evaluation and assessment are in fact completed within the 45-day period.

Every agency or person having a direct role in providing early intervention services is responsible for making a good faith effort to assist each eligible child in achieving the IFSP outcomes. But no agency or person may be held accountable if the child does not achieve the growth projected by the IFSP.

There are two important differences between Part B (IEP) and Part H (IFSP) with respect to rights. First, Part H services must be those that are "necessary" to most of the child's and family's needs. This is different from Part B, which requires "appropriate" education (a higher standard than "necessary" services). Second, the requirements for case management and transition planning do not appear at all in Part B.

But it is clear that the IFSP and Part H generally have potential for strengthening families by helping them:

1. develop great expectations for their infant-toddler and themselves;
2. see the positive contributions that the infant-toddler can make to the family, its friends, and society;
3. make choices about how they want to be involved in their infant-toddler's life;
4. create relationships with professionals and with others who are not in the business of providing disability services;
5. learn what their strengths and needs are;
6. learn what new strengths can be developed;
7. determine how they cope with difficulties and learn new coping skills;
8. improve or develop new techniques for communicating within the family and with professionals;
9. see the possibilities for the integration and independence of the infant-toddler and, indeed, of the whole family;
10. secure and coordinate services from a variety of disciplines, service providers, and funding streams;
11. learn how to take charge of their situation and become their own case manager if they wish to do so;
12. be launched successfully as families affected by a disability.

Moreover, the IFSP recognizes that families play a crucial role in the infant-toddler's development and will always play an important role in child development. The IFSP really extends the notion of "parent participation" to that of "family participation," subject to the final decision by parent(s). It recognizes that families are systems and that no one member of the family (the infant-toddler) truly can be helped unless all members of the family are strengthened and unless the whole family plays from a position of strength.

Section 504

The regulations under Section 504 [Sec. 104.33(b)] provide a third way to define appropriate education by requiring schools to furnish handicapped children with special education and related aids and services designed to meet their educational needs as adequately as the needs of nonhandicapped children are met (an *equivalence* definition). The program must be based on least restrictive placement principles and include a full and individual preplacement evaluation, a nondiscriminatory test, an annual reevaluation of special education placement, and procedural due process.

Implementing an IEP is one way to provide an appropriate education, but Section 504 does not require an IEP, nor do its regulations. Like the EHA, Section 504 addresses the requirement of appropriate or individualized education by requiring that schools follow a process and requires equivalency between the handicapped and nonhandicapped. In commenting on the present Section 104.33, the Department of Health, Education, and Welfare said:[7]

> Section 84.33(b) [now, Sec. 104.33(b)] concerns the provision of appropriate educational services to handicapped children. To be appropriate, such services must be designed to meet handicapped children's individual educational needs to the same extent that those of nonhandicapped children are met. An appropriate education could consist of education in regular classes, education in regular classes with the use of supplementary services, or special education and related services. Special education may include specially designed instruction in classrooms, at home, or in private or public institutions and may be accompanied by such related services as developmental, corrective, and other supportive services (including psychological, counseling, and medical diagnostic services). The placement of the child must, however, be consistent with the requirements of Sec. 84.34 [100.34] and be suited to his or her educational needs.
>
> The quality of the educational services provided to handicapped students must equal that of the services provided to nonhandicapped students; thus, handicapped students' teachers must be trained in the instruction of persons with the handicap in question and appropriate materials and equipment must be available. The Department is aware that the supply of adequately trained teachers may, at least at the outset of the imposition of this requirement, be insufficient to meet the demand of all recipients. This factor will be considered in determining the appropriateness of the remedy for noncompliance with this section. A new Sec. 84.33(b)(2) [100.33(b)(2)] has been added, which allows the full implementation of an individualized education program developed in accordance with the standards of the EHA. [Author's note: Section 504 regulation references have been updated, in brackets.]

POST-EHA CASES

Given the EHA's process definition of appropriate education, the IEP definition in the EHA regulations, the comparability definition of the Section 504 regulations, and the requirement that an appropriate education must be in the least restrictive environment (LRE), it was clear at the outset that courts would be called on to define *appropriate education* and its relationship to the *least restriction* requirement. For the purpose of explaining the courts' interpretations, it will be helpful to consider separately the LRE cases and their impact on the meaning of appropriate education (see chapter 6). Here, it will be useful to consider how courts have interpreted the other definitions of appropriate education.

Appropriate Education and the Supreme Court

The Supreme Court defined appropriate education in its first special education case, *Board of Education v. Rowley.* The *Rowley* decision has become the touchstone for all subsequent appropriate education cases. It incorporated much of the reasoning and results of other appropriate education cases decided by other courts. Its history and principles, therefore, are worthy of close examination (see Appendix C for the Court's opinion).

In *Rowley,* a federal district court and the Second Circuit Court of Appeals both held that a school district must provide a sign language interpreter in the classroom as part of a deaf child's individualized education program in order to comply with requirements of the EHA. The courts found that, as a matter of law, a handicapped child's education must be comparable to that given nonhandicapped children, not the best education available. Under the facts in this case, they found that comparability would not be achieved without an interpreter.

The court of appeals noted that the decision was restricted to the facts of this case (the child's parents were also deaf, and evidence at the trial showed that, without an interpreter, only 59% of what transpired in the classroom was accessible to the child). One judge filed a lengthy dissent citing the extensive efforts the school district had already made on behalf of the child.

The U.S. Supreme Court reversed the court of appeals, holding that the EHA does not require the school to provide the student an interpreter in order to comply with the mandate of an appropriate education. The Court emphasized the EHA legislative history. As the Court read that history, it concluded that Congress had not intended that the schools try to develop handicapped children to their maximum. Instead, the EHA's purpose was basically to open the schools' doors to disabled students, granting them access to educational opportunities. Accordingly, congressional intent is satisfied when the school provides the student a reasonable opportunity to learn.

Because the student in this case had progressed from grade to grade without an interpreter's help, there was evidence of the school's compliance with the "open doors" intent of Congress. In this aspect of the case, the Court essentially adopted the comparability standard (the Section 504 approach). If the open doors rule were not adopted— i.e., if comparable treatment were not required—the "maximum development" purpose would be appropriate. Because it is not, *the comparability test prevails.*

The Court also stressed the importance of the law's procedures for defining and providing an appropriate education. Specifically, it noted that all of the professionals involved in developing the child's IEP were of the opinion that the child could be educated appropriately without an interpreter. In addition, it pointed out the many ways in which the law allows the child's parents to be involved in the IEP process and otherwise.

The *Rowley* decision undoubtedly is quite limited by its facts as precedent for other cases. For example, because the student was mainstreamed, it is doubtful that the Court's emphasis on grade-to-grade promotion would apply to handicapped children who do not or cannot progress from grade to grade or whose progress cannot be measured by that standard. It also is doubtful whether the decision would apply to handicapped children who require related services in order to be educated in the mainsteam, such as the spina bifida children in *Tatro* and *Tokarcik,* two cases that are discussed later in this chapter under "Related Services." The Supreme Court's own *Tatro* decision confirmed that suspicion.

But *Rowley*'s impact—the principle of rough comparability in opportunity and the Court's reliance on professionalism and process—is great. Some of the cases summarized in the following paragraphs reflect *Rowley*'s fallout. Others were decided before *Rowley.*

Appropriate Education, Not Maximum Development

The first of *Rowley*'s principles is that the EHA was designed only to provide to handicapped children the same basic opportunities for an education as nonhandicapped children have. Opening the school doors so that handicapped children have reasonable opportunities to learn, but not assuring them an opportunity to reach their maximum potential, was considered to be Congress' intent, nothing more. *Rowley* thus addressed the goal of an education, not just how that goal is to be reached (e.g., with or without an interpreter). Several other cases also addressed the goal of special education. The trend of the cases is to hold that the EHA provides only *an* appropriate education, not the best one or one designed to help the child reach his or her maximum potential.

The principal case, *Springdale School District v. Grace,* held that the child is entitled to an appropriate education (in the public school, in this case), not the best (in a residential facility). On appeal, the Eighth Circuit affirmed, applying *Rowley* and holding that the mainstreaming goal is served by education in a local school district, where instruction is reasonably calculated to provide the child with educational benefits. The best education available does not have to be offered. Note that the court does not consider cost of implementing a school district program if it provides an appropriate education. Other cases agree with this result.[8] Under these cases, the child's maximum development is not the goal of his or her education. In other cases, however, maximum development is the goal, and the "best" or "near best" education is the appropriate one.[9]

If a state by its own laws provides that a goal of the special education program is to develop a child's maximum potential, a court will enforce that requirement and command a program of education that is appropriate to developing a child's maximum potential. That is the rule of *David D. v. Dartmouth School Committee,* and it has been followed in subsequent cases.[10] Thus, a state may set a higher standard than the EHA, and a court will enforce that standard.

The reason for this result is simple. The EHA is a national law, not one that sets standards, other than minimum ones, for each state. Moreover, its intention—as declared by Congress and interpreted by the Supreme Court in *Rowley*—is to open the doors to an appropriate education. This goal is essentially one of providing equal opportunity for education, commensurate with the student's capacities.

Thus, equal educational opportunities mean just that—equal, not exceptional in the sense that the maximum development is the goal. If maximum development were the goal, equal opportunity would not be the dominant theme of the EHA. Indeed, the three ways of obtaining equal educational opportunity for students with disabilities require only that an appropriate education be provided, not that the maximum development be sought.

Thus, equal treatment, equal treatment plus accommodations, and unequal but favorable treatment (see chapter 3 for a discussion of the concept of equality and equal treatment for students with disabilities) are the means for equal educational opportunity. If maximum development were the goal, these three means would have to be added to; another one would be "equal treatment plus favorable accommodations for extraordinary opportunity, not just ordinary opportunity."

Although this result may be desirable, it is not consistent with the EHA's goals of equal educational opportunity. Thus, it is not part of the federal law. But because it is a desirable goal, a state may adopt it, and a court will enforce it. That result—state-set goals with judicial enforcement—also is consistent with the federalism principle. This principle (explained more in chapter 3) allows a state to have discretion in the education of its students, as long as it does not deny them equal protection of the laws (i.e., as long as the state does not violate the Fourteenth Amendment). Thus, a state may set a higher standard (maximum development), but if it does not, it is bound only to the EHA standard of equal (not extraordinary) educational opportunity.

The 12-Month School Year

Another of *Rowley*'s tenets is that professionally developed, individualized education programs are deemed to be appropriate. That proposition flies squarely in the face of legislative judgments, usually based on fiscal policy, that a school year should be limited to a fixed number of days a year. Although fiscally and politically defensible, that decision does not satisfy the *Rowley* demand for individualization of education, based on professional judgment.

It was therefore predictable that inflexible school year limits would be tested by handicapped children. On 12-month education, the leading case is *Armstrong v. Kline.* In that case, the district court held that the state's refusal to pay for more than 180 days' schooling each year for severely and profoundly retarded and severely emotionally disturbed children violated their rights to an appropriate education under the EHA. An appropriate education is one that allows the children to become self-sufficient within the limits of their handicaps, not just one that allows them to share equally in programs provided to non-handicapped students or to reach one of several other goals (the court relied on legislative intent to define appropriate education). The court also noted that some children will regress significantly during breaks in their education, recoup their losses more slowly than nonhandicapped children, and thus are denied an appropriate education when they are not given year-round education. Other cases concur in this result.[11]

The *Rowley* Standard Interpreted

The essence of the *Rowley* standard is "educational benefit." A school district must ensure, through the student's IEP, that there is some educational benefit from the education provided.

Courts have interpreted this provision in several cases. For example, one court[12] held that the *Rowley* standard means that grade-to-grade advancement of a child classified as trainable mentally retarded is not valid. The "benefit" must be measured by some means other than such advancement. Otherwise, the student will be deprived of the opportunities for placement in the mainstream (regular education programs—see chapter 6). Likewise, the *Rowley* standard as applied to a child who has never attended regular classes means that the child must be given instruction that ensures some educational progress, not any regression or trivial educational advancement.[13] It is clear from these cases that the *Rowley* standard of eductional benefit is interpreted on a case-by-case basis, and that the student's present placement, diagnosis, disability, and capability must be taken into account in measuring "educational benefit."

The Process Definition

The appropriate education cases lead to other conclusions. Clearly, the process definition of appropriate education is at work: Enroll the child, evaluate, do an IEP, and place him or her in the least restrictive environment. The cases, other than *Rowley*, are *New York Association for Retarded Children v. Carey, In the Matter of the ''A'' Family*, and *Harrell v. Wilson County Schools*.

The "process definition" as set out in the EHA and in *Rowley* has been applied by several courts, with interesting results. The basic rule seems to be that the process of identification, evaluation, and program (IEP) must be followed. If it is not, and if the noncompliance results in some actual harm or some likelihood of harm, the student's IEP is inappropriate. For example, if the IEP fails to address the diagnosed aspects of the child's education (that is, it does not pay attention to the nondiscriminatory evaluation), it is not appropriate because it cannot provide an education that is reasonably calculated to benefit the child.[14] Likewise, if a school district fails to comply with the procedures for nondiscriminatory evaluation and IEPs and fails to give notice to the parents concerning their rights (in violation of the due process safeguards, chapter 7), the IEP is inappropriate.[15] Similarly, the school district's failure to properly evaluate a student results in an inappropriate and invalid IEP.[16]

The courts seem reluctant to insist on strict compliance with the process definition if there is no demonstrable harm to the student as a result of noncompliance with process. Thus, failure to give notice to the parents does not result in harm when the parents attend the IEP meeting and know its purpose.[17] This is the "harmless error" exception to the general rule.

In summary: The process definition must be followed if there is actual or potential harm to the student if it is not followed. But there is an exception for "harmless error"— the situation in which error occurred (failure to follow process) but the error caused no harm.

Judicial Reliance on Expert Judgment

Rowley made it clear that the courts should defer to the experts in matters related to the child's right to an appropriate education. This rule—judicial deference to expert judgment—comes into play after the courts determine that the educational benefit test and the process definition have been met. Thus, if there is a dispute between parents and the school district about the appropriateness of a student's education, and if there is some proof that the student is benefiting from the education offered and that the process for determining appropriateness has been met, the courts will not substitute their judgments for that of experts concerning the student's education.

For example, in *Rowley* the Court mentioned many times that the experts had determined that Amy Rowley did not need an interpreter, in large part because she was receiving an educational benefit from schooling without an interpreter; after all, benefit—progress from grade to grade—was clearly evident. Likewise, in *Lachman v. Illinois Board of Education,* a court found that if an LEA fulfills its procedural responsibilities in developing an IEP and experts differ on whether the student should be educated by one means or another (here, by one type of educational method for the deaf or another), the parents have no right to insist on the child's placement in a program that uses only cued speech instruction.

It bears mention that the rule of judicial deference to expert judgment is well settled. The Supreme Court has announced it in disability cases, such as *Honig* and *Arline* (both of which are discussed in chapter 3), *Tatro* (discussed immediately below, see Appendix D), and other disability cases.[18] As pointed out in chapter 4, the rule allows the courts to make "correct" judgments on matters that are very technical and on which experts may disagree; the courts lack capacity to make their own independent judgments and must rely on experts. But the rule also allows the courts to duck the hard issues of social policy—deferring to experts, instead, as in *PASE v. Hannon* (see chapter 4) and *Armstrong v. Kline* (discussed in this chapter).

Other Factors

An appropriate education also depends on the presence of developmental or age-appropriate peers;[19] on education with students of the same gender, where education with students of the opposite gender would be inappropriate because of the student's imitative tendencies;[20] on a healthful environment;[21] on instruction by certified teachers;[22] and on placement in residential facilities fairly near the child's home;[23] or with nonhandicapped children.[24]

Related Services

An appropriate education also depends on the availability of related services. These are transportation and such developmental, corrective, and other supportive services (including speech pathology and audiology, psychological services, physical and occupational therapy, recreation, early identification and assessment, counseling services, school health services, social work services in school, parent counseling and training, and medical and counseling services, except that such medical services shall be for diagnostic and evaluation purposes only) as are required to assist a handicapped child to benefit from special education [Sec. 300.13].

Catheterization.   The U.S. Supreme Court itself has clarified one important aspect of related services. The general issue was how to distinguish between a related service and a medical service. The specific issue was whether catheterization is a related service that schools must provide or a medical service that they are not required to provide except for diagnostic or evaluation purposes. Federal trial and appeals courts had held in *Irving Independent School District v. Tatro* that clean intermittent catheterization (CIC) is a related service. The Supreme Court affirmed, holding in a unanimous opinion that CIC is a related service that schools must provide.

In *Tatro,* the Supreme Court found as a matter of fact that CIC is a "simple procedure ... that may be performed in a few minutes by a layperson with less than an hour's training." Indeed, the student herself soon would be able to perform the service, as her parents, babysitters, and teenage brother had been doing all along.

The Court was faced with the legal issue of whether CIC is a related service under the EHA [Sec. 1401(17)]. To decide that, it had to determine whether CIC is a supportive service required to assist a handicapped child to benefit from special education and, next, whether CIC is excluded from the supportive service definition because it is a medical service serving purposes other than diagnosis or evaluation.

The Court held that CIC is a supportive service because, without it, the student could not attend school and thereby benefit from special education. Congress' intent, said the Court (relying on its earlier decision in *Rowley*), was to make a public education available to handicapped children and to make their access to school meaningful. A service that makes it possible for the child to "remain at school during the day is an important means of providing the child with the meaningful access to education that Congress envisioned." It is clear that the Court was not about to allow any violation of the zero reject principle by permitting schools to escape the obligation of this type of related service. It also is apparent that the Court was concerned that handicapped children have an opportunity for *meaningful* access. Its concern with prohibiting functional exclusion is apparent, too. And the Court may have been concerned with exclusion of the student from education with nondisabled students, although it did not refer to the LRE principle.

Next, the Court found that CIC is not a medical service that the school must provide for diagnosis or evaluation. There are two reasons for this conclusion. First, the Court deferred to the Department of Education regulations, which ruled CIC to be a related, not a medical, service. (This was its approach in *Arline,* too.) Second, the Court found that Congress plainly required schools to hire various specially trained personnel and that school nurses have long been a part of educational systems. It also noted that nurses have authority to dispense oral medication and administer emergency injections and that it is difficult to distinguish CIC from these services.

Note that *Tokarcik v. Forest Hills* also held that catheterization is a related service. Similarly, tracheotomy cleaning and reinsertion is a related service (school health service).[25]

Psychotherapy.   Several of the dispositive facts in *Tatro* and its holding that CIC is a related service are not present in cases involving psychotherapy. For example, trained lay-persons can perform CIC. Indeed, CIC can be self-administered. By contrast, psychotherapy can be performed lawfully and competently (it is presumed) only by licensed physicians with special training and qualifications in psychiatry. Rarely is it self-administered in the sense of the patient and psychiatrist being one and the same person.

In addition, the cost of CIC is relatively low, and its benefits to the child (enhanced opportunity for life and for education, particularly with nondisabled children) are great. The cost-benefit ratio favors CIC and disfavors schools' objections to providing it. On the other hand, psychotherapy is expensive and its benefits seem questionable in some cases. It is therefore no wonder that the courts have divided opinions on whether psychotherapy is a related service that school districts must either pay for (so others can provide it) or provide themselves.

In the Matter of the "A" Family held that out-of-state placement in a private residential facility for seriously emotionally disturbed children, at which the child would receive psychotherapy, is placement in the least restrictive alternative for the child and the tuition and the therapy must be paid by a local school district under the EHA's provisions for related services. Psychotherapy is a related service, not a medical service, because it is a "treatment of mental or emotional disorders or of related bodily ills by psychological means," according to *Webster's New Collegiate Dictionary.* It thus comes within the definition of psychological services [Reg. Sec. 121a.13(b)(8)— "planning and managing a program of psychological services, including psychological counseling for children and parents"]. A case reaching a similar result is *T.G. v. Board of Education of Piscataway.*

By contrast, *McKenzie v. Jefferson* held that the residential component of a psychiatric hospital placement is medical, not educational, in nature and is not to be paid for by a school district, because it is not a related service. A concurring case is *Darlene L. v. Illinois State Board of Education.*

Other cases tend to be expansive and liberal about psychotherapy, usually in the context of residential hospitalization (as contrasted with school-based special education and psychotherapy as a related service). Thus, *Gladys J. v. Pearland Independent School District* and *Kruelle v. New Castle County School District* both held that an appropriate education for severely emotionally disturbed children includes psychotherapy and 24-hour, 12-month residential placement. Other cases concur in this result,[26] holding that school nurses' and physicians' charges at a residential facility should be paid by the school district that placed the child there but the physicians' charges are for evaluations and diagnostic and prescriptive services, not treatment.

Similarly, in *Gary B. v. Cronin*, the plaintiffs were emotionally disturbed children alleging that a state rule excludes counseling and therapeutic services from special education services. The court issued a preliminary injunction preventing implementation of the rule to deny money from counseling, therapy, and so forth, failure to pay the plaintiff for costs of therapy, counseling, and so forth, and denial of a free appropriate education to the plaintiff. (Note the opposite trend in *McKenzie* and in *Darlene L.*, mentioned earlier.)

Other Medical or Health-Related Services.   Although the trend in the cases involving psychotherapy barely tilts toward holding that service to be a related service, there is a clear trend in the opposite direction in cases involving other medical or health-related services. The leading case is *Detsel v. Board of Education of the Auburn Enlarged City School District*. The student (Detsel) is an oxygen-dependent person who requires a constant supply of oxygen. The supply must be calibrated to provide a mixture of 40% oxygen. The means for providing that supply is a respirator. The respirator is operated by a trained nurse or other professional. That person must observe the respirator and be in attendance with the student and the respirator on a constant basis.

The issue in *Detsel* was whether the school district must pay for the nurse—that is, whether the provision of a nurse to constantly monitor and provide the necessary respirator-support and oxygen is a school-health service that meets the test of a related service. The federal courts held that the district does not have to provide the nurse and that the service is not a school-health or related service.

The reasons for this result have to do with the nature of the service and its relationship to the child's education. The person who must provide the service must be professionally licensed; and an aide for the principal professional usually is required. A registered nurse or licensed practical nurse is the only person professionally qualified to perform the procedure. A school nurse's duties have not included this service. The procedure itelf is complex, consisting of many separate but interrelated steps. The expense of providing the service is great. The service is life-sustaining, and the risk of a malfunction in the service—that the student experiences respiratory distress and, if not rescued, may die—is great. Provision of the service is supervised and prescribed by a physician. And the student, although clearly benefiting from the service, is not using the service directly to benefit from special education; the service is necessary, but not for the purposes of special education.

A similar result was reached in *Bevin H. v. Wright*. There the court ruled that the school district is not required to pay for nursing and related health services for a child who is severely and profoundly disabled. The services are respiratory support (breathing through a tracheotomy tube inserted into the student's throat) and nutritional support (being fed through a tube inserted into the student's stomach). Because the student's care is varied, intensive, must be provided by a nurse under a physician's supervision and prescription, cannot be provided by a layperson, is time-consuming and expensive, and involves life-threatening situations that require the constant vigilance of a professional, these health services are not related to the student's special education.

Air Conditioning. An unusual related service case, *Espino v. Besteiro*, held that a school district must provide an air-conditioned classroom for a multihandicapped child unable to regulate his body's temperature. Placing him in an air-conditioned Plexiglas™ cubicle restricted him from interacting with his peers.

Summary of Related Services Cases. Although the cases on psychotherapy are not fully consistent with each other, there are some clear criteria that determine whether a service is a related service or a medical service. These are the complexity, constancy, costs, and ultimate value of the service. If the service is very complex (in *Tatro*, the service was simple and could be self-administered or performed by a layperson with only a little training, and it did not require back-up professional help; in *Detsel* and *Bevin H.*, the service was highly complex, requiring a licensed and specially trained professional working under the supervision and prescription of a physician), it is apt to be a related service. If it is not required to be performed or monitored constantly (in *Tatro*, CIC was required only a few times a day; in *Detsel* and *Bevin H.*, the service had to be performed without interruption and required constant attention), it is apt to be a related service.

Further, if the service is low-cost or has a high cost-benefit ratio in (in *Tatro*, the service was inexpensive and very helpful to the student's inclusion in regular settings or regular programs; in *Detsel* and *Bevin H.*, the procedure was very expensive and did not ensure placement in schools but, more often, education at home), it is apt to be a related service. If it directly benefits a child to be educated or even placed in a school building or regular school program (as in *Tatro* but not *Detsel* and *Bevin H.*), it is apt to be a related service.

In addition, if the service is a traditional function of a school nurse or a modest extension of the nurse's function (in *Tatro*, CIC is not unlike other school nurse functions, whereas in *Detsel* and *Bevin H.* the service is far more like a hospital-based service), it is apt to be a related service. Clearly, the courts are concerned about the function of the school nurse because, fundamentally, they are concerned about converting the role of the schools from education to all-purpose service agencies (including health services).

Also, the courts are concerned, it seems, about the expense of a service not just because educational dollars are limited and should be spent for traditional educational purposes (that is, for roles that are consistent with the usual or slightly expanded duties of a school nurse), but also because the expenditure of huge amounts of money for one child for essentially health-related reasons may deprive other handicapped students of funds in the special education budget. The issue is a classic competing equities issue (explained fully in chapter 3): To what extent shall one person be given an advantage at the expense of another?

Finally, the courts may well be concerned about the liability that schools would incur if the medical services were to malfunction or be improperly provided. Medical malpractice or health-care negligence issues are a very real concern in the public policy debates of the 1980s. There is a great deal of debate about cost-containment and health-care expenses. There also is a real concern about the impact of huge liability judgments on physicians' willingness to provide certain kinds of service. It may be that the courts are (silently) sensitive about these issues in the related-services cases and, taking them into account, tend to rule against the student when the service is of the type that can create medical malpractice or health-care negligence claims by the student against the schools.

GOVERNMENTAL PROBLEMS ARISING FROM THE RELATED SERVICES REQUIREMENTS

New policies, such as the requirement that schools must educate handicapped children appropriately and provide them with related services, rarely are executed perfectly. Those who analyze problems (such as the total and functional exclusion of handicapped children from schools) and propose solutions to them (such as requiring the provision of related services) must be on guard to anticipate barriers to the appropriate education of handicapped children and to plan ways of overcoming these barriers. No matter how thoroughly the obstacles are anticipated and prepared for, they will inevitably pose greater problems than anticipated.

Related services are a case in point. Besides the problems in interpreting what these services shall be, difficulties arise in providing them. Essentially these are intergovernmental; they go to the heart of the functions of governmental agencies involved with handicapped children.

Intergovernmental Coordination

One major problem is intergovernmental coordination. The immediate task has been to assure that the federal, state, and local agencies that can offer special education and related services will provide those services in the least restrictive setting. Because there are so many service providers and because they often are operated by separate federal agencies (each with its own state and local counterpart), it is important, though difficult, to coordinate these agencies' activities and thereby assure that their collective resources can be brought to bear on the educational problems of disabled children.

But federal interagency agreements are not always translated into action at the point where federal services are delivered, and state and local counterparts do not necessarily enter into interagency agreements or carry out these agreements. When these fairly typical bureaucratic problems are added to the interpretation problems, the results are either a failure to deliver services or its opposite—duplication of services (with a resulting competition for funding and a waste of professional time and effort and increased cost of service).

The Single-Agency Provision

Another major problem has been caused by the section of the EHA that makes the state-level education agency ultimately responsible for assuring that each handicapped child is given special education and related services. The single-agency provision has caused some public agencies (such as those that furnish occupational therapy, physical therapy, and mental health and mental retardation services) to withdraw their services from school-aged handicapped children on the ground that the state education agency is responsible for furnishing those services. Their refusal usually occurs when the child is difficult or expensive to serve or does not fit neatly into already existing programs.

On the other hand, some agencies tend to compete to serve handicapped children. Schools try to increase their social work or psychological services; social services and mental health agencies try to retain their clients and even offer educational programs for them. Competition to serve a handicapped child typically occurs when the child is easy or inexpensive to serve or fits into already existing programs.

Thus, there exists both a symbiotic and a competitive relationship between educational agencies and other agencies. The relationship is symbiotic because schools use the other agencies as "safety valves" or outlets, placing in them children who are particularly problematic for the schools. The relationship is competitive because, for other, easier-to-serve children, educational agencies compete with other agencies to serve the children. When they provide service, they usually can draw down "outside" money (from federal or other entitlement programs), justify the maintenance or expansion of services, and retain or increase their staffs.

Several additional factors aggravate the problems caused by the single-agency requirement:

1. The state education agency does not control the funds of many providers of related services. It has the ultimate responsibility but not adequate authority and resources to discharge its duty.
2. State and local governments usually have been designed so that the single-agency provision cannot work well. Social services, mental health, and education agencies receive funds from different sources and for different purposes, are governed by independent elected or appointed boards, and have always operated with relative independence from each other.
3. Handicapped children placed in private schools by local schools still retain their rights to related services, even at the usually higher cost incurred in private education.
4. Some regions of a state lack services, even when all state and local resources are mobilized and coordinated.
5. Although transportation is a related service in federal and state law, lack of transportation remains a barrier to providing other related services. This is especially true in rural areas.
6. Schools are reluctant to have their limited funds used for related services that they believe other agencies should provide and that do not fit within the traditional functions of education. This response reflects a misunderstanding concerning the role of related services: They are provided when necessary to enable a child to benefit from special education, and they are intended to prevent functional exclusion. This reluctance also reflects the need to stretch limited public school resources by requiring other agencies

to put the "first dollar" into a related service that they traditionally furnish. (The first-dollar requirement assures that one agency will pay for services up to a set level before another agency is required to pay for them.)

It reflects still another problem concerning governmental financing: Many handicapped children are eligible for health, mental health, or social services (and thus for certain related services) only if they or their families are income-eligible (poor). After the income-eligible children are served, there still may be related-services costs to be borne by the schools or other agencies. And, of course, some handicapped children who are not income-eligible are entitled to related services. Thus, an income-eligible child might receive Early Periodic Screening, Diagnosis and Treatment (EPSDT) screening, but children who are not income-eligible may have to qualify for screening by the Crippled Children's Program.

7. A final problem is that there are few legal restraints on the demand for related services. If a child's individualized education program calls for the schools to provide related services and a due process hearing officer or court sustains the child's right to these services (ruling on the child's claim to an "appropriate education"), the schools have no choice but to provide them.

INTERESTS OF HANDICAPPED CHILDREN AND FUNCTIONS OF GOVERNMENTS

Notwithstanding the progress made at federal, state, and local levels of government to overcome intergovernmental problems by adopting interagency agreements, a fundamental problem remains with the agreements and the related services provisions. This flaw is that there is massive disagreement among service providers and policy makers concerning the nature of public education for handicapped children.

Traditional Roles of Education

Traditionally, public education had been mass education. The purpose and techniques of public education were remarkably stable until a quarter of a century ago. Gradually, however, the schools have become the battleground for beginning and carrying forward substantial changes in American life: racial desegregation, extension of public services into historically private areas of family life (health and sex education, counseling, social services, and other activities that tend to supplement or even supplant, in the eyes of some, the family's role), integration of handicapped children and adults into the mainstream of life, and individualized services to handicapped people (not the provision of mass-produced and mass-consumed services).

Education was nearly as inevitable as death and taxes. Second only to the tax collector, the school cast the largest net thrown by government. Thus it was that schools have been asked to bear the brunt of social reform. But in making schools the focal point of social reform and new government services for handicapped children, policy makers have undertaken to transform the school and probably change its function from one of education alone to one of education plus physical health, mental health, and social services. Can the schools carry this burden? Should they be asked to? If so, how can they be helped? If not, who should be active in this area? These are the questions that thoughtful observers raise.

New Functions of Education

Handicapped children have a very real and defensible interest in obtaining an appropriate education and related services. The schools have an equally real and defensible interest and responsibility in satisfying those needs. In light of the present difficulties in providing related services, however, some people think that it is only proper to ask whether schools *alone* should be required to meet every educational need of a handicapped child and, if so, how they can best carry out this responsibility and with what funds (federal, state, or local).

In this matter, the function of one agency of government (schools) is being balanced against the functions of other agencies (health, mental health, and social services) and against the interests of handicapped children and the various agencies. It is increasingly clear that this issue—the issue of government functions and whether the school alone should bear the brunt of efforts to educate (in its fullest sense, by providing related services) handicapped children—has not been addressed adequately in the context not only of handicapped children but of education as a whole. The new infants-toddlers law (P.L. 99-457), the new Medicare amendments (P.L. 100-350), and the new Technology Related Assistance Act of 1988 (P.L. 100-407) prove this point: Schools are asked to do more functions. Until the issue is adequately addressed, the present problems will continue and proposed solutions will fall short because they will not reach the underlying issue of how public agencies are to respond (or fail to respond) to the presence of disabled persons in society. This is an issue not only of behavior and function but of values and principles as well.

Values and Principles

In my judgment, the Supreme Court's *Tatro* decision (concerning clean intermittent catheterization) was correctly decided and its principles are sound, both with regard to the behavior and functions of schools and with regard to values and principles. The same is true, I believe, of the 12-month school year cases and *Rowley*. All of these cases seem to emphasize the need for integration of disabled students with nondisabled students. *Tatro* required catheterization so that the student could continue her education at school (instead of home). The 12-month school year cases seem to say that the extended school year is required so some children can continue to receive school services at all; in the absence of summer schooling, they may regress so much that it would be pointless to require schools to educate them at all. And *Rowley* made much of the fact that the student was integrated with disabled students and passing from grade to grade.

In these cases, the principle that schools must provide certain services is associated with the value of integration. The cases thus require a new *behavior* of schools—appropriate education (i.e., the opposite of functional exclusion). And the cases require a new *function* of schools—to take on some of the responsibilities of other agencies. The value is integration. The objective is to prevent exclusion.

Just how far the courts will pursue these behavior-shaping and function-changing principles and values remains to be seen. The decisive test was in *Detsel*, involving technology-supported children, and *Timothy W. v. Rochester*, involving the issue of educability. There, the courts may consider the costs of school-provided therapy, the drastic change of role from providing education to practicing medicine, the length of time required for successful intervention, the professional qualifications required of the provider, and the comparability requirements of the EHA (as interpreted in *Rowley* and as seen under the "reasonable accommodations" test of *Davis*).

Practical Considerations vs. Integration

In considering any one of these factors, and especially in considering a combination of them, the courts may decide that the integration principle should yield to practical considerations of cost, time, and professionalism and should be modified because the child could receive more effective individualized services in other service systems. In this event, the child arguably would not be denied an appropriate education (since the psychiatric and possibly educational services would still be provided by other agencies) but would receive them in a less integrated setting (e.g., in a psychiatric hospital).

Indeed, that result—exclusion from school-based services and inclusion in other service providers' systems for receipt of special education and related services—is a major issue of the EHA's requirements for least restrictive alternatives or environments (LRA/LRE). It is therefore timely to consider the LRA/LRE rules next, in chapter 6.

NOTES

1. Frederick L. v. Thomas.

2. Fialkowski v. Shapp.

3. *See* Education Commission of the States, *Final Report, Special Education in the States: Legislative Progress Report, Handicapped Children's Education Project* (Denver: Author, 1974).

4. PARC.

5. MARC.

6. PARC; LeBanks v. Spears.

7. *Federal Register,* May 4, 1977, pp. 22690-91.

8. *Concur:* Rettig v. Kent City School Dist.; Bales v. Clark; Hines v. Pitt County Bd. of Ed.; Isgur v. School Bd. of Newton; Gladys J. v. Pearland I.S.D.; Campbell v. Grissett; Buchholtz v. Iowa Dep't. of Public Instruction; Riley v. Ambach.

9. Age v. Bullitt.

10. *Concur:* Georgia ARC v. McDaniel; Crawford v. Pittman (limited to the particular plaintiffs only); Yaris v. Special School Dist.; Lee v. Thompson (in which the court appointed a master to oversee implementation of the 12-month school year, the court finding the district to be in contempt for failure to carry out the order filed 2 years before); Birmingham and Lampere School Dist's. v. Sup't.; Stacey G. v. Pasadena I.S.D. For cases denying 12-month education, *see* Rettig v. Kent City School Dist. and Bales v. Clark.

11. Geis v. Bd. of Ed. of Parsnippany-Troy Hills.

12. Thornock v. Boise Ind. School Dist.

13. Bd. of Ed. of East Windsor Regional School Dist. v. Diamond.

14. Russell v. Jefferson School Dist.

15. Jackson v. Franklin County School Bd.

16. Bonadonna v. Cooperman.

17. Scituate School Committee v. Robert B.

18. Board v. Rowley; Youngberg v. Romeo; O'Connor v. Donaldson; Honig v. Doe; PASE v. Hannon; Board v. Arline, Florida; Southeastern Community College v. Davis; S-1 v. Turlington; Roncker v. Walters; Timothy W. v. Rochester School Dist.; Tatro v. State of Texas; and Parham v. J.R.

19. Age v. Bullitt.

20. County School Bd. of Loudon County v. Lower.

21. Espino v. Besteiro.

22. Rowley v. Bd.; Age v. Bullitt; Springdale v. Grace; Monahan v. Nebraska.

23. Erdman v. State of Connecticut; Hines v. Pitt County Bd. of Ed.; and Manchester Bd. v. Connecticut State Bd.

24. Campbell v. Grissett.

25. Dep't. of Ed. v. Katherine D.

26. *Concur:* Papacoda v. State of Connecticut; Harris v. D.C. Bd. of Ed.; and Woods v. Pittman.

6

Least Restrictive Appropriate Educational Placement

THE DEBATE

No requirement of the right-to-education movement and the federal law that codified the cases was as likely at the outset to generate as much heat as light as the requirement that children with disabilities be educated in the least restrictive placement. Given the inaccurate code name "mainstreaming," this requirement had the potential for encountering the same levels of opposition, misunderstanding, and ill will as the earlier constitutional and legislative-judicial requirements for racial desegregation of the public schools. This book will largely use the term *least restrictive alternative* (LRA). It has also been called *least restrictive environment* (LRE).

This requirement also had the potential for significantly improving the education of children with disabilities, redressing some of the wrongs that schools had imposed on them and their families, and contributing to the education of all pupils, training of all educators, and enlightenment of the public at large. Interestingly, the potential for not-so-good and good results has been realized, and the debate continues even now, concerning the desirability, meaning, and implementation of the requirement that children with disabilities be educated in the least restrictive setting appropriate to their needs.

It will be useful to examine the LRA requirement along several dimensions, paying attention to (1) the constitutional basis (foundations) for the requirement, (2) the case law that preceded the EHA, (3) requirements of the EHA and Section 504, (4) reasons for the LRA requirement, (5) the nature of the requirement as a rebuttable presumption and the role of presumptions in law, (6) the public policy values that the LRA requirement seeks to achieve, (7) the relationship of the policy to the requirement for an appropriate education (the third of the six principles of the EHA), (8) the role of professional and judicial interpretation of the LRA and appropriate education requirements, and (9) an evaluation of the efficacy of the LRA doctrine—its power to accomplish its stated purposes.

CONSTITUTIONAL FOUNDATIONS

LRA as a balancing mechanism in the education of handicapped children is derived from the constitutionally-based legal doctrine of the least restrictive alternative. This doctrine states that even if the legislative purpose of a government action is legitimate (e.g., promoting public health, regulating commerce, or providing education), the purpose may not be pursued by means that broadly stifle personal liberties if it can be achieved by less oppressive restrictive means. Legislative and administrative intervention must take the form of the least drastic means for achieving the same basic purpose.[1] In Chambers'[2] memorable metaphor, LRA forbids a state from using a bazooka to kill a fly on a citizen's back if a fly swatter would do as well. LRA, then, is a constitutional principle that accommodates individual and state interests to each other. It enables government to act but does not permit it to take just any action that it might want to take.

The LRA Principle

The LRA principle generally has been applied in areas affecting state regulations of interstate commerce,[3] personal liberties,[4] and procedural rights.[5] An example of one of the earliest LRA cases involved South Carolina's purported effort to conserve natural resources off its shoreline.[6] To do this, the state imposed a $25 licensing fee on residents shellfishing off the South Carolina coast and a $2,500 licensing fee on nonresidents, in an obvious attempt to discourage out-of-state fishermen. The Supreme Court invalidated the statute, ruling that South Carolina could use a less restrictive means of accomplishing its legitimate goal of conservation (e.g., by imposing a tax on the shellfish catch by weight) while minimizing the impact upon the private right of nonresidents to earn a living.

The LRA doctrine also has been applied in cases involving handicapped citizens in public institutions. A long line of cases addresses this issue.[7] In one notable case, *Wyatt v. Stickney*, the court stated that residents shall have a right to the least restrictive conditions necessary to achieve the purpose of habilitation. This phraseology is significant because it highlights the point that achievement of the purpose of commitment (treatment) is primary, and elimination of infringement on rights (in this case, deprivation of liberty) is secondary.[8] In legal terminology this means that the LRA doctrine is a *rebuttable presumption*.[9] That is to say, when it is not possible to grant total liberty and at the same time provide effective treatment, the doctrine allows the state to deprive the citizen of his or her liberty but only to the extent necessary to provide the treatment. The presumption in favor of liberty, thus, is rebutted by the action of commitment. Rebuttable presumption is discussed in detail later in this chapter.

The LRA Doctrine in Education

The same point applies to the principle of LRA in education. The right to placement in an integrated or "regular" educational environment is not an absolute right but is secondary to the primary purpose of education in the public schools—namely, an appropriate education. Thus, under federal law, educational services are to be provided "so that all handicapped children have available to them a free appropriate public education."[10]

A Mississippi case, *Mattie T. v. Holladay,* serves as a good example of educational uses of the LRA doctrine. The case focused on the provision of inadequate educational services to handicapped children who were placed in self-contained special educational classes that separated them from nonhandicapped children. The court ruled that the state goal of providing an appropriate education for these children could be met in a more *integrated* setting, thus maximizing the handicapped students' right to associate with nonhandicapped students.

LRA's power is derived from three important constitutional principles: *procedural due process, substantive due process,* and *equal protection.*[11]

1. Procedural due process requires that a state must grant citizens an adjudication procedure, allowing them to challenge an action before it may infringe upon their private, individual rights. The state must prove that the proposed action is warranted, and the individual is given the opportunity to point out less restrictive or less drastic means of accomplishing the state's goal.

   In special education matters, due process guarantees a hearing at which the handicapped child (or his or her representative) can try to show why the rebuttable presumption against deprivation of liberty—as by exclusion from public schools or placement in an arguably stigmatizing special education program—should be overcome. The hearing requires individualized decision making and imposes an accountability device on government, all to the end of protecting the child's interest in education and against classification as handicapped.

2. Substantive due process (a doctrine now rarely used) places an outer limit on what a state may do, independent of the level of procedural protections provided. It protects certain individual rights from all forms of government intrusion and requires that the government use the least intrusive means to accomplish its goals.[12] LRA is a progeny of substantive due process in that it prohibits the state from using more restrictive means than are necessary to accomplish its purpose. In special education affairs, LRA and substantive due process regard unwarranted, inappropriate special education classification and placement as too restrictive.

3. The third and last principle, equal protection, requires that a state deal with similarly situated individuals in an even-handed manner. If a state discriminates, the equal protection clause places the burden of proof on the state to show a compelling, important, or rational reason for its discrimination. The level of justification depends on the nature of the rights being limited and the political insularity of the affected individuals. Recent equal protection developments indicate that the Supreme Court rejects a "mid-

dle tier" form of judicial review for handicapped individuals, not requiring the state to demonstrate an "important" reason for its discriminatory practices.

Equal protection was the basis for the right-to-education cases that challenged exclusion of handicapped children from public schools in the early 1970s. The courts' attitude toward educational segregation can be summarized in the following comment from PARC: "[A]mong the alternative programs of education and training required by statute to be available, placement in a regular public school class is preferable to placement in ... any other type of education and training."[13] Other court decisions have continued to expand these basic rights.[14]

Thus, the LRA doctrine is a constitutionally derived way of balancing the values surrounding provision of an appropriate education (the student's right to and need for an appropriate education) with the values of individual rights of association. It is supported by, and implemented through, the constitutional principles of procedural due process, substantive due process, and equal protection. Whether premised on substantive or procedural due process or on equal protection, LRA has been a powerful doctrine for accommodating legitimate state interests (in educating all students appropriately, not just those with disabilities) and individual interests (in an appropriate education in settings and associations with nondisabled and disabled students). Its application to involuntary commitment,[15] to conditions in institutions,[16] and to less clearly analogous areas of state-individual conflict has made it a useful doctrine for courts that were determined to correct schools' discrimination against disabled children.[17] At the same time, it established a firm judicial mind-set against institutions—firm, but not unshakable, and clearly vulnerable in right-to-education cases.

PRE-EHA CASE LAW

Preference for the LRA

In *PARC* and *LeBanks*, there was ample evidence of, among other things, functional exclusion, misclassification resulting in inappropriate placement, and general inadequacy of special education programs (in terms of financing, programs, and personnel). There was additional evidence of the indisputable denial of equal educational opportunities for handicapped children in violation of equal protection and procedural due process principles (see chapters 3 and 7). Like Hamlet, a court faced with such overwhelming evidence might have been inclined to say, "There is something rotten in the State of _____; oh, cursed spite that I was born to set things right."

Court Remedies

Given the facts, the courts had to fashion remedies. One remedy, particularly appropriate for the practice of functional exclusion, was stated as follows (in *PARC*):

> It is the Commonwealth's obligation to place each mentally retarded child in a free, public program of education and training appropriate to the child's capacity, within the context of the general educational policy that, among the alternative programs of education and training required by statute to be available, placement in a regular public school class is preferable to placement in a special public school class and placement in a special public school class is preferable to placement in any other type of program of education and training.

As far as the case law initially was concerned, least restrictive placement reflected a judicial preference for students to be placed or tracked in a "normal" track rather than in a special education track and for students to be educated in the regular school environment rather than in the confines of a special school. LRA was no more than a *preference* in favor of regular educational placement; it was not an inflexible rule. It was a guide for conduct, not a rule of conduct. As a guide, it did not prohibit alternatives to regular class and regular school placement. When children with disabilities are educated with nondisabled students, usually in the same classes, their integration is sometimes called *mainstreaming*.

Reasons for the LRA Preference

Why was LRA a judicial preference? The reasons were many. The preference was a reaction to the exclusion of children with special needs from both the *opportunity* for education (placement in a school system) and the opportunity for a *meaningful* education (placement in an appropriate program). It addressed total and functional exclusion, with an emphasis on the latter.

LRA also was a reaction to the view traditionally accepted by many educators (and institutionalized in school practices) that children with special needs are different from, and therefore should be excluded from education with, nonhandicapped children. LRA was an attempt to protect exceptional children from the stereotype that they are different and deficient. It spoke to the stigmatizing effects of special educational placement—the effects that such placement has on a child's self-image and on the school's and peers' image of the child.

Further, LRA was a method for individualizing an exceptional pupil's education, because it prevented a child from being placed in special programs without first determining that the child could not profit from regular educational placement. It simultaneously addressed the requirements of an appropriate education—an individualized education—and nondiscriminatory classification. It promoted the concept that curriculum adaptations and instructional strategies tailored to the needs of exceptional children could occur in regular classrooms as well as in special classrooms.

LRA was preferred because the existence of separate, self-contained special education programs and schools was found to be equivalent to the establishment of separate but unequal systems of education. Separate generally meant unequal, and special education was not equated with equal educational opportunities. Some commentators argued that the pattern and practice of some schools was to assign the "worst" children, typically those with special needs, to the least capable teachers, putting them in the most inferior facilities, with less than adequate educational materials. Often, special education programs were funded less generously than normal mainstream programs. In the face of such biased treatment, LRA adopted some of the strategies used to bring about racial integration of the schools.

One strategy for racial integration was to integrate a racial minority into the racial mainstream. The hope behind the strategy was that the racial majority would not neglect its children's education in integrated schools, and continued attention of the white majority to "quality education" would assure the black minority of the same quality education as the white majority. Similar hopes undergirded the preference for LRA.

LRA has more than a civil rights aspect, however; it was imbued with a sense of desperation. A court wishing to redress the manifold wrongs of functional exclusion, misclassification, and inadequate special education programs could (and we suspect did) easily contrast regular education with special education, see that nonhandicapped children were not excluded, misclassified, or shortchanged, and reach the conclusion that the quickest remedy was to order placement, to the maximum extent appropriate, with the nonhandicapped. The remedy was sure. The regular programs were already in existence and could accommodate some handicapped children without extensive revision. Extensive revision of special education programs was hardly certain to be achieved satisfactorily despite court orders for revision. The courts fired with buckshot, not single rounds, and revision undoubtedly would not be quick. LRA, then, gained popularity as an easy and readily available remedy.

Moreover, LRA was a reaction to the terminal aspects of special education. Placement of an exceptional child in a self-contained special education program usually was the last step in a child's development; it often was the terminal placement. The preference for LRA rested on the hope that the self-fulfilling prophecies and the self-limiting characteristics of special educational placement would not be the end result for children with special needs.

LRA also was preferred because it was widely and forcefully advocated by many educators. They argued that the handicapped child would learn more, and more easily, by being educated with the nonhandicapped child. They contended that there were serious doubts about the educational efficacy of special (separate) programs, and they said that handicapped children needed the educational and experiential benefits of coming into contact with nonhandicapped children.

Finally, placement in the least restrictive appropriate school program cannot be divorced from two related legal developments: (1) application of the least restrictive principle to at least two other areas of state action—(a) criminal law and placement in the least restrictive environment, and (b) civil commitment of persons dangerous to themselves or others; and (2) the trend toward deinstitutionalization—preventing mentally disabled persons from being placed in institutions except as a final resort, and discharging as many as possible from institutions.

In one sense, the deinstitutionalization movement was part of a more generalized application of the least restrictive doctrine. But it was different because of its implications for the public schools. Deinstitutionalization prevented many handicapped children from being placed in institutions. Instead, they remained in the community. By requiring that all children be given a free appropriate public education, the court cases and the EHA put pressure on the public schools, particularly in terms of the zero reject principle. In responding to this pressure, the schools had to begin training the more severely handicapped children, who were, after all, the most apt candidates for institutionalization and were traditionally most excluded from school. Schools could choose not only to create new (or more extensive) programs for severely handicapped children but also to broaden the range of nonhandicapped children by placing the mildly handicapped children in the mainstream. Thus, although the least restrictive placement doctrine was born in nonschool contexts as part of the constitutional requirement of substantive due process, it has had significant implications for the public schools, as will be discussed hereinafter.

FEDERAL LEGISLATION

The EHA

It is not surprising that many of Congress' findings reflected in the EHA are identical to conclusions of the courts and the reasons the courts required children to be placed in least restrictive educational settings. These findings include the following:

1. Handicapped children have been inappropriately educated [Sec. 1400(b)(3)].
2. They have been denied the opportunity "to go through the educational process with their peers" [Sec. 1400(b)(4)].
3. There is a lack of adequate services available to them within the schools [Sec. 1400(b)(6)].
4. Educators have the ability to provide effective special education and related services, including, presumably, education and services in the regular program [Sec. 1400(b)(7)].

Legislative requirements will be examined in regard to (1) least restrictive appropriate placement and (2) other statutory provisions.

Least Restrictive Appropriate Placement.   It was predictable that Congress would require SEAs [Sec. 1412(5)(B)] and LEAs [Sec. 1414(a)(1)(C)(iv)] to follow a policy of least restrictive placement [Sec. 300.550]. They must develop procedures to assure that, to the maximum extent appropriate, handicapped children—including children in public agencies, private institutions, or other care facilities—will be educated with children who are not handicapped. Further, the requirements stipulate that special classes, separate schooling, or other removal of handicapped children from the regular educational environment will occur only when the nature or severity of a child's handicap is such that education in regular classes with the use of supplementary aids and services cannot be achieved satisfactorily.

The regulations prohibit placement outside the mainstream program except under limited circumstances. The regulations thus create a presumption in favor of integration; integration of handicapped children into the mainstream should occur "to the maximum extent appropriate." It is clear from the legislative history and a proper interpretation of the Act that "appropriate" is to be defined in terms of what is appropriate for the handicapped child, not whether the school system can conveniently absorb that child into the mainstream or whether the child will have beneficial or detrimental effects on nonhandicapped peers. It is inescapable, in light of EHA policy, to provide handicapped children with an appropriate education. This much is clear from the EHA and regulations. But, as will be shown, the courts are not strictly adhering to the focus on only the student with a disability.

The presumption in favor of integration can be overcome (rebutted). The regulations provide that a handicapped child may not be removed from the regular educational environment unless the nature or severity of the handicap is such that education in regular classes, even with supplementary aids and services, cannot be achieved satisfactorily. This condition, too, focuses on the nature or severity of the child's disability as opposed to the convenience for the school or the consequences for nonhandicapped children. Conditions for a particular placement are inexorably linked to the concept of appropriate education and are to be child-centered, not system-centered. Again, this approach is not followed consistently by the courts.

The regulations [Secs. 300.550-556] speak to one of the most potentially troublesome aspects of placement in the least restrictive environment: placing handicapped children into regular programs without regard for their individual needs. Section 300.552 of the regulations makes it clear that each handicapped child's educational placement must be determined at least annually, be based on his or her individualized education program, and unless the IEP requires special alternative arrangements, the child must receive an education in the same school he or she would attend were it not for the handicap. In selecting the least restrictive environment, any potential harmful effect on the child or on the quality of services received is to be taken into consideration [Sec. 300.552]. This is a focus on the child's needs for an appropriate education. Comments on the regulation make it clear that if the child disrupts nonhandicapped students in the regular classroom to the degree that their education is significantly impaired, the child's needs cannot be met in that classroom and placement there is inappropriate. This is the approach used in the expulsion cases and in those involving students with AIDs.

Section 300.551 puts pressure on public agencies to develop appropriate alternative placements by requiring that the options include instruction in regular classes, in special classes, in special schools, home instruction, and instruction in hospitals and institutions.

This is a policy judgment favoring a continuum of services. The LRE doctrine permits this policy choice. The agency also must provide supplementary services such as resource rooms and itinerant teachers in conjunction with regular class placement.

Handicapped children must be given a chance to participate in nonacademic and extracurricular services and activities. They are to have access to meals, recess periods, counseling services, athletics, transportation, health services, recreational activities, special interest groups, and clubs. They should be referred to agencies that give assistance to handicapped persons, and be employed in and outside of the public agency [Sec. 300.553 and .306].

SEAs must make suitable arrangements with public and private agencies to ensure that the least restrictive placement rules are effectively carried out [Sec. 300.554]. They are to provide technical assistance to the other agencies to help them implement the rules [Sec. 300.555], and must monitor programs and assist public and private agencies in correcting noncompliance with the rules [Sec. 300.556].

Other Statutory Provisions. The policy of least restrictive appropriate placement is indivisible from other policies. It is a method for assuring an appropriate education, a technique of individualized education, a way of preventing misclassification, and, ultimately, a trigger for a due process hearing. Its success will depend, in part, on personnel development [Sec. 1413(a)(3)], and it is advanced by the requirement that schools spend EHA funds, first, for the education of handicapped children who are not receiving an education, and, second, for the most severely handicapped children within each disability who are receiving an inadequate education [Sec. 1412(3)]. Since federal funds may not be spent on mainstream (regular) programs until the other priorities have been met, schools are required to spend their own funds (state or local funds, or federal funds from other sources) for mainstream purposes.

The "ceiling" on the number of handicapped children has the same effect. No more than 12% of all children may be counted as handicapped. If there are, in fact, more handicapped children than an LEA can accommodate within the ceiling, the LEA may tend to count as handicapped only those who fit the two service priorities, and count the less handicapped children as nonhandicapped. As a result, the less handicapped children are served in the mainstream or served (outside the mainstream, in some cases) in state or locally funded programs.

Part H. The regulations under Part H clearly create a strong preference for community-based services, to the extent appropriate for the child. Thus, to the extent appropriate, services must be provided in the types of settings in which infants and toddlers without handicaps would participate. Also, early intervention centers, hospitals and clinics, and other settings appropriate to the child's age and needs are permissible. And the Department of Education recommends that services be community-based and not isolate a child or family from settings or activities in which children without handicaps would participate.

Section 504

Section 504 regulations are substantially similar to those of the EHA. Section 104.34 requires schools to provide each qualified handicapped student in their jurisdiction with regular or mainstream education to the maximum extent appropriate to the handicapped person's needs. The school must place handicapped students in the regular educational environment operated by the school unless the school can demonstrate that a student's education in the regular environment with the use of supplementary aids and services cannot be achieved satisfactorily. Although the handicapped student's *needs* determine what is a proper placement, the Department's comments on regulation Section 104.34 make it clear that if a handicapped student is so *disruptive* in a regular classroom that other students' education is significantly impaired, the handicapped student's needs cannot be met in that placement and regular setting placement is not appropriate or required.[18]

Handicapped children also are to be provided with nonacademic services in as integrated a setting as possible. This requirement is especially important for children whose educational needs require them to be solely with other handicapped children during most of each day. To the maximum extent appropriate, children in residential settings are to be provided with opportunities for participation with other children. In providing or arranging for the provision of extracurricular services and activities, including meals, recess periods, and nonacademic services and activities as set forth in Section 104.37(a)(2), a school must ensure that each handicapped student participate with nonhandicapped students to the maximum extent appropriate for the student in question.

If a school operates a facility for handicapped students, the school must ensure that the facility and the services and activities it provides are comparable to its other facilities, services, and activities. This is not intended to encourage the creation and maintenance of such facilities. A separate facility violates Section 504 unless it is necessary for providing an appropriate education to certain handicapped students. When special facilities are necessary, this provision requires that the educational services provided be comparable to those provided in the recipient's regular facilities.

Among the factors to be considered is the need to place a child as close to home as possible. Under Section 104.34, schools must take this factor into account. The parents' right to challenge their child's placement extends not only to placement in special classes or a separate school but also to placement in a distant school and, in particular, to residential placement. If an equally appropriate educational program exists closer to home, the parent or guardian may raise the issue under the least restrictive placement doctrine through a procedural due process hearing.

The Federal Agency Position.   Commenting on the proposed Section 504 regulations (which are comparable to the ones adopted as final regulations), HEW (now HHS) took the position that, within the requirements of the regulation, schools must show that the *needs* of the individual handicapped child would, on balance, be furthered by placement outside the regular educational environment. According to HEW, for many handicapped children "the most normal setting feasible is that which combines the use of special and regular classes." Education of handicapped children, including those in public and private institutions and other care facilities, in the most normal setting feasible means educating them with nonhandicapped persons "to the maximum extent appropriate." It also means educating them as close to home as possible.

Thus, as HEW conceived it, the requirement for placement in the most normal setting feasible was intended to encompass the same concept as placement in the least restrictive alternative setting. HEW chose to use the "most normal rather than the "least restrictive" terminology because placement alternatives "cannot, in many instances, be compared on the basis of relative restrictiveness: i.e., while institutional education is indeed more restrictive than noninstitutional instruction, placement in special education is not necessarily more restrictive than instruction in regular classes." Despite a change in language, it does not appear that the final regulation represents a change in policy from the proposed regulations.

As HEW's comment on the proposed regulations indicated, what is restrictive or inappropriate for one person may not be restrictive or inappropriate for another. The principle of "most normal" or "least restrictive" placement rests on the policy of individualized or appropriate education. However it is phrased, the principle is a technique for individually appropriate instruction and should be viewed in that context. This view is consistent with the case law history and with proper interpretation of the EHA, as later discussion of court cases indicates.

HEW also said that an orthopedically handicapped child may not be placed in a classroom or school that is "primarily" for handicapped children, since that placement would violate the "most normal" principle. A school district is not, however, required to make every classroom and school building barrier-free. Hence, an orthopedically impaired child may be placed away from the neighborhood school, but not in a class primarily for the handicapped. This is not true for other handicapped children; their placement must be in the "most normal" setting possible. This appears to have been followed in the final regulation, which requires the school to take into account the proximity of the alternative setting.

A separate regulation [Sec. 104.37] requires schools to provide nonacademic and extracurricular services and activities in such a manner "as is necessary to afford handicapped students an equal opportunity for participation." Because they are part of a school's education program, they must be provided in the most integrated setting appropriate. Nonacademic and extracurricular services and activities include, without limitation, counseling services, recreational athletics, transportation, health services, recreational activities, special interest groups or clubs, referrals to agencies providing assistance to the handicapped, and employment of students by the school or other employers. In giving personal, academic, or vocational counseling and placement services to handicapped students, a school may not discriminate because of handicap and must make sure that students are not counseled toward more restrictive career objectives than nonhandicapped students who have similar interests and abilities.

Physical Education.   In providing physical education courses, athletics, and similar programs to any of its students, a school may not discriminate on the basis of handicap and must provide qualified handicapped students with an equal opportunity to participate in interscholastic, club, or intramural athletics. Those activities may be separate or different from the ones offered to nonhandicapped students only if separation or differentiation is consistent with the least restrictive principle [Sec. 104.35] and only if no qualified handicapped student is denied the chance to compete for teams or to participate in courses that are not separate or different. Commenting on the physical education and athletics portion of the regulation, HEW noted that "most handicapped students are able to participate in one or more regular physical education and athletics activities. For example, a student in a wheelchair can participate in regular archery courses, as can a deaf student in a wrestling course." (See chapter 3 for recent cases of alleged discrimination in athletics brought under Section 504.)

REASONS FOR THE LRA REQUIREMENT

Dual Systems in Society and Education

The very existence of an LRA policy means that there is more than one environment in which handicapped children may be educated and handicapped people served. These multiple environments are the result of the evolution of a system for legal, social, and educational treatment of handicapped people that is separate from and external to the more general society. In effect, it is a dual system—one for handicapped people and another for nonhandicapped people.

In Society.   The legal status of disabled people is subject to procedural and substantive rules that are, generally speaking, different from those applied to nondisabled citizens. Historically, these rules were shaped by the presumption that the state acts in the interest of the disabled person rather than in a role that is potentially or actually adverse to the handicapped person's interests. Thus, the doctrine of *parens patriae* established the power of the state to intervene in the lives of disabled people, in order to provide care and treatment.[19]

Although the doctrine of *parens patriae* justified the state's protective intervention, it also curtailed the legal rights of those who came under its ambit. In contrast to their concern about autonomy when considering the civil and criminal rights of nonhandicapped people, courts and legislatures tended to rely on the judgments of professional caretakers of the disabled.[20] For example, courts have given special attention to the LRA principle and its application to mentally disabled persons and the state's protective role when they have reviewed decisions regarding commitment and institutional care and treatment.[21]

In short, the *parens patriae* doctrine led to creation of a separate legal system for handicapped people, in which less rigorous procedures to protect legal rights applied. This dual system has come under vigorous attack in the last decade, resulting in a plethora of lawsuits and legislation to correct perceived wrongs. Although progress has been made, disabled people still face a dual legal system firmly in place.

Handicapped people also have fallen outside the mainstream of the nonhandicapped community. In the late 19th and early 20th centuries, theories of biological evolution gave rise to noxious social theories (particularly, Social Darwinism), which held that "genetically inferior" human beings should be segregated from the general populace lest they "contaminate" the race. Despite a growing awareness of the role of environment on human development, traces of Social Darwinism linger. Perceptions of handicapped people as different still lead to their exclusion from educational, recreational, residential, and vocational services available to most nonhandicapped citizens. This exclusion heightens public perceptions of handicapped people's differentness and further stigmatizes them.

The principle of *normalization*[22] has helped to reduce the perception of the differentness of handicapped people and has encouraged their greater integration into society. As with the legal system, however, integration and the dissolution of a dual social system have been only partially realized.

In Education.   The dual-system approach of the legal and social status of disabled individuals predictably has been reflected in the nation's public school system. Handicapped children were routinely placed in separate programs or educational facilities because of their unalterable traits,[23] in much the same manner as minority children had been subjected to separate facilities on the basis of race.[24] The practice of excluding handicapped children from the public school system has been supported by the erroneous rationale that these children lack the capacity to learn at a rate similar to that of their nonhandicapped counterparts.[25]

Prior to 1800, few states had health or educational programs for handicapped children.[26] During the early 19th century, however, social changes in America were reflected in the establishment of state-supported free public school systems for nearly all children. Advocates for free public education saw the schools as a tool that would enable democratic government to continue and expand while assimilating newcomers to the dominant "American way of life."[27]

Not coincidentally, the educational reforms and "common schools" established in the 19th century also provided the impetus for state-supported special education programs. Educational leaders such as Horace Mann, Samuel Gridley Howe, Dorothea Dix, and Thomas Hopkins Gallaudet gave impetus to establishment of the first American residential schools for blind, deaf, epileptic, retarded, and orphaned children. These schools offered training and a protective environment. But placement within them was often permanent. Despite the achievements and innovations of these early educational and political reformers, state-supported special education efforts began to dwindle.

It was not until passage of compulsory education laws in the late 19th and early 20th centuries that the questions of what to do with children who were "different" became more urgent. The "special" public school classes that evolved during this era became a dumping ground for truants, non-English speaking immigrants, and handicapped students—all of whom were outcasts of the public school system.[28] A few school districts established separate facilities to educate their handicapped students, but most excluded them entirely. The practice of exclusion persisted until the mid-1960s, when special educational programs became less rare. Nonetheless, the programs usually were separate from, and sometimes their quality was unequal to, educational opportunities offered to nonhandicapped students.

The dual system of education for handicapped children was similar in many important ways to the segregated programs for black students. In *Brown v. Board of Education*, the Supreme Court identified the effects of segregation on blacks:

> To separate them ... generates a feeling of inferiority ... that may affect their hearts and minds in a way unlikely ever to be undone.
>
> Segregation ... has a detrimental effect upon the ... children. ... [T]he policy of separating [them] is usually interpreted as denoting ... inferiority. ... [I]n the field of public education, the doctrine of "separate but equal" has no place.

It is not difficult to argue convincingly that segregation of handicapped children results in similar detrimental effects. The stigma of being labeled handicapped is thus underscored by the additional stigma of separation. Despite current federal and legislative guidelines, the stigma imposed on handicapped children as a result of being relegated to separate educational facilities continues to have important externalities. This stigma has been perpetuated in part in the attitudes of nonhandicapped students, parents, teachers, and special educators toward handicapped students, as well as in the attitudes of handicapped students themselves.[29]

In summary, the dual system of law and social status is echoed in the public school system. Segregation of handicapped children from regular classes has been the norm since the turn of the century and, until passage of the EHA, was the accepted policy among teachers, school administrators, and other educational policy makers.

Effects of the Dual System in Education

LRA requirements of the EHA responded to a multiplicity of problems in the education of handicapped children, not the least of which was the refusal of state and local education and other agencies to educate handicapped children with nonhandicapped children. But that practice was merely symptomatic of more generalized and widespread discrimination by those agencies against handicapped children.

The dual system in education has had a variety of effects, but the overall result has been a denial of educational opportunities for handicapped children. In its early findings of fact leading to enactment of the EHA, Congress found that special education needs of the more than 8 million handicapped children in the United States were not being fully met. Specifically, more than half of these handicapped children were in educational programs that were inappropriate for their needs, and an estimated 1 million handicapped children were excluded entirely from the public school system.[30]

A variety of administrative and educational practices contributed to these results. These practices fall into four basic categories: exclusion, misclassification, inappropriate education, and restrictive placements. Parents and advocates of handicapped children were unable to correct these practices because they lacked two important safeguards: procedural due process and a systematic method of parent involvement.

Exclusion. As indicated in chapter 2, a variety of educational practices resulted in the exclusion of many handicapped children from educational services. These included placing them on long waiting lists, using disciplinary procedures to remove handicapped children with behavior problems from classrooms, initiating limited (if any) child census programs to identify children, failing to provide educational programs to some institutionalized children, choosing to educate one group of handicapped children but not another, and denying all education to some children.[31]

Handicapped children who were not denied total access to education were often functionally excluded from an appropriate education because school systems tended to group all handicapped children together, ignoring their individual strengths and weaknesses.[32] Even when school systems recognized the individual needs of handicapped children, they frequently did not provide related services, as discussed in chapters 3 and 5.

Misclassification. Historically, testing and classification procedures have been (and remain) powerful political tools, capable of regulating people, degrading them, denying them access to educational opportunity, and excluding them as undesirables, as discussed in chapter 4. Handicapped children often have been misplaced or wrongfully tracked in the educational system, primarily because of the misuse of testing and classification procedures. Many school evaluation procedures were racially and culturally biased, based on a single criterion rather than being multifactored, administered by untrained personnel, rarely based on multidisciplinary assessment, and focused on only one area of disability.[33]

Inappropriate Education. Many factors have caused disabled children to receive an inappropriate education. In addition to misclassification practices, classroom teachers often had no method for organizing handicapped children's educational needs and the services required to meet them. Special educational programs themselves seldom received periodic review, and placements typically were made without regard for the unique needs of the affected children. Teachers of handicapped students were often not only uncertified in special education but were the least skilled teachers in the system as well.[34]

By classifying a child as handicapped and referring him or her to a separately financed and organized school bureaucracy,[35] schools had established and legitimized a dual system of education:[36] "regular" education for nonhandicapped children and "special education" for handicapped or minority ones. The former was substantially better financed and staffed than the latter, which became a classroom of last resort.[37]

Restrictive Placements. Educational opportunities for handicapped children were restricted because a full range of services often was not available. Typically, the only placement available was in separate classrooms or schools. These classrooms generally were the oldest and most poorly equipped, and their location often presented many architectural barriers. Often, the physical layout of schools limited handicapped children's access to libraries, gymnasiums, and cafeterias, and therefore curtailed any opportunity to participate in extracurricular activities. In general, handicapped children were given few opportunities to interact with age-equivalent, nonhandicapped students in the school environment.[38]

Not infrequently, children who were assigned to the special education system experienced permanent segregation[39] from nonhandicapped children or, what seemed worse, placement in institutions for mentally ill, mentally retarded, deaf, or blind children and adults.[40] The sad irony of this segregated system was that it satisfied the interests of so many agencies[41]—public schools, public institutions, private schools, and regular and special educators—while depriving so many children of an opportunity to be educated appropriately,[42] to attend school with their age peers,[43] to avoid the indisputable adverse effects of institutionalization,[44] and to remain with their families,[45] by attending the schools they would attend if they were not handicapped.

Lack of Procedural Due Process. Educational practices resulting in exclusion from or reduction of educational opportunities for handicapped children were perpetuated by a system that contained no safeguards to assure correction of inappropriate action (or inaction) on the part of school officials. Educational placement and evaluation of handicapped children typically were implemented without their parents' knowledge or consent. Parents generally had neither access to their child's school records[46] nor a formal protest mechanism to appeal educational decisions concerning their child. Any children who were legal wards of the state usually were not represented by advocates, guardians, or surrogate parents.

Lack of Parental Involvement. In addition to the absence of procedures for review and appeal of educational decisions, there were few mechanisms for involving parents in their child's education. As a general rule, school systems had not encouraged parent involvement. Besides being denied legally enforceable access to their child's records, parents received little information about available programs for handicapped children,[47] had no meaningful way of participating in the process of planning the education of their child, and frequently were not represented on local or state school advisory panels.[48]

During the late 1960s and early 1970s, an increasing number of parents and special educators became committed to solving the problems caused by dual educational systems. Although more and more parents began to demand a voice in the education of their handicapped children, they were frustrated by the school system's failure to provide channels through which their voices could be heard. In their frustration they turned for solutions to the state legislature and the courts. As the decade of the 1970s began, parents turned to the federal government, particularly the courts.

THE NATURE OF LRA: REBUTTABLE PRESUMPTION

The LRA principle disguises a complex debate concerning the educational rights of handicapped children. The reasons for the complexity are twofold. One is that the principle (as set out in the EHA and the regulations under it and Section 504) is a rebuttable presumption: It sets forth a general rule of conduct (integration of handicapped and nonhandicapped children), but it allows it to be rebutted when integration is not appropriate for the handicapped child.[49] In what cases should the presumption be rebutted? The other reason for complexity is that the principle takes into account the "appropriate" education to which the child is entitled by other legal principles and policy considerations. LRA is inextricably tied to the notion of appropriateness, which makes it all the more complex because appropriate education itself is difficult to define (as chapter 5 demonstrates).

The LRA principle is examined here in the context of appropriate education and, by closely analyzing major judicial decisions involving both appropriate education and least restrictive placements, the common law of an appropriate, least restrictive education for a handicapped child.[50] More than that, the question of whether LRA is interpreted according to a "rights" to and need for an appropriate education, or a rights to integration model, is addressed. Do the courts blindly follow a traditional continuum of services or a stereotypical image of more and less restriction,[51] requiring handicapped children to receive regular, or mainstream, education even when it will have little, if any, benefit for them? Or do they infuse LRA with a sense of appropriateness so that appropriate education sometimes means more, rather than less, separation from normal or regular education? Do they recognize that the right to an appropriate education, to satisfy the child's educational or other developmental needs, is as compelling an interest as the right against unnecessarily restrictive, unprofitable placements? The answer is *yes*.

It will be helpful to consider one point of this chapter—that needs sometimes do prevail over the presumptive right to regular education placement and programming—by recognizing that the LRA principle was certain to generate as much heat as light concerning the educational rights of handicapped children. Even in 1978, just a year after the federal regulations implementing the 1975 Act became effective, it seemed

> clear that the broad-based challenges to self-contained special education (i.e., programs that are not in the mainstream or do not meet every aspect of least restrictive placement) inevitably will have to answer those parents and educators who remain unconvinced of the educational value of the principle, who can adduce research and expert testimony to indicate that placement in the least restrictive program is not an automatic assurance of an appropriate education, and who assert that the least restrictive placement principle hinges on what is most enhancing or most habilitating for the handicapped person, not what is close to "normal."
>
> The risk is great that judicial and administrative interpretations of the principle will not depend on two indispensable factors: 1) The principle has its recent history in the massive denial of an adequate education for the many handicapped children who were placed in self-contained and separate programs (a history that is not necessarily doomed to be repeated, given the other rights and access to resources that handicapped

children have under case and statutory law); and 2) the principle is best understood and applied in terms of what is appropriate for the child himself where "appropriate" is defined not only by the IEP content but also by concepts of enhancement: What is enhancing is sometimes necessarily more restrictive than "normal" (e.g., a classroom for seriously emotionally disturbed children or severely retarded children may be highly "restrictive" and separated from "regular" programs but also highly enhancing of their abilities to learn). The future issue, then, is whether courts and agencies will apply the least restrictive principle by taking into account the relative "richness" or "poverty" of educational services in separate programs and the likelihood that such programs will be more enhancing for the handicapped child than not.[52]

But more is at issue concerning LRA and its judicial interpretation than balancing the relative needs and rights of handicapped children (given the policy choice, made in the EHA, in favor of a full continuum of services). A fundamental policy issue is inherent in LRA. It is one thing to concede that, when a government has a legitimate interest in restricting a citizen's liberty, it may act only in the way that is least restrictive of his or her liberty. The "least drastic means" standard thus serves to restrict governments from unnecessarily restricting citizens. But it is another thing altogether to answer the question: What is an unwarranted or unnecessary restriction of a handicapped child when the state is required to educate him or her appropriately? Any constitutional limitation on the ability of the state to act also is a limitation on the ability of its agents—educators—to act and, in turn, on the ability of the child's parents or guardians to act, and, finally, on the rights of the child.

Taking this chain of events as a focal point for discussion of LRA as it applies to persons with mental retardation, a publication of the American Association on Mental Retardation set forth the argument (in language that applies to *all* handicapped children) that LRA should not be interpreted as an absolute restriction on placement of handicapped people in unusual, atypical, or less "normal" settings, where those settings have been chosen by Congress, SEAs, or state legislatures as legitimate options on a continuum.

> One concern in analyzing the [LRA] doctrine is with the lives of persons who are subject to these natural limitations imposed by retardation. Another concern centers on limitations that lawmakers either impose on professionals or that professionals impose on themselves, which in turn are imposed on mentally retarded persons. In a nutshell, do these presumptions and assumptions, part and parcel of the [LRA] concept, overly restrict mentally retarded persons? Do governments and professionals misunderstand and misapply the [LRA] doctrine so that it becomes a force for further limitation? ... The editors' preference is to increase the range of choice for retarded people and mental retardation professionals by infusing the [LRA] doctrine with a sense of liberation, not a sense of restriction.[53]

Have the courts given that prediction and argument a hospitable reception? By and large, they have. Close analysis of the reported decisions shows that LRA does not prevent courts from authorizing the placement of a handicapped child into more restrictive settings that also are more or equally enhancing as presumptively less restrictive (more "normal") ones. Indeed, LRA as a function of appropriate education sometimes requires such placement into a setting along a continuum away from the regular school or program. The child's rights to and need for an appropriate education prevail over his or her integration rights where appropriate, and enhancing *placement* (the need) conflicts with the presumption in favor of *integration* (the presumptive right). Were it not for the deplorable restrictiveness of most public residential institutions, and, indeed, the limitations in programming and associations in many special education programs, and if it were not for the unimaginative use of the LRA doctrine by the courts in right-to-education cases, this result might be acceptable.

LRA as a Presumption

As noted, LRA is a presumption in that it requires handicapped children to be placed in educational programs with nonhandicapped children to the maximum extent appropriate for the individual and allows removal from such settings and placement in special classes, separate schools, or other separate activities only if the nature or severity of the handicap is such that education in regular classes, even with the use of supplementary aids and services, cannot be achieved satisfactorily.

Rebuttable presumptions set forth a rule of conduct that must be followed in every case unless, in a particular case, it can be demonstrated that the general rule will have unacceptable consequences for the affected individual.[54] Thus, LRA favors integration but allows separation. One reason for presumptions and for LRA specifically is that choices about appropriate placements should be made available within reason. LRA does this by being a presumption, not an iron-clad rule.

There is another reason to prefer rebuttable presumptions such as LRA. They occupy a middle ground between irrebuttable presumptions at one extreme and unguided case-by-case decision making at the other, and have several advantages over either of the other approaches. They tend to assure more consistency of behavior and thus are useful for predicting what will be legally tolerable in like cases.

In addition to *consistency* and *predictability,* rebuttable presumptions tend to prevent people from being subjected to the perceived harm they might experience if they were not governed by a presumption. Rebuttable presumptions allow policy makers the opportunity to avoid alternatives that are perceived to be harmful. Yet, because they are rebuttable, these presumptions allow greater *freedom of choice* than irrebuttable presumptions. Iron-clad rules may not, after all, be good policy decisions for everyone. Presumptively, institutional or other segregating placement is more harmful than regular school placement.[55] Only when it is shown that such a placement is necessary for appropriate education purposes in order to satisfy the individual's interests or valid state purposes is the presumption overcome.

The federal statutes and the regulations implementing them, and the applicable judicial decisions, make it clear that LRA is a rebuttable presumption.[56] But the statutes and regulations also demonstrate that LRA depends on and must be interpreted and applied in the context of *appropriate* education for the handicapped child. Under the applicable statutes and regulations, the child's placement is determined by his or her rights to and needs for special education, related services, or both, and by the individualized education program (IEP) developed for the child. And the IEP—the document that reflects educators', parents', and sometimes the child's determination of an appropriate education—cannot be accomplished until and unless the child has been evaluated nondiscriminatorily and, even prior to evaluation, accepted for enrollment into a publicly supported school system.

Thus, at least three other principles precede LRA and affect its interpretation: the *zero reject* principle (a rule that the child must be given a free and appropriate public education—a rule against "pure exclusion"), the *nondiscriminatory evaluation* principle (which requires fair assessment so that the child's strengths can be improved and weaknesses remediated), and the *appropriate education* rule (which requires that the child be given an education that potentially benefits him or her—a rule against functional exclusion from education).

Precisely because LRA is entwined with these other principles, its interpretation and application have been the subject of many lawsuits and much controversy. Before trying to untie the knot, however, it will be useful to consider the values that underlie the LRA requirement.

LRA and Values

LRA is especially value-laden because it promotes three sets of public policy values. One is the value of an *appropriate education* for handicapped children. LRA promotes this value because it creates an impetus toward integration of handicapped children with regular education, where their education arguably is enhanced.

The second is the value of *conservation of political and fiscal capital.* Equal access of handicapped children to regular education also decreases the likelihood that unequal services (special education) will be thought to be politically untenable and fiscally unfeasible; duplication of resources in times of economic retrenchment sometimes is neither politically astute nor economical.

Third, LRA may promote an important constitutional value—the right of disabled people to associate with nondisabled people. LRA's legal history clearly is related to the First Amendment and particularly relevant to disabled people. The right of association is more than a constitutional imperative; it is also a positive force in broadening individual and cultural dimensions of the citizenry and in dispelling stigmatizing and discriminatory attitudes of nonhandicapped people concerning disabled people. As stigma is less attributable to disability and as *de jure* and *de facto* discrimination accordingly recede, persons with disability acquire greater opportunity to pursue the constitutional values of liberty and choice in association.

Two points, however, cannot escape mention. One is that the public policy value of appropriate education for handicapped children can conflict with a similar value—the appropriate education of nonhandicapped children. The other is that the families of handicapped children do not always choose integration and association with nonhandicapped children. Evidence and implementation of these facts are explored later in this chapter.

For now, it is well to note that many commentators have provided explicit or implicit goals for the LRA principle.[57] A synthesis of these with the previous analysis of values, constitutional bases, and interests can be illustrated by a matrix in which the three basic levels of the policy interact with the two major value assumptions concerning appropriate education and the right of association, to produce six dimensions of the LRA policy.

Dimensions of the LRA Policy

Value Assumptions

Value Assumptions	A. That individuals and societies benefit when all are educated to our fullest potential	B. That individuals and society benefit when all its members are free to associate with each other
Produce:		
Legal Principles	1. Right to Education	4. Right to Association
and		
Educational Strategies	2. Appropriate Education	5. Integration
Resulting in:		
Social Effects	3. Enhanced Individual Potential	6. Decreased Stigma

LRA is both a legal principle and an educational strategy that circularly produces social effects. The legal principle assures a disabled student's appropriate education and thereby the right to associate with nonhandicapped students and other citizens. As an educational strategy, LRA enhances individual potential through appropriate education. Education, in turn, is thought to mitigate the effects of disability by decreasing stigma, and thereby increasing associational rights, individual opportunity, and potential.

These six dimensions provide a framework to organize stated goals of the EHA and the LRA principle. The following list summarizes the goals of the EHA and its LRA component:

1. *Right to Education:* To provide education to all handicapped children
2. *Appropriate Education:* To provide an education that is appropriate to the unique strengths and weaknesses of each handicapped child
3. *Enhanced Individual Potential:* To provide the opportunity for handicapped children to develop to their potential[58]
4. *Right to Association:* To provide education in an environment that promotes association with nonhandicapped peers[59]
5. *Integration:* To provide the opportunity for nonhandicapped peers to develop sensitivity to individual differences; and to prepare the handicapped child for future integration into regular education as well as integration into society in general[60]
6. *Decreased Stigma:* To enhance the social status of the handicapped child.[61]

Given this understanding of the goals of LRA, the final question to be determined is how these goals are to be implemented and how the value conflicts embedded in the goals can be resolved in practice. To resolve these questions, it is necessary to return to the legal concept of LRA as a rebuttable presumption and to translate that principle into an educational strategy.

The relative restrictiveness of an educational environment should be judged only in light of the individual educational need (right to an appropriate education) of each disabled child. In light of that need, the most "normal" environment may not always be the least restrictive of the child's right to an appropriate program of education.[62] To determine the least restrictive environment for a given child, two decisions must be made. The first involves choosing the range of available programs or environments to satisfy the child's requirements for an appropriate education. Conceivably, this might include more than one possible environment. Second, decision makers, such as the individualized education planning committee, must identify the particular programs or environment, from among the range of satisfactory ones, that can contribute most substantially to the child's freedom to interact with students who are not handicapped. Thus, when making a placement decision, priority is given to providing an appropriate education, and to a consideration of provision for appropriate education in an environment that minimizes infringement on the liberty to associate with nonhandicapped peers.

The principle is illustrated below. Circle A represents the set of all appropriate educational programs or environments available for a given handicapped child. Circle B represents the set of all environments that allow the same child to interact with nonhandicapped peers. In an ideal case, circles A and B overlay one another perfectly or nearly perfectly (la). More likely, they will marginally overlap, providing decision makers with relatively fewer choices for placement (lb). Or they may not meet at all, forcing decision makers to choose environments entirely on the basis of what is available within circle A (lc). In actuality, the problem is much more complex because the interests and needs of others (e.g., parents) enter the decision process (ld). Moreover, the decision of Congress and state legislatures to have a continuum of services further complicates the choice, because the continuum supports placement in segregated or special programs and thus reduces the likelihood that appropriate programs will be developed within more, rather than less, integrated environments.

A = All possible educational environments capable of providing an education for an
      individual handicapped child

B = All possible environments capable of maximizing freedom to associate with
      nonhandicapped peers

C = Needs of other interested parties

1a. Ideal case: Numerous choices available to satisfy both A and B

1b. Few choices available to A and B

1c. No available alternatives to satisfy needs of both A and B

1d. Complex decision process considering needs of A and B as well as other interested parties

THE JUDICIAL INTERPRETATION

LRA and Appropriate Education

The threshold inquiry would appear to be: What does the law mean when it requires that a handicapped child must be educated with nonhandicapped children to the maximum extent appropriate? What is the "maximum extent?" Even before that can be answered, one must ask: What is "appropriate?" This value-laden term promised to provoke spirited litigation. As the cases discussed here show, the promise has been more than fulfilled. For present purposes, it is necessary to analyze only those cases in which both LRA and appropriate education requirements are involved. (Much of what follows also was presented in chapter 5.)

In nearly all of the appropriate education-LRA cases, parents and educators of handicapped children have disagreed with each other over the meaning of appropriate education. Parents and educators alike have sought both non-regular (non-LRA) and regular school (LRA) placements for handicapped children. In trying to obtain non-regular (non-LRA) institutional or residential placement for a handicapped child, they have desired the child's placement *out* of the least restrictive setting. ("Least restriction" is defined by the image of a continuum on which the most restrictive setting is usually homebound or residential placement and the least restrictive placement is in the mainstream, with nonhandicapped children for the entire or majority of the handicapped child's time in school;)

This was the situation as of 1985 in 12 of the reported cases.[63] In nine of them, the courts ordered institutional or other "more restrictive" placement.[64] In those nine, the children were either severely or profoundly handicapped. In four instances,[65] they were emotionally disturbed; in four others,[66] mentally retarded; and in one,[67] learning disabled. In the three cases in which parents were unsuccessful in seeking institutional or residential placement, one child was severely multiply handicapped[68] (retardation and autism), and two were mildly learning disabled.[69] It seems difficult to harmonize the first with the seven cases ordering residential placement. The latter clearly are distinguishable on the basis of the degree of handicap.

Conversely, each group also has sought least restrictive or more "normal" placement for handicapped children. Thus, of seven cases reported by 1985, school officials were successful in five[70]—two children with severe multiple handicaps and one "trainable mentally retarded" (i.e., moderately retarded, not mildly or severely retarded), one severely to moderately retarded, and one learning disabled—and unsuccessful in two others[71] (profoundly deaf and severely and profoundly mentally retarded). In a fifth case, the child's parents did not contest institutional placement.[72]

Where parents and educators have not been able to agree on the proper placement for a particular child, courts have been required to define an appropriate education and LRA. In cases in which parents have sought institutional or other "more restrictive" placement, but schools have opposed such placement, courts, as of 1985, have decided in favor of the parents in a clear majority of the cases.[73] By the same token, where schools have sought institutional placement contrary to parents' desires, courts, as of 1985, ordered such placement in a majority of the cases.[74] Clearly the courts were disposed toward institutional placement. This trend in the cases did not change between 1985 and late 1988. Several cases are particularly good illustrations of the trend (discussed in the following paragraphs).

Two initial and partial conclusions emerge from these cases. The first reflects a concern that the perspectives of the handicapped person should be taken into account. Interestingly, the children's perspectives—their self-declared interests in placement—have not been reflected in the LRA cases. Indeed, all of special education law insufficiently allows for the child's self-declared interests to be advanced. The locus of control—the power to make decisions—is never placed with the handicapped child.[75] The paradox is that, in the name of removing a restriction, the LRA rule, as practiced in schools, by parents, or both, tends to disregard the choices (and thereby restrict the autonomy) of the person who is ultimately restricted by any placement. The second conclusion is that, given a choice between more or less restriction, parents and educators more often choose the former—greater restriction—than the latter, and the courts are now prone to affirm that choice.

On its face, this latter conclusion might seem surprising for two reasons. First, it suggests that the LRA principle either is unacceptable to a majority of parents, educators, and courts and is therefore a shaky basis for law simply because of its low potential to command the assent of the governed. (Some reasons for this result are suggested in chapter 4, on nondiscriminatory education, in the portions on why and how we classify.) Second, it appears that the LRA rule is being interpreted in ways not anticipated by many who thought it would result in substantial inclusion of handicapped children in traditional public school settings.[76]

But another explanation exists. If one studies the nature[77] and extent[78] of the handicaps of the children around whom the cases have been litigated and the nature of the choices presented—the choice between a public school and a residential program—it becomes clear that courts are concerned primarily about appropriate education and its provision, not about lock-step adherence to a hard-and-fast rule of integration. Alternatively stated, the exception has become the rule in these cases. More often than not, the presumption is rebutted because of a mismatch between the child's needs for an appropriate education, through the continuum of services, and the right to least restrictive (more integrated) placement.

In a sense, these cases instruct us that presumptively least restrictive placements (where that means more, not less, movement of handicapped children into regular educational settings and programs) can be functionally more restrictive where the continuum of services is allowed a legitimate policy choice. The paradox—less restriction is more—can be resolved only if the child's needs (right to an appropriate or enhancing education) are held paramount over his or her rights to integration.

Conceptual Frameworks

Clearly, the courts are influenced by parents and educators who advocate more restrictive (less integrated) placements. That advocacy seems to confirm the courts' position that the primary emphasis should be placed upon appropriateness (not integratedness) of the education. The courts are thus able to act consistently with the familiar constitutional doctrine of LRA while at the same time deferring to the educational judgment of many parents and educators. The doctrine of LRA has promoted a great deal of debate among educators, parents, and policy makers, including courts.[79] The consensus among parents and educators regarding proper interpretation of LRA, however, is divided largely between two schools of thought. This divergence is attributable to the emergence of two different conceptual frameworks for understanding LRA.

One conceptual framework for LRA strikes a compromise between the appropriateness of education provided and the loss of associational rights. Those who apply this framework are willing to forsake a portion of academic achievement in order to increase association. This position lends greater weight to the *right of association.* The other conceptual framework employs the LRA model to ensure the *more appropriate education* but still minimizes the infringement upon private rights of association. Those who apply the second LRA model first determine the nature of the most appropriate education and then implement that education with a minimum of infringement upon the private right of association. Thus, no part of the appropriate education is compromised to achieve a greater degree of association.

Those who apply the first (compromise) model to LRA generally consider the courts as insensitive to the integrating-associational rights of handicapped children when they order placement in a segregated setting. This perception would be true if the decisions favoring residential placement were to violate the principle of LRA and permit a more restrictive placement than necessary to accomplish the state's goal of providing an appropriate education.

After reviewing the constitutional and legal history of LRA, two important conclusions can be drawn. First, parents and educators who use the compromise model lack understanding of LRA. They mistakenly view LRA as an educational product rather than an administrative strategy. The second conclusion is that the judiciary's reluctance to reshape educational practice (that is, its unwillingness to become involved in the schools' governance and in making educational policy, as announced in *Rowley, Roncker v. Walters,* and *Honig*) weakens the application of the LRA model and promotes, rather than resolves, conflict. Conflict is promoted because both parents and educators can identify the least restrictive educational changes the court is unwilling to order.

The crux of conflict lies at the point of application to individual students, particularly severely and profoundly handicapped children. At one extreme is the position that the LRA's twin goals of education and integration are not only compatible but complementary as well, and that integration is a necessary element in the attempt to enhance *any* handicapped child's individual potential. At the other extreme is the position that the two goals are incompatible, and that, especially in the case of a severely handicapped student, placement in an integrated environment may actually impair educational achievement.

Appropriate Education

Disagreement over placement clearly begins as a disagreement concerning "appropriate" education. That this is so should not be unanticipated. As chapter 5 showed, it is conceptually difficult to define appropriate education and even more danger-fraught to apply the definition to a particular child.

Process Definition. In the process definition, the handicapped child will receive an appropriate education if he or she is "processed" properly. The child is not subject to "pure exclusion" (a zero reject approach) and is evaluated nondiscriminatorily, furnished an

IEP, and placed in the least restrictive appropriate setting. Several cases demonstrate the validity of this definition, but none so well as *Rowley.*

In *Rowley,* the school district had evaluated the child, placed her in regular class programs, and developed an IEP as required by law. The IEP did not call for an interpreter. The parents of the child, however, believed a sign language interpreter was necessary to ensure the child's maximum achievement. The school resisted, arguing that the child was making satisfactory progress without an interpreter. A due process hearing officer agreed with the parents. So did the district and circuit courts. The lower courts looked to the exceptional ability of the child and said that although her education was adequate, it could not be considered appropriate until an interpreter was provided.

The Supreme Court reversed and interpreted the EHA to require individualized educational services, developed through the IEP process by educators and parents, that are individually designed to benefit the child. It laid great emphasis on professional judgments, parent-professional collaboration through the IEP process, compliance with other procedural safeguards, and a "legislative conviction that adequate compliance with the procedures (of the Act) would in most cases assure much, if not all, of what Congress wished in the way of substantive content in an IEP."

IEP Definition. A second way to define appropriate education has been to assure that the child is given the special education and related services called for by his or her IEP. This definition clearly is the statutorily accepted one. It also has received the sanction of all of the appropriate education-LRE cases, including *Rowley,* in which the Court noted that the child's IEP did not require an interpreter.

In *Laura M. v. Special School District No. 1,*[80] for example, the court not only acknowledged this definition but also set out in its order the components of a judicially acceptable IEP. By the same token, when a federal court ordered a school district to educate a severely retarded boy in the same building in which it was educating nonhandicapped children, it also specified the major contents of the child's education program.[81]

Comparability Definition. A third definition of appropriate education derives from the Section 504 regulations.[82] These require schools to provide handicapped children with special education and related aids and services designed to meet their educational needs as adequately as the needs of nonhandicapped children are met. The comparability definition has strong equal protection overtones and, as the cases demonstrate, has been a draconian sword for handicapped children. It has enabled them to obtain some, but not all, of what someone believed was due them.

The court in *Springdale v. Grace,* relying on the district court's *Rowley* opinion, concluded that, when residential and "less restrictive" educational placements are comparable and even when the residential one is preferable because it is "better" for the child, the comparability standard, coupled with the LRA presumption, requires the regular school placement. A similar result was obtained in *Isgur v. School Board of Newton,*[83] in which a state court held that the LRA principle modifies a state law provision requiring that the child be placed in the program that would benefit him to the maximum extent feasible; an appropriate education is not tantamount to maximum development, only adequate development of the handicapped child.

In adopting a process definition and requiring *some* educational benefit, the Supreme Court's *Rowley* opinion explicitly turned its back on a definition that has the purpose of maximizing a handicapped child's development. Beyond these rather traditional definitions, however, the meaning of "appropriate" has become increasingly protean. As suggested, some courts view an appropriate education as that which gives reasonable assurance that a handicapped child will be developed to the full potential. Thus, *Age v. Bullitt*[84] characterized the purpose of the EHA as being to provide for the child's maximum development. To that end, the court required the most effective instruction of the child. Other courts seem to reject the maximum development concept without simultaneously holding that the child is entitled only to a barely adequate education. This is the *Rowley* standard, now adopted by several other courts as well.[85] From the cases decided after *Rowley,* clearly the substantive right to an appropriate education, required by the EHA, is to an education that is intended to provide, and indeed does in fact provide, some educational benefit. (See chapter 5 for a discussion of these cases.)

Related Services.   It also is now clear that the availability of related services is a critical factor in determining whether a child's education and educational placement will be appropriate and in the least restrictive setting. These cases are discussed in chapter 3.

Costs as a Standard.   To what degree, if any, may courts weigh the costs of an appropriate special education in determining the LEA's duty to a handicapped child? There are mixed answers to this issue. But it is important to recognize that the EHA and its regulations, and Section 504 and its regulations, are absolutely silent on the issue of whether costs are legitimate considerations in defining an appropriate education in the least restrictive (most integrated) setting. Thus, any considerations relating to costs are created by the courts and SEAs or LEAs that seek to minimize the cost to themselves.

There are two sets of cases involving costs, appropriateness, and the LRA doctrine. The first set relates to this issue: When a residential program (i.e., a relatively nonintegrated one) is appropriate, are the SEAs or LEAs ultimately responsible for the full costs? The answer is yes, but usually the costs are shared between the SEA-LEA, on the one hand, and the state agencies providing the programs in the residential setting, on the other.

Concerning this issue, courts have not usually regarded the relatively high cost of appropriate residential placement as a factor that should mitigate against the child's right to placement in residential facilities. The cost factor usually comes into play when the child is so handicapped that residential placement is acknowledged by all the parties to be the appropriate placement and the issue is whether educational agencies will bear the full cost of residential placement or other agencies (typically mental health or social service agencies) will contribute to the cost.[86] The decisions unanimously assess the cost to educational agencies on the grounds that the EHA imposes single-agency responsibility on the state and the one agency solely responsible to implement the EHA is the state education agency, together with its local counterparts.

Two exceptions to this general rule appear to be developing, however. One seems to be a "reasonableness" rule. If the school has made good faith efforts to provide the handicapped child an appropriate education in the least restrictive environment, the school will not be charged residential school tuition.[87] Conversely, the cost of residential school tuition will be assessed to the public school, not the child's parents, unless "reasonable alternatives" to the residential placement are available.[88]

The other exception arises from the "current-status" regulations.[89] If the parents of a handicapped child remove him or her from a public school and place the child in a private school and subsequently seek to recover the tuition from the public school, some courts[90] refuse to award them tuition on the grounds that, under federal regulations, (1) the child's current educational status may not be changed during the pendency of any administrative or judicial proceedings concerning placement,[91] and (2) school-initiated private placement is free of cost to parents but parent-initiated placement is not.[92]

The second set of cases explicitly takes into account the costs of an appropriate education. These cases usually address this issue: Does the student have a right to an appropriate education in more integrated settings or in more segregated settings, and may the costs of providing the appropriate education in integrated settings legitimately be weighed against the costs of the education in less integrated settings? The trend of the cases answers the question—yes.

The Davis Standard. Although it dealt with an unrelated legal issue involving handicapped people, *Southeast Community College v. Davis,* holding that a hearing impaired applicant for admission to a school of nursing is not "otherwise qualified" for admission under Section 504 regulations, and that the regulations do not require the nursing school to make extensive, professionally indefensible adjustments in its program to accommodate the applicant, seems to provide a final layer of judicial gloss on "appropriate education." Taking a cue from the Supreme Court's decision in *Davis* that Section 504 does not mandate certain accommodations, several courts seem to conclude that, when the child's handicap is so great that his or her successful placement in a regular education program is impractical or improbable without substantial modifications in the school's facilities or regular or special education programs, the LRA principle does not require such modifications.[93]

An appropriate education, these courts reason, lawfully may be provided under the federal Act and its regulations (without violation of the LRA prescription) by special programs if the cost of modifying regular programs is too great. In a sense, this is a "competing equities" approach wherein, unlike the harmful effects test, the issue is balancing the child's interests against school system interests. In this posture, the *Davis* accommodations criteria modify the integration principle and justify the inference that courts conclude it is more appropriate for severely handicapped children to be educated in separate programs or schools.

Three recent cases illustrate the new "cost-consideration" approach. *Roncker v. Walters,* decided in 1983 by the Sixth Circuit Court of Appeals, involved the Ohio system of separate schools for students with moderate to severe disabilities. The immediate issue was whether a student classified as trainable mentally retarded should be educated in the school system that serves nonhandicapped and mildly handicapped students or in the system that serves those with more severe disabilities. The court of appeals set aside the lower court's order that the student be placed in the separate system and ordered the lower court to make a new determination of the student's placement.

A basic (rather than immediate) issue in *Roncker* was the meaning of the LRA provisions of the EHA. The Court of Appeals observed that the very strong congressional preference for mainstreaming was found in the Act's requirement that the student with a disability be educated with nondisabled students "to the maximum extent appropriate." It then said:

> The proper inquiry is whether a proposed placement is appropriate under the Act. In some cases, a placement which may be considered better for academic reasons may not be appropriate because of the failure to provide for mainstreaming. The perception that a segregated institution is academically superior for a handicapped child may reflect no more than a basic disagreement with the mainstreaming concept. Such a disagreement is not, of course, any basis for not following the Act's mandate. *Campbell v. Talladega City Bd. of Education*, 518 F. Supp. 47, 55 (N.D. Ala. 1981). In a case where the segregated facility is considered superior, the court should determine whether the services which make that placement superior could be feasibly provided in a non-segregated setting. If they can, the placement in the segregated school would be inappropriate under the Act. Framing the issue in this manner accords the proper respect for the strong preference in favor of mainstreaming while still realizing the possibility that some handicapped children simply must be educated in segregated facilities either because the handicapped child would not benefit from mainstreaming, because any marginal benefits received from mainstreaming are far outweighed by the benefits gained from services which could not feasibly be provided in the non-segregated setting, or because the handicapped child is a disruptive force in the non-segregated setting. Cost is a proper factor to consider since excessive spending on one handicapped child deprives other handicapped children. *See Age v. Bullitt County Schools*, 673 F.2d 141, 145 (6th Cir. 1982). Cost is no defense, however, if the school district has failed to use its funds to provide a proper continuum of alternative placements for handicapped children. The provision of such alternative placements benefits all handicapped children.

This statement develops a new standard by which to judge "the maximum extent appropriate" requirement of the EHA. Under the *Roncker* standard, "the maximum extent appropriate" depends on the feasibility of providing, in a nonsegregated setting, those services that make a segregated facility "superior." If it is feasible to duplicate those services, placement in the segregated setting is inappropriate. Thus, courts must determine what is and is not feasible in each case where the segregated and nonsegregated programs are the only two options presented.

This approach seems valid for two reasons, at least. First, it forces courts to make a decision based on the student's rights to an appropriate education and to an integrated setting for that education. Alternatively stated, this approach is a student-centered, individualized determination, consistent with the EHA's overall approach.

Second, this approach forces the courts to look into what can be done ("feasible") to modify the otherwise inappropriate integrated setting. Alternatively stated, it forces the courts to require the schools to show why an integrated setting cannot be modified or accommodated to the student. Under this approach, the schools bear the burden of proof that an integrated setting (that is, the student's right to an integrated, least restrictive education) cannot possibly satisfy the "educational benefit" standard of *Rowley* (the student's right to an appropriate education). The *Roncker* approach is an excellent illustration of the LRA principle at work. The principle requires that state's interests in providing an appropriate education be balanced with and, if possible (feasible), merged with and, at least, balanced with the individual student's interest in associating with nondisabled students.

But what does "feasible" mean? *Roncker* defines the term by stating three exceptions to the appropriateness/integration requirement: "(S)ome handicapped children simply must be educated in segregated facilities either because the handicapped child would not benefit from mainstreaming, because any marginal benefits received from mainstreaming are far outweighed by the benefits gained from services which could not feasibly be provided in the nonsegregated setting, or because the handicapped child is a disruptive force in the nonsegregated setting."

The three exceptions, then, are:

1. No benefit to the child;
2. Greater benefits in segregated settings even after the feasibility standard is applied (that is, after the courts determine what segregated-setting services can be created in nonsegregated settings);
3. Disruption in a nonsegregated setting.

The court then said:

> Cost is a proper factor to consider since excessive spending on one handicapped child deprives other handicapped children. ...Cost is no defense, however, if a school district has failed to use its funds to provide a proper continuum of alternative placements for handicapped children. The provision of such alternative placements benefits all handicapped children.

Here, the court clearly uses a "competing equities" approach. As explained in chapters 3 and 5, competing equities issues always raise this question: At whose expense, and at how much expense, is one person to be given an advantage? Or, to what extent will one or more people be burdened to give an advantage to another? The court's use of the competing equities approach is apparent when it says that "excessive spending on one handicapped child deprives other handicapped children." That is, the "equity" of one child can be too expensive to require other children to pay for.

As appealing as this approach might be (in light of the fact that school districts have limited local, state, and federal funds in special education and must educate all handicapped children appropriately), there is something wrong about it. Namely, the court assumes that a benefit for one student is not or cannot be a benefit for others as well.

In fact, what may seem to be excessive expenditures for one student may create benefits for others. If a school facility, program, curriculum, or faculty/staff is modified to accommodate one student's right to an appropriate education, the modification also may create benefits for others. There is no necessary or unavoidable connection between spending for one student and not having adequate funds for another. True, there may be such cases, but they are apt to be infrequent, as when a child whose accommodations are very expensive is the only one for whom the accommodations are, or most likely will be, beneficial and the school district is relatively poor. But the usual case will be the opposite: An accommodation for one will be an accommodation for others, if not immediately, then within a relatively short time.

The court said more than that excessive expenditures on one student may cause a disadvantage to others. It also pointed out that cost is "no defense" if the district has not provided a "proper continuum" of alternative placements. Thus, if a district does not provide an alternative to an integrated appropriate program, it may not complain about the cost of modifying the integrated one. This is true because the "marginal benefit" exception to integrated education requires the courts to compare segregated and nonsegregated programs. When there is no segregated program to compare to an integrated program, the school district can hardly complain that it must provide integrated education, since it must, under the EHA, provide not only an appropriate education but also, if feasible, one that is integrated. The "cost-is-a-consideration" approach does have its limitations after all: It does not apply when a court can make no choice at all between one program and another.

One other case shows that cost is a consideration in balancing the student's right to an appropriate education against the right to an integrated education. In *A.W. v. Northwest R-1 School District,* decided by the Eighth Circuit Court of Appeals in 1987, the court of appeals upheld a lower court decision to place a child with severe mental retardation into a segregated program. The district court had concluded that no certified teacher is available for the student in an integrated program, and that the addition of a teacher is not an acceptable solution because "the funds available are limited so that placing a [certified] teacher [in the integrated setting] for the benefit of a few students at best, and possibly only one child, [A.W.], would directly reduce the educational benefits provided to other handicapped students by increasing the number of students taught by a single teacher [in the segregated setting]." To educate the one child in an integrated setting creates a benefit for that child, but the benefit is "insufficient to justify a reduction in unquestionable benefits to other handicapped children which would result from an inequitable expenditure of the finite funds available."

The court of appeals upheld the district court. In doing so, it relied on *Roncker* as allowing a court to consider cost to the district and benefit to the child (as cost-benefit approach). It also relied on *Rowley's* observation that available financial resources must be equitably distributed among all handicapped children.

Reasons for the Cost-Consideration Approach. It is clear that the courts are applying an economic analysis to the EHA requirement that appropriate education be provided in the integrated setting to the maximum extent appropriate. Why are the courts taking this approach? The obvious reason is that they are very reluctant to become involved in issues of school financing. This is a familiar posture for the courts.

The Political Thicket and Separation of Powers. The Supreme Court's decision in *San Antonio Independent School District v. Rodriquez* in 1973 clearly is the basis for this reluctance to get involved in school financing. In that case, the issue before the Court was whether the state's system of supporting local school districts discriminated against the poorer districts in favor of the wealthier ones. The Court refused to rule on the matter, holding that there is no federal constitutional right under the equal protection doctrine to equal subsidies in school financing.

In *Rodriquez,* the Court made it very clear that it wanted to avoid the "political thicket" that would entangle it if it were to hold that such a right exists. Holding that such a right exists would require it to determine whether the states have violated such a right. That decision, in turn, would require it to create remedies to correct a violation. To create remedies, however, is to become involved in the most fundamental of all legislative decisions—namely, how a state and its political subdivisions should raise and spend money to apportion equally among its school districts. Thus, the Court's concern about the separation of powers doctrine—that legislatures enact laws and appropriate funds to carry them out, and courts interpret and apply the laws in disputes—impelled the Court to steer clear of the fiscal-allocation and legislative-determinations involved in school financing.

That is one political thicket that the Court earlier learned to avoid. After all, it had been embroiled in school governance and legislative matters as a result of its school desegregation decision in *Brown.* And it had been equally involved in state legislative matters as a result of its decisions in the legislative reapportionment cases that began with *Baker v. Carr* and *Reynolds v. Sims.* Clearly, it was not going to become involved in another such thicket, and thus it ducked the school financing issue in *Rodriquez* and continued to avoid it in *Rowley.* Thus, the doctrine of separation of powers justified the courts in avoiding these matters that are fundamentally legislative, not judicial, dispute-resolutions.

Congressional Intent and Majoritarian Decision Making. But there is another reason for the courts' reluctance to become involved as a superordinary school board, or even as a supervisor of state legislative decisions. It is, as the Supreme Court pointed out in *Rowley,* that "(t)he primary responsibility for formulating the education to be accorded to a handicapped child, and for choosing the educational method most suitable to the child's needs, was left by the [Education of the Handicapped] Act to state and local educational agencies in cooperation with the parents or guardian of the child."

Alternatively stated, the Congress has chosen to limit the courts' role in making educational decisions. For the courts to make any incursion into educational policy matters, therefore, would be opposite congressional intent. That is to say, it would violate the decisions made by the elected representatives of the people. It would be "undemocratic" in the very basic sense that it would violate the will of the people. It would be "anti-majoritarian." As long as the Constitution itself does not prohibit a certain legislative result, there is no reason, the Court in *Rowley* is saying, for courts to substitute their judgments for those of the representatives of the people.

This principle of majoritarian democracy—that the will of the people is expressed in laws enacted by their representatives—is the foundation for judicial restraint, or for judicial conservatism. It also is the principle that allows the courts to escape from making educational—that is, "professional" or "scientific"—decisions and for deferring to the judgment of experts in those fields.

State-Local Government, Federal Government, and Federalism. There is a third reason for the courts' reluctance to become too closely involved in matters of school governance and educational policy making. It is based on the principle of federalism. Federalism (as explained in chapters 1 and 2) is a principle of government that allocates responsibility and power between the federal government, on the one hand, and among the states, on the other. It rests on the premise that shared responsibility and power are means for checking and balancing powers of all governments, and checks and balances are necessary and desirable to advance the interest of the people in liberty and the pursuit of their interests (including the pursuit of "happiness" and property) by various means.

Federalism also rests on the assumption that the pursuit of people's interests requires a great deal of flexibility and variability in the ways chosen by the federal, state, and local governments. Because people are so different and have so many different interests, no single government and certainly no single response ("answer") to their needs and interests will do the whole job.

The EHA takes the federalism principle into account by allowing states to create a continuum of services and to satisfy students' rights to an appropriate education in the least restrictive setting-program by choosing not only from the continuum but also from various means of delivering services (such as curriculum, methodology, teacher certification, staff-student ratios) within the continuum.

As the Supreme Court said in *Rowley,* the EHA leaves the primary responsibility on these matters to the state and local education agencies and to parents. Thus, the principle of federalism is another reason explaining the courts' reluctance to become the super-ordinary school boards.

Parental and Professional Decision Making; Judicial Deference. Finally, the rights and interests of parents and educators constitute a reason for the courts to avoid becoming too involved in matters of education. If the courts begin to become heavily involved, they will begin to displace parents' rights and natural instincts to rear their children in ways suitable to or chosen by the parents, consistent with parents' duties to act in ways that do not hurt their children. The Supreme Court itself has recognized the important and valuable role that parents have in their children's education and care, most recently in the *Parham* decision, involving the parents' right to place their children in state psychiatric or mental retardation institutions.

In addition, if the courts become heavily involved in educational decision making, they will displace the experts, substituting judicial opinion for that of educators. The Supreme Court is clearly reluctant to do this, as its decisions in *Davis* (see chapter 3) and *Rowley* (see chapter 3, also) point out. And courts as a whole have reasons not to substitute their judgment of professionals, as the discussion on classification (see chapter 4) indicates.

REBUTTING THE PRESUMPTION

It should be fairly evident by now that the LRA presumption has been overcome more often than many "integrationists" wanted or expected. Some of the justifications for rebuttal clearly emanate from the appropriate education principle, as construed and applied. And there are additional reasons why LRA has not compelled integration.

The Harmful Effects Issue

Is the harmful effect of institutional placement a standard for defining appropriate education? Curiously, none of the courts, save one,[94] appear to have been faced with an argument that placement in institutional or residential settings would have a harmful effect on the handicapped child and therefore not be appropriate, despite the well known data and cases indicating that such placement can cause the handicapped child to regress.[95] Indeed, one court explicitly adopted the contrary view, saying that the child would regress if he were excluded from an institution for emotionally disturbed chidren.[96] Another court ordered residential placement of a schizophrenic child because evidence showed that she had made no meaningful progress in a regular school environment and was experiencing some intellectual regression there.[97] The only court that did consider the institutional regression factor could not have failed to do so, for the parties had entered into a prior consent decree requiring the defendants to deinstitutionalize the plaintiff-class children.[98]

Statutory and regulatory language excuses the LRA from being applied to a child who cannot be educated satisfactorily in regular programs or schools even with the use of supplementary aids and services. This is the harmful effects standard. The harmful effect of integrating the handicapped child is a legitimate concern. Likewise, departmental comments about regulations under Section 504 entitle schools to place the handicapped child outside of regular education if placement in a regular classroom would significantly impair the education of nonhandicapped children. The harmful effect of integration on nonhandicapped children, thus, is another legitimate concern.

As chapter 3 demonstrates, this is precisely the approach adopted in *Honig* and the other expulsion cases and in the AIDS cases. Both of these harmful effects criteria reflect a more general "competing equities" concern: To what extent should children (handicapped or not) be disadvantaged (by LRA integration) at the expense of others or at their own expense?

The harmful effects application of the competing equities doctrine (essentially, a familiar "balancing" test) is at work in several cases. For example, in *Tatro v. Texas,* the court was faced with deciding whether clean intermittent catheterization is a related service that a school must furnish to a spina bifida child with normal intelligence. The school sought to avoid that responsibility and assigned the student to homebound status, effectively blocking her presence in any programs at school sites. The court weighed the catheterization "burden" the schools would face with the exclusion the child would face and ruled in her favor. Similar balancing occurred in *Cox v. Brown,* [99] where the competing interests were those of the Department of Defense in avoiding the cost of residential placement of two learning disabled youths and the certainty that they would experience the humiliation of failure in DoD programs.

It appears, then, that the harmful effects test is solidly entrenched as a factor in determining whether a handicapped child will be educated appropriately. Its effect, however, is far from singular: It does not always prevent residential or institutional placement (more restrictive placement, in the stereotypic view); nor does it always command regular education placement. It is an important factor and requires careful attention to individualized, child-specific considerations.

The harmful effects issue is especially important because of its direct relationship to one of the values that LRA seeks to advance—the *appropriate* education of handicapped children. But the states' responsibilities extend to nonhandicapped children, too. If placing a handicapped child in a program with nonhandicapped children negatively affects the education of the latter, the states' responsibilities to them are compromised. And if it does no good for the handicapped child either, the states' responsibilities to all students are jeopardized.

Prediction and Placement

Most of the cases relying on the harmful effects exception have involved children whose education in less restrictive programs has been demonstrably unsatisfactory. Evidence of failure was so compelling as to require the children to be placed in a more restrictive (less integrated) program or school. It is not beyond the pale of fair inference to suggest that the more normal placements or programs would have been more restrictive, because less beneficial, for these children.

But these cases raise a disturbing question: Must the child always be subjected to experiences (placements or programs) in which he or she predictably will not be educated satisfactorily before he or she can be placed in more restrictive programs? Or will educators, related services personnel, and parents be able to place the child in the less integrated placements or programs on the basis of reasonable, professionally defensible expectations, projections, or predictions that the child will benefit from less restrictive programs as much as from more restrictive ones? In one case,[100] the clear answer is that professionally defensible predictions are permissible foundations for placements; the risk of unsatisfactory integration does not have to be undertaken.

Besides legitimizing a common practice, this decision seems to venture into the morass of uncertainty raised by the involuntary commitment cases—the quagmire of prediction of dangerousness.[101] Upon closer analysis, however, it is not so easy to make the analogy stick. The prediction of dangerousness is bogged down in the muddy soil of psychiatry, whereas the prediction of unsatisfactory school experiences seems to be on firmer soil—namely, the ability of educators to assess school programs and placements, fairly accurately measure handicapped children's potential, and make a not unhappy match between the two.

How a person will behave in future environments that are not clearly foreseeable is a different matter than how a child will function in well known educational settings or programs. On the whole, prediction of future educational success or failure seems acceptable, albeit unenviable for courts, particularly in light of the procedural safeguards afforded by special education law, IEPs, periodic review of the child's placement or classification as a handicapped child, and parent participation in the child's education. There are, moreover, critical differences between the deprivation of liberty through involuntary commitment and concomitant institutionalization and special education placement.

None of this is meant to suggest that prediction of failure in integrated settings should be made lightly (the evidence should be clear and convincing) or that the pressure on public education to accommodate all handicapped children, regardless of the nature or extent of their handicaps, in community-based programs should be diminished. It *is* acceptable to predict; it is not acceptable to subject handicapped children (and their parents) to the probable effects of failure.

As indicated previously, an exception to the LRA presumption is permissible under the Section 504 regulations (as interpreted by the enforcing agency) when the handicapped child poses (a prediction issue again) or is a danger to nonhandicapped children or educators. Although courts have applied this exception to permit the LRA presumption to be rebutted, they also seem to graft two other conditions onto this exception: If the child is dangerous to self[102] or to property,[103] the presumption can be overcome. In these cases, there was concurrent evidence of dangerousness to others and the children were severely handicapped. If there were isolated evidence of dangerousness to self only or to property only, it remains to be seen if the exception would obtain.

Educability

Courts seem to weigh other competing equities considerations in deciding whether to apply the harmful effects exemption. As indicated by *Timothy W. v. Rochester* (discussed in chapter 3), the child's educability—or ineducability—is a dispositive factor in whether the zero reject rule will prevent a profoundly retarded child from being excluded from *any* educational programs, much less those that are comparably more or less restrictive. Until that case, the issue had yet to be decided.

In *Matthews v. Campbell,* the surface issue was the placement of a profoundly re-tarded child. The placement choices were a residential facility for retarded children and adults or a community-based public school program. With blatant gratuity, the court on its own initiative raised the underlying issue of the case: If a child cannot be educated in any sense of the word—totally incapable of learning anything—and if progress in either the public school program or the institutional program is nil, what responsibilities does a school system or any residential program have to that child?

The educability issue was latent in *Matthews:* If the child is ineducable, does the law entitle him (or her) to any educational program at all, however restrictive or atypical it might be? Or does the law permit the child to be totally excluded from the educational system or from placement in residential programs at the expense of educational agencies? Does the least restrictive placement principle have an end? Is there a point along any con-tinuum when, because of the child's ineducability, the continuum terminates? If so, LRA arguably no longer applies since, by definition, an ineducable child cannot be educated. In its legal posture, this is a question of zero reject and equal protection: Do federal or state special education laws tolerate any zero reject exceptions and, if so, does the ex-cluded child suffer an equal protection violation because he or she, unlike any other stu-dent, is excluded?

The answer in *Timothy W.* was unfavorable to the child at the district (trial) court level; the prospect for it being unfavorable in *Matthews* certainly existed. As Judge Merhige said:

> Candor compels the Court to admit that it is not optimistic about plaintiff's future. The Court is especially concerned about what options, if any, it will have should it become apparent that a residential placement is not the appropriate setting for plaintiff. Neither the language of the Act nor the legislative history appears to contemplate the possibility that certain children may simply be untrainable. Should the Court ultimately conclude that, contrary to the still unsupported expert opinions, plaintiff is not trainable, what options are then available?
>
> At least one commentator has observed that the "Act contains no exclusions for ex-ceptionally severe handicaps." ... The Court, however, may be faced with considering if there are any reasonable exceptions from this absolute position. A reading of the legislative history suggests that Congress was primarily concerned with handicapped children who, despite their limitations, are capable in some ways of learning and even of being creative and productive. The instant plaintiff, regrettably, almost certainly does not fall in this category.
>
> That there may be some latitude for equitable relief based upon a common sense reading of the Act is perhaps suggested by the Supreme Court's recent decision in *South-eastern Community College v. Davis.* ... In *Davis* the Court found the critical language of Section 504 of the Rehabilitation Act of 1973 (a precursor in some respects to the Ed-ucation for All Handicapped Act) not to be so absolute as to require petitioner to admit respondent, who was legally deaf, to its nursing school. In this regard, should it become apparent that a residential placement cannot provide plaintiff an appropriate education, the Court suggests the parties be prepared to address the question of what options, if any, will then be available to the Court. [Citations omitted]

It seems significant that at least two federal courts have taken a different view of educability. In *Gladys J. v. Pearland Independent School District,* a schizophrenic child, who may also have been moderately to severely mentally retarded, was placed in a residential school, but the court rejected the idea that the child was unable to learn despite her severe multiple disabilities. And in *Campbell v. Talladega,* the court explicitly found, on the basis of the evidence, that a severely retarded boy had demonstrated his ability to learn. Yet, the *Timothy W.* district court seemed to say this: LRA does not apply to an educable child, at least as a matter of the EHA. What is or is not "restrictive" is a moot point when the child cannot be educated at all.

Competing Equities (Other than Costs)

Competing equities problems arise in other troublesome guises in the appropriate education-LRA cases. Thus, the risk that an interpreter for a hearing impaired child might distract nonhandicapped children was discounted by the *Rowley* district court as essentially a *de minimus* (minimal) concern. And in *New York ARC v. Carey,* the hazard of infection from retarded carriers of hepatitis B likewise was found inconsequential. The very fact, however, that distraction and contagion were considered to be competing equities factors suggests that, in a different case (where the interests of nonhandicapped children are more substantial, as in the danger-to-others cases such as the expulsion or AIDS cases), the exception might apply and a sort of reverse discrimination judgment could be entered—the harmful effects standard being the ostensible justification but the realignment of competing interests being the real one.

Expulsion: Not an LRA Option

Unlike the harmful effects cases, which are statutorily grounded in appropriate education-LRA concepts, cases involving the attempted expulsion of handicapped children rely instead on statutory zero reject[104] principles. These cases appear to have only an indirect relevance to LRA, but the fact of the matter is that they are well positioned within an LRA ambit. The most restrictive educational placement, after all, is outside any educational program—total exclusion of the purest kind. Courts recognize this when they prohibit a handicapped child from being expelled when the cause of the disruptive behavior is the handicap. The harmful effect of the behavior on self and others is the bedrock factual issue in these cases. Instead, courts allow only a change of placement from a more regular/normal program to a more restrictive/special one, pursuant to a modification in the child's IEP.

The courts thus silently recognize not only that expulsion would be the greatest harm the handicapped child might experience but also that the LRA presumption is properly rebutted when the justification is keeping the child in *some* educational program. Yet the courts have not articulated this rationale for their decisions. Instead, they rely on congressional intent and statutory zero reject rules.

There can be no doubt, however, concerning the effect of these decisions: They bring the handicapped child's interests into sharp relief by preventing expulsion—the most harmful effect of all and the most restrictive placement of all. The zero reject principle thus limits the power of schools to expel some handicapped children, and simultaneously it limits the LRA continuum: The most restrictive placement is necessarily one within the continuum (i.e., within a free appropriate education, wherever furnished), not outside it (i.e., beyond a free appropriate education, wherever furnished). Exclusion is not an option. It is, by definition, too restrictive.

Conclusion

What defensible conclusions can be drawn from the cases and the foregoing analysis of them? Surely, one is that the courts are capable of tremendous sensitivity toward handicapped children and their parents. This is particularly encouraging in light of the Supreme Court's *Parham* decision, which was hardly a paradigm for the expression of concern for mentally disabled children, and *Davis,* a decision that reeked of paternalism.

Beyond this sensitivity lies a sense that there are so many complexities in the nature and degree of handicapping conditions that marching lock-step down a stereotypical least restrictive continuum is bound to result in inappropriate education for some children. The child's needs—his or her rights to and interest in appropriate education, even when furnished in residential or institutional settings—seem to prevail when the extent of the disability is more severe or profound than mild or moderate. The contrary seems to obtain when the disability is less handicapping: The right to an appropriate education is more likely to be satisfied when the child is placed in regular settings or programs. In some cases, rights to appropriateness (to satisfy the need) and to integration occur simultaneously, leading to the same recommendations for placement. In others, courts are applying LRA by taking into account the relative "richness" or "poverty" of educational services in separate, nonintegrated programs and the likelihood that such programs will be more enhancing for a handicapped child than not.

Still another conclusion emerges. Judicial interpretation and application of LRA rest on a sense of *appropriate education,* a concept that, by using a continuum approach does not exclude separate and segregated placements or programs. It appears, then, that courts do not so misunderstand and misapply the LRA principle in the context of the continuum options that it becomes a force for limiting handicapped children by denying them an appropriate education or for limiting educators by restricting their ability to educate handicapped people appropriately.

One concern expressed in the AAMR publication on LRA—namely, that LRA should become infused with a sense of liberation, not of restriction[105]—seems to be shared by many courts. The courts seem to construe LRA as a tool for making sure that handicapped children, their parents, and their educators have available to them choices that restrict their freedom to the minimum extent necessary. In a sense, then, the child's needs do prevail over his or her rights, where appropriate, and enhancing placement (the need) conflicts with a presumption in favor of integration (the presumptive right to LRA).

The risk of complacently accepting and sanctioning this result is that judicial legitimization of separate (segregating) or institutional placement is tantamount to judicial approval of the separate schools, programs, and institutions themselves. This is both paradoxical and unfortunate.

The paradox comes about because many courts have condemned institutional conditions on constitutional (Eighth Amendment) and other (*quid pro quo*) grounds.[106] It is odd that other courts, not squarely facing the institutional reform case, would bless institutional placement in right-to-education cases.

The misfortune arises because there are unacceptable consequences of institutionalization.[107] At the least, the child is put at risk of regression;[108] public school systems are relieved of the pressure to accommodate severely handicapped children in their own programs (but not of the enormous cost of institutionalization); family ties can be attenuated (but family stress can be reduced); and "throw-away" children are put out of sight and out of mind.

In all of this, there is special irony. One of the values that LRA explicitly seeks to advance is that of the right of association. If handicapped children are free to associate with nonhandicapped children in the public schools, the argument goes, the stigma and discrimination visited upon them *de facto* or *de jure* will dissipate and handicapped people will be less restricted, more liberated. Yet, parents also share the stigma that attends their handicapped children. Some have sought to (or thought they could) escape their child's and their own stigmatization by institutionalizing their children or having them educated only with other handicapped children (in special classes, special schools, or special school districts). Thus, some parents seem to contribute to the very stigma they seek to avoid.

To the extent that the LRA doctrine creates educationally enhancing programs for handicapped children in the public schools, it may be a technique for reducing public opinion that less able people are less worthy and increasing public acceptance of different (handicapped) children and their families. But if some parents, some educators, and some courts continue to rely on institutional, residential placements, LRA will not be as useful as it might be in achieving either the values of an appropriate education or the right of (stigma-free) association.

LRA as a constitutional principle seeks to curtail overreaching by government. It was not intended, and should not be used, to restrict reasonable choices by courts, families, professionals, or handicapped people. But, as used by the courts upon the initiative of some parents and educators in the LRA education cases, it does not realize one of its greatest potentials: It does not compel the creation of more acceptable, more enhancing, less harmful placement options that are noninstitutional. In implementing LRA in these cases, the courts have not focused on the *creation* of appropriate educational placements, only on the selection of one of two available choices, both apparently reasonable in the context of education of a handicapped child and given the continuum approach to educational services.

The legally and educationally defensible placement is the one that is least restrictive of rights of education and association among those available that would adequately serve the child. The courts, however, are myopic and unimaginative because they have failed to use LRA, as it has been used in other disability cases, to create acceptable alternatives to institutions.[109] True, they recognize the handicapped child's needs and decline to restrict those charged with his or her care.

But that posture, though necessary, is hardly sufficient. To refuse to eliminate or limit restrictive alternatives may inhibit the creation of less liberty-restrictive ones that can serve a person's interests equally well. Until the courts use LRA as an affirmative, rights-creating tool, their decisions will merit only qualified approval. In the words of the AAMR book, "The focus of LRE implementation must remain in the creation of less restrictive alternatives, rather than on the reduction of unduly restrictive choices."[110]

It is true that the courts have failed on the whole to require SEAs or LEAs to create programs of appropriate education within integrated settings. Even *Roncker's* test of feasibility (of modifying the integrated setting) does not seem to be forceful enough. Instead, they have been content to defer to expert judgment about the student's educational needs and, depending on the extent of the child's disability and the experts' opinion, have chosen between the existing alternatives.

Those who favor judicial restraint (judicial conservatism) will argue that such an approach is proper. Those who favor judicial creativity (judicial activism) will object to this approach.

Yet it is clear that the forced choice—between one type of program and setting and another—is one that the EHA and state law creates. That is, Congress and state legislatures have decided to rely on a continuum-of-services approach. Given this policy choice, courts themselves are reluctant to undo the policy by forcing one program and setting (e.g., an "integrated" one) to become more appropriate for the student's education. Of course, they could use their remedial powers to change the policies, and perhaps they should.

Is it only the courts' fault that the LRA doctrine still allows, indeed encourages, segregated placements? The answer has to be no. Institutions and other segregated special education are the creation of some policy makers in Congress and in state legislatures; of some educators, psychologists, physicians, and other professionals; and of some parents. As chapter 4 pointed out, the reasons for classification, and thus for segregation, are powerful, longstanding, and not always correctable by law made by judges.

The "fault" that there is a continuum from which courts may choose thus is attributable to those who created the continuum in the first place. It is entirely defensible to criticize the courts for allowing the presumption in favor of integration (the LRA doctrine in education) to be rebutted (in my judgment, too often). But it also is worth remembering: Reducing the continuum, so that certain placements are no longer possible, and concurrently expanding appropriate programs in integrated settings, is a choice for policy makers in legislatures and executive agencies, and for professionals and parents alike.

As pointed out earlier in this chapter (under the discussion about why costs are a consideration), there are reasons why courts are reluctant to be more active in prescribing remedies that exceed the policy choices made by legislatures. Whether these reasons are satisfactory is for the reader to determine.

NOTES

1. *See, e.g.,* Covington v. Harris, Lake v. Cameron, Shelton v. Tucker; Ellis, Boggs, Brooks, and Biklen, *The Least Restrictive Alternative: Principles and Practices,* edited by Turnbull (Washington, D.C.: American Association on Mental Retardation, 1981) (hereafter called Least Restrictive Alternative). *See also* Chambers, "Alternatives to Civil Commitment of the Mentally Ill: Practical Guides and Constitutional Imperatives," 70 *Michigan Law Review* 1108 (1972) (least restrictive alternative in context of civil commitment).

2. Chambers, *supra* n. 1, at pp. 1108, 1150.

3. *See, e.g.,* Pike v. Bruce Church, Dean Milk v. City of Madison. *See also* Wormuth and Mirkin, "The Doctrine of the Reasonable Alternative," 9 *Utah Law Review* 254 (1964) (application of LRA to commerce clause, police power, and due process, first amendment, and procedural rights).

4. *See, e.g.,* Dunn v. Blumstein (voting rights); U.S. v. Robel, *citing* NAACP v. Button (freedom of association); Griswold v. Connecticut (right of privacy); Aptheker v. Sec'y. of State (right to travel); and Talley v. California (freedom of speech).

5. *See, e.g.,* Brenneman v. Madigan. *See generally,* "Constitutional Limitations on the Conditions of Pretrial Detention," 79 *Yale Law Journal* 941 (1970) (use of LRA in context of pretrial detention); and Wormuth and Mirkin, *supra* n. 3, at pp. 293-96.

6. Toomer v. Witsell, 334 U.S. 385 (1948).

7. *See, e.g.,* Covington v. Harris; Lake v. Cameron (*en banc*) ("Deprivation of liberty solely because of dangers to the ill persons themselves should not go beyond what is necessary for their protection"); Halderman v. Pennhurst State School and Hosp.; Dixon v. Weinberger; Lessard v. Schmidt; Wyatt v. Stickney. *See also* Least Restrictive Alternative, *supra* n. 1, at pp. 21-22.

8. *See* Least Restrictive Alternative, *supra* n. 1, at p. 28. *See also* Youngberg v. Romeo ("The state is under a duty to provide respondent with such training as an appropriate professional would consider reasonable to ensure his safety and to facilitate his ability to function free from bodily restraints").

9. Yarbrough, "The Burger Court and Unspecified Rights," *Duke Law Journal* 143, 154 (1977).

10. 20 U.S.C. Sec. 1413(a)(1976).

11. *See* Least Restrictive Alternative, *supra* n. 1, at pp. 21-25.

12. *E.g.,* the right to an abortion within the first 3 months of pregnancy. *See* Doe v. Bolton and Roe v. Wade. *See also* Bellotti v. Baird and Planned Parenthood of Central Missouri v. Danforth, both on the right to contraception; and O'Connor v. Donaldson, on right to liberty.

13. PARC, at p. 307 (amended consent agreement).

14. *See, e.g.,* LeBanks v. Spears, Panitch v. Wisconsin, and State of Wisconsin *ex rel.* Warren v. Nusbaum.

15. *See* O'Connor v. Donaldson, Jackson v. Indiana, Shelton v. Tucker, Covington v. Harris, Dixon v. Attorney General, and Lake v. Cameron.

16. *See* Pennhurst v. Halderman, Wyatt v. Stickney, Welsch v. Likins, New York ARC v. Rockefeller, Wouri v. Zitnay, and Evans v. D.C. Bd. of Ed. *See also* Stone, "Overview: The Right to Treatment—Comment on the Law and Its Impact," 132 *American Journal of Psychology* 1125 (1975).

17. An explicit origin of the minimum intrusion principle is found in Dean Milk v. Madison, at pp. 354-56, where the court found a city ordinance unconstitutional under the commerce clause. The ordinance prohibited the sale of milk within the city that had been processed more than 25 miles outside of the city. The court found that less drastic measures could protect the citizens from bad milk without banning the sale of nonlocally processed milk. For an earlier case in which LRA-

minimum intrusion is applied, *see* Toomer v. Witsell. The minimum intrusion principle has also been used in other cases that necessitated the balancing of individual interests against governmental needs: Dunn v. Blumstein (right to vote); U.S. v. Robel and NAACP v. Button (right to associate); Griswold v. Connecticut (right to privacy); Aptheker v. Sec'y. of State and Kent v. Dulles (right to travel); Sherbert v. Verner (freedom of religion); and Talley v. California (right to free speech). In all of these cases, government activity and infringement of a constitutional right both triggered the minimum intrusion LRE/LRA principle. For a discussion of LRA, *see* Struve, "The Less-Restrictive Alternative Principle and Economic Due Process," 80 *Harvard Law Review* 1463 (1967) and Note, "Less Drastic Means and the First Amendment," 78 *Yale Law Review* 464 (1969).

18. *Federal Register*, May 4, 1977, p. 22691.

19. *See* Lessard v. Schmidt (discussed right of state to deprive an individual of liberty due to mental disability); Cohen, Oosterhout, and Leviton, "Tailoring Guardianship to the Needs of Mentally Handicapped Citizens," 6 *Maryland Legal Forum* 91 (1976); and Horstman, "Protective Services for the Elderly: The Limits of Parens Patriae," 40 *Missouri Law Review* 215 (1975) (discusses *parens patriae* as applied to the elderly).

20. *See* Youngberg v. Romeo: "[T]here certainly is no reason to think judges or juries are better qualified than appropriate professionals in making such decisions [about what is a reasonable restraint on a retarded individual's liberty interest consistent with his safety]. ... For these reasons, the decision, if made by a professional, is presumptively valid; [42 U.S.C. Sec. 1983 (1976)] liability may be imposed only when the decision by the professional is such a substantial departure from accepted professional judgment, practice or standards as to demonstrate that the person responsible actually did not base the decision on such a judgment." *See also* Parham v. J.R. (commitment of children under age 18 is largely a medical and parental decision).

21. *See, e.g.,* Halderman v. Pennhurst State School and Hosp., Wyatt v. Stickney, and Covington v. Harris. *Cf.* Heryford v. Parker ("likelihood of involuntary incarceration ... commands observance of the constitutional safeguards of due process"). For informative analyses of this problem, *see* Wexler, *Mental Health Law: Major Issues* (New York: Plenum Press, 1981), pp. 11-59; Morse, "Crazy Behavior," 51 *Southern California Law Review* 527 (1978); Cohn, "Standards for Civil Commitment and the Right to Liberty," in 1 *Legal Rights of Mentally Disabled Persons,* edited by Friedman et al. (New York: Practicing Law Institute, 1979); Burt, "The Constitution of the Family," in *Supreme Court Review,* edited by Kurland and Casper (Chicago: University of Chicago Press, 1979), pp. 329-95; Teitelbaum and Ellis, "The Liberty Interest of Children: Due Process Rights and Their Application," 12 *Family Law Quarterly* 153 (1978); Ennis and Litwack, "Psychiatry and the Presumption of Expertise: Flipping Coins in the Courtroom," 62 *California Law Review* 693 (1974).

22. *See generally* Wolfensberger, *The Principle of Normalization in Human Services* (Toronto: National Institute of Mental Retardation, 1972); and Kugel and Wolfensberger, editors, *Changing Patterns in Residential Services for the Mentally Retarded* (Washington, D.C.: President's Committee on Mental Retardation, 1969).

23. *See, e.g.,* Mills and PARC.

24. *See, e.g.,* Brown v. Bd. of Ed. (abolished "separate but equal" doctrine; ordered desegregation of public schools); Gong Lum v. Rice (natural citizen, child of Chinese extraction, not denied equal protection when assigned to "separate but equal" school); Cumming v. Bd. of Ed. (federal government should not interfere with state economic reasons for closing school for blacks while leaving open school for whites); Plessy v. Ferguson (doctrine that "separate but equal" facilities satisfies equal protection).

25. *See* Watson v. City of Cambridge.

26. *See generally* Kanner, *A History of the Care and Study of the Mentally Retarded* (Springfield, Ill.: Charles Thomas, 1964); and Kauffman, "Nineteenth Century Views of Children's Behavior Disorders: Historical Contributions and Continuing Issues," 10 *Journal of Special Education* 335 (1976).

27. Sarason and Doris, *Educational Handicap, Public Policy, and Social History: A Broadened Perspective on Mental Retardation* (New York: Free Press, 1979), pp. 179-80.

28. *Ibid.*, pp. 282-95.

29. *See generally* Gleidman and Roth, *The Unexpected Minority: Handicapped Children in America* (New York: Harcourt Brace Jovanovich, 1981).

30. *See* P.L. 94-142, Sec. 3(b), (3) and (4) [commentary to 20 U.S.C. Sec. 1401 (1982)]; *Congressional Record* 25,526 (statement of findings and purpose), 25,537-38 (daily ed. July 29, 1975) (statement of Rep. Ford).

31. *See generally* Levine and Wexler, *PL 94-142: An Act of Congress* (New York: Macmillan, 1981); Comment, "The Least Restrictive Environment Section of the Education for All Handicapped Children Act of 1975: A Legislative History and An Analysis," 13 *Gonzaga Law Review* 717 (1978).

32. For a good recent illustration of functional exclusion, *see* Campbell v. Talladega County Bd. of Ed. *See also* Mattie T. v. Holladay, LeBanks v. Spears, PARC, and MARC v. Maryland.

33. *See* Gleidman and Roth, *supra* n. 29, at pp. 178-82, 204-8. *See also* Nazzaro, "Comprehensive Assessment for Educational Planning," in *Public Policy and the Education of Exceptional Children,* edited by Weintraub, Abeson, Ballard, and LaVor (Reston, Va.: Council for Exceptional Children, 1976) (hereafter called Public Policy); and Miller and Miller, "The Education for the Handicapped Act: How Well Does It Accomplish Its Goal of Promoting the Least Restrictive Environment for Education?" 28 *DePaul Law Review* 321, 339 (1979).

34. *See* Sarason and Doris, *supra* n. 27, at pp. 321-54; Miller and Miller, *supra* n. 33, at pp. 339-40.

35. Milofsky, "Why Special Education Isn't Special," 44 *Harvard Educational Review* 437 (1974).

36. *See* Kirp, Buss, and Kuriloff, "Legal Reform of Special Education: Empirical Studies and Procedural Proposals," 62 *California Law Review* 40; Kirp, "Schools as Sorters," 121 *Pennsylvania Law Review* 705 (1973); and Children's Defense Fund, *Children Out of School in America* (Cambridge, Ma.: Author, 1974).

37. *See* New York State Commission, *Report on the Quality, Cost and Financing of Elementary and Secondary Education,* 9 B. 2 (1972), *cited* in Kirp et al., *supra* n. 36; Hobbs, *The Futures of Children* (San Francisco: Jossey-Bass, 1975); Education Commission of the States, *States with Comprehensive Legislation and Education Services for Handicapped Children* (Denver: Author, 1974); Marinelli, "Financing the Education of Exceptional Children," in Public Policy, *supra* n. 33; Dunn, "Special Education for the Mildly Retarded—Is Much of Is Justifiable?" 35 *Exceptional Children* 5 (1968); Mercer, *Labeling the Mentally Retarded* (Berkeley: University of California Press, 1973); Budoff, "Providing Special Education without Special Classes," 10 *Journal of School Psychology* 199 (1972); and Lilly, "Special Education: A Tempest in a Teapot," 37 *Exceptional Children* 43 (1970).

38. Education of the Handicapped Act, P.L. 94-142 [commentary to 20 U.S.C. Sec. 1401 (1982) Sec. 3(b)(4), (6), (7)].

39. *See* Mills and PARC.

40. *See* Pennhurst v. Halderman and Wyatt v. Stickney.

41. *See* Turnbull, "Two Legal Analysis Techniques and Public Policy Analysis," in *Models for Analysis of Social Policy: An Introduction,* edited by Haskins and Gallagher (Norwood, N.J.: Ablex, 1981).

42. Over half of the more than 8 million handicapped children in the United States did not receive an appropriate education. *See* P.L. 94-142, Sec. 601(b)(1), (3).

43. One million handicapped children in the United States received no public education and were not educated with their peers. *See* P.L. 94-142, Sec. 601(b)(7).

44. If appropriately funded, state and local educational agencies could provide for the educational needs of handicapped children. *See* P.L. 94-142, Sec. 601(b)(7).

45. Because public education was not serving the needs of handicapped children, many were educated away from their families. *See* P.L. 94-142, Sec. 601(b)(6).

46. *See generally* Abeson, "Confidentiality and Record Keeping," in Public Policy, *supra* n. 33.

47. Gorham, Des Jardins, Page, Pettis, and Scheiber, "Effect on Parents," in *Issues in the Classification of Children* (vol. 2), edited by Hobbs (San Francisco: Jossey-Bass, 1975), p. 154.

48. *See* Nazzaro, *supra* n. 33, at pp. 33-47; Turnbull, Turnbull, and Wheat, "Assumptions About Parental Participation: A Legislative History," 3 *Exceptional Education Quarterly* 2 (1982).

49. 20 U.S.C. Secs. 1412(5)(B) and 1414(a)(1)(C)(iv)(1976).

50. *See* Note: "Enforcing the Right to an 'Appropriate' Education: The Education for All Handicapped Children Act of 1975," 92 *Harvard Law Review* 1103 (1979).

51. Deno, "Special Education as Developmental Capital," 37 *Exceptional Children* 229 (1970).

52. Turnbull, "The Past and Future Impact on Court Decisions in Special Education," *Phi Delta Kappan* 523 (Apr. 1978).

53. *See* Least Restrictive Alternative, *supra* n. 1.

54. *See* Tribe, "Childhood: Suspect Classifications and Conclusive Presumptions: 3 Linked Riddles," 38 *Law and Contemporary Problems* 8 (1975).

55. *See* Pennhurst v. Halderman, Welsch v. Likins, Wyatt v. Stickney, and Covington v. Harris.

56. 20 U.S.C. Secs. 1412(5)(B) and 1414(a)(1)(C)(iv) and 34 C.F.R. Secs. 300.550 *et seq.* (1980); Bd. v. Rowley; and Roncker v. Walters.

57. *See generally* Turnbull, *Preschool Mainstreaming: A Policy and Implementation Analysis* (paper presented at Annual Meeting of American Educational Research Ass'n., April 1980; on file with author, Univ. of Kansas, Dep't. of Sp. Ed.).

58. *See* Karnes and Lee, "Mainstreaming in the Preschool," in 13 *Current Topics in Early Childhood* (1979); Cooke, Appolloni, and Cooke, "Normal Preschool Children as Behavior Models for Retarded Peers," 43 *Exceptional Children* 531 (1977); Neisworth and Madle, "Normalized Day Care: A Philosophy and Approach to Integrating Exceptional and Normal Children," 4 *Child Care Quarterly* 163 (1975); Devoney, Guralnick, and Rubin, "Integrating Handicapped and Nonhandicapped Preschool Children: Effects on Social Play," 50 *Childhood Education* 360 (1974).

59. *See* Hobbs, *supra* n. 37, at p. 180.

60. *See* Oversight of Public Law 94-142, the Education for All Handicapped Children Act Hearings before the Subcommittee on Select Education of the Committee on Education and Labor, Part I, 96th Congress, 1st Session (1979) (prepared statement of Deborah Olson, Sp. Ed. teacher, Laconia, N.H.); Wynne, Brown, Dakof, and Ulfelder, *Mainstreaming and Early Childhood Education for Handicapped Children: A Guide for Teachers and Parents* (1975) (on file with author, Univ. of Kansas, Dep't. of Sp. Ed.).

61. *See* 1979 Hearings, *supra* n. 60, at pp. 75-77. *See generally* Hobbs, *supra* n. 37.

62. *See* Least Restrictive Alternative, *supra* n. 1.

63. *See* Abrahamson v. Hershman, Erdman v. Connecticut, Kruelle v. Biggs, Cox v. Brown, North v. D.C. Bd. of Ed., Matthews v. Campbell, Isgur v. School Bd. of Newton, In the Matter of the "A" Family, Manchester Bd. v. Connecticut Bd., Gladys J. v. Pearland I.S.D., Harris v. D.C. Bd. of Ed., and Zvi D. v. Ambach.

64. Erdman v. Connecticut, Kruelle v. New Castle, Cox v. Brown, North v. D.C. Bd. of Ed., Matthews v. Campbell, Manchester Bd. v. Connecticut Bd., In the Matter of the "A" Family, Gladys J. v. Pearland I.S.D., and Harris v. D.C. Bd. of Ed.

65. Erdman v. Connecticut, North v. D.C. Bd. of Ed., In the Matter of the "A" Family, and Gladys J. v. Pearland I.S.D.

66. Kruelle v. New Castle, Matthews v. Campbell, Manchester Bd. v. Connecticut Bd., and Harris v. D.C. Bd. of Ed.

67. Cox v. Brown.

68. Abrahamson v. Hershman.

69. Isgur v. School Bd. of Newton and Zvi D. v. Ambach.

70. DeWalt v. Burkholder, Victoria L. v. Dist. School Bd. of Lee County, Roncker v. Walters, Campbell v. Talladega, and Town of Burlington v. Dep't. of Ed.

71. New York ARC v. Carey and Springdale School Dist. v. Grace.

72. Hines v. Pitt County Bd. of Ed.

73. *Supra* n. 64.

74. DeWalt v. Burkholder, Hines v. Pitt County Bd. of Ed., and Victoria L. v. Dist. School Bd. of Lee County.

75. The statute allows the child to participate where appropriate and the regulations allow the child to attend the IEP meetings, if appropriate. 20 U.S.C. Sec. 1401(19)(1976) and 34 C.F.R. Sec. 300.344(a)(4)(1980).

76. *See* Gilhool, "The Right to Community Services," 173 *The Mentally Retarded Citizen and the Law* (1976).

77. Of the cases that have been analyzed here (all that have been reported through Dec. 1984): Roughly 14% involved children who were deaf (Age v. Bullitt, DeWalt v. Burkholder, Bd. v. Rowley, and Springdale School Dist. v. Grace).

78. The cases also can be categorized by the extent or degree of the child's disability. Thus: Five children were mildly handicapped (Isgur v. School Bd. of Newton, Tatro v. Texas, Tokarcik v. Forest Hills, Espino v. Besteiro, and Zvi D. v. Ambach); two were mildly to moderately handicapped (Laura M. v. Sp. School Dist. and Town of Burlington v. Dep't. of Ed.); one was moderately handicapped (Gary B. v. Cronin); fourteen were severely handicapped (Abrahamson v. Hershman, Age v. Bullitt, Cox v. Brown, DeWalt v. Burkholder, Erdman v. Connecticut, Hines v. Pitt County Bd. of Ed., Victoria L. v. Dist. School Bd. of Lee County, North v. D.C. Bd. of Ed., Manchester Bd. v. Connecticut Bd., In the Matter of the "A" Family, Campbell v. Talladega, Gladys J. v. Pearland I.S.D., Harris v. D.C. Bd. of Ed., and *In re* Claudia K.); two were severely to profoundly handicapped (New York ARC v. Carey and Kruelle v. New Castle); two were profoundly handicapped (Springdale School Dist. v. Grace and Matthews v. Campbell).

79. The previous (1986) edition of this book reviewed that debate.

80. *See also* Age v. Bullitt and Cox v. Brown.

81. Campbell v. Talladega.

82. 29 U.S.C. Sec. 706, 34 C.F.R. Secs. 300.1 *et seq.* (1980).

83. *See also* Gladys J. v. Pearland I.S.D.

84. *See also* Town of Burlington v. Dep't. of Ed.

85. *See* Hines v. Pitt County Bd. of Ed., Springdale School Dist. v. Grace, Isgur v. School Bd. of Newton, Gladys J. v. Pearland I.S.D., Campbell v. Grissett, and Bales v. Clark.

86. Erdman v. Connecticut, Matthews v. Campbell, North v. D.C. Bd. of Ed., Manchester Bd. v. Connecticut Bd., and In the Matter of the "A" Family.

87. *See* Laura M. v. Sp. School Dist.; *contra,* Matthews v. Campbell.

88. Cox v. Brown.

89. 34 C.F.R. Secs. 300.500 *et seq.* (1980). *See* Honig v. Doe.

90. *See* Adams Central School Dist. v. Deist, Zvi D. v. Ambach, Abrahamson v. Hershman, Monahan v. Nebraska, and Victoria L. v. Dist. School Bd. of Lee County; *contra,* Cox v. Brown.

91. 34 C.F.R. Sec. 300.513 (1980).

92. 34 C.F.R. Sec. 300.403 (1980).

93. *See* New York ARC v. Carey, Kruelle v. Biggs, and Espino v. Besteiro.

94. New York ARC v. Carey.

95. *See* Halderman v. Pennhurst.

96. Gary B. v. Cronin.

97. Gladys J. v. Pearland I.S.D.

98. New York ARC v. Carey.

99. *See also* Kruelle v. New Castle and Espino v. Besteiro.

100. DeWalt v. Burkholder.

101. Stone, *Mental Health and Law: A System in Transition* (published in conjunction with the Center for Studies of Crime and Delinquency, National Institute of Mental Health, Dep't. of HEW, Washington, D.C., 1976).

102. In the Matter of the "A" Family.

103. Hines v. Pitt County Bd. of Ed.

104. *See* Blue v. N. Haven Bd. of Ed., Stanley v. School Admin. Unit, S-1 v. Turlington, and Stuart v. Nappi.

105. *See* Least Restrictive Alternative, *supra* n. 1.

106. The Supreme Court's decision in Youngberg v. Romeo established only a liberty-based interest in treatment for involuntarily committed profoundly retarded people and left in doubt the Eighth Amendment and substantive due process rationale.

107. *Id.*

108. *See* Halderman v. Pennhurst.

109. *See* Dixon v. Weinberger.

110. *See* Least Restrictive Alternative, *supra* n. 1, at pp. 43, 46, 52.

7

Procedural Due Process

CONSTITUTIONAL FOUNDATIONS

The legal expression of fairness is procedural due process—the right of a citizen to protest before a government takes action with respect to him or her. In the case of the handicapped child, that means having the right to protest actions of the state education agency (SEA) or the local education agency (LEA). For those who pioneered the right-to-education doctrine, the procedures for implementing the right were as crucial as the right itself. Procedural due process is a means of challenging the multitude of discriminatory practices that the schools had habitually followed. It also is a way of enforcing the first four principles of the EHA and of putting them to work. Without due process, the children would have found that their right to be included in an educational program and to be treated non-discriminatorily (to receive a free appropriate education) would have a hollow ring. Procedural due process—the right to protest—is a necessary educational ingredient in enforcing every phase of the handicapped child's right to an education.

Procedural due process also is a constitutional requisite under the requirements of the Fifth and Fourteenth Amendments that no person shall be deprived of life, liberty, or property without due process of law. In terms of the education of handicapped children, this means that no handicapped child can be deprived of an education without the opportunity of exercising the right to protest what happens to him or her.

The success of the right-to-education movement reaffirmed a belief widely held by lawyers—namely, that fair procedures tend to produce acceptable, correct, and fair results. Due process took many forms in the right-to-education cases decided before Congress enacted P.L. 94-142 as part of the Education of the Handicapped Act.

PRE-EHA COURT DECISIONS

Notification

A person who is adversely affected by the action or inaction of an SEA or LEA is helpless to protect himself or herself from the agency or to protest the decision unless he or she has adequate prior notice of what the agency proposes to do and for what reasons. The notion of *prior notice* clearly applies when a handicapped child is actually involved with an agency—when he or she has applied for admission to a program, has been placed or refused placement, has or has not been identified as handicapped, or has or has not been evaluated as handicapped. All of these actions can occur only after the child comes to the school's attention.

Many handicapped children, however, had been totally excluded from the schools, and often parents (or guardians) had been unaware of their child's right to an education. In the earliest right-to-education cases, *Pennsylvania Association for Retarded Children (PARC) v. Commonwealth of Pennsylvania* and *Mills v. D.C. Board of Education,* an initial issue for due process consideration was parental ignorance of a child's right to an education. In response, *PARC* ordered local school boards to conduct door-to-door canvasses and directed the Department of Public Education and other state agencies serving children to comb their records for names of handicapped school-aged persons. *Mills* ordered the D.C. Board of Education to locate all handicapped children and advise them of their right to an education. In addition, *Mills* required that a notice be published in D.C. newspapers stating that all children, regardless of their handicap, have a right to publicly supported, appropriate education. The notice informed parents of procedures for enrolling children in appropriate educational programs. *Mills* also required the school board to arrange for presentation of information on local radio and television stations.

Notice of the right to an education is related not only to the notion of fairness but also to the principle of *zero reject*—the idea that all handicapped children have the right to a free appropriate public education, *without regard to the nature or severity of their handicaps* (see chapter 3). It is one thing to notify a child or his parents of legal rights. It is quite another to deal fairly with the child once he or she is enrolled in the public schools. Procedural due process speaks to both issues.

Evaluation and Placement

After handicapped children are located, schools are required to evaluate them and place them in appropriate educational programs. *PARC* provided the first detailed set of requirements for placing a child or changing the placement, but these requirements applied only to the evaluation and placement of mentally retarded children. *Mills* extended basically the same procedure to *all* handicapped children. Later cases included the same procedural requirements.[1] The cases were unanimous in requiring three basic procedural safeguards.

First, the child's parent or guardian must be notified in writing. There are special provisions, not specified in the orders, for parents who cannot read English or who cannot

read at all. The notice must describe the action the school proposes to take, the reasons
for it (including references to results of any test or reports on which the action is based),
and available alternative educational opportunities.[2] The right to a hearing prior to educational evaluation or placement includes the right to a conference before the school evaluates or places a child.[3] It is logical for a conference to precede formal notice of proposed
action or inaction because the development of a child's individualized education program
in the requisite conference also becomes, at the least, the basis for the child's placement.

In a natural extension of the principle of notice prior to placement, notice must be
given prior to reassignment as well[4] since both the initial placement and any subsequent
placement affects the child's right to an appropriate education. The notice must inform the
parent of the reasons for the proposed action and of his or her right to object to the proposed action, to receive a hearing on his objection, and to obtain free medical, psychological, and education evaluations.[5]

One of the purposes of written notice is to give actual notice—to inform the parent
of the proposed action—and it is doubtful that actual notice can be conveyed without a detailed explanation of what the school proposes to do and why. A statement of proposed
action is meaningless unless the *action* is fairly described, the details of the action clearly
set forth. Likewise, a statement of proposed action is meaningless unless the *reasons* for
the proposed action are fully described. The formality of notification is constitutionally
insufficient; it is the reality of the notice—the *details of proposed action and the reasons
therefor*—that is constitutionally required.

*Second, if a parent requests a hearing, it must be conducted by a hearing officer in-
dependent of the local school authorities, at a time and place convenient to the parent.*
The hearing must be held within a specified period after the parent requests it, and is generally closed to the public unless the parent requests otherwise.[6]

Procedural due process not only allows a potentially adversely affected person to protest proposed governmental action but it also furnishes him or her with a forum to present
the objections and have them heard and ruled on by a disinterested party. The parent is
not just entitled to a hearing; he or she has a *meaningful* right to have the hearing before
an impartial tribunal and at a time and place convenient to the parent.

Justice delayed is justice denied, and the right to a reasonably prompt hearing is a prerequisite to any procedural safeguard. And because the hearing may involve evidence that
divulges highly personal aspects of a child's or family's life (e.g., whether the child is emotionally disturbed or why he or she is physically disabled), the notion of a *right to privacy*
permits hearings to be closed to the public unless the parent does not object to open
hearings.

Third, the hearing must be conducted according to due process procedures. The parent must be informed of the right to be represented by counsel at the hearing, to present
evidence and testimony, to confront and cross-examine witnesses, to examine school records before the hearing, to be furnished with a transcript of the hearing if he or she wishes
to appeal the hearing officer's decision, and to receive a written statement of the findings
of fact and conclusions of law.[7] The parent also has the right to be assured that the evidence

he or she presents will come before the hearing officer,[8] that it will be considered by the officer, and that no evidence *not* offered by the parent or the school will be considered.

The results of a hearing significantly affect a child's right to an appropriate education and thereby affect the explicitly guaranteed constitutional rights of liberty and property as well. Sometimes (although not necessarily), due process hearings take on aspects of an adversarial hearing. The hearing, however, is governed by rules of procedure that offer each party in the hearing equal opportunity to present his or her "case." In a proceeding of such importance, an absence of legal counsel makes a mockery of the concept of fairness and due process. Parents must be made aware of their right to counsel.

The right to present evidence and examine and cross-examine witnesses is the foundation of the right to be heard. Moreover, the right to call expert witnesses speaks directly to the issue that is often the very reason for the hearing—namely, evaluation and placement of the handicapped child. Access to school records is part and parcel of the right to examine and cross-examine witnesses. The right to appeal, to a record of the hearing, and to a statement of the hearing officer's decisions and reasons are indispensable in assuring a parent that arbitrariness will not govern the hearing and its results—that the hearing will have both the appearance *and* the reality of fairness.

Periodic Reevaluation

Another important requirement of the cases was that student assignments must be reevaluated periodically. *PARC* required automatic biennial reevaluation of any educational assignment other than to regular class; annual reevaluation was available at the request of the child's parent. Prior to each reevaluation, there was to be full notice and opportunity for a due process hearing. *Mills* also required periodic reevaluation of the child's status.

Without mandatory periodic reevaluation and notice thereof to the child's parent, the opportunity for protest (i.e., the opportunity for due process) might be effectively lost, since schools would not likely encourage parents to exercise their due process rights. Some parents, having been put off by their first hearing—not having achieved a decision they wanted, or having learned not to challenge the professionals—would not continue to assert their child's rights without the enforced reevaluation.

Misuse of Disciplinary Procedures

In the past, some disciplinary procedures were misused to exclude handicapped children from the public school. *Mills* directly addressed the problem of misused disciplinary procedures by setting out in detail the procedural safeguards to be used in any disciplinary proceeding.

Mills required that the D.C. schools "shall not suspend a child from the public schools for disciplinary reasons for any period in excess of two days without affording him a hearing pursuant to the [due process] provision ... and without providing for his education during the period of any such suspension." The provisions for notice and hearing in disciplinary cases were much like those that apply to placement, transfer, and exclusion. The essential elements were *notice* to the parent of the action to be taken and the *reasons* for it, and the procedural *rights* of the parent, including the right to an evaluation and to examine the school records.

Classification Criteria

A different type of concern for the procedures used in placing children within the school system was shown in the cases challenging use of various evaluation and testing materials and procedures for purposes of determining intelligence and student tracking. At issue was the validity of the criteria used in evaluation and placement—the alleged linguistic and cultural bias of the materials. In the leading cases in which classification was an issue, procedural due process became an essential element to safeguard the child against discriminatory classification.[9]

Expunction or Correction of Records

Mills provided for the expunction from or correction of records of any handicapped children with regard to past expulsions, suspensions, or exclusions, through either academic classifications or disciplinary actions, that violated their rights. If a child is incorrectly placed in a program for the mentally retarded, his or her records can be examined and, if found in error, they must be corrected. Only then can the effects of an incorrect record be ameliorated.

It is not surprising that the case law requirements of due process are reflected, almost in perfect mirror image, in the applicable federal statutes.

FEDERAL LEGISLATION

To receive the formula grant authorized by Part B of the EHA for the education of handicapped children, the SEA and each public agency must give assurances to the federal Office of Special Education that they have adopted appropriate due process procedures [Sec. 1412(5)(A) applicable to the SEA; Sec. 1414(a) (7) applicable to the LEA and IEU; and Sec. 1415, applicable to all three]. The requirement of *procedural safeguards* is consistent with the EHA intent to assure that the rights of handicapped children and their parents and guardians are protected [Sec. 1400(c)]. The differences between Part H and Part B are set out in the following paragraphs.

As members of Congress made clear when they were introducing P.L. 99-457, the legislation is a "pro-family" bill. Thus, the focus of P.L. 99-457's Part H, infants and toddlers, is on the person with a disability and the person's family. This is very different from the other major provisions of EHA—namely those in Part B that provide for the free appropriate public eduction of children with disabilities, because Part B focuses on the person and then on the parent, not the family.

Access to Records

Under Part B, a child's parents or guardians must have an opportunity to examine all relevant records relating to the child's identification, evaluation, or placement and the provision of a free appropriate public education for the child. Under Part H there is a specific right to confidentiality of personally identifiable information; and the general requirements of the Family Educational Rights and Privacy Act also apply to Part H programs.

Evaluation

Under Part B, the parents are entitled to an independent (non-agency) educational evaluation of their child. Section 300.500 defines evaluation as "procedures used to determine whether a child is handicapped and the nature and extent of the special education and related services that the child needs." This refers to procedures used selectively with an individual child and does not include basic tests administered to or procedures used with all children in a school, grade, or class. Section 300.503 defines who may make an independent evaluation—namely, a qualified examiner not employed by the public agency responsible for educating the child. A qualified person is one who has met certification, licensing, registration, or other such requirements of the SEA in the area in which he or she provides special education or related services [Sec. 300.12].

Section 300.503 also provides that public agencies must, upon request, give parents information about where they may have independent educational evaluations made. Under some circumstances, the independent evaluation must be made at public expense; the public agency either pays for the full cost of the evaluation or ensures that the evaluation is otherwise provided to the parent without cost to him or her.

Parents have the right to an independent evaluation at public expense if the hearing officer requests one for use in a due process hearing or if the parents disagree with the evaluation made by the public agency. But, if in a due process hearing that it initiates, the agency can prove that its evaluation was appropriate, the parents may be required to pay for the new evaluation. When parents obtain an independent evaluation at their own expense, the agency must take it into consideration as a basis for providing the child an appropriate education or as evidence in a due process hearing, or both [Sec. 300.503].

Parental consent must be obtained for preplacement evaluation and for the child's initial placement in a special education program [Sec. 504(b)]. Consent, in this context and all others, means that (1) the parents have been fully informed in their native language, or in another suitable manner of communication, of all information relevant to the activity (e.g., evaluation) for which consent was sought; (2) the parents understand and agree in writing that the activity may be carried out; (3) the consent describes the activity and lists the records (if any) that will be released and to whom; and (4) the parents understand that they give their consent voluntarily and may revoke it at any time [Sec. 300.500]. The Department of Education comments on Section 300.504 make it clear that any changes in a child's special education program, after the initial placement, are not subject to the parental consent rule but are subject only to the requirement of notice and opportunity for changes in the IEP.

If parents refuse to consent when consent is required, the parties must first attempt to resolve the conflict by complying with any applicable state law. If there is none, the agency may initiate a due process hearing. Should the hearing officer rule in favor of the agency, the parents' refusal will be overruled and the agency may evaluate or place the child, notifying the parents of its actions so that they may appeal [Sec. 300.504 and .510 through .513].

Part H (infants and toddlers) has its own rules about consent. Early intervention service providers must obtain parental consent before (1) conducting the initial evaluation and assessment of the child and (2) initiating the provision of early intervention services for the first time. If the parents do not give consent, the providers must make reasonable efforts to ensure that the parent (1) is fully aware of the nature of the evaluation and assessment or the services that would be available and (2) understands that the child will not be able to receive the evaluation and assessment or services unless consent is given. Also, if the parents do not give consent, the provider may initiate a due process hearing or other procedures to override the parents' refusal to consent to the initial evaluation of the child.

Surrogate Parents

Under Part B, Section 1415 and Section 300.514 require the SEA to ensure that the child's rights are protected if his or her parents are unknown or unavailable or if the child is a ward of the state. (The child's rights are not the responsibility of the SEA when the parents are simply uncooperative or unresponsive.) The SEA may comply with this requirement by assigning a parent surrogate. There are other ways, but Section 1415 and Section 300.514 mention only this one.

If the SEA goes the route of parent surrogate, it must devise methods for determining whether a child needs a surrogate, and then for assigning one. The regulations give no guidance on the methods. They do, however, set out the criteria for selecting a surrogate—primarily, there should be no conflict of interest and the individual should have the skill to represent the child. A superintendent or other employee of an institution in which a child resides may not serve as a surrogate. If there is disagreement about who the surrogate will be, the conflict may be resolved by a due process hearing. The regulations also make clear that a person paid by a public agency solely for the purpose of being a surrogate does not thereby become an agency employee. The surrogate may represent the child in matters affecting his or her identification, evaluation, and placement, and right to a free appropriate public education.

Under Part H, the rights of infants and toddlers whose parents are unknown or absent or who are wards of the state also are protected by procedures similar to Part B, including surrogacy.

Notice

Under Part B, the agency must give prior written notice to parents, guardians, or surrogates whenever it proposes to initiate or change, or refuses to initiate or change, a child's identification, evaluation, or placement and the provision of a free appropriate public education [Sec. 1415(b)(1)(C) and (D)]. Section 300.505 requires the notice to contain:

(1) A full explanation of all the procedural safeguards available to the parents ...;

(2) A description of the action proposed or refused by the agency, an explanation of why the agency proposes or refuses to take the action, and a description of any options the agency considered and the reasons why those options were rejected;

(3) A description of each evaluation procedure, test, record, or report the agency uses as a basis for the proposal or refusal; and

(4) A description of any other factors which are relevant to the agency's proposal or refusal.

It also requires that the notice be:

(1) Written in language understandable to the general public; and

(2) Provided in the native language of the parent or other mode of communication used by the parent, unless it is clearly not feasible to do so.

If the parents' native language or other mode of communication is not a written language, the SEA or LEA must take steps to ensure:

(1) That the notice is translated orally or by other means to the parent in his or her native language or other mode of communication;

(2) That the parent understands the content of the notice; and

(3) That there is written evidence that the requirements (of oral translation and parent understanding) have been met.

Under Part H there are similar requirements for notice in the family's native language when there is a proposed change or refusal to change the identification, evaluation, placement, or provision of early intervention services to the infant or toddler.

Complaints and Due Process Hearings

Under Part B, the agency must give the parents, guardians, or surrogates an opportunity to present complaints relating to any matter concerning the child's identification, evaluation, or placement, or right to a free appropriate public education [Sec. 1415(b)(1)(E)]. If the parents (or guardians) file a complaint with an agency, they are entitled to an opportunity for an impartial hearing conducted by the agency, as determined by state law or the SEA. The agency must inform the parents about any low-cost or free legal aid in the geographical area [Sec. 300.506].

The right to a due process hearing is not limited to consumers. Under Section 300.504 and Section 300.506, an agency also may initiate a due process hearing on its proposal or refusal to initiate or change the identification, evaluation, or placement of a handicapped child, or the free appropriate public education provided to the child.

Unless the parties agree to an extension, the hearing must be held and a final decision reached within 45 days after the hearing is requested, and a copy of the decision must be mailed to the parties. (The hearing officer may extend this deadline.) The time and place of the hearing and each review involving oral argument must be reasonably convenient to the parents and child.

The Department of Education comments on Section 300.506 make it clear that a state may use mediation prior to a due process hearing. In fact, many states now require mediation. But the Department also makes it clear that mediation may not be used to deny or delay a parent's rights to procedural due process. It is not clear when mediation will deny or delay rights, but if mediation takes a long time (perhaps more than the 45 days in which the parent has a right to a hearing after requesting one), the parent may argue successfully that mediation has delayed the rights to procedural due process.

Each agency must keep a list of the hearing officers and their qualifications. The hearing may not be conducted by an employee of the agency involved in education or caring for the child [Sec. 1415(b)(2)]. Section 300.507 prohibits a due process hearing from being conducted by any person having a personal or professional interest that might conflict with objectivity in the hearing. A person who otherwise qualifies to conduct a hearing is *not* considered an employee of the agency solely because he or she is paid by the agency to serve as a hearing officer.

At the initial hearing and on appeal, each party has the right to be accompanied and advised by an attorney and by other experts (persons with special knowledge or training with respect to the problems of handicapped children); to present evidence and confront, examine, cross-examine and compel the attendance of witnesses; to make written and oral argument; to receive a written or electronic verbatim record of the hearing; and to receive a written account of findings of fact. No evidence may be introduced by any party unless it was disclosed at least 5 days before the hearing. The parents must have the opportunity to have their child present and to have the hearing open to the public [Sec. 1415(d) and Section 300.508]. The decision must be sent to the state advisory panel established under Section 1413(a)(12).

Unless a party appeals from the initial hearing or begins a court action after the appeal, the decision of the initial hearing is final [Sec. 1415(e)]. If the hearing is conducted by an LEA, an aggrieved party may appeal to the SEA, which is required to conduct an impartial review of the hearing, reach a decision, and send a copy of the decision to the parties within 30 days. The hearing officer on appeal must make an independent decision after reviewing the matter [Sec. 1415(c)].

Persons who are aggrieved by the findings and decision in the initial hearing but who do not have the right to appeal to the SEA (the Act and regulations do not say who these people may be) and persons who are aggrieved by the findings and decision on appeal (that is, any party in the appeal) may file a civil action in either a state court or federal district court. (For purposes of the federal suit, the jurisdictional rules about dollar amounts in controversy do not apply.) The court, whether state or federal, is to receive the records of the administrative proceedings, hear additional evidence if offered, and, on the basis of the preponderance of the evidence, grant appropriate relief [Sec. 1415(e)(2) and (4)].

During the initial hearing or appeal, the child remains in his or her current educational placement unless the SEA or LEA and the parents or guardians agree otherwise. If applying for initial admission to school, the child will be placed in the public school program, if the parents and guardians agree, until all hearings (including appeals) have been completed [Sec. 1415(e)(3)]. The agency may, of course, use its normal procedures for dealing with children who are endangering themselves or others.

The Supreme Court's decision in *Honig,* discussed in chapter 3, makes it clear that the stay-put rule prohibits the LEA from making a unilateral placement of the child—that is, from placing the child outside of the child's present placement without parental consent—while a due process dispute is ongoing. But the Court also gave the LEA the right to seek appropriate judicial relief if the stay-put rule was creating an intolerable situation (as in preventing a placement that would reduce danger to the child, other students, or staff).

In another stay-put case, *Corbett v. Regional Center for the East Bay, Inc.,* a federal district court ruled that the LEA, not the parent, has the burden of overcoming the presumption that the child will remain in the present placement. The burden is overcome, the court said, if the child's present placement is "substantially likely to cause injury to himself or herself, or to others."[10] This decision allocates the burden of proof to the school to justify the change in placement—that is, to create an exception to the stay-put rule. That result follows the settled law that, where the stay-put rule is at issue, the burden is with the schools, as announced in *Doe v. Brookline School Committee,* a 1983 decision of the First Circuit Court of Appeals.[11]

Under Part H (infants and toddlers), the state must provide for the timely administrative resolution of complaints by parents. States have two options: (1) to adopt the Part B due process procedures; or (2) to develop new impartial procedures for resolving individual child complaints. The procedures, whether under either option, require that an impartial decision-maker resolve the dispute. The service provider is bound by that decision and must implement it unless it is reversed on appeal.

In addition, a state that does not use the Part B procedures must nonetheless ensure that its procedures result in speedy resolution of individual child complaints. A state may offer mediation as an intervening step before implementing due process procedures, but it may not require parents to use mediation. All disputes must be resolved within 30 days after the lead agency receives a complaint. All hearings must be in places and at times convenient to the parents. Parents have the rights to be accompanied and advised by counsel or other people with special knowledge or training in early intervention; present evidence and cross-examine witnesses; prohibit the use of evidence not disclosed to them at least 5 days before the hearing; obtain a transcript; and obtain written findings of fact and decisions. A provider or parent who is aggrieved by a decision may appeal it to a state or federal court.

As in the case of Part B, the infant-toddler also is protected by a specific stay-put rule under Part H. The rule is this: If a complaint is pending at any administrative level or on appeal to a federal or state court, then, unless the state agency and parents or guardians agree otherwise, the infant-toddler is entitled to continue to receive the appropriate early intervention services currently being provided; or, if applying for initial services, is entitled to receive those services that are not in dispute.

These rules under Part H deal only with complaints about individual children. Part H's regulations also require the state lead agency to establish procedures to resolve complaints about how the state itself—so-called systemic complaints—implements Part H and its site plan.

Section 504

The Section 504 regulation (Sec. 104.36) provides that an SEA or LEA may satisfy Section 504 due process requirements by complying with the procedural safeguards of Section 1415 of P.L. 94-142. The alternative, and minimum, requirement for the SEA and LEA is to furnish notice, to make the child's records accessible, to guarantee an impartial hearing, to afford the right to counsel, and to assure an impartial review.

POST-EHA CASES

Lawyers love procedures. They have a continuing *affair d'amour* with procedures for many reasons. Two are especially relevant here. First, they believe (and with good justification) that fair procedures will provide fair results. This fundamental premise undergirds the EHA, which is ripe with procedural requirements (e.g., nondiscriminatory evaluation, IEPs, procedural due process). Second, they often successfully use procedural requirements to establish or to circumvent the substantive rights of their clients. Out of these two reasons have grown a plethora of judicial decisions.

Exhaustion of Remedies

The most vexsome issue is whether handicapped children or their representatives (typically, their parents) must exhaust their administrative remedies (fully use up their EHA procedural safeguard rights) before they may file a lawsuit in a federal or state court. By and large, the courts agree that they must exhaust their remedies, but as is their wont, courts create exceptions to the general rule. Usually the "futility" exception will allow some courts to hear the lawsuit before the administrative proceedings have been completed. The other exceptions involve cases in which the school district does not insist on exhaustion or the lawsuit is not one that deals with students' procedural rights under the EHA.

Establishing the general rule, *Sessions v. Livingston Parish* held that parents must exhaust their administrative remedies before filing a federal court lawsuit.[12] A similar result is well explained in *Davis v. Maine Endwell Central School District.* Joining a 504 claim with an EHA claim does not mean that the requirement of exhaustion will be avoided; the plaintiff still must exhaust the EHA remedies.[13] Simply because administrative due process under the EHA is protracted does not excuse failure to use administrative due process.[14] Moreover, exhaustion is not excused in a case involving many plaintiffs where factual questions concern needs particular of a child, where exhaustion does not result in duplication of effort, and where any resulting delay will flow from prior failure to exhaust.[15]

Although the general rule is that the parties must exhaust their administrative remedies before suing in court, there are instances when that rule will not apply. Generally, plaintiffs are excused from exhaustion of remedies when the exhaustion is apt to be "futile"—that is, when it will accomplish little to nothing in resolving the parties' dispute.[16] For example, if the LEA or the SEA does not argue that the plaintiff handicapped child must exhaust administrative remedies and if there already has been an adjudication of part of the case, exhaustion will not be required.[17]

Plaintiffs also need not exhaust their administrative remedies under state law before filing a class action lawsuit in federal court because, first, the city board of education had failed in the past to carry out its obligations to handicapped children (and a court had so found), and, second, the defendant's attorney conceded that exhaustion in each case in the class action "could not be expeditiously processed."[18] Similarly, *New Mexico Association for Retarded Citizens v. State of New Mexico* held that exhaustion of administrative remedies under Section 504 is not required where the only remedy is cut-off of federal funds upon petition by the Office of Civil Rights because, in that case, pursuing a cut-off would be futile since the plaintiffs sought a restructuring of the state's entire system of special education.

By the same token, a non-profit organization (UCP) and individual students filing a class action suit against the New York City school board and officials did not have to exhaust their administrative remedies under Section 504 or the EHA for the following reasons: (1) Two different federal agencies and offices were responsible for enforcing compliance with the EHA and Section 504 (the Commissioner of Education in the former case, the Secretary of the Department of Health, Education, and Welfare in the latter); (2) the sole means available to them to enforce the statutes was to cut off federal funds, and that alternative would be far more disruptive of the legislative scheme under the EHA than a private lawsuit; and (3) the administrative remedies themselves were meaningless (because there were too many plaintiffs with common complaints).[19]

When there is proof that school officials have made extensive efforts to provide a handicapped child with an appropriate education, the plaintiff must exhaust his or her administrative remedies. Exhaustion is not required, however, when there are undisputed facts conclusively showing that the child was receiving no education at all and that school officials would take no action to provide an appropriate education.[20] Moreover, residents of a state institution for people who are mentally retarded, for whom the state failed to appoint surrogate parents as required, are not compelled to exhaust their administrative remedies before suing under the EHA, Section 504, the federal Developmental Disabilities Act, and the federal Constitution. The state's failure to appoint surrogates cannot benefit the state; children without parents have had no access to procedural remedies so they may bring their lawsuit without exhausting remedies.[21] Finally, exhaustion is not required because it would be futile where there were challenges to SEA regulations, to the state commissioner's performance of his duties under federal law, and to an alleged violation of due process (expulsion without hearing).[22]

In addition, a plaintiff claiming damages under the EHA is not required to exhaust the state administrative remedies because the state procedures are designed only to handle challenges to evaluation or placement, or both, not a claim of whether there is private remedy for damages implicit in the EHA; there is no such remedy.[23] Also, a plaintiff who has exhausted administrative remedies under the EHA need not also exhaust them under Section 504 because the legislative history of the EHA indicates Congress' intent that compensatory damages are available under the law; a federal court may award damages.[24]

Burden of Proof

When one party brings a lawsuit against another, the law typically requires the party bringing the suit to prove his or her claim. Another way of stating that the party bringing the suit must do this is to say that the burden of proof falls on the party bringing the suit. Since the EHA does not assign the burden of proof to any potential party, the courts have relied on state law to determine which party has the burden of proof. Generally, the courts have held that the party bringing the case has the burden of proof. In most cases, the party bringing the case is the handicapped child or the parents, so they have the responsibility of proving that their claim is worthy of judicial protection.

For example, they must prove the inappropriateness of education in the LEA or that private school placement is appropriate and the state residential school or institution is not[25] or that the child is entitled to a vocational program, not an academic one, and that the LEA is unable to provide such a program.[26] Moreover, the burden of overturning a decision of a state due process hearing officer by a court falls on the party appealing the LEA-level decision, and that party must show that the SEA-level decision was not supported by substantial evidence, was arbitrary or capricious, or is clearly erroneous under law.[27]

Retroactive Application of the EHA

Normally an Act of Congress speaks only to the future: It is "prospective" in its application. Sometimes, however, courts have found the EHA to be "retrospective"—to apply to children who were discriminated against, in violation of the Act or other law, before the Act became effective. The cases—*Stemple v. Board of Education of Prince George's County,* and *Frankel v. Commissioner of Education of New York*—reached opposite results. The general rule, however, is that laws are prospective.

In *Stemple,* parents of a multiply handicapped child had placed her in a private residential school before the EHA became effective. After it became effective, they sought reimbursement in due process hearings called by them. The district court held that it was not entitled to review the hearings because the EHA's procedural guarantees were not in effect when the child was placed.

A similar result was reached in *Alexopulos v. Riles*,[28] which disallowed retroactive application of the EHA in a case that claimed compensatory education. The court relied on Congressional intent for the law to apply prospectively and noted that if the law applied retroactively to a claim for denial of appropriate education in the 1973 school year (2 years before it was enacted), compensatory damages would have to be awarded; because such damages are so much like money damages and because Congress did not authorize money damages to be awarded, retroactive application of the law clearly would violate Congressional intent.

A different result was obtained in another case. The plaintiff's parents, in *Frankel*, sought to recover tuition costs they had paid for their handicapped child's out-of-state private tuition, claiming that the school had failed to timely classify him and provide him with an appropriate education. The state commissioner of education denied their request, and they filed a civil action in federal court. The state and local schools filed motions to dismiss, arguing that the EHA should not be applied retroactively.

The court denied the motion to dismiss, holding that, since the Act and its legislative history are silent on the issue of retroactivity, the U.S. Supreme Court's decision in *Bradley v. Richmond School Board* controls. The *Bradley* test is whether retroactive application would work an injustice in light of the nature and identity of the parties, the nature of their rights, and the nature of the impact of the change in law. Here, the court held that the EHA may be applied retroactively.

Due Process Hearing Officer

The impartiality of due process hearing officers has come under scrutiny in several cases. Each of these demonstrates that the courts are meticulous about ensuring the officers' impartiality.

Robert M. v. Benton held that the state superintendent of schools was not an impartial hearing officer, because he was an employee of an agency involved in the education of handicapped children.[29] But *Vermont Association for Children with Learning Disabilities v. Kaagan* held that the state board of education members were not employees because they were appointed for fixed terms by the governor with the advice and consent of the state senate.[30] Also, *Smith v. Cumberland School Committee* held that employees of the state education agency may serve as due process hearing officers at the appeals (state-level hearings).[31]

Silvio v. Commonwealth of Pennsylvania held that the use of a state college professor as a due process hearing officer does not violate the EHA. Simply because the professor was being paid by the state did not make him a partial person. Notwithstanding this early decision, later cases have held that university personnel who help formulate state special education policies are not impartial and may not serve as hearing officers.[32]

Helms v. McDaniel held that under the EHA a state may continue to use a procedure in which the local school board treats the findings of a local due process hearing officer as a report that it can accept as final or automatically appeal; the process (automatic appeal if not accept) is merely a "decision to appeal" and does not mean that the board itself is hearing the case. But the state violated the EHA by treating the findings of the state-level hearing officer as the findings of a "special master" and not as a final decision; the law requires a final decision at the SEA level.

Likewise, *Cothern v. Mallory* upheld the state's procedures for selecting the due process hearing panel (the procedure calls for three panelists—one selected by the state, one by the parents, and another by both the two previously designated members). But the EHA allows a single panelist.[33]

When a Hearing Is Not Available

Although the EHA grants a due process hearing as a matter of right to any party (typically, parents of a handicapped child or the LEA charged with educating the child) in matters involving the child's identification, classification, or services, there are limitations on the right to obtain a hearing. The cases described in the following paragraphs show that the courts are unwilling to grant a hearing in every instance of an educational dispute.

The reasons for the court's reluctance to grant a hearing in every case of any minor change in a student's placement or program are fairly well grounded. First, Congress intended a hearing to be available when there is a change in placement (the child is moved from one type of program, such as a residential one, to another, such as an integrated one; or from one type of setting, such as a resource room, to another, such as a fully integrated program). Unless the change in placement or program substantially affects the student's rights to an appropriate education, there is no reason to create a due process right.

Second, allowing a due process hearing in all changes of placement or program, even those that are minor and not likely to affect the student's rights to an educational benefit, would open up the floodgates for many insubstantial claims. The administrative and judicial hearing process could become clogged with essentially frivolous cases.

Third, allowing a due process hearing in all changes of placement and program would involve the courts in oversight of school district decisions that are based on administrative grounds. To function effectively and efficiently, school authorities have to redraw school boundaries, open or close schools, move students from one building to another, and so on. If every such administrative decision can be challenged, the courts will become superordinary school boards and the administrative efficacy of the schools will be impaired.

Finally, allowing a due process hearing in all such changes may put the courts in the position of having the opportunity to substitute their educational policy decisions or their administrative policy decision for those of the elected or appointed school boards and their professional staff. As has been argued throughout this book, courts are reluctant to take on that kind of authority, preferring to defer to the experts in those matters.

Thus, there is a line of cases that disallow hearings when parents seek to prevent SEAs or LEAs from carrying out administrative or organizational decisions affecting more than one child or school. For example, parents of handicapped children placed by an LEA or their parents in a private school lack standing under the EHA to use due process procedures to challenge a state-level decision to terminate funding for a private school.[34]

A case reaching a similar result is *Concerned Parents and Citizens for Continuing Education at Malcolm X (P.S. 79) v. New York City Board of Education.* The Second Circuit there concluded that prior notice and a hearing are not required when a handicapped child is transferred from a special class at one school to a substantially similar class at another school within the same school district, because there has been no official change of placement under the EHA.

In that case, the plaintiffs filed suit in federal court to prevent the closing of an experimental school in New York City that employed innovative techniques to integrate and educate handicapped and nonhandicapped students. The school was closed, and the children were transferred to other schools in the district in a very secretive way. Many parents learned of the decision after their handicapped child had been reassigned to a different school in the fall. The lower court ruled that this transfer constituted a change of placement and under federal law there should have been notice and a hearing. Since the school was already closed, however, the court did not reopen the school; instead, it ordered remedial improvements in the new programs.

The Second Circuit reversed the lower court, concluding that the transfer of students from one program to another in the same district was not a change in placement as contemplated under the EHA, even though it noted that the transfer was "poorly planned" and the new placements did not duplicate the innovative program at the old school. The court was persuaded by several factors: (1) Under Section 1415(b)(1)(C) of the EHA, placement seemed to be "limited to certain fundamental decisions regarding the existence and classification of the handicap, and the most appropriate type of educational programs for assisting a child with such a handicap"; (2) the regulations implementing the EHA also interpret the term "placement" to refer only to the general educational placement. A broad interpretation would "cripple the Board's ability to implement even minor discretionary changes." The court emphasized, however, that the decision did not leave parents without a remedy. They still could file a complaint, request a full administrative hearing, and appeal any adverse decision to the courts.

Likewise, a due process hearing is not available when children placed in one school are transferred to another and there is no change in their educational instruction. But if the transfer involves a change in their IEPs, if only to incorporate additional supportive services, a hearing is available.[35]

Dima v. Macchiarola held that the wholesale transfer of students from a private school to alternative placements, because the school district terminated contact with the private school after auditing it, was not a change of placement that triggers a due process hearing. Likewise, a state decision to reduce its tuition reimbursement rate to a private school does not trigger a due process hearing.[36] This New York decision has been followed consistently in that state, with *Lowell School, Inc. v. Ambach* holding that a private school for children with disabilities has no right to challenge (under due process safeguards) the decision of the state education commissioner to reduce future tuition payments to the school, and *Language Development Program of Western New York, Inc. v. Ambach* holding that a private school has no right to a hearing before the state modifies the scope of disabling conditions the school may serve at public expense. These cases, as well as the

Tilton case, digested below, indicate that the courts will not tolerate use of the federal special education law to obstruct or modify state fiscal decisions.

Tilton v. Jefferson County Board of Education held that the stay-put provision of the EHA (requiring that a handicapped child's placement not be changed while administrative or legal remedies are being exhausted) does not prohibit a state from closing, for financial reasons, a regional mental retardation facility in which disabled children had been given special education. To apply the due process protections of the EHA to school closings, even when the children receive substantially different programs as a result, would thwart the state's fiscal policies, a situation that Congress did not intend.

In a result slightly different from the New York cases and *Tilton,* a federal district court has held that the state of Oregon violated its duties under the EHA and state law by discontinuing funding of a private education program.[37] In that case, the private residential center was certified by the federal government as an intermediate care facility for the mentally retarded and by the state as a residential training center. The center's students participated in a local school district's special education program, which received federal and state special education funds. When the state declined to fund the students' education adequately, the school district proposed to reduce the amount of services it provided and refused to grant the students any procedural safeguard (due process) opportunities to challenge its decision, and the state denied that it had any further responsibility to the students.

The court concluded that the students were participating in a state-operated program (the ICF-MR program), not a school district program, and, because the EHA, its regulations, and state law all impose a responsibility on the state to provide an appropriate education to those students, the state would be required to provide such an education and to fund it. The students' failure to exhaust administrative remedies, further, does not prohibit the federal court from acting to prevent the state from discontinuing the students' funding; the school district had refused to allow due process hearings, and thus there could be no exhaustion of remedies. This result is distinguishable from the New York cases and *Tilton* on the basis that the New York cases and *Tilton* did not result in the denial of an appropriate education, only a change in funding patterns or opportunities.

Statute of Limitations

General law is that a lawsuit or administrative action (such as a due process hearing) must be begun within a certain period of time. This rule ensures that disputes are heard when evidence is relatively fresh—when the witnesses are only recently removed from the time during which the facts arose. The rule also prompts parties to resolve their disputes sooner or later so that they may get on with their lives without the inevitable uncertainty and burdens that come with a lawsuit.

The means by which the rule for prompt litigation is enforced is called the *statute of limitations.* It is a law (statute enacted by a legislature) that places a limitation on the period of time beyond which a lawsuit may be filed. The EHA contains no statute of limitation, and the courts have been compelled to create one. In every case, they have borrowed the statute of limitations that applies to administrative actions (a due process hearing) as enacted by the state legislature in which the hearing is heard.[38]

THE REALITY

The reality of due process in the EHA is fairly stark. It helps one to realize at the outset that parents or an LEA may pull at least 36 "triggers," or grounds for either party to seek a due process hearing.[39] This alone makes due process a provision that can be wielded in good faith or in bad, for the legitimate purpose of correcting deficits in a handicapped child's educational rights or for purposes of harassment.

It also helps to realize that implementation of due process requirements early on was a matter of some concern. The requirements in the EHA and its implementing regulations were hardly self-explanatory or self-executing.[40] Much of the ambiguity of the EHA and its regulations has been eliminated by judicial interpretation, state-agency regulations and guidelines, and common practice (the so-called common law on conducting hearings). For example, the likelihood of due process hearing officers' being not totally impartial or even well trained was great,[41] but by the mid-1980s, most states have provided for a careful selection and training process.

Nonetheless, problems remain. The largest one seems to be the cost of due process. Cost consists of three elements: (1) the actual *financial cost* of the hearings—preparing for them, hiring attorneys and expert witnesses, paying for the documents required for evidence, and pursuing an appeal; (2) the *emotional or psychic cost*—the enormous energy and stress involved in a hearing and its appeal; and (3) the cost that consists of *time spent,* and perhaps lost, when the child may (or may not) be receiving an appropriate education.

A good measure of the actual costs involved in due process is the dramatic increase in the number of due process hearings since the EHA was enacted and due process was made available under the EHA.[42] Another measure of the actual cost is the increased use of *mediation* as a way of preventing due process. Mediation involves the use of less formal, less adversarial, more negotiated-settlement meetings for resolving disputes.[43]

It is increasingly evident that the psychic costs—the exacerbation of ill will that parents and educators already feel about each other—are the more serious ones, from the viewpoint of both the parents and the educators involved in due process.[33] That is not to minimize the huge financial costs, which are increasingly affordable only by the middle and upper classes and by schools.

Moreover, there is evidence that due process hearings do not satisfactorily resolve the disputes between parents and school systems.[34] There is a perception on the part of some parents that schools have the "home court advantage" in due process and that parent-initiated due process will not be particularly helpful even if the parents gain the legal victory they seek. That is why many parents, especially those whose income level is upper-middle class and upper-class, can afford to withdraw their children from public education if they fail, in a due process hearing, to obtain the private school placement or other expensive service they seek.[35]

For all of its problems, however, due process remains an important—indeed, an indispensable—element of the EHA and the right to education. Like many other aspects of the legal process, it is flawed because it requires extraordinary amounts of energy, time, and money. The fault lies mainly with the system of dispute resolution in our society and with an inadequate understanding of the causes of due process in special education (an understanding that would help prevent due process). The necessity of due process, however, is beyond dispute.

NOTES

1. *See, e.g.,* LeBanks v. Spears, Guadalupe Org. v. Tempe Elem. School Dist., and Larry P. v. Riles.
2. Doe v. Kenny.
3. Cuyahoga ARC v. Essex.
4. Doe v. Kenny.
5. Mills, Cuyahoga ARC v. Essex, and Doe v. Kenny.
6. LeBanks v. Spears, and Mills; *contra,* PARC.
7. Cuyahoga ARC v. Essex.
8. *Id.*
9. Diana v. State Bd. of Ed., LeBanks v. Spears, and Larry P. v. Riles.
10. __ F. Supp. ____ EHLR 559:373 N.D. Cal. 1988.
11. 722 F. 2nd 910.
12. *See also* Riley v. Ambach, Dima v. Macchiarola, Harris v. Campbell, Armstrong v. Kline, Monahan v. Nebraska, Timms v. Metro. School Dist., Doe v. Koger, Ezratty v. Puerto Rico, Akers v. Bolton, Greg B. v. Bd. of Ed., McGovern v. Sullins, Mitchell v. Walter, San Francisco Unified School Dist. v. California, Lombardi v. Ambach, Smith v. Ambach, and Davis v. Maine Endwell Cent. School Dist.
13. Smith v. Ambach, and Shannon v. Ambach.
14. Cluff v. Johnson City Cent. School Dist., and Kresse v. Johnson City Cent. School Dist.
15. Phipps v. New Hanover County Bd. of Ed., Riley v. Ambach, and Calhoun v. Illinois State Bd.
16. Christopher T. v. San Francisco U.S.D., Monahan v. Nebraska, Howard S. v. Friendswood I.S.D., ARC in Colorado v. Frazier, and Miener v. Missouri.
17. North v. D.C. Bd. of Ed., a case in which the parties were bound by the prior order of the same court in Mills.
18. Jose P. v. Ambach; but normally exhaustion is required: Riley v. Ambach, Lombardi v. Ambach, Vermont ACLD v. Kaagan (ruling on constitutional and statutory challenges to redefinition of "learning disabilities"), and Darlene L. v. Illinois State Bd. of Ed.
19. United Cerebral Palsy of NYC v. Bd. of Ed. of City of N.Y.
20. Harris v. Campbell.
21. Garrity v. Gallen, and (Ruth Anne) M. v. Alvin I.S.D.
22. J.G. v. Bd. (suit designed to correct alleged system-wide violation of EHA's procedures).

23. Loughran v. Flanders.

24. Boxall v. Sequoia Union H.S. Dist.

25. Bales v. Clark.

26. Fitz v. Intermediate Unit #29, and Savka v. Pennsylvania Dep't. of Ed.

27. Levy v. Pennsylvania Dep't. of Ed.

28. __ F. 2d EHLR 557:296 (9th Cir. 1986).

29. *Concur:* Vogel v. School Bd., involving deputy state superintendent; Monahan v. Nebraska, where the state commissioner had authority to overrule the decision of the state-level hearing officer; East Brunswick Bd. of Ed. v. New Jersey State Bd. of Ed., holding that an SEA employee is not an impartial hearing officer.

30. *See also* Timms v. Metro. School Dist.

31. *Contra:* Compochiaro v. Califano.

32. Mayson v. Teague; Kotowicz v. Mississippi State Bd. of Ed.

33. Nevada County Office of Ed. v. Sup't.

34. Windward School v. State.

35. Brown v. D.C. Bd. of Ed.

36. *Concur:* Fallis v. Ambach.

37. Kerr Center Parents Ass'n. v. Charles.

38. *Supra* n. 32.

39. Turnbull, Turnbull, and Strickland, "Procedural Due Process: The Two-Edged Sword that the Untrained Should Not Unsheath," *Boston University Journal of Education* 40-59 (Summer, 1979).

40. *Id.*

41. Turnbull, Strickland, and Turnbull, "Due Process Hearing Officers: Characteristics, Needs, and Appointment Criteria," 48 *Exceptional Children* 48-54 (1981).

42. U.S. Dep't. of Education, Annual Reports to Congress on the Implementation of Public Law 94-142: The Education for All Handicapped Children Act (Washington, D.C.: U.S. Government Printing Office).

43. U.S. Dep't. of Education, *Sixth Annual Report to Congress* (Washington, D.C.: U.S. Government Printing Office, 1984).

44. Budoff, "Special Education Appeals Hearings: Are They Fair and Are They Helping?" *Exceptional Education Quarterly* 37-48 (Aug. 1981).

45. *Id.*

46. *Id.*

8
Parent Participation and Shared Decision Making

CONSTITUTIONAL FOUNDATIONS

Participatory democracy is a term that describes shared decision making in the schools or in other public agencies. It refers to the legal right or political opportunity of those affected by a public agency's decisions to participate in making those decisions. It is a long-standing tenet of government in this country, but it has not always been in good standing. Too often it has been given little more than lip-service. But, as this chapter will show, the EHA—like the cases—has started to make inroads on unilateral decision making in the schools.

Although the constitutional foundations for parent participation in the education of handicapped children are not well articulated by the courts—probably because they involve the children's rights instead of the parents'—they nevertheless exist and can be identified and explained. At the core of the constitutional principles is the common law doctrine that parents have a duty to support their children and a corollary right to their children's services and earnings for as long as the children have the legal status of minors. Under common law and even by today's statutes, these rights and interests mean that parents may control their children in various ways.

For example, parents are empowered to consent (on the minor's behalf) to medical treatment for the minor and, more recently, to educational diagnosis and evaluation. The compulsory school attendance laws usually make the parents criminally liable if they do not require their child to attend the public schools. Also, state statutes make parents criminally liable for failing to support their minor children. The reason for these and similar laws is that a minor is presumed incapable, because of age, of acting on his or her own behalf except in limited ways, as granted by statute or as recently recognized under the constitutional "privacy interest" by the courts (for example, the rights to abortion, contraception, or treatment for substance abuse). Parents, then, have rights that they exercise on behalf of their child, and in many instances the child's right to have an education is exercised by the parents.

Children's rights to procedural due process, to a proper evaluation and appropriate classification, and to be included in school can be enforced by their parents acting in their representative capacity (acting on the child's behalf).

The cases have made an indirect but nevertheless damning criticism of the schools by recognizing that children have rights of their own and their parents have rights in a representative capacity. They have said that schools have been making unilateral decisions about handicapped children's education but that, in the future, those decisions must be shared with the parents and other representatives of handicapped children.

FEDERAL LEGISLATION

The EHA declares that the Act is intended to "assure that the rights of handicapped children and their parents or guardians are protected" [Sec. 1400(c)]. It carries out its policy in the following ways (in addition to those already mentioned in conjunction with classification, evaluation, individualized education programs, least restrictive placement, and procedural due process).

Notice, Consultation, and Hearings

The EHA requires SEAs to give assurances to the U.S. Department of Education that, in carrying out the Act's requirements to provide a free appropriate public education, the state will establish procedures for consultation with persons involved in or concerned with the education of handicapped children, including the handicapped individuals and their parents or guardians [Sec. 1412 (7) and Sec. 300.137]. The EHA also requires SEAs to establish procedures for making the state plan available to the public and to the parents [Sec. 300.284]; for having public hearings [Sec. 300.280] and for giving adequate notice of those hearings; and for allowing the general public to comment on proposed policies, programs, and procedures required by the EHA before they are adopted [Sec. 1412(7) and Sec. 300.282].

As is more fully discussed later in this chapter, the regulations require SEAs to give public notice of policy hearings, to provide an opportunity for public participation and public comment, to review public comments before adopting the annual plan, and to publish and make the plan generally available [Secs. 300.280-.284]. In addition, the Act requires LEAs to give assurances that, in offering full educational opportunities to all handicapped children, they will provide for the participation and consultation of the parents or guardians of the children [Sec. 1414(a)(1)(C)(iii) and Sec. 300.226].

Advisory Panels

The Act requires SEAs to create an advisory panel whose members are to be appointed by the governor or other official authorized to make such appointments. The panel should be composed of individuals involved in or concerned with the education of handicapped children, including at least one representative of handicapped individuals, teachers of handicapped children, parents of such children, state and local educational officials, and administrators of programs for handicapped children [Sec. 1413(a)(12) and Sec. 300.651]. The panel is to advise the SEAs on the unmet needs of handicapped students, make public comment on the annual plan and on pertinent state rules or regulations to be issued by the SEA, and assist the state in developing and reporting whatever data and evaluations the Secretary might require.

Access to System Records

The Act requires that certain information about school programs for handicapped children and about the children themselves be treated as public information, available to all, including parents of the handicapped children. An LEA must give assurances that its application for federal funds and all documents related to the application are available to parents, or guardians, and other members of the general public. This includes information that is necessary for an SEA to perform its evaluation duties and information relating to the educational achievement of handicapped children in programs financed under the Act [Sec. 1414(a)(3) and (4)]. Likewise, before submitting an amendment to the State plan, an SEA must give to parents, or guardians, and other members of the general public at least 30 days' prior notice of the amendment [Sec. 1412(2)(E)].

Protection of Student Records

The EHA also provides for the confidentiality of student records and access to those records by parents or guardians [Secs. 1417(c) and 1412(2)(D)]. Both the SEAs and LEAs are subject to action by the Secretary, in accordance with the Family Educational Rights and Privacy Act (FERPA), codified at 20 U.S.C. Sec. 1232g, and regulations, 34 C.F.R. Parts A-E).

FERPA requires recipients of federal education grants to give parents, or guardians, and in some cases, pupils, access to their own public school records. Parents must be given an opportunity for a hearing to challenge the content of the records, and certain parts of the records cannot be released without parental consent. The EHA confidentiality regulations [Sec. 300.560-.576] conform to FERPA.

Part H

Part H defines "parent(s)" to be a parent, guardian, person acting as a parent, or surrogate parent. A person acting as a parent may be a grandparent or stepparent with whom the child lives or a person legally responsible for the child's welfare.

There are other Part H rules for parent participation. The law establishes a State Interagency Coordinating Council and requires that family members be on the Council. In addition, all of the parent rights available under Part B relating to access to and confidentiality of information apply to Part H programs.

Parents and other members of the public may have access to information about state and local early intervention programs. Also, not all information about every student is accessible, but generally parents and other members of the public may obtain all information concerning the *programs* that the state or local agency runs. (This is different from the rights of parents to have access to their child's education records. That type of access does not belong to the public.)

Parents have the right to consent or object to the release of personally identifying information about their children. This protects family privacy. In addition to the right to assure confidentiality, parents also have the right of access to their own children's educational records. This assures the basis for a long-term and constructive relationship.

The state also must publish its proposed plan, give notice of when hearings will be held, allow for public opportunity to comment on the plan, hold public hearings, and review and comment on the public comments. It also must establish a public awareness program, comprehensive child find system, and a central directory of information.

Section 504

There is only one requirement under Section 504 regulations. That is that LEAs must annually try to identify and locate every qualified handicapped person in the school district who is not receiving a public education and notify those persons and their parents or guardians of the school's duty to provide them with a free education [Sec. 104.32].

JUDICIAL INTERPRETATIONS

Perhaps reflecting the fact that "family" nowadays includes more than just parents, incorporating brothers, sisters, grandparents, other blood or by-marriage relatives, and even "extended family" who are not related by blood or marriage, the term "parent" includes more than simply the natural (biological) parent of a child with a disability. Thus, permanent foster parents, appointed by the state welfare agency to be the student's "parents," are entitled to exercise all of the rights that the LEA gives to natural parents, and the foster parents, not the state agency, are entitled to make decisions about enforcing rights under the EHA; likewise, the state may not appoint surrogate parents for the student who has permanent foster parents.[1]

Even when a surrogate parent has been appointed for the student, the natural parents may still sue an LEA to enforce their—if not their child's—rights under the EHA. This is true even if the child has attained the age of majority. The reason for this result is that the appointment of a surrogate is for the purpose of enforcing the child's rights; the appointment does not displace the natural parents' own rights.[2] Moreover, even after the child reaches the age of majority, the natural, adoptive, or foster parents retain the right to enforce their rights—if not their child's—under the EHA.[3]

When a child's natural parents have separated or divorced, the general practice has been for the LEA to deal only with the parent to whom the child's custody has been awarded. This has proven to be sound practice and probably should not be modified except in one situation. That situation is one in which the noncustodial parent is responsible for the child's education expenses; in that case, the LEA must seek to involve the noncustodial parent in all parent-rights matters and must accede to that parent's wishes to be involved as fully as the custodial parent, such as in the IEP development.[4]

A natural parent can lose the rights of participation, however, by his or her own action. Thus, when a parent, in order to obtain the child's admission to a state psychiatric institution, arranges for the county department of human services appointed as the child's conservator (guardian) and for a lawyer appointed as the guardian *ad litem* (a guardian for the purpose of a lawsuit only), and when the same parent fails to obtain a court appointment as the child's "next of friend" (a legal term designating the continuing parent-child relationship), the parent loses his or her right to sue on the child's behalf.[5] A foster child whose natural parents have moved out of state but who lives with foster parents is a resident of the state in which the foster parents live, and is entitled to obtain a free appropriate education at that state's expense, because to prohibit that result would apply residency requirements to bar the children in foster homes from having or enforcing rights under the EHA.[6]

RIGHTS TO INFORMATION

A major implication of the parent participation regulations is that both LEAs and SEAs have new responsibilities for providing educational information to consumers. For example, an SEA must provide notice to parents of handicapped students (in the parents' native language) that personally identifiable information (including the name of the child, parents, and other family members, address, any personal identifier such as a social security number or student number, or any list of personal characteristics or other information that would make it possible to identify the child [Sec. 300.500]) is on file. Further, it must explain the type of information it plans to collect and how it plans to use the information. An SEA might, for example, collect information on the number of children with a particular handicapping condition, or it might seek data for a description of the educational achievement of a group of handicapped children.

In addition, parents must be provided with a summary of policies and procedures to be used by "participating agencies" (*any* agency or institution that collects, maintains, and uses or provides information) for storing information, releasing it to third parties, or destroying it, as well as the agency's plan for protecting personally identifiable information. An SEA must publicly announce, through the newspapers or some other appropriate media, any child identification and evaluation activities it plans [Sec. 300.561]. Thus, the SEA has responsibility for developing policies for access to system records and protection of student records, to be followed by all participating agencies. Representatives from LEAs may wish to request an opportunity to participate in the SEA's development of these policies.

Parents and their representatives have the right to inspect personally identifiable information in their child's records within 45 days, maximum, after requesting to inspect the records. If the record includes information on more than one child, parents are entitled to see or be informed about only the portion relating to their child [Sec. 300.564]. The agency may presume that the parent has access rights unless it is advised otherwise in cases of guardianship, separation, and divorce. Parents may request an explanation or interpretation of the information and must be provided with copies if failure to provide copies would result in their being unable to inspect or review the information [Sec. 300.562]. A fee for copies may be charged, unless the fee would prevent a parent from having access to the record [Sec. 300.566]. Upon request, parents also must be provided with a list of the types and locations of information collected and used by the agency [Sec. 300.565]. The school must keep a record of access [Sec. 300.563].

There are further requirements for the protection of student records. After reading the records and having them appropriately interpreted, parents may request that the participating agency amend the information. The agency must consider the request and give an affirmative or negative response within a reasonable time. If the agency disagrees with the request, it must inform the parents of their right to a hearing to protest this decision [Secs. 300.567-.570]. Thus, parents not only have rights of access to student records, but they also have rights to informally or formally challenge the contents of student records. This underscores the necessity for educators to recognize the importance of their responsibilities in maintaining accurate student records and developing skills in documenting educational progress.

The regulations safeguarding the confidentiality of student information set forth clear implementation guidelines for public schools. First, one official must be appointed at each participating agency to assume overall responsibility for ensuring that personally identifiable information remains confidential [Sec. 300.572(b)]. This person might be the director of special education, the director of special services, or some other administrator who has concomitant responsibility for implementation of the EHA and Section 504. All persons who participate in the collection or use of confidential information must receive training related to the state's policies and procedures on confidentiality of personally identifiable information [Sec. 300.572(c)]. The participating agency also must maintain an updated roster of persons (and their positions) employed by the agency who have access to personally identifiable information. This list is to be available for public inspection [Sec. 300.572(d)].

Public agencies must obtain parental consent before releasing personally identifiable information to anyone other than the agency officials authorized to collect and use this information, unless otherwise authorized to do so under the Buckley-Pell Amendment in the federal Family Educational Rights and Privacy Act. The SEA must establish policies and procedures to be followed when a parent refuses to give consent [Sec. 300.571].

Public agencies must notify parents when personally identifiable information that had been collected and maintained is no longer needed for educational services; upon the parent's request, the information must be destroyed. Permanent information that can be kept without regard to time limitations includes a student's name, address, phone number, grades, attendance record, classes attended, grade level completed, and year completed [Sec. 300.573]. Public agency officials should advise parents that their child's records may be needed for purposes such as securing social security benefits or qualifying for certain income tax deductions. In addition, the safeguards for maintaining confidentiality of records should be fully explained to parents before they make a decision about having the records destroyed.

In their annual program plans, SEAs are required to specify policies and procedures to assure the rights of children as well as the rights of their parents. Consideration should be given to the child's age and the type or severity of disability [Sec. 300.574]. The Family Educational Rights and Privacy Act requires the rights of parents pertaining to educational records to be transferred to the student at age 18. This requirement has major implications for schools serving handicapped students in the 18 to 21 age range.

NOTES

1. Criswell v. State Dep't. of Ed.
2. John H. v. McDonald.
3. *Id.*
4. Doe v. Anrig.
5. Susan R.M. v. Northwest I.S.D.
6. Catlin v. Ambach.

SECTION III
Enforcing the Law

9

Case Law Techniques

COMPLIANCE

Litigation has been a major—and, indeed, was the original—source for establishing the educational rights of handicapped children. Were it not for the landmark decisions (e.g., *PARC, Mills, LeBanks, Larry P.,* and *Diana*), it is doubtful if subsequent litigation would have had such widespread success, if the "second-generation" litigation (defining appropriate education) would have had any useful precedents, or if state and federal legislation would have been enacted, much less mirror the case law so closely.

Court decisions and orders are not self-executing. They demand compliance by the parties involved, but they cannot assure or guarantee it. Court orders in the right-to-education movement are effective only if the defendants (school authorities) are willing or able to carry them out. When, as sometimes happens, the defendants are neither willing nor able, the plaintiffs are compelled to return to court and seek additional relief. The alternative types of relief they usually seek are described in the sections that follow.

PRE-EHA COMPLIANCE TECHNIQUES

These sections describe only the compliance cases that were decided before the EHA was enacted. They illustrate various techniques for compliance. The cases that have been decided after the EHA was enacted are described in the latter part of this chapter.

Contempt Citations

In *Mills,* the court required the defendants to provide handicapped children with an appropriate or suitable education. Three years later, their "victory" having proven shallow because the defendants were unwilling or unable to comply, the plaintiffs filed a motion to enforce the court's earlier order. The court granted the motion and found the superintendent, the board of education, and the director of the department of human resources to be in contempt of court for failing to make appropriate placements and to notify the court of problems that prevented them from complying with the court's order. The court chose not to impose any penalities because funds had been made available to appropriately place some of the handicapped children.

A similar contempt citation was issued in *Rainey v. Tennessee.* In 1974, a consent decree was entered obligating the defendants to provide appropriate programs for handicapped children. Two years later, the plaintiffs petitioned the court for a contempt citation, alleging that the defendants had not complied with the consent decree and were in continuing violation of the state's 1972 Mandatory Education Law for Handicapped Children and Youth. Two years after the plaintiffs filed the petition, the court found the defendants to be in violation of the consent decree and issued a contempt order, rejecting the defense that they should not be held in contempt because they did not have sufficient funds to comply with the order. The defendants were ordered to submit an implementation plan by March 1977, and to put the plan into effect by July 1977.

The New York City School Board was held in contempt in *ASPIRA of New York, Inc. v. Board* for failing steadily and repeatedly to exercise its power and authority to make the board's employees proceed promptly and in good faith to accomplish the tasks commanded by a consent decree (to provide a broad program of bilingual education in New York City schools). The court found that there had been clear and convincing proof that the board, though not willfully flaunting the consent decree, had not been reasonably diligent and energetic in attempting to accomplish what the decree had ordered.

The board had failed to marshal its own resources, assert its "high" authority, and demand the results needed from subordinate agencies in order to accomplish the terms of the decree. It had allowed deadlines to pass without volunteering explanations and had tolerated long periods of nonperformance, inadequate performance, and outright defiance from community school boards. Furthermore, it had tolerated slipshod procedures, failed to enlist or order the placement of needed and available personnel, and had displayed a sense of non-urgency that bordered on indifference.

Court-Appointed Masters

Although a contempt order is an indication of the failure or unwillingness (or both) of the defendants to comply with court orders, its initial effect in both *Mills* and *Rainey* was to hold the individual defendants and the school systems potentially liable to the court through imposition of a fine. It is not intended to assure that the court's orders will be carried out—it only holds out the threat of punishment to those who fail to carry them out. Thus, it is of limited value for accomplishing the education of handicapped children.

In both *Mills* and *Rainey,* however, the contempt order was accompanied by orders that the defendants must report to the court on the identification of other children needing services and how the defendants will provide those services, and file with the court a plan for implementing its orders. Like the original orders, the ones accompanying the contempt order in *Mills* required the defendants to make extensive changes in the way they provided special education services. And, as perhaps could have been predicted from the defendants' reaction to the 1972 orders, the defendants once again failed to adequately comply. Thus, a scant 2 months after finding the defendants in contempt, the court appointed a special master to oversee implementation of its order that the defendants furnish a suitable education to handicapped children. A *master* is an agent of the court, appointed to accomplish certain court-assigned tasks to ensure that the defendants carry out the court's orders.

In *Mills,* the court assigned the master extensive duties: (1) to investigate and evaluate the appropriateness of special education programs in the public schools, institutions operated by the D.C. department of human resources, and alternative educational services furnished outside the school system; (2) to review the defendants' child-census and tuition-subsidy programs to determine if they were adequate; (3) to report on the status of procedures and programs formulated to carry out the court's order by the school board, the department of human resources, and the D.C. government; (4) to review the defendants' procedures for estimating the budgets, justifying special education needs, identifying budgetary shortages, and obtaining supplemental funding to make up deficits; (5) to help the defendants prepare a plan to implement the court's orders; and (6) to file periodic interim reports, file a final report with the court, and make recommendations to the court. The court did not grant the master power to give directions or orders to the school board or to supervise its operations. It did, however, order the board to pay the master for his services.

Other Judicial Remedies

There are judicial remedies other than contempt citations and masters. Indeed, courts have extensive power to enforce their decrees. For example, they may order a defendant school to regularly file with the court its plans for implementing a court decree or state statute.[1] They may retain jurisdiction over a case in order to monitor the school's implementation of the court's order,[2] and set dates by which certain of the orders must be carried out.[3]

Financial Reallocation and Withholding of Funds

One of the earliest defenses in right-to-education suits, which has fared least well in the courts, is the defendants' contention that they do not have sufficient funds to provide an appropriate education to all handicapped children. In *Mills,* the court made short shrift of this argument, stating (in now well known dicta) that absence of funds is no defense of a failure to provide constitutional rights (equal educational opportunities) to handicapped students, and that the burden of inadequate funds may not fall more heavily on handicapped pupils than on nonhandicapped ones. In *MARC,* the Maryland Circuit Court also gave little heed to the defense claims of financial difficulty when it ordered the defendants to take appropriate action to request additional funds from the state legislature.

It is one thing to say that defendants must be equitable in the use of funds or that they should request more from their funding sources. It is altogether another to step into the budget process. Throughout the right-to-education cases, the courts have been extremely reluctant to interfere in any way with the financing of public education.[4]

The *Mills* court hesitated to appoint a master because it recognized that compensation to the master would drain off funds that would otherwise be available to educate handicapped children. When it finally did appoint a master, it ordered only that he review the school board's budget process. Further evidence of judicial reluctance to interfere with the traditional legislative function of taxation and appropriation is shown in *Rainey,* where, in response to the defendants' claim that they could not comply with the consent decree because they had insufficient funds, the court ordered them to submit an implementation plan by March 1977 and to put it into effect by July. Voicing a threat it had the power to enforce, the court said, "From and after that date, the defendants shall be enjoined from expending money for the operation of a public school system in this state unless the plan to be submitted is incorporated into the operation of the department of education and fully pursued to implement the consent decree." The appeals court reversed the trial court's enjoining the state from spending any money for the education of any children in the state if children with disabilities were not receiving special education by July 1, 1977; the court of appeals held that the trial court's remedy was excessive and would cause more damage than it would yield benefits.

Federal Abstention, Mootness, Dormancy, and Voluntary Dismissals

Not every case reaches the stage at which judicial remedies become necessary; indeed, there are several avenues "out" of litigation and enforcement of court orders. One way out is through use of the doctrine of *federal abstention.* When a right-to-education suit is filed in a federal court (on the grounds that the defendants are violating the equal protection and due process guarantees of the Fifth and Fourteenth Amendments), this doctrine permits the court to rule that the case, although involving federal claims, should be tried first in state courts because it also involves state issues that may dispose of the case and make it unnecessary for the federal constitutional issues to be tried. It is not uncommon for federal courts to dodge right-to-education cases on this ground[5] and to remit the plaintiffs to state courts. Defendants favor the abstention doctrine because it enables them to try their cases in forums traditionally less hostile to school systems and less inclined to find constitutional violations.

The federal trial court's power to abstain is discretionary. It may choose to abstain or not, and if its order of abstention or nonabstention is appealed, the appellate court will inquire only whether the trial court abused its discretion. In *Frederick L. v. Thomas,* the plaintiffs alleged that the Philadelphia school district did not provide learning disabled students with a minimally appropriate education, did not test all students in order to identify those with learning disabilities, and instead placed primary reliance on teacher referrals to school psychologists. The trial court held that the referral method was inadequate for identifying learning disabled students and ordered the district to submit a plan for identifying all learning disabled students in the district.

Responding to the defendants' claim that the trial court should have abstained because the case raised a constitutional claim of functional exclusion (see chapters 3 and 5) and an accompanying claim based on state law—which the defendants argued was ambiguous and should have been resolved by a state court before the federal court ruled on it—the appellate court found that the trial court had not abused its discretion and was not required to abstain. It said that: (1) the state statutes were not wholly ambiguous, (2) the defendant's abstention motion was not filed until more than a year after the plaintiffs had filed their complaint, and (3) ordering abstention now would mean that many members of the plaintiff's "class" (the case was a class action suit) would go through school without obtaining the education they claim they are entitled to under state law and the federal constitution.

If a federal court does not wiggle out on abstention grounds, it sometimes may avoid the issues on the ground of *mootness*. State courts, too, may defer or escape trying a case on that ground. Typically, a case is moot (and thus need not be tried) if state legislation or state agency regulations provide a sufficient answer to the claims that the plaintiffs have raised in their lawsuit. For example, a classic right-to-education case was brought in Michigan in a federal district court in 1972. After the case was filed, the state legislature enacted a right-to-education law, and, after that law was enacted, the defendant school officials successfully persuaded the court to dismiss the case because it was moot; the legislation ostensibly satisfied the plaintiffs' requests for relief.[6]

Some cases do not become moot. They simply become dormant or inactive. For example, in both North Carolina[7] and North Dakota,[8] federal right-to-education cases filed in 1972 were nearly a decade later still awaiting a final disposition, largely because the state legislatures enacted mandatory legislation and the plaintiffs and court were waiting to determine what effect, if any, the legislation would have on the plaintiffs' claims. In both cases, the legislation set a future date for full implementation. *Dormancy* gives plaintiffs the opportunity to resist any motion the defendants might make to dismiss the case, but it also gives the defendants temporary freedom from judicial intervention.

It is possible for plaintiffs to dismiss their cases voluntarily—on their own motion. Apparently the only case in which they have taken a *voluntary dismissal,* however, is the Colorado right-to-education suit.[9]

Access to Student Records in Class Action Suits

In *Mattie T. v. Holladay,* a class action suit that challenged classification practices, exclusion from mainstream programs, inadequacy of special education programs (functional exclusion), and absence of compliance with due process safeguards, the plaintiffs sought access to the records of individual members of the class bringing the suit. Although the plaintiffs stipulated that names and other information that would allow the students to be personally identified could be deleted, the defendant school districts declined to release the records, claiming that they were to be treated confidentially under provisions of the Family Educational Rights and Privacy Act of 1972[10] (see chapters 7 and 8).

The court granted the plaintiffs' request, holding that their request allowed personally identifying information to be deleted, and that the plaintiffs did not have the burden of notifying the students or their parents that the records were being subpoenaed. The decision opens up wide avenues of discovery for plaintiffs in class action suits.

POST-EHA COMPLIANCE TECHNIQUES IN COURT

As the pre-EHA cases illustrate, it has never been easy to enforce court decisions in right-to-education cases. This is particularly evident in cases involving the racial desegregation of public schools, and it is now apparent in cases involving the education of handicapped children. In an effort to enforce the EHA, advocates for handicapped children have resorted to an imaginative array of lawsuits.

Damages—Malpractice

First, plaintiffs have sought to hold school districts liable in monetary damages for failing to comply with the EHA. These new *educational malpractice* cases generally have been unsuccessful. The majority of the courts have held that the EHA does not authorize a suit for monetary damages.

Denying Damages.   The lower courts prohibit plaintiffs from recovering money damages for alleged violation of the EHA for several reasons:

1. Congress has not expressly granted a right to sue for damages, so courts are reluctant to imply one. The exclusive remedy is due process hearings; damages are therefore not allowed.
2. To imply a right to sue for damages would involve the courts in the thicket of deciding what constitutes "good" or "bad" educational practice. Such a determination is necessary if a court is to find that malpractice exists.
3. If courts become involved in determining damages, they also will become involved in the daily governance of schools. Traditionally, the governance and curriculum of schools are matters courts have preferred to avoid.
4. Malpractice suits are apt to discourage implementation of the law by educators, who, because of the threat of litigation, will be more concerned about their liability than about the education of handicapped children.
5. Malpractice suits will usurp the Act's present remedies (which are largely procedural, not substantive, in nature). Provision of an appropriate education is achieved by comp-

lying with certain procedural safeguards (nondiscriminatory evaluation, IEPs, LRE, and parent participation).

6. Moreover, courts are concerned whether the Eleventh Amendment to the federal Constitution (granting states immunity from suit unless they expressly consent to be sued) prohibits a child from suing the state. Their concern is that a state's participation in the EHA does not amount to consent to be sued. Ordinarily, courts duck constitutional issues when they can.

For reasons set out in the following discussion, it is strongly arguable that the U.S. Supreme Court will agree with the majority trend and disallow monetary damages in suits brought by handicapped children against local or state education agencies. Its 1984 decision in *Smith v. Robinson* specifically side-stepped the damages question but contained language suggesting that the Court will rule consistent with the majority trend.

The major issue in *Smith* was whether a student who successfully sues a school district for violating his or her educational rights may recover attorneys' fees from the district. The Court held that the student could not (as more fully explained later in this chapter, under "Attorney Fees, Private Right of Action, and Exclusive Remedy").

Relationship of the EHA to Section 504. In reaching that result, however, the Court was required to discuss the relationship of the EHA to Section 504 of the Rehabilitation Act and Section 1983 of the Civil Rights Act. Under Section 504, a recipient of federal aid (including programs of public education) may not discriminate solely on the basis of a handicap against any otherwise qualified person. Under Section 1983, anyone who, acting under "color of law" (i.e., in an official capacity, not a personal one), deprives another of federal constitutional or statutory rights may be held liable in monetary damages to the aggrieved person. Since both of these laws seek to prohibit discrimination and illegal conduct and both are civil rights protections, Congress also has permitted the plaintiffs (i.e., students who are disabled) to recover their attorneys' fees from the school officials or districts. Section 505 implements Section 504 and allows the recovery of attorneys' fees, and Section 1988 implements Section 1983 and allows the recovery of attorneys' fees.

The issue in *Smith* was whether a student may sue under the EHA, Section 504, and Section 1983 where the alleged discrimination is prohibited under EHA; that is, may the student use Section 504 and Section 1983 to enforce a right already granted by the EHA and, if successful, recover attorneys' fees under Section 505 and Section 1988, although the EHA does not allow attorneys' fees? The Court held that the student could not do that, since the EHA provides the "exclusive remedy" and comprehensive scheme to correct violations of its provisions.

First, the Court observed that Congress intended the EHA to be the exclusive remedy for asserting certain types of claims to educational discrimination based on handicap. In addition, Congress intended children with constitutional claims to pursue them through the "carefully tailored administrative and judicial remedies" set out in the EHA. Further, the EHA is a "comprehensive scheme" to aid the states in complying with their constitutional obligations to educate children with disabilities. In light of Congress' intent and the nature of the EHA, the Court concluded, it would be inconsistent with Congress' "carefully tailored ... scheme" to allow a student to circumvent the EHA's administrative remedies. Moreover, Congress itself "perceived the EHA as the most effective vehicle" for protecting a student's constitutional rights. That was the reason that it made the EHA the "exclusive avenue" for pursuing a claim.

It is easy to use this same reasoning—which resulted in the EHA being the only method for redress and the disallowance of Section 504 and Section 505, as well as Section 1983 and Section 1988, as additional remedies, in the attorneys' fee situation—to infer that the Court would follow the same approach in a damages case and hold that the EHA is the sole remedy. And, since Congress did not specifically grant a remedy of monetary damages in the EHA (but did in Section 1983 and arguably did in Section 504), no such remedy exists for a violation of the EHA.

Another aspect of *Smith* seems to support that inference. In addressing the attorneys' fees issue, the Court resolved the conflict between the EHA (which does not expressly allow recovery) and Sections 504 and 505 (which do) in favor of the EHA. In addition, the Court noted that if the EHA is not available for redress of educational discrimination or Section 504 guarantees substantive rights that are greater than the EHA's, then there is a different situation: The statutes do not grant equal rights, and the EHA would not be the controlling one. That is, the EHA will not prevent a party from recovering attorneys' fees under Section 504, because the EHA simply does not apply. Again, the inference is that the EHA will prevail when there is conflict between them. Since the EHA does not grant a right to monetary damages but Section 504 arguably does, the result would be that a student cannot obtain such damages in an EHA lawsuit and cannot use Section 504 (or Section 1983, for that matter) to bootstrap himself or herself into a position to obtain such damages.

To conclude, in *Smith* the Court expressly avoided the damages issue of the EHA, Section 504, or Section 1983. But there is enough language and reasoning in *Smith* to support an inference that, when it must deal with that issue, it will rule that the EHA is the exclusive remedy and that, because it does not expressly grant monetary damages, none are available.

Other Cases Denying Damages.   In one of the earliest cases, *Loughran v. Flanders,* a plaintiff who claimed he was entitled to damages under the EHA was held not entitled to damages. In another ruling in the case, he was not required to exhaust his state administrative remedies because the state procedures were designed only to handle challenges to evaluation or placement, or both, not a claim of whether there is a private remedy for damages implicit in the EHA; there is no such remedy.

In the leading case, *Miener v. Missouri,*[11] a federal district court in Missouri dismissed that portion of the suit, filed by a 17-year-old resident of a state mental hospital, which sought *compensatory education* under the EHA and Section 504 of the Rehabilitation Act. The court viewed the compensation as *damages,* which are barred by the Eleventh Amendment. The district court held that the patient could bring suit for injunctive relief under Section 504 and the EHA, but not one for monetary relief. The context in which the claim was raised suggested that there was no difference ("Damages ... are meant to compensate a party for a past violation of some duty"). Therefore, *Edelman v. Jordan* is controlling. In that case, the lower courts had awarded plaintiffs a retroactive award of monetary relief as equitable restitution, but the Supreme Court found that the Eleventh Amendment barred such an award, even though phrased in equitable terms.

On appeal of *Miener,* the Eighth Circuit Court of Appeals affirmed in part and reversed in part. The court held that the plaintiffs had a private cause of action under Section 504; where administrative remedies were inadequate, a private action for damages was allowable for violations of Section 504 and may be instituted before administrative remedies are exhausted; the EHA does *not* provide for damages, only for injunctive relief; the Eleventh Amendment does not preclude damages against a local education agency, only against the state; the EHA does not abrogate the state's immunity under the Eleventh Amendment, nor does state participation in P.L. 94-142; and the Eleventh Amendment precludes an award of compensatory education.

The trend to deny damages for "educational malpractice" is evidenced in several recent cases. In *DeRosa v. The City of New York,* and *Agostine v. School District of Philadelphia,* for example, the courts refused to award damages to students placed in special education programs where the students complained that they were improperly classified as handicapped.

Some courts, however, seem so upset with school districts' actions that they award compensatory education to plaintiffs, often using the compensatory education award as a substitute for a damages award. For example, in *White v. State of California,* the state court determined that it may not award money damages, as that would be against public policy (for the reasons stated earlier in this section of this chapter). But it did hold that the plaintiffs, who had been illegally excluded from special education in violation of the EHA, are entitled to compensatory special education services to remedy any past denial of services for which they were eligible. The court reasoned that the award of compensatory education is preferable to the award of monetary damages because the EHA entitles individuals to services, not money.

Granting Damages. Other cases (clearly a minority) allow whole or partial recovery of damages under the EHA or Section 504. They include *Monahan v. Nebraska* and *Boxall v. Sequoia.*

A recent award of money was made in *Allen v. School Committee of Boston,* decided by a state court. There, the LEA had contracted with a private company for the busing of children to special education programs. When the private company's drivers went on strike, the students were unable to attend school for 12 days. The court awarded damages to the students for the time they missed, reasoning that the school district could have decided not to have a private company provide transportation and thereby could have retained control over transportation. In "abdicating" its responsibilities by entering into the private-company contract, the district is held liable for the company's drivers' action. Because the daily cost of educating each student was $20, the award of that daily amount times the number of days missed was a proper remedy under the theory of a *compensatory fine.* The difference between compensatory damages and a compensatory fine is not great in their effect; the students still obtain compensation. In theory, the difference is that the "damages" are for malpractice whereas the fine is for contempt of court. The court itself had previously held the school district in contempt (as explained earlier in this chapter) for failing to comply with its duties to educate children with disabilities.

The lesson of the damages cases seems to be this: An LEA will be free of damages if it does something for the children, however poorly it does that job, because an award of damages for malpractice is almost never granted; but not if it does nothing, for in that case, compensatory education rights will be granted.

Granting Tuition. Courts generally will not award tuition if the parents unilaterally place a child in a private program. The reason for this rule is the provision of the EHA that requires the provision of a "public" education—i.e., one at public expense and in public programs. Underlying this reason is the general understanding that public funds should not be spent for private education. There is an explicit exception in the EHA for children who are placed in private schools by their LEAs or with the consent of their LEAs.

On the other hand, recovering tuition the child's parents have paid to a private school is a viable remedy when there is proof that the public schools have denied the child an appropriate education and there is no unilateral placement before exhaustion of administrative remedies or without notice to the school.

The U.S. Supreme Court ruled, in the 1985 case *School Committee of the Town of Burlington v. Department of Education of Massachusetts,* that courts may order school districts to reimburse tuition to parents who make a private school placement in order to obtain an appropriate education for their children. By making such a placement, parents do not waive their rights to seek reimbursement. In addition, courts must determine that the private school placement, not the placement of the proposed IEP, is appropriate. Without making that determination, courts may not order tuition reimbursement. The Supreme Court noted that tuition reimbursement is not an award of damages, since reimbursement merely requires the school district to pay belatedly what it should have paid all along.

The rule can adversely affect an LEA. Thus, in *Parks v. Parkovic* the court held that a handicapped child and his parents were entitled to a preliminary injunction to prevent the state from refusing to pay tuition in a private school placement that the LEA and state agreed was appropriate. The injunction assures the child's continued placement and the provision of necessary services. The LEA and state may not agree to a placement and then refuse to fund it on the ground that the facility is not approved or the placement is inappropriate. Once they decide on the placement, they must fund it because the child is entitled to a free education.

Likewise, *Leo P. v. Board* charged the LEA with tuition at a private school. The LEA had agreed to private school placement for one academic year plus the summer after it. After the new academic year began, and while the child was still in private placement, the LEA refused payment on the basis that its own program was appropriate. The court held that the LEA must continue to pay tuition during due process and appeals. The LEA had failed to act timely to object to the private school (acting after the school year had begun).

If it is impossible for a court to determine, on the record before it, the effect of residential placement on learning disabled children, and if it appears that IEPs for the children would not provide them an appropriate education, it is correct for the children to continue to be educated in a residential facility while new IEPs are developed.[12]

Some cases—apparently a minority—have reached an opposite result from the stay-put rule established by the cases noted above. They have created an exception to the stay-put rule for cases involving risk to the child's health or school district bad faith.[13] In addition, school districts may not unilaterally stop paying tuition. For example, once a court has determined that an LEA is responsible for paying for the costs of residential placement that it recommends, no subsequent change in the student's placement may be made solely on account of the cost of the placement; changes may occur only upon recommendation of the pupil personnel team, made prior to the change.[14] Also, by illustration, *Grymes v. Madden* held that parents are entitled to tuition reimbursement (for private school placement made before they began due process) during pendency of due process appeal.[15]

By the same token, a parent who must spend funds to obtain related services that the school district agreed in the child's IEP to provide is entitled to recover the costs of the services when the school later refused to pay for them. The district's refusal to comply with its IEP agreement is the basis for the parent's recovery. Also, tuition reimbursement is a proper remedy where the schools illegally suspended a child and the parents incurred educational expenses during the period of suspension.[16]

There have been many recent cases on the award of tuition. The basic rule still is that private school placement unilaterally made by parents is not reimbursable by the schools. Thus, if a school offers an appropriate IEP and placement, it is not required to reimburse the parents who place the child in a private school *(Rouse v. Wilson)*, and the parents' decision to make such a placement is at their own risk *(Evans v. District No. 17)*.

Moreover, the parents' rights to reimbursement, if they are entitled to it at all, are not unlimited. Although the LEA must reimburse for tuition paid for a child with learning disabilities during the period that the LEA proposed the child be placed in a program with children with emotional disturbance (i.e., in an inappropriate program), once the school changes its recommendations and offers an LD placement, the parents' rights to reimbursement terminate *(Hudson v. Wilson)*. The LEA does not have an unlimited obligation; once it cures its default, it puts an end to its obligation of reimbursement.

Similarly, the parents' rights to reimbursement are available only if the parents notify the schools that they seek private placement *(Evans v. District No. 17, Garland Independent School District v. Wilks,* and *Quackenbush v. Johnson City School District)*. The reason for this result is that compliance with the procedural safeguards of the EHA is a prerequisite for achieving a free apppropriate public education; it is essentially unfair to require the schools to pay tuition if they do not comply but to allow parents to recover tuition costs even when they do not comply.

It is perfectly clear that the LEA's procedural failures constitute denial of an appropriate education if the failures are so great that the student is functionally or actually excluded from an appropriate program, as seen in *Board of Education of County of Cabell v. Dienelt*. In that case, the LEA failed to conduct triennial reevaluations; did not notify the student's parents of their rights; failed to use an interdisciplinary team to evaluate the student; failed to conduct proper evaluations (that is, those tailored to the student's handicaps; drafted an IEP before the student had been evaluated; and failed to provide an appropriate curriculum. In that case and probably because of the egregious noncompliance by the LEA with the EHA, the court awarded damages to the parents for their lost wages when they were seeking to have the LEA comply with the EHA.

Finally, the LEA is not required to pay tuition for placement in an "unapproved" school. The EHA itself provides that special education and related services are those that are provided by programs that meet the standards of the state education agency. If a school is not on the SEA's approved list, it cannot—because of the definition in the EHA of a free appropriate public education—be considered appropriate. Thus, the parents may not recover tuition for the child enrolled in that school *(Schimmel v. Spillane)*.

Attorneys' Fees, Private Right of Action, and Exclusive Remedy

For several years before 1984, enforcement of the EHA had been complicated by the facts that: (1) Section 504 prohibits schools that receive federal funds from discriminating against otherwise qualified handicapped children, (2) the regulations under Section 504 are nearly identical to those of the EHA, and (3) the Rehabilitation Act is unclear on several critical enforcement issues—namely (a) whether an aggrieved party has a private right of action (a right to sue in court, rather than using administrative remedies exclusively) to enforce Section 504, (b) whether damages are allowable under Section 504, and (c) whether the aggrieved party can recover attorneys' fees under Section 505 of the Rehabilitation Act if successful in the Section 504 lawsuit.

These enforcement issues had been further confounded because Section 1983 of the Civil Rights Act allows a person whose federal statutory or constitutional rights are violated by a state or local official (acting in an official, not a personal, capacity) to sue the official for damages. The question thus arose as to whether a child whose rights under the EHA or Section 504 are violated may sue under Section 1983 to redress his or her rights. If so, may attorneys' fees, as allowed by Section 1988 of the same Civil Rights Act, also be recovered?

The U.S. Supreme Court had addressed related matters (and perhaps thereby contributed to the confusion) in several recent cases. In *Maine v. Thiboutot* and *Maher v. Gagne,* the Court held that persons who are unlawfully denied their rights under the federal Constitution or federal statutes may sue a state or local official who, in the discharge of his or her duties, violated such rights; they may bring their lawsuits under Section 1983 of the Civil Rights Act. In a subsequent decision, *Middlesex County Sewage Authority v. National Sea Clammers Association,* the Supreme Court narrowed the scope of these decisions by holding that where Congress has provided a comprehensive enforcement mechanism for protection of a federal right, and those mechanisms did not include a private right of action (recourse to the courts after administrative hearings), the litigant cannot obtain a private right of action by asserting a claim under Section 1983.

Under related law, The Civil Rights Attorneys' Fees Act, codified as Section 1988 of the Civil Rights Act,[17] a court has discretion to award attorneys' fees to a plaintiff who prevails (wins the case) in a lawsuit brought under Section 1983. Both *Maine* and *Maher* had caused some courts to conclude that they may award attorneys' fees to plaintiffs who prevail in lawsuits they bring against school districts for violation of the EHA, Section 504, and federal constitutional guarantees (under the Fourteenth Amendment) of equal protection and due process.

This issue about attorneys' fees was clarified by the Supreme Court when it held in 1984 in *Smith v. Robinson* that a child who has a claim under the EHA may not also sue under Section 1983 and Section 504 and thereby use Section 1983 and Section 504 as vehicles for recovering attorneys' fees under Section 1988 and Section 505. As noted earlier in this chaper, the Court held in *Smith* that attorneys' fees were not recoverable for two reasons: (1) Congress intended the EHA to be the *exclusive avenue* through which a claim of educational discrimination on the basis of handicap is to be brought to enforce the child's constitutional Fourteenth Amendment rights to equal protection; and (2) the EHA is a *comprehensive scheme* to aid the states in complying with their constitutional obligations to provide public education for children with disabilities, and it would be inconsistent with that scheme to allow the child to circumvent the EHA's administrative remedies by relying on Section 1983 of the Civil Rights Act as a remedy for a substantial equal protection claim that is identical to a claim made and remediable under EHA.

In addition, the Court held that the child is not entitled to recover legal fees under Section 505 of the Rehabilitation Act because, again, Congress intended the child to follow EHA, not Section 504, in enforcing a claim that also is enforceable under EHA. To allow the child to rely on both the EHA and Section 504, the Court said, would be to upset the balance that Congress struck in clarifying and making enforceable the rights of children with disabilities to a free appropriate public education and endeavoring to relieve the financial burden imposed on the educational agencies responsible for guaranteeing the child's rights to such an education. Thus, *Smith* effectively settled that identical EHA, Section 1983, and Section 504 claims may not be pursued simultaneously, with eventual recovery of legal fees if the plaintiff is successful; the EHA is the exclusive remedy, and it does not provide for legal fees.

The Supreme Court also indicated in *Smith* that the constitutional claim—based on a violation of the equal protection clause of the Fourteenth Amendment—would not be allowed if there also is a ground under EHA to sue to remedy the violation. Again, the EHA provides the exclusive remedy for a violation that otherwise (i.e., without the EHA) would constitute a constitutional violation. But the Court was careful to note that a constitutional claim—based on the due process clause of the Fourteenth Amendment—could be pursued (and attorneys' fees awarded under Section 1988) where the plaintiff (in a Section 1983 case) challenges the state's procedural guarantees as not being constitutionally sufficient (as denying the plaintiff the process [procedural safeguards] that is due).[18]

Private Right of Action and Exclusive Remedy.   Although the courts have been divided on the issue of whether an aggrieved party has a private right of action under Section 504, most hold that the right exists.[19] But does the private right of action extend to a right to recover damages or only a right to an injunction to prohibit further discrimination? On this question, there is mass confusion.

In the right-to-education area, some cases[20] hold that damages are recoverable, but others[21] hold to the contrary. The explanation for the two diverse results is this: The cases divide on the issue of whether the legislative history of Section 504 can be read to imply a right to damages. Some say so; others not. Those that say so also argue that administrative remedies (cutting off federal funds) are futile ones for individual plaintiffs, so damages must have been intended to make the Act effective. The courts that disallow damages argue that administrative remedies, coupled with injunctive relief (but not damages), constitute an effective remedy, so a damage remedy may not be implied. Aside from the issue of damages, however, the courts are unanimous in agreeing that a right to an injunction under Section 504 exists.

As to recovery of damages, the leading case is *Anderson v. Thompson.* It holds that compensatory damages are not available under the EHA, absent exceptional circumstances, because the Act has its own exclusive remedy.[22]

THE HANDICAPPED CHILDREN'S PROTECTION ACT: REVERSING SMITH V. ROBINSON

After the Court's decision in *Smith v. Robinson,* the advocates for students with disabilities and many members of Congress realized the need for legislation to overturn *Smith* and to make it clear that the EHA permits the award of attorney fees to a prevailing party. They were motivated not only by the desire to seek clarity in the EHA but also by a recognition that all of the EHA's rights are meaningless without effective enforcement techniques. When a student's family cannot afford a lawyer to help enforce the EHA, an effective enforcement technique is missing.

Accordingly, Senator Weicker, joined by Senator Harkin and other members of the Senate Subcommittee on the Handicapped, introduced legislation to overturn *Smith.* Their bill was successful and eventually was enacted as The Handicapped Children's Protection Act of 1986, P.L. 99-372 (HCPA).

The HCPA provides that in any action or proceeding brought under the EHA, a court may award reasonable attorneys' fees as part of the costs to the parents or guardian of a handicapped child or youth who is the prevailing party. Fees are to be based on the rates prevailing in the party's community for the kind and quality of services rendered. No bonus or multiplier (e.g., 3 times the actual fee) is allowable.

There are some exceptions to the right to recover attorneys' fees. No fees may be awarded after the time the LEA makes a written offer of settlement to the parents or guardian if (a) the offer is timely (according to the Federal Rules of Civil Procedure or within 10 days before an administrative procedure—due process hearing—begins), (b) the offer is not accepted within 10 days after it is a made, and (c) the court or administrative-hearing officer finds that the relief finally obtained is not more favorable to the parents or guardian than the offer of settlement. Notwithstanding these exceptions, fees may be awarded if the parents or guardian prevail and if they are substantially justified in rejecting the settlement offer.

The court may reduce the fees if the parent or guardian unreasonably protracts the final resolution of the controversy, if the amount of the fees unreasonably exceeds the prevailing rate in the community, or if the time spent and legal services rendered were excessive in light of the nature of the action or proceeding. None of these reduction provisions applies if the court finds that the LEA itself unreasonably protracted final resolution of the controversy or if there was a violation of Section 615 of the EHA. (Section 615 contains the procedural safeguards, particularly those relating to due process hearings; thus, if an LEA effectively denies the parents or guardian an opportunity for due process hearings, it may not later complain if the court awards attorneys' fees that were incurred because there were no opportunities for due process hearings and the matter had to be taken directly to court.)

The HCPA applies retroactively to all actions or proceedings that were pending on July 4, 1984, the date of the decision in *Smith v. Robinson.* Naturally, several issues have arisen under the HCPA, and the courts have been involved in litigation over it. One question is whether the retroactivity provision is constitutional. Most courts hold that the HCPA is not unconstitutional; Congress has the power to make laws retroactive as long as it is absolutely clear about its intent to do so. Congress has the power to enforce the Fourteenth Amendment; the EHA is enacted to enforce that amendment; and the HCPA is enacted to enforce the EHA. Thus, retroactivity is constitutional. The leading cases are *Rollison v. Biggs, Jackson v. Franklin County School Board, Board of Education of East Windsor Regional School District v. Diamond, Counsel v. Dow, Fontenot v. Louisiana Board of Elementary and Secondary Education, Yaris v. Special School District of St. Louis County,* and *Dodds v. Simpson.*

Similarly, the HCPA's retroactivity provision allows a Section 504 claim to be heard if it, too, was pending when HCPA was pending *(Board v. Diamond).* And if there also was pending a claim under Section 1983 of the Civil Rights Act, that claim can go forward and attorneys' fees can be awarded if the party prevails on that (and on a Section 504) claim *(Robinson v. Pinderhughes).*

The courts also have considered cases relating to the amount of the fees authorized by the HCPA. Some LEAs have argued that the fees should be proportional to the relief that the parents or guardian obtained; the less the relief, the less the fee. That argument has been rejected by *Rollison v. Biggs,* reasoning that the award of fees in a civil rights case is determined according to the public benefit created by the litigation.

May the fees be increased because of the SEA's or LEA's delay in complying with payment of the awarded fees? Yes, according to *Rollison v. Biggs* and *Moore v. D.C. Board of Education.*

May fees be awarded for work done in connection with a trial as well as in connection with the appeal? Yes, under *Board v. Diamond.*

May fees be awarded for work done solely in the due process hearing? Yes, under *USD No. 259 v. Newton, Burpee v. Manchester School District, Michael F. v. Cambridge School District,* and *School Board of the County of Prince William v. Malone;* but, no, according to *Rollison v. Biggs.*

Often a case is concluded when the parties enter into a *consent decree* (as in the case *PARC*). Under a consent decree, the parties agree that a certain order shall be entered by a court, and the court agrees to enter such an order. Unlike the usual case, cases with a consent decree have been resolved largely by the parties themselves, with the court adopting (in whole or large part) their agreement. Typically, court orders are adversary—not agreed to by the parties. May fees be awarded for consent decree cases? Yes, under *Barbara R. v. Tirozzi.*

If a parent or guardian enters into a settlement agreement with an LEA or an SEA and the agreement does not provide for attorneys' fees, the fees may not be recovered under the HCPA (*Abu-Sahyun v. Palo Alto Unified School District*).

Finally, only attorneys, not "lay advocates," may be paid under the HCPA, which speaks only about attorneys' fees and not about any other kind of fees (*Arons v. New Jersey State Board of Education*).

THE SUPREME COURT'S
CONSERVATIVE APPROACH AND EHA

The *Smith* case illustrates that the Supreme Court is taking a conservative or narrow approach in interpreting the EHA. But *Smith* also is just one of many cases that illustrate the Court's "strict construction" approach to disability issues. It is important to understand not just *Smith* and its approach but also the more general doctrines that underlie that case and the Court's approach to the EHA and other disability issues.

Although *Smith* was rendered in 1984, the Court previously had made it clear that it was not inclined to create new rights for people with disability. It had indicated, however, that it would enforce the rights that Congress created—if Congress would make it perfectly clear that it was creating new rights.

Pennhurst

The original case in the disability field was *Pennhurst State School (Pennhurst I) v. Halderman,* decided in 1981. In that case, the surface issue was whether the Developmental Disabilities Assistance and Bill of Rights Act (the "DD Act") created a right of residents of the Pennhurst state institution for people with mental retardation to live in the community. The DD Act provided:

Congress makes the following findings respecting the rights of persons with developmental disabilities.

(1) Persons with developmental disabilities have a right to appropriate treatment, services, and habilitation for such disabilities.

(2) The treatment, services, and habilitation for a person with developmental disabilities should be designed to maximize the developmental potential of the person and should be provided in the setting that is least restrictive of the person's personal liberty.

(3) The Federal Government and the States both have an obligation to assure that public funds are not provided to any institution ... that—(A) does not provide treatment, services and habilitation which is appropriate to the needs of such person; or (B) does not meet the following minimum standards.

In *Pennhurst,* residents sued to be discharged and provided with community-based residences and services. They based their claims on alleged violations of a variety of federal and state laws: (1) the Eighth Amendment, prohibiting cruel and unusual punishment, and the Fourteenth Amendment, guaranteeing equal protection and due process; (2) Section 504 of the Rehabilitation Act, prohibiting discrimination solely on the basis of disability; (3) the DD Act, creating programs and stating that people with disabilities have rights to live in the least restrictive setting; and (4) state law.

The trial court found for the residents under the constitution, Section 504, and state law, but it did not rule on their rights under the DD Act. The Court of Appeals modified the trial court's order; it ruled that the DD Act had been violated, but it refused to consider the constitutional or the Section 504 claims. It also ruled that the state law had been violated.

The Supreme Court reversed the Court of Appeals, finding that the DD Act did not create any substantive right to residence in the least restrictive environment. The Supreme Court reasoned that the DD Act did not create such a right because Congress had not explicitly said that there is a right to community placement; instead, Congress had declared only that there is a preference to such a placement, as a matter of federal policy.

The Supreme Court said:

> Turning to Congress' power to legislate pursuant to the spending power, our cases have long recognized that Congress may fix the terms on which it shall disburse federal money to the States. [citations omitted] Unlike legislation enacted under § 5, however, legislation enacted pursuant to the spending power is much in the nature of a contract: in return for federal funds, the States agree to comply with federally imposed conditions. The legitimacy of Congress' power to legislate under the spending power thus rests on whether the State voluntarily and knowingly accepts the terms of the "contract." [citations omitted] There can, of course, be no knowing acceptance if a State is unaware of the conditions or is unable to ascertain what is expected of it. Accordingly, if Congress intends to impose a condition on the grant of federal moneys, it must do so unambiguously. [citations omitted] By insisting that Congress speak with a clear voice, we enable the States to exercise their choice knowingly, cognizant of the consequences of their participation.

Indeed, in those instances where Congress has intended the States to fund certain entitlements as a condition of receiving federal funds, it has proved capable of saying so explicitly....

[T]he, specific language and the legislative history of § 6010 are ambiguous. We are persuaded that § 6010, when read in the context of other more specific provisions of the Act, does no more than express a Congressional preference for certain kinds of treatment. It is simply a general statement of "findings" and, as such, is too thin a reed to support the rights and obligations read into it by the court below. The closest one can come in giving § 6010 meaning is that it justifies and supports Congress' appropriation of money under the Act and guides the Secretary in his review of state applications for federal funds. [citations omitted] As this Court recognized [citations omitted], "Congress sometimes legislates by innuendo, making declarations of policy and indicating a preference while requiring measures that, though falling short of legislating its goals, serve as a nudge in the preferred directions." This is such a case.

On reconsideration of the case, the Court of Appeals held that state law created a right to community placement and rejected the state's argument that the Eleventh Amendment prohibited the federal court from enforcing a state-law claim against state officials. The Court of Appeals did not reach the other federal constitutional issues—namely, due process, equal protection, and cruel and unusual punishment.

The state again appealed the Court of Appeals judgment to the Supreme Court, which held in *Pennhurst II* that the Eleventh Amendment does, in fact, prohibit a person from suing a state official in federal court to enforce a right under state law. The importance of the Supreme Court's decision—prohibiting a person from requiring state officials to conform to state law by suing them in federal court—is twofold: (1) the decision reemphasized the Court's reluctance, first declared in *Pennhurst I,* to create rights unless the Congress and the states clearly agree that the rights exist; and (2) the decision created a precedent for other disability-rights cases, including *Dellmuth v. Muth,* decided in 1989.

Sovereign Immunity

The fundamental legal issue in *Pennhurst II* was whether a state, which may not be sued without its consent, agreed to be sued by participating in the DD Act. The Eleventh Amendment, as previously interpreted by the Court, effectively prevents a state from being sued without its consent. That result rests on the principle of *sovereign immunity*—the rule that the state (the sovereign) may not be sued (is immune) unless it consents to be sued. Thus, the issue was whether Pennsylvania could be sued in federal court simply because it took federal funds allocated to it under the DD Act.

To determine whether the state had waived its sovereign immunity and agreed to be liable to a suit, the Supreme Court began by stating the basic rule that a state's consent to be sued must be "unequivocally expressed." This rule is subject to another rule, however. The second rule is that Congress may override the state's sovereign immunity, so that a state may be sued without its consent, if it does so by a law enacted to enforce the rights of citizens under the Fourteenth Amendment. But even this second rule is subject to the doctrine of "unequivocal expression."

Thus, the basic approach in interpreting the Eleventh and Fourteenth Amendments is to study the language that the state and Congress use. If the state is not unequivocally clear that it may be sued, or if the Congress is not equally clear that it overrides the Eleventh Amendment when it passes a law to enforce the Fourteenth Amendment, a state may defend against a suit by claiming the sovereign immunity defense. This is, after all, a basic tenet of the doctrine of federalism: A state's sovereign immunity extends not only to *whether* it may be sued, but also *where* it may be sued (whether in federal court or not).

Given these precedents and the "unequivocal expression" rule of interpretation, the Court held in *Pennhurst II* that federal courts do not have jurisdiction to require that officials and state institutions comply with state law. The DD Act was not unequivocally clear that a state waives its sovereign immunity by taking federal funds under the DD Act. And no other act of the state indicated clearly and without any doubt that it had waived its immunity to be sued, much less to be sued in federal court.

Pennhurst I and *II* signaled a very important trend for the 1980s—the disinclination of the Supreme Court to be involved in cases that rest on constitutional issues and a very high reluctance to have federal courts, especially itself, involved in issues of state policy. After all, the fundamental issue underlying the legal issue of sovereign immunity and the approach to interpreting acts of Congress was the policy of deinstitutionalization. That policy—to close down the state institutions and create community-based placements for their residents—was a most controversial policy during the late 1970s and early 1980s; indeed, it remains controversial even as this book is being revised (fall and winter, 1988). Advocates for and against deinstitutionalization were strong and numerous, and they all advanced various arguments for their cause. The matter was fundamentally one for state policy to resolve, because the institutions were created and operated by the states, and much of the money to operate them was state money.

The way to keep the federal courts out of state policy issues was to limit the ability of plaintiffs (in *Pennhurst I* and *II,* its residents) who challenge state policy to use the federal courts to enforce alleged constitutional or federal statutory claims that the state policy of institutionalization is illegal, as violating federal constitutional doctrines or federal statutes. The way to reach this result is to allow the state to defend against the lawsuit by claiming sovereign immunity from suit in federal court. And, ultimately, the way to reach the result that the state may defend on the ground of sovereign immunity is to interpret the DD Act in a strict, narrow way, requiring a clear and unequivocal expression of congressional intent that the state may be sued. If Congress wants the state to be sued, so that the federal courts will have jurisdiction over challenges to state policies, state officials, and state expenditure decisions, Congress must be crystal clear about its intent.

Federalism

The Supreme Court's reluctance to have federal courts become involved in state policy and expenditure decisions, and its inclination to use the principle of federalism as a way of keeping the federal courts out of state policy matters, was demonstrated again in *Smith v. Robinson.* As pointed out earlier, the Court ruled that Congress intended the EHA to be the exclusive remedy, because it was a comprehensive scheme of enforcement, for violations under the EHA.

In *Smith,* one sees again the Court's reluctance to have federal courts dragged into the state policy-making and policy-enforcing arena. The fundamental issue in *Smith* was not the EHA and rights to attorneys' fees. That was the legal issue, true. But the fundamental issue was again the federal courts' potential involvement in policy making; thus, the challenge for the Court was to find a way out of deciding the issue of attorneys' fees and the allocation of federal and state EHA dollars (since a finding that the plaintiff could recover attorneys' fees necessarily creates a claim on special education dollars to pay the fees).

If, in *Smith,* the Court could determine that there is no right to attorneys' fees, on the basis that the EHA is not unequivocally clear that there is right to them, it could avoid a decision about allocation of federal-state special education funds and the related policy problems of how much money shall be spent to educate children with disabilities and how it shall be spent.

As in *Pennhurst I* and *II,* so in *Smith:* The Court sought to avoid an issue of state policy by using the statutory interpretation doctrine of "unequivocal expression." More than that, however, resulted from *Pennhurst I* and *II* and from *Smith.* Not only did the Court avoid having the federal courts decide these issues about rights and rights enforcement, but it also clearly conveyed to the residents of Pennhurst and the students in special education—that is, to people with disabilities—that they must go to Congress and state legislatures to create rights and obtain the means to enforce rights. This is the result when the Court basically says that the federal courts will not deal with federal and state policy issues unless the Congress and states make it crystal clear that people with disabilities may sue in federal court to enforce rights that are intricately involved with controversial policy issues.

In effect, the Court says: If people with disabilities want new rights created or existing ones interpreted in their favor when the existing ones are subject to more than one interpretation, they may not look to the federal courts for help but must return to the legislatures for help. It is in the legislatures—in Congress and state legislatures—after all, that the original rights under the DD Act and the EHA were created; and it is there, not in court, where the ambiguities must be resolved. Moreover, it is in Congress and the state legislatures that people with disabilities must resolve the fundamental policy issues—namely, how many rights do people with disabilities have, what are those rights, how and by whom will they be funded, and at whose disadvantage do those rights and their enforcement exist?

In the Court's view, as expressed in *Pennhurst I* and *II,* and in *Smith,* the policy issues should be resolved under the democratic majoritarian process—the process of open debate by those seeking rights and those affected by the creation of rights. Not only does majoritarian democracy require this result, but so too does the principle of federalism. After all, the Court is saying, the federal government, in the guise of the federal courts, should not require states to make certain policy decisions. To do so would be to have a federal government absolutely supreme over state governments; it would be to wipe out the opportunity and rights of states and their citizens to decide issues that are closer to them than to the federal government.

Antidiscrimination

The approach to statutory and constitutional interpretation that the Court followed in *Pennhurst I* and *II* and in *Smith* is consistent with the approach it used in other important civil rights cases involving hard issues of public policy.

Conrail and Grove City. In two cases decided in 1984, *Conrail v. Darrone* and *Grove City College v. Bell*, the Court again faced difficult policy issues. In *Conrail*, the question involved the extent to which the antidiscrimination provision of the Rehabilitation Act could be applied to a public agency—namely, the Consolidated Railroad system—and in *Grove City*, the extent to which the antidiscrimination provisions of the Civil Rights Act, prohibiting discrimination based on gender, could be applied to a private college that received some federal funds.

In both cases, then, the basic issue was essentially a policy issue—namely, the extent of federal antidiscrimination statutes. Alternatively stated, the issue was the extent to which quasi-public entities such as Conrail or fundamentally private agencies such as Grove City College could be required to accommodate people in minority status (disabled or female), sometimes at the expense of other people and, in the case of Grove City College, in violation of its organizing principles and underlying values.

In *Conrail v. Darrone*, the first issue was whether the antidiscrimination provision of the Rehabilitation Act—Section 504—authorized a disabled person (and, after his death, his estate) to sue the railroad for discrimination on the basis of handicap. The second issue was, if a suit is permitted by Section 504, whether the suit is restricted only to discrimination related to employment. The Court held that Section 504 authorizes the lawsuit and that any lawsuit under Section 504 may extend beyond discrimination in employment. Thus, Section 504 allows a plaintiff to sue for discrimination in employment and in any activities other than employment.

The Court gave four reasons for this result. First, the language of Section 504 contains no limitation of suits to employment discrimination only. Second, the legislative purpose clearly was to allow suits for employment discrimination, as this was. Third, the Court defers to executive agency interpretations. Finally, the statute is a broadly remedial one that permits the use of Section 504 to enforce discrimination in "all programs receiving federal financial assistance." Note the Court's careful attention to the statutory language, the clearly expressed congressional intent, and then to other criteria for deciding the scope of Section 504.

In *Grove City*, however, the result was different. There the Court had to construe the meaning of Title IX (sex discrimination) as applied to a college that receives no federal financial assistance other than student loan funds. The narrow issue was whether the college is a program or activity that receives federal financial assistance. The Court held that the College is a recipient and based this result on the language of the statute (the same consideration as in *Conrail*), the broad remedial scope of Title IX (the same consideration as in *Conrail*), congressional intent (the same as in *Conrail*), and agency interpretation (the same as in *Conrail*).

But that result—that the college is a recipient—did not dispose of the issue of whether Title IX applied to all of the college's activities or just to those of the financial aid office that administered the student loan funds. The issue then was whether the "program or activity" subject to Title IX is the entire college or just part of it.

The Court held that Title IX is "program-specific," applicable only to the student aid office. Again, the basis of the decision is the language and the congressional intent (the same factors as in *Conrail's* decision). The federal financial assistance was earmarked for the college's financial program; it was not a general underwriting of anything except the college's ability to award financial aid.

By holding that the "program or activity" language of the statute does not subject the college to "institutionwide coverage," the Court avoided the underlying issue: Does Title IX apply to all aspects of private education when only one aspect is federally aided? Alternatively stated, will the Court, or Congress, decide on the scope of antidiscrimination laws, and if the Court is not the body of government to do that, how may it avoid that task and remit the parties to the majoritarian processs? The answer is that the Court may construe the language of a statute in such a way as to avoid or limit its involvement in policy issues raised by an interpretation of the statute.

Atascadero.   The trend of the cases, *Pennhurst I* (D.D. Act), *Pennhurst II* (Eleventh Amendment), *Conrail* (Sec. 504), and *Grove City* (Title IX), was against results that would involve the courts in the political thickets in policy making. This trend was restated in *Atascadero State Hospital v. Scanlon,* a 1985 decision.

There the issue was whether a disabled person may sue a state for enforcement of Section 504 rights, filing the action in federal courts, or whether the Eleventh Amendment bars such an action. The general rule is that the Eleventh Amendment bars a suit against a state; as noted earlier, there are two exceptions: A state may consent to suit, or the Congress may abrogate the Eleventh Amendment, when it enacts legislation to enforce the Fourteenth Amendment. The Court said: "But because the Eleventh Amendment implicates fundamental constitutional balance between the federal government and the States, this Court consistently has held that these exceptions apply only when certain specific conditions are met."

These are the "unequivocal expression" or "overwhelming implication" rules. The Court found that the state constitution does not waive the State's right to not be sued in federal court; and the Rehabilitation Act does not clearly enough subject the state to suits in federal court. To quote the Court: "A general authorization for suit in federal court is not the kind of unequivocal statutory language sufficient to abrogate the Eleventh Amendment. When Congress chooses to subject the States to federal jurisdiction, it must do so specifically."

Here again, the Court gives a strict or narrow reading to the statute—one that is defensible, but one that enables it to avoid the basic policy issue, which is whether the individual may sue a state in federal court to enforce a claimed right against discrimination based on disability. And here again the Court remits the parties to the majoritarian process; it sends them back to Congress to determine whether it, not the Court, wants to take the position that receipt of federal funds subjects the state to suit in federal court.

DOT v. PVA. When the Court again had the opportunity to duck the policy issues of the scope of antidiscrimination legislation, it did so again, in the 1986 decision *United States Department of Transportation v. Paralyzed Veterans of America (DOT v. PVA).* There, as in *Grove City,* the issue was the meaning of "program or activity." Although *DOT v. PVA* was a Section 504 case and *Grove City* was a Title IX case, there was no difference in the result, the Court holding in *DOT v. PVA* that the federal aid to airports does not entitle a plaintiff who has been discriminated against—not by the airports but by air-carriers—to use Section 504 to sue the carriers. Again, the Court's approach is language-based (the carriers are not "recipients") and intent-based (Congress intended to cover only recipients, not all who benefit, however indirectly, from federal financial assistance). But the Court also was concerned about opening floodgates of litigation. It announced the new criterion of the "contractual-manageability" ground (the states must be free to decide whether to take aid in exchange for their commitment not to discriminate, and the power of the courts to enforce that contract of money for pledge to not discriminate must be kept within "manageable bounds").

Summary of Policy Issues. As was to be expected, the Court's decisions in *Smith v. Robinson, Conrail, Grove City, Atascadero,* and *DOT v. PVA* did result in a revisiting of the policy issue, but in a different forum. The parties' surrogates—females *(Grove City)* and people with disabilities *(Smith, Conrail,* and *Atascadero)*—did seek remedies in Congress, and they succeeded. The HCPA, P.L. 99-372, reversed *Smith* and granted a right to attorneys' fees to a prevailing party in EHA actions or proceedings. P.L. 99-506 reversed *Atascadero* and provided for Section 504 to be enforced against state defendants and states themselves in federal courts. And P.L. 100-259, the Civil Rights Restoration Act, made it clear that "program or activity" means *all* the operations of a recipient, both for Title IX and Section 504 purposes. And P.L. 99-435 reversed *DOT v. PVA.*

Dellmuth v. Muth. The Supreme Court confronted the issue of the "strict" or "conservative" reading of the EHA and the Eleventh Amendment in its 1988–89 term. It had before it the case *Dellmuth v. Muth,* which raised two issues.

The first was whether parents who challenge a special education placement may sue the states for the cost of private education. This is a question to which the lower courts had answered both "yes" and "no." The Court's decision, "no," resolved the issue.

The second issue was whether the Eleventh Amendment bars the parents' lawsuits against the states. Alternatively stated, the issue was whether the EHA sufficiently overrides the states' sovereign immunity (from suit without consent, as guaranteed by the Eleventh Amendment) in pursuance of the Congress' power to enforce the Fourteenth Amendment. The Court held that the Eleventh Amendment does prohibit parents from suing states under the EHA. It gave three reasons for this result:

1. There is no unmistakable and unambiguous expression of congressional intent to make the states subject to lawsuits;
2. The expression of such intent must be found in the text of the statute itself; and
3. Congressional history may not be used to furnish evidence of such intent.

As disappointing as this result is for many people, it is not surprising. The battle to overturn the *Dellmuth* decision now forms in Congress.

NOTES

1. Frederick L. v. Thomas, and Panitch v. Wisconsin.
2. Panitch v. Wisconsin.
3. Frederick L. v. Thomas, and Panitch v. Wisconsin.
4. San Antonio v. Rodriguez may be explained partially on the basis that the Supreme Court was more worried about becoming embroiled in school financial issues and related matters of taxation for public services than in dealing with the difficult constitutional issues the case posed.
5. Reid v. Bd. of Ed. of City of N.Y., Rhode Island Society for Autistic Children, Inc. v. Rhode Island Bd. of Regents, Silva v. Bd. of Ed., and Tidewater Ass'n. for Autistic Children v. Tidewater Bd. of Ed.
6. Harrison v. Michigan, Florida ARC v. State Bd. of Ed., and Radley v. Missouri.
7. North Carolina ARC v. North Carolina.
8. North Dakota ARC v. Peterson.
9. Colorado ARC v. Colorado.
10. 20 U.S.C. Sec. 1232(g).
11. The other leading case is Anderson v. Thompson. Cases that concur with "no damages" include Flavin v. Connecticut State Bd., Stemple v. Bd. of Ed. of Prince George's County, Akers v. Bolton (holding that the Eleventh Amendment bars suit against the state and the EHA does not authorize private damage remedy), Hessler v. State Bd. of Ed., Reineman v. Valley View Comm. School Dist., Jaworski v. Rhode Island Bd. of Regents (denying compensatory damages for violation of P.L. 94-142 but allowing nominal compensatory damages for violation of state procedural due process regulations), Dep't. of Ed. v. Katherine Dorr, (Ruth Anne) M. v. Alvin I.S.D., Colin K. v. Schmidt, Foster v. D.C. Bd. of Ed., Hines v. Pitt County Bd. of Ed., Davis v. Maine Endwell Cent. School Dist., Newport-Mesa U.S.D. v. Hubert, Carter v. I.S.D., Dore T. v. Board of Education, Mark R. v. Bd., Calhoun v. Illinois State Bd., Stacey G. v. Pasadena I.S.D., Marvin H. v. Austin I.S.D., Scokin v. Texas, Sanders v. Marquette Public Schools, Christopher T. v. San Francisco U.S.D., Timms v. Metro. School Dist., Christopher N. v. McDaniel, Max M. v. Thompson, and William S. v. Gill (damages only under Sec. 1983, not Sec. 504 or EHA).

Ezratty v. Puerto Rico suggests that a state, simply by participating in the EHA, does not thereby give its consent to be sued for monetary damages. Cases that also rely on the Eleventh Amendment approach—no consent to be sued for monetary damages simply by participating in the EHA— include M.R. v. Milwaukee Public Schools, Miener v. Missouri, Stemple v. Bd. of Ed. of

Prince George's County, Riley v. Ambach, Hark v. School Dist. of Philadelphia, and Anderson v. Thompson.

Powell v. Defoe held that parents are not entitled to damages under the EHA for alleged negligent (mis)classification of the child; they are not entitled to damages under Section 504 for alleged misplacement in special education because there is no implied right of action under Section 504 when placement was made for bona fide educational reasons, in good faith, and not because of discrimination because of handicap; and the Civil Rights Act (Sec. 1983) does not give parents basis for relief because the EHA contains its own exclusive remedy.

A case that reached a similar result is D.S.W. v. Fairbanks North Star Borough School Dist., which held that students who claimed their school district had been negligent in classifying, placing, and teaching them may not sue the district under the EHA for damages.

Other cases denying "malpractice" damages are Loughran v. Flanders, Smith v. Alameda County School Services Agency, Donohue v. Copiague Union Free School Dist., Doe v. Rockingham County School Bd., Christopher N. v. McDaniel, Brosnan v. Livonia Public Schools (negligent diagnosis of learning disability not actionable), and Lindsay v. Thomas (negligent diagnosis of learning disability not actionable under state law).

12. Colin K. v. Schmidt.

13. Bloomstrom v. Massachusetts Dep't. of Ed. (entitlement to the portion of costs corresponding to the cost of an appropriate education); Walter v. Cronin (child's physical health and bad faith of LEA as exceptions to "stay-put" rule, per Anderson v. Thompson); New York City Bd. of Ed. v. Ambach (LEA delays); Doe v. Anrig and Lillian S. v. Ambach (both cases conclude that bad faith by school justifies court award of tuition reimbursement); Stacey G. v. Pasadena I.S.D. (unreasonable delay in evaluation, causing harm to child); William S. v. Gill (allowing tuition reimbursement in case where parents made unilateral private school placement when evidence indicated child's physical health would have been endangered by remaining in current placement). Anderson v. Thompson, Colin K. v. Schmidt, Jaworski v. Bd. of Regents, Foster v. D.C. Bd. of Ed., (Ruth Anne) M. v. Alvin I.S.D., Walter v. Cronin, Mountain View-Los Altos Union H.S. Dist. v. Sharron B.H., and Matthews v. Ambach. A case that explicitly rejects the "bad faith" doctrine is Sanders v. Marquette Public Schools.

14. Michael P. v. Maloney.

15. *Concur:* Stemple v. Bd. of Ed. of Prince George's County, Doe v. Anrig; Lillian S. v. Ambach; Abrahamson v. Hershman; VanderMalle v. Ambach, holding that LEA must continue to pay private placement costs pending new placement decision (triggered because state moved school from approved list of schools), where LEA made the initial placement.

16. Adams Cent. School Dist. v. Deist. *Concur:* Harris v. D.C. Bd. of Ed. and Dep't. of Ed. v. Katherine Dorr.

17. 20 U.S.C. Sec. 1988.

18. For such a case, *see* Quackenbush v. Johnson City School Dist.

19. *See, e.g.,* Miener v. Missouri and Kampmeier v. Nyquist.

20. Patton v. Dumpson, and Poole v. S. Plainfield Bd. of Ed.

21. Anderson v. Thompson, Miener v. Missouri, Boxall v. Sequoia Union H.S. Dist., Powell v. Defoe, and (Ruth Anne) M. v. Alvin I.S.D.

22. *Concur:* Stemple v. Bd. of Ed. of Prince George's County, Akers v. Bolton, Loughran v. Flanders, Hessler v. State Bd. of Ed., Reineman v. Valley View Comm. School Dist., Jaworski v. Rhode Island Bd. of Regents, Dep't. of Ed. v. Katherine Dorr, (Ruth Anne) M. v. Alvin I.S.D., and Timms v. Metro. School Dist.

10
Statutory Techniques

ENFORCEMENT

The donkey chasing a carrot while running from a possible beating with a stick is a familar image, and it is an appropriate one in the case of the EHA because Congress seeks to achieve the education of handicapped children through similar approaches. To enforce the six principles of the law—zero reject, nondiscriminatory evaluation, individualized appropriate education, placement in the least restrictive setting, protection of rights through due process, and parent participation in school decisions—Congress holds out the promise of federal funds to SEAs and LEAs while requiring certain behaviors under threat of withdrawal of federal funds.

On closer examination, however, the image is somewhat misleading, for it suggests that congressional altruism is tinged with more than a bit of cynicism. In fact, Congress legislates the establishment of effective special education programs and demands normal fiscal accountability for them. It is helpful to look at the EHA in this light: Congress puts money where the problems are; it seeks ways to require that programs for handicapped children be accountable to the Congress and to the intended beneficiaries of the EHA; it imposes normal requirements of fiscal accountability to ensure that the federal funds are in fact used as they were intended to be used; and it empowers the appropriate federal officials and agencies to review, correct, and impose sanctions on noncomplying recipients.

PUTTING MONEY WHERE THE PROBLEMS ARE

In 1975, Congress found that there were more than eight million handicapped children in the United States whose special education needs were not being fully met [Sec. 1400(b)(1) and (2)]. Having concluded that it is proper to see that all of those children have a free appropriate public education available to them [Sec. 1400(c)], it was logical for Congress

249

to attempt to solve the national problem through already existing state and local governmental mechanisms. Through the use of those mechanisms—not by establishing separate and distinct federally operated programs of public education—Congress has traditionally sought to respond to educational needs.

Congress' initial step was to provide money for state and local school programs. The second step was to ensure that the public agencies would spend the money on the children it was intended for. The third step was to assure that the money would be shared between local and state agencies (that is, between the agencies most directly responsible for educating handicapped children and the agencies with overall supervision and some direct responsibility). The techniques were: authorization of expenditures, appropriation of funds, and pass-through requirements. Before describing these principal techniques for putting federal funds where they are most needed, it is appropriate to recite some of the facts Congress was responding to.

A Bit of History

In very general terms, financing for the education of handicapped children is the stepchild of public school financing. Many handicapped children were without programs because funds had not been appropriated. Others were fortunate enough to be admitted to programs (although some of their handicapped peers were not), but these programs often were inadequately funded. The use of labels by special educators and others involved in serving handicapped children put them into categories—a convenient practice for serving those children and receiving appropriations for them, but of no use to the handicapped children who were not labeled and categorized. In many school districts, handicapped children were not sought out through child census or child identification programs and therefore were excluded from school planning, programming, and appropriations.

Because of the lack of free public programs, parents frequently were forced into starting private school programs or buying into existing private programs. In either case, parents were required to make tuition payments that parents of nonhandicapped children did not have to make, and in some cases the programs were located far from the parents' homes or in residential institutions. Some states did decide to help defray the tuition for private schooling, but they often did not appropriate sufficient funds to meet the needs of all affected parents.

Unhappily, not all state institutions for handicapped children provided them with an education. Centers for the mentally retarded and hospitals for the mentally ill were notoriously deficient in school programs, especially when compared to state schools for the deaf or blind. State governments were often organized in a way that prevented institutional school programs from being supervised by public school authorities. Departments of public instruction lacked jurisdiction over departments of social services or human resources, and they did not have the authority or the will to supervise other departments' education of handicapped children.

Federal Funding Techniques

Authorization and Appropriation of Monies. Congress authorized the expenditure of federal funds for handicapped children ages birth to 21, inclusive. The authorized funds are allocated to the states through the SEAs, and to local agencies through the LEAs and IEUs in each state. Each SEA must have its application for funds approved by the Office of Special Education and Rehabilitative Services; the LEAs and IEUs must have their applications approved by the SEAs [Secs. 1412, 1413, and 1414]. All authorizations for state and local appropriations are keyed to a formula. In the case of an LEA, the allocation is based on the number of handicapped children in the state, aged 3 through 21, who are receiving special education and related services, multiplied by 40% of the average per-pupil expenditure in the public elementary and secondary schools for the immediately preceding fiscal year. There is a special allocation for children birth through age 2, under Part H of the EHA.

The *basis of the authorization* is the number of handicapped children in all states. The *basis of the allocation* to each state is the number of handicapped children in the state in proportion to the number in the United States. The *amount of the allocation* to each state is 40% of the average per-pupil expenditure for handicapped children receiving special education and related services in all public elementary and secondary schools in the United States.

The following formula is used to compute the average per-pupil expenditure: The aggregate expenditures (without regard to source) for all LEAs in the United States (including the District of Columbia) are determined for the second fiscal year prior to the one the computation is being done for. If satisfactory data for that year are not available, suitable data for the most recent preceding fiscal year may be used. That figure, along with any direct expenditures by the state for operation of the LEAs (without regard to their source), must be divided by the aggregate number of children in average daily attendance who were provided with free public education by the LEAs during that fiscal year [Sec. 300.701(c)]. The 12% and 2% ceilings, as well as the exclusions (handicapped children funded under Section 121 of the Elementary and Secondary Education Act of 1965), apply—those children are not to be taken into consideration [Sec. 300.701(c)].

Pass-Through Requirements. Having devised a way to get money to the states, Congress had to make it trickle down to where the problems and the handicapped children are—the LEAs. Congress accomplished this by requiring that the funds "pass through" the SEA to the LEAs. No more than 25% of the funds may be retained by the SEA. What is not retained by the SEA must be passed through to the LEAs. The SEA may, if it wants, pass through more than the statutory minimum [Sec. 1411(b)(1) and (c)(1) and Sec. 300.705 and .706].

To determine how much each LEA and IEU is entitled to receive from the SEA, Congress used a simple formula based on the proportionate population of each LEA and IEU to its SEA population. The funds are allocated in the same ratio to the total amount available for pass-through that the number of handicapped children (aged 3 through 21) receiving special education and related services in the LEA or IEU bears to the total number of handicapped children in all LEAs and IEUs applying for funds [Sec. 1411(d) and Sec. 300.707]. If an SEA determines that an LEA is adequately providing a free appropriate education to all of the handicapped children in its jurisdiction by using state and local funds otherwise available to it, the SEA may reallocate all or part of the funds the LEA would have received under the pass-through provisions; that allocation must be made to other LEAs that are not adequately providing such an education [Sec. 300.708].

"Average Expenditures"

The LEA and IEU entitlement depends on the number of handicapped children in the state who receive special education and related services. This number is defined as the average number of children receiving those services on December 1 of the school year [Sec. 1411(a)(3) and Sec. 300.75]. LEA entitlement also depends on the average per-pupil expenditure in public elementary and secondary schools of the United States (defined previously, under "Authorization and Appropriation of Monies").

Ceiling

Referring to Section 1411(a)(5) and Section 300.702, the following children may not be counted in determining the LEA allotment:

- the number of handicapped children in excess of the 12% limitation; and
- handicapped children counted under Section 121 of the Elementary and Secondary Education Act (ESEA) of 1965 (called "Head Start handicapped children").

Limitation on "Allowable" Administrative Costs

SEAs are limited in how they may use funds not passed through. They may not use more than 5% of the funds, or $200,000, whichever is greater, for administrative costs related to Section 1412 (state eligibility) and Section 1413 (state plans) [Sec. 1411(b)(2) and (c)(2) and Sec. 300.620 and .621]. The funds available to the SEA for administration may be spent only for the following "allowable costs" [Sec. 300.621]:

1. Administration of the annual program plan and for planning at the state level, including planning, or assisting in the planning of, programs or projects for the education of handicapped children;
2. Approval, supervision, monitoring, and evaluation of the effectiveness of local programs and projects for the education of handicapped children;
3. Technical assistance to local education agencies;
4. Leadership services for program supervision and management of special education activities for the handicapped; and
5. Other state leadership activities and consultative services.

The SEA must use the remainder of the funds (those not allocated to allowable costs of administration) to provide support and direct services for the benefit of handicapped children in accordance with the service priorities [Sec. 1411(b) and (c)]. Section 300.370 defines support and direct services as follows:

1. "Direct services" provided to a handicapped child directly by the State, by contract, or through other arrangements.
2. "Support services" include implementing the comprehensive system of personnel development, recruitment and training of hearing officers and surrogate parents, and public information activities relating to a free appropriate public education for handicapped children.

In the fiscal years beginning in 1978, the amount SEAs spent from federal funds not passed through for support or direct services must be matched, "on a program basis," with state funds for the provision of support or direct services for the fiscal year involved. The matching funds may not be federal funds [Sec. 1411(c)(2)(B) and Sec. 300.371]. "Program basis" refers to the major programs such as personnel development and training hearing officers.

Disentitled LEAs

No LEA may receive funds if it is entitled to less than $7,500 in any fiscal year; if it has not submitted an application that meets the requirements of Section 1414 (SEA applications); if it is unable or unwilling to establish programs of free appropriate education; if it is unwilling to consolidate with another LEA; or if it has one or more handicapped children who can best be served by a state or regional center specially designed to meet their needs [Sec. 1411(c)(4) and Sec. 300.360]. If an LEA has no right to funds, the SEA must use the funds the LEA would otherwise receive to assure a free appropriate education to the handicapped children in the LEA's jurisdiction [Sec. 300.360].

Funds for Territories and BIA

Congress also has provided for federal funds to Guam, American Samoa, the Virgin Islands, the trust territory of the Pacific Islands [Sec. 1411(e)], and the Bureau of Indian Affairs in the Department of the Interior [Sec. 1411(f)].

Ratable Reductions

If Congress does not appropriate enough funds for the states to receive what they are authorized to receive, there will be a ratable reduction in the amount each state receives [Sec. 1411(g)(1)]. By the same token, there will be a ratable reduction of funds available to LEAs [Sec. 1411(g)(2) and Sec. 300.703].

Research, Innovation, Training, and Dissemination Activities

Under Section 1424 of the Act, the Secretary may make specific grants for the benefit of severely handicapped children and youth. These are for research (to identify and meet the needs of handicapped children), development or demonstration activities (new or improved methods, approaches, and techniques for the education and adjustment of handicapped children), training (of personnel to work with them), and dissemination (of materials and information about their education).

Post-Secondary Education Programs

Under Section 1424(a) of the Act, the Secretary may make grants to or enter into contracts with SEAs, institutions of higher education, junior and community colleges, vocational and technical schools, and other non-profit educational agencies, for developing, operating, and disseminating programs in post-secondary, vocational, technical, continuing, and adult education.

In addition, the Secretary may make grants to or enter into contracts with SEAs, LEAs, institutions of higher education, or other non-profit agencies to strengthen and coordinate education, training, and related services for handicapped youths. These contracts are for assistance in the transition from school to post-secondary education, vocational training, competitive employment, continuing education, or adult services, and to stimulate programs for secondary special education.

Antidilution Provisions/Excess Costs

Recognizing that inclusion of handicapped children would be necessary but insufficient to help them, Congress set out to make sure that federal funds would not be diluted—that it would get the biggest bang for its buck. It required LEAs and IEUs to assure the SEAs that federal funds would be spent only for "excess costs" related to child identification, confidentiality of records, full-service goals (including personnel development, adherence to the service priorities, parent participation, and least restrictive placement). Congress also established a timetable for accomplishing the full-service goal and implementing that goal [Sec. 1414(a)(1) and Sec. 300.182 through Sec. 300.186].

An LEA meets the excess-cost requirement if it spends a certain minimum amount of its *own* money on each handicapped child. This does not include costs of capital outlay or debt expenditure. The purpose of the excess-cost requirement is to ensure that children served with federal funds have at least the same average amount spent on them (from sources other than federal funds) as on children in the school district as a whole.

The minimum amount that must be spent for educating handicapped children is computed under a formula. Any costs that exceed the amount determined by the formula are excess costs (they exceed the minimum). Only if an LEA can prove that it has spent the minimum may it use EHA funds to educate handicapped children.

The minimum average amount is computed as follows: (1) The LEA adds all of its expenditures from the prior year except capital outlay and debt service, for elementary or secondary students (depending on whether the minimum is being computed for elementary or secondary handicapped children); (2) the following sums then are subtracted from that amount: (a) amounts spent from EHA funds and Title I and Title VII of ESEA (1965); and (b) amounts from state and local funds spent for programs for handicapped children, programs to meet the special educational needs of educationally deprived children, and programs of bilingual education; and (3) the resulting amount is divided by the average number of students enrolled in the LEA's elementary or secondary programs in the preceding year (depending on whether the minimum is being computed for an elementary or a secondary child). The following example of an elementary school computation comes from the comments on the regulation:

a. First, the local educational agency must determine its total amount of expenditures for elementary school students from all sources—local, State and Federal (including Part B)—in the preceding school year. Only capital outlay and debt service are excluded.

Example: A local educational agency spent the following amounts last year for elementary school students (including its handicapped elementary school students):

(1) From local tax funds		$ 2,750,000
(2) From State funds		7,000,000
(3) From Federal funds		750,000
		10,500,000

Of this total, $500,000 was for capital outlay and debt service relating to the education of elementary school students. This must be subtracted from total expenditures:

$10,500,000
−500,000

Total expenditures for elementary school students (less capital outlay and debt service)................................. 10,000,000

b. Next, the local education agency must subtract amounts spent for:

(1) Programs for handicapped children;

(2) Programs to meet the special educational needs of educationally deprived children; and

(3) Programs of bilingual education for children with limited English-speaking ability.

These are funds which the local educational agency actually spent, not funds received last year but carried over for the current school year.

Example: The local educational agency spent the following amounts for elementary school students last year:

(1) From funds under Title I of the Elementary and Secondary Education Act of 1965		$ 300,000
(2) From a special State program for educationally deprived children		200,000
(3) From a grant under Part B		200,000
(4) From State funds for the education of handicapped children		500,000
(5) From a locally-funded program for handicapped children		250,000
(6) From a grant for a bilingual education program under Title VII of the Elementary and Secondary Education Act of 1965		150,000
Total		1,600,000

(A local educational agency would also include any other funds it spent from Federal, State, or local sources for the three basic purposes: handicapped children, educationally deprived children, and bilingual education for children with limited English-speaking ability.)

This amount is subtracted from the local educational agency's total expenditure for elementary school students computed above:

$$\begin{array}{r} \$10,000,000 \\ -1,600,000 \\ \hline 8,400,000 \end{array}$$

c. The local educational agency next must divide by the average number of students enrolled in the elementary schools of the agency last year (including its handicapped students).

Example: Last year, an average of 7,000 students were enrolled in the agency's elementary schools. This must be divided into the amount computed under the above paragraph:

$$\frac{\$8,400,000}{7,000 \text{ students}} = \$1,200/\text{student}$$

This figure is the minimum amount the local educational agency must spend (on the average) for the education of each of its handicapped students. Funds under Part B may be used only for costs over and above this minimum. In this example, if the local educational agency has 100 handicapped elementary school students, it must keep records adequate to show that it has spent at least $120,000 for the education of those students (100 students times $1,200/student), not including capital outlay and debt service.

This $120,000 may come from any funds except funds under Part B, subject to any legal requirements that govern the use of those other funds.

If the local educational agency has handicapped secondary school students, it must do the same computation for them. However, the amounts used in the computation would be those the local educational agency spent last year for the education of secondary school students, rather than for elementary school students. [Sec. 300.184]

The basic intent of the excess-cost provision is to ensure that SEAs and LEAs provide the same support for handicapped children as for all other children, and that EHA funds are used to supplement the state and local commitment. The regulations stipulate that SEAs and LEAs may not use EHA funds to pay *all* of the special education and related services given to a handicapped child [Sec. 300.186]. The excess-cost requirement, however, does not prevent an LEA from using EHA funds to pay for all of the costs directly attributable to the education of a handicapped child in any of the age ranges 3 through 5 and 18 through 21 if no local or state funds are available for nonhandicapped children in that age range. The LEA, however, must comply with the nonsupplanting and other requirements in providing the education and services.

In another step to prevent dilution, Congress required LEAs to give satisfactory assurances to the SEAs that federal funds received under the EHA will be used to pay only the excess costs directly attributable to the education of handicapped children, to supplement and increase the amount of state and local funds expended for the education of handicapped children, and to provide services in program areas that are comparable to services provided to other handicapped children in the LEA [Sec. 1414(a)(2) and Section 300.229-.231]. Congress also stipulated that LEAs required by state law to carry out a program for educating handicapped children are entitled to receive pass-through payments for use in carrying out that program, but pass-through funds may not be used to reduce state and local expenditures for the program below the level of such expenditures in the preceding fiscal year. In effect, LEAs must maintain their effort in order to qualify for funds [Sec. 1414(f)].

Another antidilution provision prohibits SEAs from using federal funds to match other federal funds [Sec. 1414a]. In a sense, too, the requirement that private schooling be paid for by the LEA is an antidilution requirement.

Consolidated Applications

Some LEAs may not be eligible for funds because they do not generate $7,500 annually, because their application is not approvable, or because they are unable to establish and maintain programs of sufficient size and scope to effectively meet the educational needs of handicapped children. To maintain control of these LEAs, Congress authorized SEAs to require consolidated LEA applications and to allocate funds to LEAs submitting a consolidated application [Sec. 1414(c) and Sec. 300.190-.192]. This provision clearly prevents LEAs from escaping the provisions of the Act.

SEA Direct Services

An SEA may provide direct services to handicapped children, thus displacing an LEA's authority, if the LEA does not seek EHA funds or submits an unapprovable application, or if the SEA determines that the LEA is unable or unwilling to establish and maintain a free appropriate public education. If the LEA is unable or unwilling to be consolidated with another LEA in order to meet those requirements, or has one or more handicapped children who can best be served by a regional or state center, the SEA also can provide direct services [Sec. 1414(d) and Sec. 300.360]. In such instances, the SEA may use payments that would have gone to the LEA and may provide appropriate services at locations it considers appropriate (including regional or state centers), subject to the general requirements of the Act, including least restrictive placement. An LEA that is able but unwilling to comply with the Act would, of course, be subject to the sanctions of that Act. Moreover, it would be in violation of Section 504.

Through all of these measures, Congress has attempted to put its money where the problems are—in the local schools. It has authorized funds, provided for their allocation, required that they be shared by state and local agencies, mandated that they be spent for excess costs and not used in any manner that would dilute their intended effect, and closed the door to LEAs' attempting to escape the requirements of the Act. Having done this much, Congress turned to the problem of making the recipients' programs effective and accountable.

EFFECTIVE SPECIAL EDUCATION

Congress' intent to provide a free appropriate public education to all handicapped children [Sec. 1400(c) and Sec. 1401(18)] is accomplished through six techniques that are intended to enhance the effectiveness of SEA and LEA programs: (1) assistance and involvement in state and local programs; (2) state and local program conformity with other federal legislation affecting the handicapped; (3) state and local program effectiveness; (4) state and local program accountability; (5) limitations on administrative costs to be charged against EHA funds; and (6) sanctions. Although it is organizationally convenient to discuss each technique separately, they are inseparable as a means of accomplishing congressional intent.

Federal Assistance and Involvement in State and Local Programs

Recognizing that it was appropriate for the federal government to assist, assess, and assure the effectiveness of state and local agency programs for educating handicapped children [Sec. 1400(c)], Congress, in Section 1402, first created the Bureau of Education for the Handicapped. (Now, BEH is the Office of Special Education Programs—OSEP). It was designated as the principal agency for administering and carrying out programs and projects to train teachers of the handicapped and to conduct research in education and training [Sec. 1402].

To advance its role in EHA programs, Congress required the Secretary of Education to assist states in implementing the EHA by providing short-term training programs and institutes if necessary, disseminating information, and making sure that each state certified the number of children included in its child count [Sec. 1417(a)(1)]. The Secretary also was authorized to issue regulations for SEA financial reports [Sec. 1417(a)(2)], for implementation of the EHA [Sec. 1417(b)], and to assure the confidentiality of information received from SEAs and LEAs [Sec. 1417(c)]. The Secretary also may hire personnel to help execute the duties of that office [Sec. 1417(d)]. Congress provided for evaluation of SEA and LEA programs by requiring the Secretary to measure and evaluate the impact of EHA programs and the effectivensss of SEA efforts to furnish a free appropriate public education to handicapped children [Sec. 1418(a)]. The Secretary has the right to conduct studies, investigations, and evaluations to assure effective implementation of the EHA [Sec. 1418(b)], and the duty to report certain data and results of evaluations to Congress [Sec. 1418(f)].

Congress empowered the Secretary to authorize use of EHA funds by SEAs and LEAs for acquiring equipment and constructing necessary facilities if he or she determines that a program for education of the handicapped will be improved by the use of federal funds for those purposes [Sec. 1404]. In addition, the Secretary may make grants to SEAs and LEAs to remove architectural barriers and alter existing buildings or equipment so that they may be used by handicapped children [Sec. 1406].

Conformity with Other Federal Programs

Approaching implementation of the EHA on several fronts, Congress required SEAs to make plans for the proper use of EHA funds [Sec. 1413(a)(1)] containing programs and procedures to assure that SEAs, LEAs, and other political subdivisions (such as cities, counties, and special districts) use federal funds in a manner consistent with the goal of establishing a free appropriate education for handicapped children [Sec. 1413(a)(2)].

In an effort to make the education of handicapped people meaningful by providing them with job opportunities after they leave school, Congress ordered the Secretary to make sure that each recipient of EHA funds make "positive efforts" to employ and advance in employment qualified handicapped individuals in programs assisted by those funds [Sec. 1405]. This requirement is consistent with other federal legislation prohibiting employment discrimination against otherwise qualified handicapped individuals (Secs. 101, 501, 503, and 504, Rehabilitation Act Amendments).

Program Effectiveness

Although the regulations just described will contribute to the free appropriate education of handicapped children, nothing can accomplish that goal better than making SEA and LEA programs effective. Unless those programs deliver effective special education services to handicapped children, federal, state, and local funds will not have been wisely spent, the hopes of consumers and educators will be crushed, discriminatory practices illegally foisted upon the handicapped will not be fully redressed, and the notion that handicapped children are not worth the investment of substantial amounts of time, money, and energy will not be dispelled.

To ensure program effectiveness, Congress first required special education programs to be appropriate to the child and individualized, for full benefit. Second, it required public school personnel to become more competent in educating and training handicapped children through personnel development programs [Secs. 1413(a)(3) and 1414(a)(C)(i), and Sec. 300.380-.387]. Third, it limited the number of children who may be counted as handicapped for EHA purposes (the "exclusion" "and "ceiling"). Fourth, it extended the EHA to private programs and established single-agency responsibility. Finally, it required both OSEP and SEAs to create procedures for at least annual evaluation of the effectiveness of state and local programs [Sec. 1413(a)(11)].

Program Accountability

Program accountability is another means of helping special education do the job it is designed to do. The techniques for accomplishing this end are multifaceted. Among them are requirements for single-agency responsibility, SEA preemption, LEA consolidation, public notice of LEA and SEA programs, parental access to records, and requirements that SEAs and LEAs provide information or assurances to OSEP or to the SEA, as appropriate [Secs. 1413, 1414, 1417, and 1418].

Accountability is also advanced by creation of advisory panels [Sec. 1413(a)(12) and Sec. 300.650], establishment of timetables for implementation of the Act, and formulation of full-service goals. The provisions for program evaluation are also a means of producing program accountability.

Limitations on Administrative Costs

By limiting the amount of administrative costs that SEAs or LEAs can charge against EHA funds [Sec. 1411(b)(2), (c)(2), and (e)(3)], and by other techniques designed to put the money where the problems are, Congress clearly intends that programs for the handicapped be made as effective as possible, as well as accountable for how they operate.

Sanctions

It might become necessary to apply stronger measures to recipients of EHA funds if they do not comply with requirements of the Act. Accordingly, Congress provided four types of sanctions:

1. In spite of provisions dealing with exclusion, ceiling, and nondiscriminatory classification of students, children still might be erroneously classified as eligible so that the LEA could count them for receipt of federal funds. Obviously, the LEA should not receive federal funds for such children. Congress required the state plan to contain policies and procedures for seeking to recover federal funds available under the Act that are allocated for incorrectly classified children [Sec. 1413(a)(5) and Sec. 300.141].

2. An SEA may refuse to approve an LEA application that does not meet the requirements of Section 1414(a), setting out the contents of the LEA application, including child census, confidentiality, full-service goals, and related assurances [Sec. 1414(b)(1) and Sec. 300.193]. If, after reasonable notice and opportunity for a hearing, an SEA determines that an LEA has failed to comply with any requirement set forth in an SEA-approved application, the SEA must take one of two steps: (a) withhold payments to the agency until satisfied that the default has been cured; or (b) take the determination into account in reviewing any later application the LEA or IEU might make. It might even take both steps. In any event, the noncomplying agency must give public notice that it is subject to sanction [Sec. 1414(b)(2)(A) and (B) and Sec. 300.194].

3. If, after providing reasonable notice and an opportunity to be heard, the Secretary of Education finds that an SEA or LEA has failed to comply substantially with any provision of Section 1412 (SEA eligibility) or Section 1413 (state plan), or has failed to comply with any provision of the Act or with any requirements set forth in an SEA-approved application from an LEA, he or she must withhold any further payments to the state and may stop further payments to the state of handicapped education funds under his or her jurisdiction, granted pursuant to Section 121 and ESEA and the Vocational Education Act.

The Secretary may limit the withholding of federal funds to specific programs or projects under the state plan (Sec. 1416), or portions of the state plan that are affected by the noncompliance. He or she also may order SEAs not to make further payments to noncomplying LEAs, and may continue to withhold funds until the noncompliance is ended. A noncomplying SEA or LEA must give public notice of the sanction [Sec. 1416(a)]. (Secs. 300.580 and .589 govern Department of Education sanction procedures.)

4. After exhausting all statutory appeals, any aggrieved party in a due process hearing has the right to bring a civil action in a state or United States district court concerning the identification, evaluation, or educational placement of a child, or the provision of a free appropriate public education to a child [Sec. 1415(e)(2)].

FISCAL ACCOUNTABILITY

Another way to accomplish the major principles of the Act is to require fiscal accountability of SEAs and LEAs. The Act imposes fiscal accountability in a variety of ways. It requires the state plan to set forth policies and procedures to assure that federal funds are spent according to provisions of the Act [Sec. 1413(a)(1) and Sec. 300.112].

In order to trace the expenditures and determine if the funds have been spent in accordance with the Act, Sections 1413(a)(6), (9), and (10) require public control of federal funds, prohibit co-mingling or supplanting by the state (Sec. 300.145), and require the state to impose fiscal control and fund accounting procedures. Section 1414(a)(2) requires LEAs to give assurances of public control of funds. The requirement of fiscal control by the state also applies to the LEAs [Sec. 1413(a)(10)].

SECTION IV

Free Appropriate Public Education and the American Value System

11
Objections to the EHA and Answers to Them

A person with even the most casual knowledge about the EHA can recognize that it makes revolutionary changes in the education of handicapped children and in the relationships between the individuals and interest groups involved in educating them. No law as complex and innovative as the EHA can escape severe criticisms. They come from sources such as the regular education constituency, administrators, and teacher associations and unions. They are based on educational and ethical grounds. And they can all be answered more or less satisfactorily.

This chapter gives the most common objections and some of the answers to them. Because the history of the EHA, its implications, and some methods of implementation have already been discussed, the objections and answers will be concise, although more complete statements could be given. The purpose of this book, and particularly this chapter, is *not* to justify the EHA in terms of how it has been implemented, nor to describe its implementation. Accordingly, the objections are not answered in terms of how schools and other agencies have responded since the EHA became effective. I seek to set out the objections and answers. Readers must look elsewhere for data on implementation.

Objection 1: Congress requires compliance, but it does not appropriate sufficient funds. He (or she) who regulates should appropriate.

Answer: The education of handicapped children is an obligation that each state has assumed for itself in its constitution or mandatory education laws. It is not an obligation that the federal government initially or traditionally has undertaken. The federal government seeks to help the states comply with their own self-imposed responsibilities. Its presence is designed to underwrite some, but not all, of the costs of special education that state and local governments have inadequately funded in the past. Nonetheless, it is true that the federal authorization for EHA (the amount that Congress says it may spend) has not been equalled by the appropriation (the amount of money that Congress actually sets aside for the EHA each year). Indeed, the EHA has caused the states and local school authorities to substantially increase their funding for special education. Yet the federal share has not kept pace with what the federal government may spend, if it wants to.

Objection 2: Educating handicapped children is too expensive.

Answer: Although it may cost more to educate handicapped children than nonhandicapped children, the states have a constitutional duty to do so. Federal funds help state and local education agencies comply with that duty. The costs of educating handicapped children required additional tax levies, and present state and local educational funds have been reallocated. Funds spent on the far more costly task of maintaining handicapped persons in institutions during the school-age years and afterwards can be reduced and diverted to educating them. The long-term cost of maintaining handicapped people at public expense is far greater than the short-term cost of educating them when they are children. Indeed, the costs of educating a child with a disability increase in proportion to the severity of the child's disability. Still, there is abundant evidence that all children with disabilities can be workers, and the long-term benefit therefore justifies the short-term cost.

Objection 3: Granted, it is cheaper in the long run to educate a handicapped person than to have the state pay for lifetime care, but state and local education agencies look only to their own funds and have little concern about the wider fiscal benefits of educating a handicapped person.

Answer: Short-sightedness is common among all agencies of government, but it is not forgivable. The EHA addresses the wider concerns through provisions allowing SEAs to use funds not passed through to LEAs for service contracts with state and private agencies, requiring state and local agencies (other than educational ones) to educate handicapped children in their care or custody and providing increased levels of federal funds.

The 1988 amendments to the Social Security Act, entitled The Medicaid Catastrophic Health Amendments Act (see chapter 5), provide the SEA and LEA with a pool of funds for educating children who have severe health-related disabilities, essentially by allowing EHA and Medicaid funds to be combined to provide related services. These amendments reduce the burden on the education budget and partially answer the objection.

Objection 4: The EHA requires funding of *related services,* which are really not *special education* services.

Answer: The related services are essential to the appropriate education of a handicapped child. Without them, special education is an inadequate education.

Objection 5: Requiring SEAs and LEAs to provide related services will encourage them to create their own capacities to furnish those services, in spite of the fact that other agencies (such as mental health, social services, or human resources) have the necessary capacities. The resulting interagency competition will dilute already inadequate state fiscal and personnel resources.

Answer: Through the state plan and single-agency responsibility, SEAs can orchestrate the efforts of various agencies so that they cooperate rather than compete.

Objection 6: The EHA tips the scales of state-federal relationships so drastically toward the federal that state and local discretion in the education of handicapped children is all but eliminated. This represents an intolerable intrusion on the concepts of federalism and state and local autonomy in education.

Answer: The EHA is a formula-grant act that does not require the states to participate. Moreover, state and local autonomy has permitted the states to fail in their legal duties to educate handicapped children. Were it not for such massive failure, federal regulations governing the use of federal funds would not be necessary. The federal government must correct violations of citizens' Fifth and Fourteenth Amendment rights. To that end, it can legislate even without appropriating funds.

Objection 7: The requirement for single-agency responsibility runs against the grain of the Tenth Amendment, which provides that states retain powers not specifically delegated by the U.S. Constitution to the federal government.

Answer: As a condition for allocating federal funds to states that seek them, the federal government constitutionally may require administrative convenience through the single-agency device. Moreover, the single-agency requirement seals service gaps that previously excluded handicapped children from a free appropriate education.

Objection 8: The EHA represents an unwarranted shift in educational philosophy, requiring individualized education when, as a rule, mass education has been acceptable.

Answer: There is no shift in philosophy—only an extension of the accepted philosophies of education. Individualized education is necessary if handicapped children are to be adequately educated (that is, if public policy is to be accomplished).

Objection 9: The law omits the gifted child, whose educational needs are clearly exceptional.

Answer: Gifted children have not been subjected to the same discrimination and violation of their constitutional rights as have handicapped children. Federal programs already provide funds for their education. And, like the nonhandicapped child, they have been receiving at least a minimum level of education.

Objection 10: The EHA should not authorize SEAs and LEAs to provide education to handicapped children during the preschool years, because those children are better dealt with by health and social service systems, not school systems. In addition, the EHA should not authorize SEAs and LEAs to provide education to handicapped children who are over the age of majority (usually 18) and in transition from school to adult services or post-secondary education, because those children are better dealt with by existing service systems, such as vocational rehabilitation, developmental disabilities programs, mental health and mental retardation programs, social and human services programs, and institutions of higher education, including the vocational and technical institutes.

Answer: The schools are one part—and a very important part—of the system of services that federal, state, and local governments have created for people with disabilities. As part of that system, schools have legitimate roles to perform. In the case of preschool children, they can and should work with other service providers to assure that the children are prepared for elementary school. When other service providers do not furnish preschool training, the schools themselves may do so, benefiting both the children and the schools themselves.

In the case of young adults, the schools also can and should work with other service providers to assure that the young adults are moved effectively from their secondary education programs into post-secondary education or adult services. Schools have an important role to play in the transition of students into other service systems. That role includes providing transition services (which other service systems may not provide) so that the students' education is made most effective.

Objection 11: The EHA creates a special law for special (handicapped) people, thus contradicting one of its own principles—the integration of all students. Its concepts are internally inconsistent.

Answer: If handicapped people are to be included in the benefits of a public education, integration through least restrictive appropriate placement and equal opportunities (the same as extended to nonhandicapped students) are a must. The longstanding and severe discrimination against handicapped people justifies remedial legislation that redistributes public benefits in compliance with federal and state constitutional requirements and laws. Both integration and preferential treatment of disabled persons is justified in light of past wrongs and within the principles of distributive justice.

Objection 12: The EHA places unwarranted emphasis on handicapped children by putting an inordinate amount of public resources behind their education. More to the point, it says that handicapped students are entitled to more of society's benefits than other children, thereby misconstruing the contribution—the "return"—that handicapped children will make to society.

Answer: The issue of competing equities—who is to be inconvenienced so that the needs of handicapped students may be met, and to what degree they are to be inconvenienced—is at the heart of all legislation that advances the interests of any minority group, whether the group is characterized by race, sex, handicap, or some other trait. The answers have not yet been generally articulated, but in the case of the EHA, they can be easily set forth.

The Act corrects massive past discrimination; it redresses the balance of fiscal equities by providing a limited portion of the additional costs of educating handicapped children; it requires only that LEAs spend at least the same amount on handicapped children as on nonhandicapped ones; it cures the imbalance of educational equities by enabling many handicapped persons to make substantial contributions to society through the requirement that they be given education for work and equal educational opportunities; and it institutionalizes values that the majority holds dear. It is not likely to overbalance the competition for equities or put children with handicaps in a position of significant advantage.

Objection 13: Leaving aside the issue of competing equities, the EHA grants to the handicapped special rights, such as the right to an IEP and individualized appropriate education.

Answer: Although nonhandicapped students do not have the same legal claims as the handicapped, they have generally received a far more appropriate education. The Act extends to the handicapped the soundest current educational principles, including least restrictive appropriate placement, individualized programming, and procedural safeguards.

It may, and indeed should, set the stage for nonhandicapped students to receive those same benefits. It can help special educators make important contributions to the education of all children.

Objection 14: The EHA sets a policy that is simply disagreeable. Handicapped children really should not be educated; they should be placed in institutions or in special schools with their own kind.

Answer: Besides the fact that the states have a legal obligation to educate handicapped children and have violated the state and federal constitutional rights of those children, it is definitely in the public interest to educate them outside institutions whenever possible. Only with education can the handicapped contribute to society rather than be dependent on it. All the evidence shows that they can learn if appropriately trained, and appropriate training usually occurs outside of institutions.

Objection 15: The EHA imposes such an excessive administrative burden that it will divert educators from their proper role—educating handicapped children. Bureaucrats will devise coping behaviors, resulting in mere paper compliance with the law.

Answer: Although more paperwork is required, *better* paperwork is also called for, and SEAs and LEAs may charge some administrative costs against federal funds. Some educators may take approaches that undermine or diminish children's rights under the law, but this reaction certainly will not be universal. The required personnel development programs for preservice and inservice personnel and federal and state technical assistance should make the administrative "costs" more manageable. Educators' time should be increasingly available for the actual education of handicapped students. Moreover, much of the administrative burden is created by the states themselves.

Objection 16: The state will simply certify to the federal government that the public agencies have complied with the EHA when, in fact, they have not.

Answer: The EHA is full of accountability devices that consumers and the OSERS may invoke if they believe that noncompliance exists. The Act's sanctions are strong enough to induce the states to comply.

Objection 17: To avoid certifying that something is true when it is not, states will try to reduce their responsibilities under the Act. They will lower their program standards to a level at which they will become relatively meaningless for handicapped children.

Answer: An appropriate education entails not only compliance with state standards but also the avoidance of functional exclusion. Handicapped children may invoke (and have invoked) the procedural safeguards, including their right to sue in federal or state courts, to ensure that they are not denied an appropriate education even though their educational program may comply with state standards.

Objection 18: In an effort to make compliance easier, educators will write IEPs that call for easily obtainable goals and objectives.

Answer: Although educators may seek to minimize IEP goals and objectives, parents and other participants at IEP conferences can see to it that the IEP is realistic.

Objection 19: A child's failure to achieve the goals and objectives set forth in the IEP does not make the educators liable. The IEP is really not a technique for holding educators accountable.

Answer: The Act has procedural safeguards that allow parents to raise the issue of the school's failure to write an IEP, and courts may hold the schools as well as individual educators liable for failing to write an IEP. The claim of such a case would be that the schools and educators failed to perform a statutory duty owed to the child, not that they or the child failed to perform as the IEP required. This is the *Rowley* process definition of appropriate education. Moreover, the *Rowley* substantive definition of appropriate education (that there be an educational benefit for the student) ensures that the educators can be held accountable.

Objection 20: The procedural safeguards of the EHA are inconsistent with procedural safeguards under the laws of many states. The EHA creates confusion and conflicts with some state laws.

Answer: The EHA is a federal law that rightly seeks uniformity in its application and interpretation. For this reason, it is appropriate to include a single set of procedural safeguards. Although the safeguards in the EHA may differ slightly from, or even conflict in some respects with, state laws, they reflect the basic provisions of case law and of state law to a surprisingly accurate degree. The differences or conflicts are minimal.

Objection 21: The costs of complying with the procedural safeguards are high and may require that funds be diverted from the education of handicapped children to pay for the safeguards.

Answer: The safeguards are an integral part of the legislation. Without them, there would be no way to make the schools accountable or enable them to do their jobs properly. The safeguards do require administration, time, and personnel, but they are indispensable to the statutory guarantee of a free appropriate education. Compliance with child census, nondiscriminatory evaluation, the IEP, and other provisions is a means of forestalling due process hearings.

In states where similar safeguards have been in the law for several years, the number of cases has been well below educators' fearful expectations, and not all were decided against the schools. Educators are far from defenseless in due process hearings.

Objection 22: The EHA requires the schools to answer to too many masters; there is an excess of "enforcers."

Answer: Although both the OSERS in the Department of Education and the Office for Civil Rights have enforcement powers (as do hearing officers and courts), the principles of *res judicata* (the same matter has been adjudicated before) and the *stare decisis* (the precedent for this case has been set by an earlier case with similar facts involving the same issue of law) can prevent duplication of enforcement. For that matter, educators' compliance is the best guarantee against sanctions.

Objection 23: The EHA creates potential liability for school systems and educators; both institutional and personal liability are likely. Educators may start to practice "defensive education," just as some physicians practice defensive medicine and some mental health professionals practice defensive treatment.

Answer: The EHA may encourage the practice of defensive education, but it is more likely to require and enable educators to do what they have been trained to do and should have been doing all the time—giving each handicapped child a free appropriate public education. The Act takes the best practices of special education and writes them into the law, thereby both requiring and enabling educators to practice as professional standards require. Moreover, the requirements for IEPs, nondiscriminatory testing, and parent participation should actually forestall lawsuits against educators if they comply with those requirements. The due process hearing itself can protect educators against later liability if they comply with the orders of hearing officers.

Objection 24: The EHA is a lawyer's dream, creating a multitude of potential lawsuits against educators and schools.

Answer: Certainly, litigation is necessary to enforce the EHA and to define or refine the rights of handicapped children under it. But litigation also can show school systems how to carry out their obligations and give them desirable political clout in dealing with state and local funding sources. Moreover, the duties and the potential liabilities litigation creates exist independently of the EHA. They are based on federal and state constitutional claims and state mandatory education laws.

Objection 25: The requirement of least restrictive appropriate placement guarantees some form of educational integration, but it does not and cannot guarantee social integration or a change in attitudes about the handicapped.

Answer: Not only does school integration lead to social integration (to the extent that any student chooses to make friends with any other student, handicapped or not), but it also has long-term social integration effects. It positively influences the attitudes of nonhandicapped toward handicapped people.

Objection 26: The requirement for nondiscriminatory evaluation cannot always be satisfied, and the requirement institutionalizes the undesirable practice of classifying and labeling children.

Answer: The nondiscriminatory evaluation techniques found to be effective with handicapped children in some minority populations can be adapted for use with handicapped children in other minority populations. Moreover, classification itself is not entirely invidious. It does have educational benefits. The nondiscriminatory testing requirement attempts to encourage fairness in evaluation procedures and assumes, with justification, that fair procedures will yield acceptable results.

Objection 27: The requirement for parental consent to initial evaluation and nondiscriminatory testing may prevent school psychologists from testing a child and thereby deny the child the educational opportunities needed.

Answer: The school may invoke due process hearings if the parents refuse to consent to an initial evaluation. The requirement for fair testing procedures does not prevent testing. It requires testing to be accurately and appropriately performed. If anything, it results in greater accuracy in tests and a better basis for judgments by school personnel.

Objection 28: Realizing that a child who is designated *handicapped* has substantial rights, schools may be reluctant to classify a child as handicapped and might instead treat him or her as nonhandicapped, perhaps to the child's detriment.

Answer: Although this may occur, at least the child would not suffer the stigma of being labeled *handicapped.* The child's parents may, of course, invoke a due process hearing if the school refuses to identify or evaluate their child or if it refuses to grant an appropriate education.

Objection 29: The practice described in Objection 28 would leave the "hardest" cases in special education and remove the "best" children from programs for the handicapped.

Answer: If this occurs, it may prove to be consistent with the principle of least restrictive appropriate placement, thus making special education programs and classes truly special. This reflects the service priorities Congress set forth for the expenditure of EHA funds. Also, some handicapped children are not so different from nonhandicapped children—in the way they learn, the rate at which they learn, or the methods they need to be taught with—that they should be left out of the mainstream.

Objection 30: Teachers are inadequately prepared to implement the law; this is especially so of "regular" teachers.

Answer: SEAs have the responsibility and available federal funds to carry out preservice and inservice personnel development programs.

Objection 31: Although SEAs have the authority for personnel development, the law does not make any demands on colleges or universities that engage in teacher training. It does not require them to change their preservice curriculum to enable future regular and special educators to carry out provisions of the law such as least restrictive placement.

Answer: Congress could extend the regulations to colleges and universities receiving federal funds, but it chose not to impose requirements on them, singling out the SEAs as the agency responsible for statewide implementation. The SEAs may contract with colleges and universities for preservice and inservice training. And colleges and universities are funded under the EHA for personnel development, research, and demonstration projects directed at implementing the EHA.

Objection 32: The law requires too much of the schools, which must cope with severe personnel shortages in some school programs and inadequately trained personnel throughout.

Answer: The personnel development mandate should ease those immediate concerns, and the requirements for long-range planning (full-service goals), child census, and the ability of SEAs to contract with colleges and universities also will help schools with implementation. The Act simply requires schools to do what they were supposed to be doing all along.

Objection 33: Personnel problems are serious enough in metropolitan areas, but they are extreme in rural areas. In fact, rural school systems have a hard time complying with the law.

Answer: In addition to the provisions of the EHA just mentioned in reply to Objection 32, the Act provides for consolidated grant applications, which should be especially appropriate for rural areas. The Act also provides for direct services by the SEAs and optional purchase of services from private agencies, colleges, and universities.

Objection 34: The EHA creates unequal services for handicapped children by setting priorities for some but not for others.

Answer: First-priority children are entitled to the first priority in the use of EHA funds because they must be included in school programs. Equal protection and zero reject demand no less. Second-priority children are entitled to the second priority because the inadequate education they receive amounts to functional exclusion and may be tantamount to no education at all. Handicapped children who are not in the first or second priorities do not have the same needs as other handicapped children. School systems are already serving them better than the children in the first two priorities.

Objection 35: The EHA creates artificial ceilings for the classification of handicapped children for federal funding purposes. For example, some school systems typically have more learning disabled children than 2% of all their children.

Answer: The ceilings place reasonable limits, based on available data, on the responsibility of the federal government to fund state and local programs. Open-ended funding would be disastrous. At present, a school may serve more than the number of children covered by the federal ceilings by using its own funds. The ceilings force the school systems to adhere to the priorities by counting only the most needy children as eligible for federal funds.

Objection 36: The foregoing criticisms all make the point that the EHA goes too far in regulating and falls short in appropriating. More money is needed to educate handicapped children, and the EHA does not provide enough. For example, it does not include children ages birth through 5 in mandatory programs, does not establish a right to compensatory education for children who were denied their rights to education when they were of school age, and sets low ceilings on federal funding.

Answer: The rights to preschool and compensatory education are not generally granted by state constitutions or laws, and one purpose of the federal law is to be generally consistent with state laws. The federal presence is designed to assist states in complying with *self-imposed* laws. Without the ceilings there would be an unlimited—and unrealistic—federal obligation. The EHA is a remarkable beginning, one of the most important federal education laws ever enacted. It builds on case law, sets forth rights and techniques for securing those rights, commits the federal government to the education of handicapped children, moves them into the mainstream of the schools, and gives them a means of joining the mainstream of society.

Objection 37: The EHA does not create in-school advocacy systems despite ample evidence that child advocacy with school systems is necessary for the implementation of children's rights.

Answer: Although it does not create a single formal advocacy system within the schools, the EHA does offer many techniques for monitoring, such as the procedural safeguards, parent participation, and administrative sanctions.

Objection 38: Whether the EHA goes too far or not far enough in creating rights for handicapped children is beside the point. What is important is whether the law over-promises and under-performs, creates unintended consequences (negative reactions to handicapped children), or acts as a proper vehicle for interpreting and applying educational principles.

Answer: The EHA is based on court decisions and congressionally gathered data that prove that handicapped children have suffered longstanding and severe discrimination in the public schools. It promises them a redress of their grievances and follows up that promise with federal funds, accountability techniques, and the requirement of sound educational principles. Of course there will be negative reaction to any act that regulates, especially if it affects the traditionally sacrosanct practices of state and local schools. The EHA, however, can positively shape attitudes about handicapped children, show the schools how to perform duties they must perform as a matter of state law, provide financial support to the schools, and make important contributions to the education of nonhandicapped children. The educational practices that it mandates are sound and have been sound for a long time. If, for some reason, they *are* found to be unsound after careful research and review, they can be deleted from the law, but there is no present reason to change them.

Objection 39: The "bottom line" is not the EHA or the cases; it is the values they enforce. Simply stated, the Act and the cases do not articulate the values of the majority.

Answer: The objection is untrue, as the next chapter will demonstrate.

12

Underlying Beliefs and Values in Right-to-Education Laws

No radical change of public policy occurs and is sustained unless there are generally accepted beliefs to support the change. This is particularly true of the right-to-education movement, and although our beliefs and values may not have been well articulated in the past, they do exist and can be put forward.

To make clear the underlying beliefs and values in the right-to-education movement, this chapter first reviews the role of law in the right-to-education cases. It then examines the dual system of law to which children and adults with disabilities had been subjected and the objectionable principle that sustained that dual sustem. Third, it discusses briefly the civil rights movement that began in 1954 with the Supreme Court's decision in *Brown v. Board of Education* and the meaning of that movement for disabled children and youth. Fourth, it sets forth the basic concepts that underlie the right-to-education movement, explains the interactive relationship of political ideologies, human service and special education concepts, and legal principles, and shows how the interaction of these ideas gave support to the right-to-education movement. Fifth, it discusses the techniques of law reform, followed by a discussion of the nature of law reform in the context of the right to education for disabled children and youth, and how advocates have resorted to federal and state legislatures, executive agencies, and courts to secure equal educational opportunity. Seventh, it sets forth the underlying beliefs in special education law (the so-called right-to-education credo). Eighth, it defines the law, the underlying beliefs and values, and shows how they are harmonized through the EHA. Finally, it describes the trade-offs that are made to obtain certain results in the education of disabled children.

ROLE OF LAW

It should be obvious by now that the role of law in our society is basically twofold. First, the law seeks to regulate the affairs of individuals in relation to each other. Consider how the EHA does this. The EHA makes it possible for parents, school personnel, and disabled children to have certain regularized relationships with each other, mainly through the principles of nondiscriminatory evaluation, appropriate and individualized education, least restrictive placements, due process, and parent participation. In each of these principles, the EHA sets forth certain rules that parents, school personnel, and disabled children must follow to assure the child's education. In this way, the EHA regulates the relationships of individuals to each other.

Second, the law seeks to regulate the affairs of an individual to his or her government. The EHA does this in the same way that it regulates the affairs of individuals to each other, but simply by substituting the SEA or LEA for school personnel. Here, too, the EHA emphasizes procedures and process. And, to make those procedures and processes meaningful, the courts have interpreted them and other relevant laws (e.g., the Civil Rights Act and Section 504 of the Rehabilitation Act), thereby regulating the relationships of the governed (parents and children) to the government (SEA and LEA).

In these respects, then, the EHA is very traditional. This is so even though its provisions may have seemed (or still may seem) to be thoroughly innovative, even radical.

DUAL SYSTEM OF LAW

The fact that the right-to-education movement for handicapped children had to begin in the courts and be legitimized by Congress attests to a distressing historical fact: People with disabilities have been treated as second-class citizens in America. Not only has popular and some professional opinion usually treated them as less worthy of protection and improvement, but the law itself also has perpetuated the same treatment and a wrong idea—that those who are less able are indeed less worthy.

In the area of education, the right-to-education cases (especially the early ones) and EHA frontally respond to this odious notion. For example, it was not uncommon for SEAs and LEAs to exclude disabled children from school; hence the zero reject principle. It was not uncommon for SEAs and LEAs to discriminate against disabled children in testing and classification, often for reasons wholly unrelated to the educational capacities of those children; hence the nondiscriminatory evaluation principle. It was not uncommon for SEAs and LEAs to fail to provide handicapped children an appropriate education, particularly with nondisabled children; hence the principles of appropriate, individualized education and least restrictive environment. Finally, there was precious little due process and parent participation in the education of handicapped children; hence the necessity for those two principles.

Because public and some professional opinion so influenced the law that the principle of "less able is less worthy" became the rule, it was necessary to make a radical and complete rejection of that principle. The right-to-education cases and the EHA do this by affirming another principle: *Less able does not mean less worthy.*

LAW REFORM MOVEMENT

Brown v. Board of Education, the 1954 Supreme Court decision holding that separate education of the races in public education is inherently unequal and therefore forbidden by the equal protection doctrine, lighted the way for development of widespread civil rights reforms. The law's attention was drawn to segregation of people by race, first in public schools and then in public accommodations (such as restaurants and buses). Next, the law was broadened to protect students and minors generally so that they would have the same or substantially the same rights as adults have under the federal Constitution. At nearly the same time, the rights of persons charged with crimes were expanded under constitutional doctrines. Finally, the civil rights movement reached out to protect women and aliens from practices and laws that treated them discriminatorily.

The 18 years from 1954 until 1972—the time span between *Brown* and the *PARC* and *Mills* decisions—represented a long time for disabled people who were victims of discrimination. Today, children and adults with disabilities, their families, and the professionals who serve them owe a tremendous debt to the civil rights frontiersmen who radically changed the meaning of the Constitution, particularly the equal protection and due process provisions of the Fourteenth Amendment. Without those constitutional pioneers and their risk-taking clients, the legal groundwork for the right-to-education movement would not have been laid and the "silent revolution" in education would have been much longer in coming.

The *Brown* decision was more than a landmark in the development of the law and the application of constitutional principles. It was a landmark, as chapters 1–3 showed, because it had such a profound and long-lasting influence on the law's application to other minority groups, including in particular those with disabilities. But *Brown* also reflected a developing moral sentiment—one not universally held but one that at least the Court's members and some others believed needed to be articulated. This sentiment was that segregation by race was ethically intolerable. Today, many people who challenge segregation by disability or other indicia of inferiority also premise their arguments on moral and ethical grounds. Finally, *Brown* stimulated an inchoate political movement and gave first voice to a renaissance in political ideology—an ideology of equality in oppportunity. In these three regards, *Brown* was a progenitor of the right-to-education movement on behalf of children with disabilities. Just how this is so is the topic of the next section.

NATURE AND SOURCES OF RIGHT-TO-EDUCATION POLICY

One of the remarkable aspects of the civil rights movement was the interaction of political beliefs and constitutional doctrines. It is not appropriate here to say which came first—the political belief or the legal doctrine. It is important, however, to note that there was a happy and necessary coincidence of doctrine.

Egalitarianism, Equal Protection, and Due Process

The belief in egalitarianism (that all citizens are inherently equal and should be treated that way) was the corollary of the constitutional doctrines of equal protection (equally situated people should be treated equally, as a general rule) and due process (governments may not act arbitrarily, treating some people one way and others another way, without reason). Egalitarianism held that it is not consistent with the democratic principles upon which the country was founded for blacks and whites to be treated differently (by being segregated), for women to be barred from various occupations, or for children to be without legal protection. The equal protection and due process doctrines held that the Constitution prohibits such discrimination against racial and other minorities.

In the right-to-education movement, there was a similar convergence of beliefs and ideologies. But there was more—the infusion of certain concepts of human services and special education. Thus, the right-to-education movement rests on three separate but complementary grounds: political egalitarianism, constitutional equal protection and due process, and the human services and special education doctrines of normalization and integration/least restriction/mainstreaming.

Egalitarianism holds that all citizens, and hence all children and youth, are essentially equal and should be treated that way. In education, this came to mean that disabled children should have the right to a free appropriate public education—which is what most nondisabled children obtain from the political process as a matter of right. *Equal protection* and *due process* hold, respectively, that governments may not treat essentially similar people differently or arbitrarily (i.e., without sufficient reason to make the distinctions). In education, these doctrines came to mean that disabled children may not be excluded from education; they, like nondisabled children, constitute a "class" of similar people—namely, students—each of whom is capable of learning. Accordingly, it is arbitrary, and therefore a violation of equal protection and due process, to treat one group of students (those who are disabled) different from another (those who are not) by denying them educational opportunities that are less than comparable to those of nondisabled children.

Just as egalitarianism gave impetus to the doctrine of equal educational opportunity, and just as the equal protection and due process doctrines gave a legal underpinning for equal educational opportunity, so, too, did certain human service and special education doctrines support the political and legal doctrines and receive legitimacy from them in turn. These doctrines were normalization and integration/least restriction/mainstreaming.

Normalization and Integration/Least Restriction/Mainstreaming

Normalization is a principle that came to America from the Scandinavian countries and was articulated here by Wolf Wolfensberger, now a professor of special education at Syracuse University. In his first formulation, normalization meant making the lives of mentally retarded people as normal as practicable; the principle of normalization sought to create human service systems, including special education, that were as normal as practicable for the clients in those systems. In his second formulation, normalization has given way to a new principle—*social role valorization:* the creation, support, and defense of "valued social roles" for disabled people and others who are at risk of social devaluation.[1] Both principles seek to reduce or prevent the overt signs and differentness that may devalue a person in the eyes of others and to change societal perceptions and values in regard to such a person so that his or her disability is no longer devalued.

The doctrine of *integration/least restrictive alternative/mainstreaming* really is three separate concepts rolled into one. As chapter 6 of this book shows, the legal doctrine of least restrictive alternative placement in education attempts to maximize the disabled student's education as well as the opportunity to associate with nondisabled students and adults. Similarly, chapter 6 describes mainstreaming as a related concept, one that addresses the placement of disabled students into educational settings—classes, other activities, and buildings—with nondisabled students. Both doctrines emphasize the integration of disabled and nondisabled students, and both regard integration as a strategy for educating disabled students.

It should be obvious that normalization/social role valorization and integration/least restriction/mainstreaming are powerfully related to political egalitarianism and constitutional equal protection. Like egalitarianism and equal protection, these two human service concepts seek equal educational opportunities for disabled students. They promote equal treatment when such treatment will render equal opportunities, and they seek unequal treatment when that kind of treatment is necessary to render equal educational opportunities. They also affirm that disabled students are not so different from, and actually are so much like, nondisabled students that it is not justified always to treat them less favorably by segregating them and providing them with less than comparable educational opportunities.

For those who believe in the education of handicapped students, it is fortunate that the climate of the 1970s was such that it was possible and even desirable as a matter of national politics to extend the benefits of egalitarianism to disabled students. Likewise, it was a happy matter that the courts had developed the equal protection and due process doctrines in such a way that they could be brought to bear on the education of disabled children and that the children's advocates could persuade the courts to apply the constitutional precedents of the civil rights movement in creative and positive ways to the education of disabled students.

Finally, it also was a matter of extreme good luck that human services and special education programs were developing and accepting ideologies that welcomed and were accommodating to these political and constitutional ideologies. The trio of ideologies—

egalitarianism, equal protection and due process, and normalization and integration—were ideally suited to each other. They supported each other, complemented each other, and drove the law and the right-to-education movement in the same direction, toward enactment of the EHA.

RELATIONSHIP OF THE RIGHT-TO-EDUCATION MOVEMENT TO OTHER FEDERAL POLICIES AND LAWS

During the same time that political, constitutional, and human-service ideologies were converging to create the theoretical underpinnings of the right-to-education movement and the EHA, other important legal developments were affecting people with disabilities. These were largely complementary of the right-to-education ideologies; they were based in major part on the same constitutional principles; and they were reflected in various federal laws.

To understand how these separate movements—the right-to-education movement and the "general-rights" movement—developed, it will be helpful to review the four major forces that influenced federal laws, including the EHA. It then will be useful to consider the major concepts of the federal laws and their relationship to the EHA, and also to consider the laws' relationships to the four motivating forces behind them.

Forces Influencing Federal Laws

Four major forces influence the enactment of federal laws. The first is the constitutional doctrine of *equal protection,* with its corollaries of egalitarianism (a political doctrine), normalization (a human services doctrine), and due process (with its insistence on fair procedures and its assumption that, generally, fair procedures will produce or tend to produce fair or acceptable results). This book has explained in detail how these doctrines have influenced and been reflected in the EHA (see especially chapters 1 through 8).

The second major force is *social altruism.* This refers to the concern that most people have, and that the EHA clearly has, for ameliorating the effects of a disability through provision of a free appropriate public education. The power of the federal government to enact the EHA is based on the Constitution, but the power of the states to have their own education laws and carry out the federal law in cooperation with the federal government rests on their inherent powers of *parens patriae.* This is a centuries-old legal doctrine that asserts that government is responsible for taking care of those who, because of their youthfulness (status as minors), disability (having a handicap), or vulnerability (such as being victims of abuse or neglect), cannot take care of themselves without assistance from the government. Literally, *parens patriae* means "parent/father of the country," referring to the state as the father of the citizens. Clearly, the EHA seeks to ameliorate the effects of a disability and to ensure that the former discrimination in education to which children with disabilities were subjected is not repeated.

The third major force is *deinstitutionalization,* more recently characterized as anti-institutionalization. Deinstitutionalization has sought to prevent people from being placed in institutions (such as those for people with mental retardation or other developmental disabilities or those for people with mental illness). It also has sought to change the conditions of those institutions so that those who are placed there do not have to experience the horrid conditions in many of the institutions as they existed in the early 1970s, when deinstitutionalization became a federal and state goal. Finally, it has sought to prevent people from being placed in institutions in the first place by providing them with the necessary and appropriate services in home or community settings.

The EHA is linked to the deinstitutionalization movement by its zero reject principle (ensuring that the state and local education agencies serve all children, regardless of the type or extent of their disabilities); its principle of appropriate education (ensuring that services, whenever provided, are suitable and educationally beneficial); its least restrictive placement/environment principle (ensuring that, to the maximum extent appropriate, children with disabilities are educated in regular schools, regular classrooms, or other integrated settings and programs); and its twin principles of accountability—procedural due process and parent participation (ensuring that the schools be made accountable for their actions). Indeed, the EHA has had a profound effect on many state institutions, enabling many children who otherwise would be placed or kept in those institutions to be educated in the community. As chapter 6 points out, however, the effect of the EHA on the institutions is not as wholesome as it ought to be: Schools and parents still seek institutional placement, and courts are still inclined to grant it.

The fourth and final impetus for federal legislation is the desire to *re-balance power* between people with disabilities and the professionals who serve them. As this book has indicated, there is a long and unsavory history of discrimination in education against people with disabilities. Those who had the power to educate persons with disabilities (the state and local school authorities) often did not exercise that power to include them in an appropriate education but, rather, to exclude them from any education at all or to provide only a barely appropriate education (see chapters 1 through 8). The EHA accordingly seeks to change the relationship between the education officials, who have had power, and the students with disabilities and their parents, who have not had power. Its six principles all work toward that goal, as explained in detail previously in this book.

Major Concepts of the Federal Laws

As Turnbull and Barber indicated in their discussion of federal laws affecting adults with developmental disabilities,[2] these motives—the impetus in federal laws—are reflected in various concepts that underlie not only the EHA but other federal laws as well. But to merely acknowledge that four major forces have been influencing the enactment of federal laws is not enough. It is important also to consider the major concepts of those federal laws and (a) their relationships to the EHA and (b) their connections to those four major forces.

Normalization.   The doctrines of normalization, social role valorization, integration, mainstreaming, and the least restrictive alternative are reflections of the constitutional doctrine of equal protection (see chapter 6), of altruism (an effort to bring persons with disabilities into a more "normal" way of life, where they can be more valued as contributing citizens), and of deinstitutionalization (an effort to provide community-based, integrated education instead of programs in segregated institutional settings). The fourth major principle of the EHA—that of education in the least restrictive environment—sets forth the presumption that children with disabilities will be educated to the maximum extent appropriate with children who do not have disabilities.

Unity and Integrity of Families.   Many federal laws seek to keep families together, recognizing that the family is the most important and the basic structure of civilization. In the EHA, the effort to maintain the family's participation in the student's education is the sixth major principle: parent participation. And the principle of the least restrictive alternative also is relevant to this effort in that it seeks to have children with disabilities educated in the community and thereby in settings where they can continue to live with their families. Moreover, the provision in the EHA for home-based education as an alternative in the continuum of services is an explicit recognition of the desirability of having children educated in the care of their families so that families may stay unified and not have to place the child into an institution.

Accountability and Due Process.   The Constitution provides for procedural safeguards, and the EHA simply describes those safeguards as applicable to the education of children with disabilities (see chapter 7). Moreover, the 1986 enactment of the Handicapped Children's Protection Act, overturning *Smith v. Robinson* and granting the prevailing party in a due process hearing or appeal from such a hearing the right to recover attorneys' fees, is a more recent statement of the concept of accountability and due process.

Advocacy and Advocates.   Accountability and due process will not be obtained unless parents and students with disabilities have advocates. The EHA's procedural safeguards (e.g., the right to a surrogate parent, the right of natural and surrogate parents to consent to certain procedures such as the initial evaluation and placement and to have a due process hearing if they and the schools disagree about the child's right to a free appropriate public education, and the right to recover counsel fees if prevailing in due process hearing or appeal—see chapter 7) are explicit recognitions that advocacy and advocates are essential to the child's educational rights' enforcement.

Consent, Choice, and Client Participation.   It is a hallmark of constitutional government in this country that government exists by and with the consent of the governed. The EHA recognizes that special education, as a service of the government, should be consistent with the principle of government by consent, and it therefore provides for the consent of parents for initial evaluation and placement, their and the student's participation in certain evaluations and in the development of the student's educational program through the right to an IEP, and the family's right to be involved in the development of early education programs for the child through the individualized family service plan (described in chapters 3 and 5).

Individualization. The due process principle requires that government make individual determinations when allocating benefits and burdens; it eschews the "meat ax" approach of treating all students with disabilities exactly alike. The principle of individualization is reflected in the IEP and IFSP.

Developmental Model. The developmental model recognizes that all people with disabilities, no matter the nature or extent of their disabilities, have inherent capacities, including the ability to learn and be educated. *PARC v. Commonwealth,* discussed in detail in chapters 2 and 3, is explicit about that capacity, finding that all children with mental retardation can learn. And the EHA, which rests on and was greatly influenced by *PARC* (see chapters 1 through 3), reflects the developmental model, too, through its principles of zero reject and appropriate education, especially as designed and carried out by the IEP and IFSP.

Economic Productivity. Madeleine Will, the Assistant Secretary of Education from 1983 through 1989 (the date of the revision of this book), has often said that the implied promise of special education is a job. Granting that her statement is accurate, and no responsible people dispute it, the EHA clearly seeks to build the capacities of people with disabilities so that they may take their place in the workforce of America. It does this not only by the general principles of zero reject, nondiscriminatory evaluation, appropriate education, and least restrictive placement, but it does so also by the specific provisions for incentive grants for transition (see chapter 5), by providing for the education of youth up to age 21 (see chapter 3), and by provisions for the employment of people with disabilities in special education programs (see chapter 10).

Prevention, Cure, and Amelioration. A large number of disabilities, and many of the conditions that aggravate a disability, are caused by social or environmental conditions; only a few disabilities are "organic" and caused by biological or inherent conditions in a person. Because of this, many federal laws seek to prevent, cure (absolutely reverse), or ameliorate (reduce the effects of) a disability. Clearly, the EHA is consistent with those laws. By its principle of zero reject, it seeks to open the doors of education and its ameliorating effects to all children; by its principles of appropriate education and the least restrictive environment, it seeks to provide educational benefit in the community instead of deprivation—absolute or relative, it does not matter—by institutional placement; and by its principle of parent participation, and especially through the IFSP for children ages 0–2 and the provision of some related services for families, it seeks to ensure that families themselves receive some benefits from the child's education and that their circumstances, which sometimes can add to the child's handicap, receive some attention, too.

TECHNIQUES AND NATURE OF LAW REFORM

Notwithstanding the convergence of ideologies and the recent history of the civil rights movement, the right-to-education movement did not happen and indeed could not have happened without the skills of the many advocates who understood how to change the laws that barred handicapped children from equal educational opportunities. Those advocates were led at first by parents whose mentally retarded and otherwise disabled children successfully sued the states for their rights to an education (such as in *PARC* and *Mills*) and then were joined by the Council for Exceptional Children (CEC). Above all, they knew that they must master the techniques of, and control the nature of, law reform.

To achieve the right-to-education movement's goals of a free and appropriate public education for all handicapped children, it was necessary to have a general purpose. That purpose was to change the nature of the public schools so that there would be no more second-class students, so that the dual system of education would be abolished. This goal required two strategies: (1) to chip away at and eventually dismantle the restrictions that the states' laws and the schools' practices and policies imposed on disabled children (chapters 2 though 8 describe those pre-EHA practices in detail; they consisted by and large of pure and functional exclusion and misuse of classification procedures); and (2) to create rights, such as the rights to zero reject laws, nondiscriminatory evaluation, and individualized appropriate education.

The first technique was (and almost always is) negative in nature; it seeks to tear down that which time, tradition, and law have created. The second technique was (and also almost always is) positive; it seeks to replace the destroyed system with something more accommodating and effective. Simply accomplishing the dismemberment of a system would be a half measure only; the right-to-education movement required that something of value replace the old. That is why the right-to-education movement not only made illegal the old ways but also enacted new ones.

Since the object (with its two strategies) was to abolish the dual system and replace it with a system of equal educational opportunities, the techniques for achieving that object had to include a sophisticated understanding of the meaning of *equal educational opportunities*. Advocates had to begin by explaining equal educational opportunity for disabled children. As chapter 3 shows, equality for disabled students consists of three sub-types:

1. It is possible to obtain equal educational opportunities for some disabled students by treating them exactly like nondisabled students; educating an orthopedically impaired student in the same academic classes as nondisabled students is an example of "pure equal treatment" (assuming the school is barrier-free).
2. It is possible to obtain equal educational opportunities for other disabled students by treating them substantially like nondisabled students but also by making simultaneous accommodations to them; for example, educating a deaf child in the same classroom as children who do not have a hearing deficiency may require only a few adaptations by the teacher or school system.

3. It is possible to obtain equal educational opportunities for still other students by treating them very differently, but not less effectively, than nondisabled students; for example, educating severely disabled students in separate classes, using a different curriculum and different methods of instruction, may provide those students with educational opportunities that, for them, are comparable to the opportunities provided to nondisabled students who are educated in their own classes with a different curriculum and different methods of instruction.

Thus, the first technique for the right-to-education movement was to develop and announce a well-thought-out concept of equal educational opportunity.

Next, advocates in the right-to-education movement had to target their efforts on all branches of federal and state government. In this respect, they adopted a bifurcated approach: They pursued law reform from federal and state governments alike. They knew they had to achieve a uniform, national result—one that secured equal educational opportunities to all handicapped children, without regard to where they lived or by which government they were served. This required reforms at both levels of government. At the federal level, for example, advocates sought enactment of the 1973 and 1975 amendments to the Education of the Handicapped Act (see chapter 2 for a discussion of the EHA's history). At the state level, they pursued mandatory education laws and the enforcement of existing ones.

As just suggested, one of the most obvious forums for the federal-state approach to a uniform, national result was the *elected legislature*—the Congress in the federal route and the state legislatures in the state route. Advocates therefore sought passage of laws, appropriation of money to carry out the laws, and implementation of those laws at state and local levels. Legislatures, then, were a collective forum in which the right-to-education movement had to be established.

A second forum was directly related to the first—the *executive agencies* of the federal government (at first, the Department of Health, Education, and Welfare and, later, the Department of Education) and the executive agencies of the states (the state departments of education or public instruction). The executive agencies, after all, are charged with implementing the laws that the legislatures enact. They do this by issuing regulations and guidelines, providing technical assistance, and performing monitoring and overseeing functions. Clearly, such complex legislation as the EHA required detailed regulations. For example, the EHA itself has little in it concerning the principle of the least restrictive education of handicapped children. By contrast, the regulations implementing the EHA itself are quite specific and broad in setting forth the way in which the principle is to be carried out.

Finally, advocates had to resort to the courts to establish the educational right of handicapped children, either as a matter of federal constitutional law or as a matter of state educational law. In addition, advocates sought judicial relief when state education agencies were reluctant or recalcitrant in carrying out state laws.

Thus, advocates had to adopt a *bifurcated* approach—to seek the educational rights of disabled children by federal and state routes. And they had to adopt an *integrated* approach—to seek those rights in the legislatures, executive agencies, and courts of the federal and state forums. Only by taking this *comprehensive* approach would they be able to achieve their complex goals.

But advocates were obliged to use still another technique of law reform. It was to obtain both substantive and procedural reforms in the education laws of the federal and state governments. By *substantive* reforms, they had in mind, and eventually obtained, law that created a new body of rights for disabled children. For example, the zero reject principle is a substantive reform. It creates a right to a free public education for all handicapped children. Likewise, the principles of nondiscriminatory evaluation, appropriate education, least restrictive environment, due process, and parent participation are substantive in nature. Each grants to handicapped children certain rights that SEAs and LEAs are obliged to satisfy. There are correlating rights (for the students) and duties (upon the SEAs and LEAs).

By *procedural* reforms, the advocates wanted, and also eventually obtained, laws that specify how the substantive rights are to be carried out and made effective. For example, the zero reject principle becomes effective when SEAs and LEAs conduct an annual census of disabled children. The nondiscriminatory evaluation principle is made effective through multifaceted testing. The appropriate education principle is carried out when IEPs are developed for each student. The least restrictive alternative placement rule is satisfied when the child receives a placement that is both educationally effective and more integrated than not with nondisabled students. And, of course, the due process and parent participation principles are complied with when certain procedures (e.g., notice, consent, access to records, and impartial hearings) are made available.

Clearly, then, it was imperative for advocates to pursue and secure their goal by a well-grounded understanding of how schools operate and can be made to operate, and by an equally sophisticated understanding of how law can be created to affect schools' operation. In summary, the techniques of law reform were exceedingly complex. They entailed:

- *bifurcated* advocacy at both the federal and the state levels;
- *comprehensive* and *integrated* advocacy in all three forums of law making (legislative, executive, and judicial); and
- a highly developed understanding of the *substantive* and *procedural* approaches to law reform.

All of this was undergirded by a well developed *definition* of equal educational opportunity as the concept applies to disabled students.

Given this background to the right-to-education movement, it is now appropriate to set forth the EHA's underlying beliefs (credo), their relationship to the law and values, and their implementation at law.

THE UNDERLYING BELIEFS:
A RIGHT-TO-EDUCATION CREDO

We believe that education makes a difference in a person's life. That was one of the foundations of *Brown v. Board of Education* and is supported by the six principles of the EHA.

We know and believe that handicapped children can profit from an education appropriate to their capacities. Hence, the EHA and the case law grant each handicapped child the right to a suitable education. In the case of the EHA, an affirmative duty to hire handicapped people is also imposed on the public schools.

We also believe in equity—that is, in equal educational opportunity. Thus, the EHA and the cases grant the right of education to all handicapped students.

We believe in the value of an education for all people—the universality of education. Accordingly, the EHA and case law grant the right to an education to all handicapped students.

Most of us believe that governmental benefits should not be parceled out on the basis of the recipients' unalterable characteristics. We believe that such a practice says something demeaning and invidious about the person who is denied benefits, and it places the government in the position of causing that person to feel and act inferior simply because he or she is different from those who are receiving the benefits. Our acceptance of this belief is seen in racial discrimination cases and in both criminal and civil law where a person is denied benefits because he or she is indigent, an alien, a member of one sex or the other, or handicapped. In the case of the handicapped, the right-to-education cases and the EHA challenge the old distribution of governmental benefits (education) and attempt to redistribute them more equitably. They attack a system of distribution founded on the false premise that persons who have handicaps are expendable and that the bulk of benefits in education should be given to the most meritorious (where merit was measured by intelligence or conformity to the nonhandicapped norm).

We believe in the essential sameness of all persons. Grounded in concepts of normalization, egalitarianism, and equal protection, this belief leads us to assert that students with handicaps are no less worthy of constitutional protection and statutory benefits than are students without handicaps. Although people may be classified, their rights to an education should not be denied because of a classification. The principle of free appropriate public education for *all* handicapped children illustrates this belief.

We also believe that the economic investment of furnishing a person with handicaps an education appropriate to his or her needs will yield long-term returns in the increased productivity and decreased dependency of that person. On humanitarian grounds, we also point out that students with handicaps have been seriously short-changed in the competition for governmental benefits. Each principle of the right-to-education movement attests to this belief.

We believe that the longstanding state and local neglect of the educational claims of children who have handicaps, with its ample evidence, will not be abated in the foreseeable future. We even believe that it will be permanent. For that reason, permanent federal funding and control are amply justified.

We believe that, because we choose who governs us, we have the right to ask our representatives to be accountable to us. To that end, the EHA and case law require several types of accountability.

We believe that people should treat each other fairly and decently and that government should deal fairly and decently with the governed. Alternatively stated, we believe that a fair process of governing will produce fair and acceptable results—thus, the EHA and the case law requiring that procedural safeguards be made available to handicapped students and their parents.

We believe that the best government is one we can influence or affect. We believe in participatory democracy in the education of children, and the EHA may well be the high-water mark of participatory democracy in public education.

The EHA translates our beliefs into public policy for the education of handicapped children, assigns legal rights that reflect our collective decency, and defines and refines our relationships to each other and among the governments and the governed.

THE LAW, OUR BELIEFS, AND OUR VALUES

More often than not, our beliefs harmonize with our values. In this respect, and particularly in the right-to-education movement, the word *value* has a familiar meaning. A value is something we, as individuals and as a society, highly prize and cherish. It is something we do not want to be without and we do not want others to be without. In a constitutional sense, a value is a "fundamental interest."[3] There are many values, and the right-to-education movement reflects at least four of them.

1. We do not want to be without access to courts or other forums for the peaceful solution of our differences with others. Expressed in another way, we do not want to be without a way of being heard and heeded when we have disagreements with others. Access to the courts as an avenue for redress of grievances is constitutionally required and is provided in the EHA and in the right-to-education cases through requirements for procedural due process.

2. We do not want to be denied a right to participate in self-government. Thus, the right to vote is constitutionally protected, and the right to participate in school (as a "government") is provided for in the EHA and the case law under the concept of parental participation.

3. We do not want to be without the opportunity to acquire property or fulfill ourselves. The principles of substantive due process guarantee us these opportunities as a matter of constitutional law, and the EHA and the case law address them through the requirements of nondiscriminatory evaluation (protection from classifications that inevitably forestall or retard the opportunities of handicapped children to develop to their max-

imum potential) and least restrictive appropriate placement (protection from programs that will have equally debilitating results).

4. We do not want our unalterable traits, such as race, gender, ancestry, or place of birth, to be used as a basis for government distribution of benefits. Thus, the EHA and the case law provide for free appropriate public educational opportunities for all handicapped students.

PUTTING OUR BELIEFS AND VALUES TO WORK: CONCEPTS INTO LAW

It is remarkable to see how effectively the EHA puts our beliefs and values to work for the education of handicapped children. The Act shows how we develop our resources to allow our beliefs and values to flourish. This function is performed by the requirements for IEPs, personnel development, OSERS technical assistance, parent involvement, full-service goals, timelines for educating handicapped children of certain ages, the child census, priorities for the use of funds, early intervention programs, and affirmative action in employing the handicapped.

The EHA also shows how we allocate status to people as a reflection of our values and beliefs.[4] We allocate power to handicapped children through provisions such as permanent funding of the EHA, service priorities, zero reject principles, and least restrictive placement requirements. We distribute power to their parents through participation in IEP conferences, procedural safeguards, membership on advisory panels, and participation in developing state and local plans. Finally, we allocate status to educators through requirements for personnel development, by legitimizing the truly special functions of special education (through the service priorities), and by changing the roles of educators with respect to each other (through the principle of least restrictive placement).

The EHA changes not only the status or power of people involved in the right-to-education movement, but also the procedures by which power and status are allocated. That is the ultimate meaning of the procedural safeguards and parent participation provisions.

The EHA changes more than the procedures. It changes the very rights that government distributes, the beneficiaries of those rights, and the methods of distributing them. It guarantees a free appropriate public education to *all* handicapped children, changes the nature of their education so that it will be appropriate to them, prefers some handicapped children over others (the service priorities), grants rights to parents of handicapped children, and demonstrates that federal funds are a means of enforcing those rights (by funding the excess costs of educating handicapped children, requiring the pass-through of funds, setting limits on administrative costs that may be charged against federal funds, and making federal funding permanent).

A Concluding Note

It is always somewhat risky to try to tie up so many divergent points as have been made in this chapter. But it is equally risky to leave them to stand on their own, without a concluding note. To introduce that concluding note, it helps to ask a simple question: Where did the EHA originate, where has it been, and where is it going?

Where did it originate? It originated with the articulation of legal, political, and human-service values, ideologies, and principles. These were, in a nutshell, equal protection, due process, egalitarianism, normalization, and integration.

What happened with these articulated values? They became the underlying principles of various federal and state laws, notably the EHA, the Rehabilitation Act, and the Developmental Disabilities Assistance and Bill of Rights Act, and their respective regulations.

Laws without funds, however, are rather toothless. And so it was that the special education programs' effectiveness depended on appropriations by Congress and state and local government. The same was—and always will be—true with respect not only to the EHA but also the Rehabilitation Act and the DD Act.

At least two other ingredients are necessary to bring life into the law and to give effect to its language and values. Those are changed behaviors by professionals and, of course, by people with disabilities and their families. It is beyond argument that the law has changed professional behavior, individual capacities, and the expectations and lives of people with disabilities and their families.

Finally, the power to enforce the laws is requisite. Just as rights often run with revenues, so do rights depend on their enforcement. Just how well the courts have enforced the EHA is a matter of some dispute.

To summarize: Values are translated into laws and regulations; laws and regulations are implemented with funds; laws, regulations, and funds are made effective when professionals, people with disabilities, and their families change their behaviors; and the proper interpretation of values and laws and the careful monitoring of practices is the role of enforcement techniques.

The EHA—it should be clear by now—follows this paradigm of legal reform. Its values (chapters 1, 2, 11, and 12) are reflected in the law through the six principles (chapters 3 through 8) and the provision of funds to carry them out (chapter 10). These legal principles have changed professional practice and the way of life of people with disabilities, their families, and people without disabilities—the "norms and forms" of society. Withal, there are various ways of enforcing the law (chapters, 7, 8, 9, and 10).

The EHA and the case law thus perfectly illustrate the unique role of law and law makers in changing existing institutions of society and building new ones, in changing the "norms and forms" of society, in which the norm was second-class citizenship of disabled people and the form was discrimination in education. But these laws are not without their detractors.

Some people argue that society has paid in the redistribution of governmental power over the education of handicapped children; the balance of power now clearly rests with the federal government, and the principles and values of local autonomy in education have been diminished. But that is not an argument unique to the EHA and the right-to-education cases. Indeed, *Brown* had a remarkable effect on public education by federalizing it in an important respect. *Brown* made clear *where* the schools were to educate children: Blacks and whites were to be educated together. In special education, *PARC* and *Mills* specified *which* children were to be educated and the terms of their education. *Rowley* federalized public education by setting out the general principles of curriculum for disabled students: The curriculum must be comparable to that for nondisabled students, and developed through a specified process (the IEP). *Tatro* federalized public education by specifying the principles governing the indispensible accessories of a disabled child's education—the related services the school must furnish. Yet, *PARC, Mills, Rowley, Tatro,* and a host of other special education cases must be seen in the light of *Brown's* initial federalization of education. It undoubtedly is true that the EHA has further federalized education, but it did so upon the precedent of *Brown* and other federal legislation.

Others also argue that society has legislated a change in the competition for equities and weighted the law in favor of handicapped children by requiring state and local education agencies to make their own investments in the education of those children (by way of the excess-cost provision). But the EHA and the cases interpreting it simply help the states do what they already had agreed to do by enacting their own constitutions and public education laws. That was to educate *all* children, without regard to their disabilities. In a very real sense, the states already had provided disabled children with leverage in the competition for funds by assuring them as a matter of state law that they would receive an education. The EHA and the cases do have the effect, however, of making the states live up to their promises. They put some bite into the teeth of the states' laws, so that disabled children now can partake of the same meal—education—furnished to other children.

Still others say that we have given advocates for handicapped children a quantum increase in ammunition. They contend that the "first-generation" issues—whether all handicapped children have a right to an appropriate education at public expense—have faded and been replaced by "second-generation" issues dealing with the specifics of the right to a free appropriate public education. They further contend that the second-generation cases show that disabled children have too many rights, especially in comparison to nondisabled children.

A Caveat

A brief answer is that it is quite true that disabled children and their advocates still have powerful arrows in their quivers—namely the EHA itself, its regulations, and the precedents of the many cases decided in their favor. This means that, as advocates select their ammunition to advance the claims of handicapped children in second-generation matters, they must be on their guard as to the forums they choose for their battlegrounds and the issues around which battle is joined. This is so because they would not want to add fuel to an unnecessary backlash by overzealously implementing the rights of handicapped children. Nor would they want to cause the EHA's underlying beliefs and values to be denied by those in the majority (the nonhandicapped) whose very beliefs, values, and attitudes are so crucial to the success of the law and the acceptance of children with handicaps.

Accordingly, advocates for handicapped children must: (1) continually articulate the beliefs and values that are the foundations for the EHA and the case law, (2) be willing and able to say that the educational rights of handicapped children should be made available to nonhandicapped children as well, and (3) be able to arouse the sympathetic imagination of nonhandicapped people so that *their* claims to better educational opportunities will be supported by, and give support to, the claims of handicapped children.

Zero reject and protection from functional exclusion, individualized appropriate education, nondiscriminatory and nonstigmatizing classification procedures and placement, rights to procedural safeguards, and the rights of participation are six principles that are supported by widely and deeply held beliefs and values. They are, however, more than that. They have a touch of justice—and no child, handicapped or nonhandicapped, has a monopoly on justice.

NOTES

1. Wolfensberger, "Social Role Valorization: A Proposed New Term for the Principle of Normalization," 21 *Mental Retardation* 224 (Dec. 1983).

2. Turnbull and Barber, "Federal Laws and Adults with Developmental Disabilities," in Summers, (Ed.) *The Right to Grow Up* (Baltimore, Md.: Paul H. Brookes, 1986).

3. Michelman, "Foreword: On Protecting the Poor through the Fourteenth Amendment," 83 *Harvard Law Review* 7 (1969).

4. *See* Gil, *Unravelling Social Policy* (Cambridge, Ma.: Schenkman, 1977).

APPENDIX A

BROWN V. BOARD OF EDUCATION

(excerpts from the Supreme Court's unanimous opinion, with only Footnote 11 included)

OLIVER BROWN, et al., Appellants,

v.

BOARD OF EDUCATION OF TOPEKA, Shawnee County,
Kansas, et al. (No. 1.)

Mr. Chief Justice Warren delivered the opinion of the Court.

These cases come to us from the States of Kansas, South Carolina, Virginia, and Delaware. They are premised on different facts and different local conditions, but a common legal question justifies their consideration together in this consolidated opinion.[1]

In each of the cases, minors of the Negro race, through their legal representatives, seek the aid of the courts in obtaining admission to the public schools of their community on a nonsegregated basis. In each instance, they had been denied admission to schools attended by white children under laws requiring or permitting segregation according to race. This segregation was alleged to deprive the plaintiffs of the equal protection of the laws under the Fourteenth Amendment. ...

The plaintiffs contend that segregated public schools are not "equal" and cannot be made "equal," and that hence they are deprived of the equal protection of the laws. ...

The most avid proponents of the post-War Amendments undoubtedly intended them to remove all legal distinctions among "all persons born or naturalized in the United

States." Their opponents, just as certainly, were antagonistic to both the letter and the spirit of the Amendments and wished them to have the most limited effect. What others in Congress and the state legislatures had in mind cannot be determined with any degree of certainty.

An additional reason for the inconclusive nature of the Amendment's history, with respect to segregated schools, is the status of public education at that time.[4] In the South, the movement toward free common schools, supported by general taxation, had not yet taken hold. Education of white children was largely in the hands of private groups. Education of Negroes was almost nonexistent, and practically all of the race were illiterate. In fact, any education of Negroes was forbidden by law in some states. Today, in contrast, many Negroes have achieved outstanding success in the arts and sciences as well as in the business and professional world. It is true that public school education at the time of the Amendment had advanced further in the North, but the effect of the Amendment on Northern States was generally ignored in the congressional debates. Even in the North, the conditions of public education did not approximate those existing today. The curriculum was usually rudimentary; ungraded schools were common in rural areas; the school term was but three months a year in many states; and compulsory school attendance was virtually unknown. As a consequence, it is not surprising that there should be so little in the history of the Fourteenth Amendment relating to its intended effect on public education.

In the first cases in this Court construing the Fourteenth Amendment, decided shortly after its adoption, the Court interpreted it as proscribing all state-imposed discriminations against the Negro race.[5] The doctrine of "separate but equal" did not make its appearance in this Court until 1896 in the case of Plessy v. Ferguson, ... involving not education but transportation.[6] ... In more recent cases, all on the graduate school level, inequality was found in that specific benefits enjoyed by white students were denied to Negro students of the same educational qualifications. ... In none of these cases was it necessary to re-examine the doctrine to grant relief to the Negro plaintiff. And in Sweatt v. Painter ..., the Court expressly reserved decision on the question whether Plessy v. Ferguson should be held inapplicable to public education.

In the instant cases, that question is directly presented. Here, unlike Sweatt v. Painter, there are findings below that the Negro and white schools involved have been equalized, or are being equalized, with respect to buildings, curricula, qualifications and salaries of teachers, and other "tangible" factors.[9] Our decision, therefore, cannot turn on merely a comparison of these tangible factors in the Negro and white schools involved in each of the cases. We must look instead to the effect of segregation itself on public education.

In approaching this problem, we cannot turn the clock back to 1868 when the Amendment was adopted, or even to 1896 when Plessy v. Ferguson was written. We must consider public education in the light of its full development and its present place in American life throughout the Nation. Only in this way can it be determined if segregation in public schools deprives these plaintiffs of the equal protection of the laws.

Today, education is perhaps the most important function of state and local governments. Compulsory school attendance laws and the great expenditures for education both demonstrate our recognition of the importance of education to our democratic society. It is required in the performance of our most basic public responsibilities, even service in the armed forces. It is the very foundation of good citizenship. Today it is a principal instrument in awakening the child to cultural values, in preparing him for later professional training, and in helping him to adjust normally to his environment. In these days, it is doubtful that any child may reasonably be expected to succeed in life if he is denied the opportunity of an education. Such an opportunity, where the state has undertaken to provide it, is a right which must be made available to all in equal terms.

We come then to the question presented: Does segregation of children in public schools solely on the basis of race, even though the physical facilities and other "tangible" factors may be equal, deprive the children of the minority group of equal education opportunities? We believe that it does.

In Sweatt v. Painter ..., in finding that a segregated law school for Negroes could not provide them equal educational opportunities, this Court relied in large part on "those qualities which are incapable of objective measurement but which make for greatness in a law school." In McLaurin v. Oklahoma State Regents, ... the Court, in requiring that a Negro admitted to a white graduate school be treated like all other students, again resorted to intangible considerations: "... his ability to study, to engage in discussions and exchange views with other students, and, in general, to learn his profession." Such considerations apply with added force to children in grade and high schools. To separate them from others of similar age and qualifications solely because of their race generates a feeling of inferiority as to their status in the community that may affect their hearts and minds in a way unlikely ever to be undone. The effect of this separation on their educational opportunities was well stated by a finding in the Kansas case by a court which nevertheless felt compelled to rule against the Negro plaintiffs:

"Segregation of white and colored children in public schools has a detrimental effect upon the colored children. The impact is greater when it has the sanction of the law; for the policy of separating the races is usually interpreted as denoting the inferiority of the Negro group. A sense of inferiority affects the motivation of a child to learn. Segregation with the sanction of the law, therefore, has a tendency to [retard] the educational and mental development of Negro children and to deprive them of some of the benefits they would receive in a racial[ly] integrated school system."[10]

Whatever may have been the extent of psychological knowledge at the time of Plessy v. Ferguson, this finding is amply supported by modern authority.[11] Any language in Plessy v. Ferguson contrary to this finding is rejected.

We conclude that in the field of public education the doctrine of "separate but equal" has no place. Separate educational facilities are inherently unequal. Therefore, we hold that the plaintiffs and others similarly situated for whom the actions have been brought are, by reason of the segregation complained of, deprived of the equal protection of the laws guaranteed by the Fourteenth Amendment. This disposition makes unnecessary any discussion whether such segregation also violates the Due Process Clause of the Fourteenth Amendment.[12] ...

NOTES

11. K.B. Clark, Effect of Prejudice and Discrimination on Personality Development (Midcentury White House Conference on Children and Youth, 1950); Witmer and Kotinsky, Personality in the Making (1952), ch VI; Deutscher and Chein, The Psychological Effects of Enforced Segregation: A Survey of Social Science Opinion, 26 J Psychol 259 (1948); Chein, What are the Psychological Effects of Segregation Under Conditions of Equal Facilities?, 3 Int J Opinion and Attitude Res 229 (1949); Brameld, Educational Costs, in Discrimination and National Welfare (MacIver, ed., 1949), 44-48; Frazier, The Negro in the United States (1949), 674-681. And see generally, Myrdal, An American Dilemma (1944).

APPENDIX B

SOUTHEASTERN COMMUNITY COLLEGE V. DAVIS

SOUTHEASTERN COMMUNITY COLLEGE

v.

FRANCIS B. DAVIS.

Mr. Justice Powell delivered the opinion of the Court.

This case presents a matter of first impression for this Court: Whether § 504 of the Rehabilitation Act of 1973, which prohibits discrimination against an "otherwise qualified handicapped individual" in federally funded programs "solely by reason of his handicap," forbids professional schools from imposing physical qualifications for admission to their clinical training programs.

I

Respondent, who suffers from a serious hearing disability, seeks to be trained as a registered nurse. During the 1973-1974 academic year she was enrolled in the College Parallel program of Southeastern Community College, a state institution that receives federal funds. Respondent hoped to progress to Southeastern's Associate Degree Nursing program, completion of which would make her eligible for state certification as a registered nurse. In the course of her application to the nursing program, she was interviewed by a member of the nursing faculty. It became apparent that respondent had difficulty understanding questions asked, and on inquiry she acknowledged a history of hearing problems and dependence on a hearing aid. She was advised to consult an audiologist.

On the basis of an examination at Duke University Medical Center, respondent was diagnosed as having a "bilateral, sensori-neural loss." App. 127a. A change in her hearing aid was recommended, as a result of which it was expected that she would be able to detect sounds "almost as well as a person would who has normal hearing." App. 127a-128a. But this improvement would not mean that she could discriminate among sounds sufficiently to understand normal spoken speech. Her lipreading skills would remain necessary for effective communication: "While wearing the hearing aid, she is well aware of gross sounds occurring in the listening environment. However, she can only be responsible for speech spoken to her, when the talker gets her attention and allows her to look directly at the talker." App. 128a.

Southeastern next consulted Mary McRee, Executive Director of the North Carolina Board of Nursing. On the basis of the audiologist's report, McRee recommended that respondent not be admitted to the nursing program. In McRee's view, respondent's hearing disability made it unsafe for her to practice as a nurse.[1] In addition, it would be impossible for respondent to participate safely in the normal clinical training program, and those modifications that would be necessary to enable safe participation would prevent her from realizing the benefits of the program: "To adjust patient learning experiences in keeping with [respondent's] hearing limitations could, in fact, be the same as denying her full learning to meet the objectives of your nursing programs." App. 132a-133a.

After respondent was notified that she was not qualified for nursing study because of her hearing disability, she requested reconsideration of the decision. The entire nursing staff of Southeastern was assembled, and McRee again was consulted. McRee repeated her conclusion that on the basis of the available evidence, respondent "has hearing limitations which could interfere with her safely caring for patients." App. 139a. Upon further deliberation, the staff voted to deny respondent admission.

Respondent then filed suit in the United States District Court for the Eastern District of North Carolina, alleging both a violation of § 504 of the Rehabilitation Act of 1973, 87 Stat. 394, as amended. 29 U.S.C. § 794,[2] and a denial of equal protection and due process. After a bench trial, the District Court entered judgment in favor of Southeastern. 424 F. Supp. 1341 (1976). It confirmed the findings of the audiologist that even with a hearing aid respondent cannot understand speech directed to her except through lipreading, and further found that,

> "[I] in many situations such as an operation room, intensive care unit, or post-natal care unit, all doctors and nurses wear surgical masks which would make lip-reading impossible. Additionally, in many situations a Registered Nurse would be required to instantly follow the physician's instructions concerning procurement of various types of instruments and drugs where the physician would be unable to get the nurse's attention by other than vocal means." *Id.*, at 1342.

Accordingly, the Court concluded that:

> "[Respondent's] handicap actually prevents her from safely performing in both her training program and her proposed profession. The trial testimony indicated numerous situations where [respondent's] particular disability would render her unable to function properly. Of particular concern to the court in this case is the potential danger to future patients in such situations." *Id.*, at 1345.

Based on these findings, the District Court concluded that respondent was not an "otherwise qualified handicapped individual" protected against discrimination by § 504. In its view, "[o]therwise qualified, can only be read to mean otherwise able to function sufficiently in the position sought in spite of the handicap, if proper training and facilities are suitable and available." *Ibid.* Because respondent's disability would prevent her from functioning "sufficiently" in Southeastern's nursing program, the Court held that the decision to exclude her was not discriminatory within the meaning of § 504.[3]

On appeal, the Court of Appeals for the Fourth Circuit reversed. 574 F. 2d 1158 (1978). It did not dispute the District Court's findings of fact, but held that the Court had misconstrued § 504. In light of administrative regulations that had been promulgated while the appeal was pending, see 42 Fed. Reg. 22676 (May 4, 1977),[4] the appellate court believed that § 504 required Southeastern to "reconsider plaintiff's application for admission to the nursing program without regard to her hearing ability." *Id.*, at 1160. It concluded that the District Court had erred in taking respondent's handicap into account in determining whether she was "otherwise qualified" for the program, rather than confining its inquiry to her "academic and technical qualifications." *Id.*, at 1161. The Court of Appeals also suggested that § 504 required "affirmative conduct" on the part of Southeastern to modify its program to accommodate the disabilities of applicants, "even when such modifications become expensive." *Id.*, at 1162.

Because of the importance of this issue to the many institutions covered by § 504, we granted certiorari. 439 U.S. _____ (1979). We now reverse.[5]

II

This is the first case in which this Court has been called upon to interpret § 504. It is elementary that "[t]he starting point in every case involving the construction of a statute is the language itself." *Blue Chip Stamps* v. *Manor Drug Stores,* 421 U.S. 723, 756 (1975) (Powell, J., concurring); see *Greyhound Corp.* v. *Mt. Hood Stages, Inc.,* 437 U.S. 322, 330 (1978); *Santa Fe Industries, Inc.* v. *Green,* 430 U.S. 462, 472 (1977). Section 504 by its terms does not compel educational institutions to disregard the disabilities of handicapped individuals or to make substantial modifications in their programs to allow disabled persons to participate. Instead, it requires only that an "otherwise qualified handicapped individual" not be excluded from participation in a federally funded program "solely by reason of his handicap," indicating only that mere possession of a handicap is not a permissible ground for assuming an inability to function in a particular context.[6]

The court below, however, believed that the "otherwise qualified" persons protected by § 504 include those who would be able to meet the requirements of a particular program in every respect except as to limitations imposed by their handicap. See 574 F. 2d. at 1160. Taken literally, this holding would prevent an institution from taking into account any limitation resulting from the handicap, however disabling. It assumes, in effect, that a person need not meet legitimate physical requirements in order to be "otherwise qualified." We think the understanding of the District Court is closer to the plain meaning of the statutory language. An otherwise qualified person is one who is able to meet all of a program's requirements in spite of his handicap.

The regulations promulgated by the Department of Health, Education, and Welfare (HEW) to interpret § 504 reinforce, rather than contradict, this conclusion. According to these regulations, a "[q]ualified handicapped person" is, "[w]ith respect to postsecondary and vocational education services, a handicapped person who meets the academic and technical standards requisite to admission or participation in the [school's] education program or activity...." 45 CFR § 84.3 (k)(3) (1978). An explanatory note states:

> "The term 'technical standards' refers to *all* nonacademic admissions criteria that are essential to participation in the program in question." 45 CFR pt. 84, App. A, at p. 405 (emphasis supplied).

A further note emphasizes that legitimate physical qualifications may be essential to participation in particular programs.[7] We think it clear, therefore, that HEW interprets the "other" qualifications which a handicapped person may be required to meet as including necessary physical qualifications.

III

The remaining question is whether the physical qualifications Southeastern demanded of respondent might not be necessary for participation in its nursing program. It is not open to dispute that, as Southeastern's Associate Degree Nursing program currently is constituted, the ability to understand speech without reliance on lipreading is necessary for patient safety during the clinical phase of the program. As the District Court found, this ability also is indispensable for many of the functions that a registered nurse performs.

Respondent contends nevertheless that § 504, properly interpreted, compels Southeastern to undertake affirmative action that would dispense with the need for effective oral communication. First, it is suggested that respondent can be given individual supervision by faculty members whenever she attends patients directly. Moreover, certain required courses might be dispensed with altogether for respondent. It is not necessary, she argues, that Southeastern train her to undertake all the tasks a registered nurse is licensed to perform. Rather, it is sufficient to make § 504 applicable if respondent might be able to perform satisfactorily some of the duties of a registered nurse or to hold some of the positions available to a registered nurse.[8]

Respondent finds support for this argument in portions of the HEW regulations discussed above. In particular, a provision applicable to postsecondary educational programs requires covered institutions to make "modifications" in their programs to accommodate handicapped persons, and to provide "auxiliary aids" such as sign-language interpreters.[9] Respondent argues that this regulation imposes an obligation to ensure full participation in covered programs by handicapped individuals and, in particular, requires Southeastern to make the kind of adjustments that would be necessary to permit her safe participation in the nursing program.

We note first that on the present record it appears unlikely respondent could benefit from any affirmative action that the regulation reasonably could be interpreted as requiring. Section 84.44 (d)(2), for example, explicitly excludes "devices or services of a personal nature" from the kinds of auxiliary aids a school must provide a handicapped individual. Yet the only evidence in the record indicates that nothing less than close, individual attention by a nursing instructor would be sufficient to ensure patient safety if respondent took part in the clinical phase of the nursing program. See 424 F. Supp., at 1346. Furthermore, it also is reasonably clear that § 84.44 (a) does not encompass the kind of curricular changes that would be necessary to accommodate respondent in the nursing program. In light of respondent's inability to function in clinical courses without close supervision, Southeastern with prudence could allow her to take only academic classes. Whatever benefits respondent might realize from such a course of study, she would not receive even a rough equivalent of the training a nursing program normally gives. Such a fundamental alteration in the nature of a program is far more than the "modification" the regulation requires.

Moreover, an interpretation of the regulations that required the extensive modifications necessary to include respondent in the nursing program would raise grave doubts about their validity. If these regulations were to require substantial adjustments in existing programs beyond those necessary to eliminate discrimination against otherwise qualified individuals, they would do more than clarify the meaning of § 504. Instead, they would constitute an unauthorized extension of the obligations imposed by that statute.

The language and structure of the Rehabilitation Act of 1973 reflect a recognition by Congress of the distinction between the evenhanded treatment of qualified handicapped persons and affirmative efforts to overcome the disabilities caused by handicaps. Section 501 (b), governing the employment of handicapped individuals by the Federal Government, requires each federal agency to submit "an affirmative action program plan for the hiring, placement, and advancement of handicapped individuals...." These plans "shall include a description of the extent to which and methods whereby the special needs of handicapped employees are being met." Similarly, § 503 (a), governing hiring by federal contractors, requires employers to "take affirmative action to employ and advance in employment qualified handicapped individuals...." The President is required to promulgate regulations to enforce this section.

Under § 501 (c) of the Act, by contrast, state agencies such as Southeastern are only "encourage[d]...to adopt such policies and procedures." Section 504 does not refer at all to affirmative action, and except as it applies to federal employers it does not provide for implementation by administrative action. A comparison of these provisions demonstrates that Congress understood accommodation of the needs of handicapped individuals may require affirmative action and knew how to provide for it in those instances where it wished to do so.[10]

Although an agency's interpretation of the statute under which it operates is entitled to some deference, "this deference is constrained by our obligation to honor the clear meaning of a statute, as revealed by its language, purpose and history." *International Brotherhood of Teamsters v. Daniel,* 439 U.S. ____, ____ n. 20 (1979). Here neither the language, purpose, nor history of § 504 reveals an intent to impose an affirmative action obligation on all recipients of federal funds.[11] Accordingly, we hold that even if HEW has attempted to create such an obligation itself, it lacks the authority to do so.

IV

We do not suggest that the line between a lawful refusal to extend affirmative action and illegal discrimination against handicapped persons always will be clear. It is possible to envision situations where an insistence on continuing past requirements and practices might arbitrarily deprive genuinely qualified handicapped persons of the opportunity to participate in a covered program. Technological advances can be expected to enhance opportunities to rehabilitate the handicapped or otherwise to qualify them for some useful employment. Such advances also may enable attainment of these goals without imposing undue financial and administrative burdens upon a State. Thus situations may arise where a refusal to modify an existing program might become unreasonable and discriminatory. Identification of those instances where a refusal to accommodate the needs of a disabled person amounts to discrimination against the handicapped continues to be an important responsibility of HEW.

In this case, however, it is clear that Southeastern's unwillingness to make major adjustments in its nursing program does not constitute such discrimination. The uncontroverted testimony of several members of Southeastern's staff and faculty established that the purpose of its program was to train persons who could serve the nursing profession in all customary ways. See, *e.g.,* App. 35a, 52a, 53a, 71a, 74a. This type of purpose, far from reflecting any animus against handicapped individuals, is shared by many if not most of the institutions that train persons to render professional service. It is undisputed that respondent could not participate in Southeastern's nursing program unless the standards were substantially lowered. Section 504 imposes no requirement upon an educational institution to lower or to effect substantial modifications of standards to accommodate a handicapped person.[12]

One may admire respondent's desire and determination to overcome her handicap and there well may be various other types of service for which she can qualify. In this case, however, we hold that there was no violation of § 504 when Southeastern concluded that respondent did not qualify for admission to its program. Nothing in the language or history of § 504 reflects an intention to limit the freedom of an educational institution to require reasonable physical qualifications for admission to a clinical training program. Nor has there been any showing in this case that any action short of a substantial change in Southeastern's program would render unreasonable the qualifications it imposed.

V

Accordingly, we reverse the judgment of the court below, and remand for proceedings consistent with this opinion.

So ordered.

NOTES

1. McRee also wrote that respondent's hearing disability could preclude her practicing safely in "any setting" allowed by "a license as L[icensed] P[ractical] N[urse]." App. 132a. Respondent contends that inasmuch as she already was licensed as a practical nurse, McRee's opinion was inherently incredible. But the record indicates that respondent had "not worked as a practical nurse except to do a little bit of night duty," App. 32a, and had not done that for several years before applying to Southeastern. Accordingly, it is at least possible to infer that respondent in fact could not work safely as a practical nurse in spite of her license to do so. In any event, we note the finding of the District Court that "a Licensed Practical Nurse, unlike a Licensed Registered Nurse, operates under constant supervision and is not allowed to perform medical tasks which require a great degree of technical sophistication." 424 F. Supp., 1341, 1342-1343 (EDNC 1976).

2. The statute provides in full:"No otherwise qualified handicapped individual in the United States, as defined in section 706 (6) of this title, shall, solely by reason of his handicap, be excluded from the participation in, or be denied the benefits of, or be subjected to discrimination under any program or activity receiving Federal financial assistance *or under any program or activity conducted by any Executive agency or by the United States Postal Service. The head of each such agency shall promulgate such regulations as may be necessary to carry out the amendments to this section made by the Rehabilitation, Comprehensive Services, and Developmental Disabilities Act of 1978. Copies of any proposed regulation shall be submitted to appropriate authorizing committees of the Congress, and such regulation may take effect no earlier than the thirtieth day after the date on which such regulation is so submitted to such committees.'* The italicized portion of the section was added by § 119 of the Rehabilitation, Comprehensive Services, and Developmental Disabilities Act of 1978, 92 Stat. 2982. Respondent asserts no claim under this portion of the statute.

3. The District Court also dismissed respondent's constitutional claims. The Court of Appeals affirmed that portion of the order, and respondent has not sought review of this ruling.

4. Relying on the plain language of the Act, the Department of Health, Education, and Welfare (HEW) at first did not promulgate any regulations to implement § 504. In a subsequent suit against HEW, however, the United States District Court for the District of Columbia held that Congress had intended regulations to be issued and ordered HEW to do so. *Cherry* v. *Mathews,* 419 F. Supp. 922 (1976). The ensuing regulations currently are embodied in 45 CFR pt. 84.

5. In addition to challenging the construction of § 504 by the Court of Appeals, Southeastern also contends that respondent cannot seek judicial relief for violations of that statute in view of the absence of any express private right of action. Respondent asserts that whether or not § 504 provides a private action, she may maintain her suit under 42 U.S.C. § 1983. In light of our disposition of this case on the merits, it is unnecessary to address these issues and we express no views on them. See *Norton* v. *Mathews,* 427 U.S. 524, 529-531 (1976); *Moor* v. *County of Alameda,* 411 U.S. 693, 715 (1973); *United States* v. *Augenblick,* 393 U.S. 348, 351-352 (1969).

6. The Act defines "handicapped individual" as follows:"The term 'handicapped individual' means any individual who (A) has a physical or mental disability which for such individual constitutes or results in a substantial handicap to employment and (B) can reasonably be expected to benefit in terms of employability from vocational rehabilitation services provided pursuant to subchapters I and III of this chapter. For the purposes of subchapters IV and V of this chapter, such term means any person who (A) has a physical or mental impairment which substantially limits one or more of such person's major life activities, (B) has a a record of such an impairment, or (C) is regarded as having such an impairment." Section 7 of the Rehabilitation Act of 1973, 87 Stat. 359, as amended, 88 Stat. 1619, 89 Stat. 2, 29 U.S.C. § 706 (6).This definition comports with our understanding of § 504. A person who has a record of or is regarded as having an impairment may at present have no actual incapacity at all. Such a person would be exactly the kind of individual who could be "otherwise qualified" to participate in covered programs. And a person who suffers from a limiting physical or mental impairment still may possess other abilities that permit him to meet the requirements of various programs. Thus it is clear that Congress included among the class of "handicapped" persons covered by § 504 a range of individuals who could be "otherwise qualified." See S. Rep. No. 1297, 93d Cong., 2d Sess., 38-39 (1974).

7. The note states:"Paragraph (k) of § 84.3 defines the term 'qualified handicapped person.' Throughout the regulation, this term is used instead of the statutory term 'otherwise qualified handicapped person.' The Department believes that the omission of the word 'otherwise' is necessary in order to comport with the intent of the statute because, read literally, 'otherwise' qualified handicapped persons include persons who are qualified except for their handicap, rather than in spite of their handicap. Under such a literal reading, a blind person possessing all the qualifications for driving a bus except sight could be said to be 'otherwise qualified' for the job of driving. Clearly, such a result was not intended by Congress. In all other respects, the terms 'qualified' and 'otherwise qualified' are intended to be interchangeable." 45 CFR pt. 84, App. A, at p.405.

8. The court below adopted a portion of this argument: "[Respondent's] ability to read lips aids her in overcoming her hearing disability; however, it was argued that in certain situations such as in an operating room environment where surgical masks are used, this ability would be unavailing to her. "Be that as it may, in the medical community, there does appear to be a number of settings in which the plaintiff could perform satisfactorily as an RN, such as in industry or perhaps a physician's office. Certainly [respondent] could be viewed as possessing extraordinary insight into the medical and emotional needs of those with hearing disabilities. "If [respondent] meets all the other criteria for admission in the pursuit of her RN career, under the relevant North Carolina statutes, N.C. Gen. Stat. §§ 90-158, *et seq.*, it should not be foreclosed to her simply because she may not be able to function effectively in all the roles which registered nurses may choose for their careers." 574 F. 2d 1158, 1161 n. 6 (CA4 1978).

9. This regulation provides in full:"(a) *Academic requirements.* A recipient [of federal funds] to which this subpart applies shall make such modifications to its academic requirements as are necessary to ensure that such requirements do not discriminate or have the effect of discriminating, on the basis of handicap, against a qualified handicapped applicant or student. Academic requirements that the recipient can demonstrate are essential to the program of instruction being pursued by such student or to any directly related licensing requirement will not be regarded as discriminatory within the meaning of this section. Modifications may include changes in the length of time permitted for the completion of degree requirements, substitution of specific courses required for the completion of degree requirements, and adaptations of the manner in which specific courses are conducted. "(d) *Auxiliary aids.* (1) A recipient to which this subpart applies shall take such steps as are necessary to ensure that no handicapped student is denied the benefits of, excluded from participation in, or

otherwise subjected to discrimination under the education program or activity operated by the recipient because of the absence of educational auxiliary aids for students with impaired sensory, manual, or speaking skills. "(2) Auxiliary aids may include taped texts, interpreters or other effective methods of making orally delivered materials available to students with hearing impairments, readers in libraries for students with visual impairments, classroom equipment adapted for use by students with manual impairments, and other similar services and actions. Recipients need not provide attendants, individually prescribed devices, readers for personal use or study, or other devices or services of a personal nature." 45 CFR § 84.44.

10. § 115(a) of the Rehabilitation Act of 1978 added to the 1973 Act a section authorizing grants to state units for the purpose of providing "such information and technical assistance (including support personnel such as interpreters for the deaf) as may be necessary to assist those entities in complying with this Act, particularly the requirements of § 504." 92 Stat. 2971, codified at 29 U.S.C. § 775. This provision recognizes that on occasion the elimination of discrimination might involve some costs; it does not imply that the refusal to undertake substantial changes in a program by itself constitutes discrimination. Whatever effect the availability of these funds might have on ascertaining the existence of discrimination in some future case, no such funds were available to Southeastern at the time respondent sought admission to its nursing program.

11. The Government, in a brief *amicus curiae* in support of respondent, cites a report of the Senate Committee on Labor and Public Welfare on the 1974 amendments to the 1973 Act and several statements by individual Members of Congress during debate on the 1978 amendments, some of which indicate a belief that § 504 requires affirmative action. See Brief for the Government as *Amicus Curiae* 44-50. But these isolated statements by individual Members of Congress or its committees, all made after the enactment of the statute under consideration, cannot substitute for a clear expression of legislative intent at the time of enactment. *Quern* v. *Mandley,* 436 U.S. 725, 736 n. 10 (1978); *Los Angeles Dept. of Water & Power* v. *Manhart,* 435 U.S. 702, 714 (1978). Nor do these comments, none of which represents the will of Congress as a whole, constitute subsequent "legislation" such as this Court might weigh in construing the meaning of an earlier enactment. Cf. *Red Lion Broadcasting Co.* v. *FCC,* 395 U.S. 367, 380-381 (1969). The Government also argues that various amendments to the 1973 Act contained in the Rehabilitation Act of 1978 further reflect Congress' approval of the affirmative action obligation created by HEW's regulations. But the amendment most directly on point undercuts this position. In amending § 504, Congress both extended that section's prohibition of discrimination to "any program or activity conducted by any Executive agency or by the United Postal Service" and authorized administrative regulations to implement only *this amendment.* See n. 2, *supra.* The fact that no other regulations were mentioned supports an inference that no others were approved. Finally, we note that the assertion by HEW of the authority to promulgate any regulations under § 504 has been neither consistent nor long-standing. For the first three years after the section was enacted, HEW maintained the position that Congress had not intended any regulations to be issued. It altered its stand only after having been enjoined to do so. See n. 4, *supra.* This fact substantially diminishes the deference to be given to HEW's present interpretation of the statute. See *General Electric Co.* v. *Gilbert,* 429 U.S. 125, 143 (1976).

12. Respondent contends that it is unclear whether North Carolina law requires a registered nurse to be capable of performing all functions open to that profession in order to obtain a license to practice, although McRee, the Executive Director of the state Board of Nursing, had informed Southeastern that the law did so require. See App. 138a-139a. Respondent further argues that even if she is not capable of meeting North Carolina's present licensing requirements, she still might succeed in obtaining a license in another jurisdiction. Respondent's argument misses the point. Southeastern's program, structured to train persons who will be able to perform all normal roles of

a registered nurse, represents a legitimate academic policy and is accepted by the State. In effect it seeks to ensure that no graduate will pose a danger to the public in any professional role he or she might be cast. Even if the licensing requirements of North Carolina or some other State are less demanding, nothing in the Act requires an educational institution to lower its standards.

APPENDIX C

BOARD V. ROWLEY

(excerpts from Court's majority opinion only; concurring and dissenting opinions are omitted, as are some footnotes from the majority opinion)

BOARD OF EDUCATION OF THE HENDRICK HUDSON CENTRAL SCHOOL
DISTRICT BD. OF ED., WESTCHESTER COUNTY, ET AL., PETITIONERS
v.
AMY ROWLEY, BY HER PARENTS AND NATURAL GUARDIANS,
CLIFFORD AND NANCY ROWLEY, ETC.

Justice Rehnquist delivered the opinion of the court.

I

The Education for All Handicapped Children Act of 1975 (Act), 20 U.S.C. § 1401 *et seq.*, provides federal money to assist state and local agencies in educating handicapped children, and conditions such funding upon a State's compliance with extensive goals and procedures. The Act represents an ambitious federal effort to promote the education of handicapped children, and was passed in response to Congress' perception that a majority of handicapped children in the United States "were either totally excluded from schools or [were] sitting idly in regular classrooms awaiting the time when they were old enough to 'drop out.' " H.R. Rep. No. 94-332, p. 2 (1975). The Act's evolution and major provisions shed light on the questions of statutory interpretation which is at the heart of this case.

Congress first addressed the problem of educating the handicapped in 1966 when it amended the Elementary and Secondary Education Act of 1965 to establish a grant program "for the purpose of assisting the States in the initiation, expansion, and improvement of programs and projects ... for the education of handicapped children." Pub. L. No. 89-750, § 161, 80 Stat. 1204 (1966). That program was repealed in 1970 by the Education for the Handicapped Act, Pub. L. No. 91-230, 84 Stat. 175, Part B of which established a grant program similar in purpose to the repealed legislation. Neither the 1966 nor the 1970 legislation contained specific guidelines for state use of the grant money; both were aimed primarily at stimulating the States to develop educational resources and to train personnel for educating the handicapped.[1]

Dissatisfied with the progress being made under these earlier enactments, and spurred by two district court decisions holding that handicapped children should be given access to a public education,[2] Congress in 1974 greatly increased federal funding for education of the handicapped and for the first time required recipient States to adopt "a goal of providing full educational opportunities to all handicapped children." Pub. L. 93-380, 88 Stat. 579, 583 (1974) (the 1974 statute). The 1974 statute was recognized as an interim measure only, adopted "in order to give the Congress an additional year in which to study what if any additional Federal assistance [was] required to enable the States to meet the needs of handicapped children." H.R. Rep. No. 94-332, *supra,* p. 4. The ensuing year of study produced the Education for All Handicapped Children Act of 1975.

In order to qualify for federal financial assistance under the Act, a State must demonstrate that it "has in effect a policy that assures all handicapped children the right to a free appropriate public education." 20 U.S.C. § 1412(1). That policy must be reflected in a state plan submitted to and approved by the Commissioner of Education,[3] § 1413, which describes in detail the goals, programs, and timetables under which the State intends to educate handicapped children within its borders. §§ 1412, 1413. States receiving money under the Act must provide education to the handicapped by priority, first "to handicapped children who are not receiving an education" and second "to handicapped children ... with the most severe handicaps who are receiving an inadequate education," § 1412(3), and "to the maximum extent appropriate" must educate handicapped children "with children who are not handicapped." § 1412(5).[4] The Act broadly defines "handicapped children" to include "mentally retarded, hard of hearing, deaf, speech impaired, visually handicapped, seriously emotionally disturbed, orthopedically impaired, [and] other health impaired children, [and] children with specific learning disabilities." § 1401(1).[5]

The "free appropriate public education" required by the Act is tailored to the unique needs of the handicapped child by means of an "individualized educational program" (IEP). § 1401(18). The IEP, which is prepared at a meeting between a qualified representative of the local educational agency, the child's teacher, the child's parents or guardian, and, where appropriate, the child, consists of a written document containing

> "(A) a statement of the present levels of educational performance of the child, (B) a statement of annual goals, including short-term instructional objectives, (C) a statement of the specific educational services to be provided to such child, and the extent to which such child will be able to participate in regular educational programs, (D) the projected date for initiation and anticipated duration of such service, and (E) appropriate objective criteria and evaluation procedures and schedules for determining, on at least an annual basis, whether instructional objectives are being achieved." § 1401(19).

Local or regional educational agencies must review, and where appropriate revise, each child's IEP at least annually. § 1404(a)(5). See also §§ 1413(a)(11), 1414(a)(5).

In addition to the state plan and the IEP already described, the Act imposes extensive procedural requirements upon States receiving federal funds under its provisions. Parents or guardians of handicapped children must be notified of any proposed change in the "identification, evaluation, or educational placement of the children of the provision of a free appropriate public education to the child," and must be permitted to bring a complaint about "any matter relating to" such evaluation and education. § 1415(b)(1)(D) and (E).[6] Complaints brought by parents or guardians must be resolved at "an impartial due process hearing," and appeal to the State educational agency must be provided if the initial hearing is held at the local or regional level. § 1415(b)(2) and (c).[7] Thereafter, "[a]ny party aggrieved by the findings and decisions" of the state administrative hearing has "the right to bring a civil action with respect to the complaint ... in any State court of competent jurisdiction or in a district court of the United States without regard to the amount in controversy." § 1415(e)(2).

Thus, although the Act leaves to the States the primary responsibility for developing and executing educational programs for handicapped children, it imposes significant requirements to be followed in the discharge of that responsibility. ...

II

This case arose in connection with the education of Amy Rowley, a deaf student at the Furnace Woods School in the Hendrick Hudson Central School District, Peekskill, New York. Amy has minimal residual hearing and is an excellent lipreader. During the year before she began attending Furnace Woods, a meeting between her parents and school administrators resulted in a decision to place her in a regular kindergarten class in order to determine what supplemental services would be necessary to her education. Several members of the school administration prepared for Amy's arrival by attending a course in sign-language interpretation, and a teletype machine was installed in the principal's office to facilitate communication with her parents who are also deaf. At the end of the trial period it was determined that Amy should remain in the kindergarten class, but that she should be provided with an FM hearing aid which would amplify words spoken into a wireless receiver by the teacher or fellow students during certain classroom activities. Amy successfully completed her kindergarten year.

As required by the Act, an IEP was prepared for Amy during the fall of her first-grade year. The IEP provided that Amy should be educated in a regular classroom at Furnace Woods, should continue to use the FM hearing aid, and should receive instruction from a tutor for the deaf for one hour each day and from a speech therapist for three hours each week. The Rowleys agreed with the IEP but insisted that Amy also be provided a qualified sign-language interpreter in all of her academic classes. Such an interpreter had been placed in Amy's kindergarten class for a two-week experimental period, but the interpreter had reported that Amy did not need his services at that time. The school administrators likewise concluded that Amy did not need such an interpreter in her first-grade classroom. They reached this conclusion after consulting the school district's Committee on the Handicapped, which had received expert evidence from Amy's parents on the importance of a sign-language interpreter, received testimony from Amy's teacher and other persons familiar with her academic and social progress, and visited a class for the deaf.

When their request for an interpreter was denied, the Rowleys demanded and received a hearing before an independent examiner. After receiving evidence from both sides, the examiner agreed with the administrators' determination that an interpreter was not necessary because "Amy was achieving educationally, academically, and socially" without such assistance. App. to Pet. for Cert. F-22. The examiner's decision was affirmed on appeal by the New York Commissioner of Education on the basis of substantial evidence in the record. ... Pursuant to the Act's provision for judicial review, the Rowleys then brought an action in the United States District Court for the Southern District of New York, claiming that the administrators' denial of the sign-language interpreter constituted a denial of the "free appropriate public education" guaranteed by the Act.

The District Court found that Amy "is a remarkably well-adjusted child" who interacts and communicates well with her classmates and has "developed an extraordinary rapport" with her teachers. 483 F. Supp. 528, 531. It also found that "she performs better than the average child in her class and is advancing easily from grade to grade," *id.*, at 534, but "that she understands considerably less of what goes on in class than she would if she were not deaf" and thus "is not learning as much, or performing as well academically, as she would without her handicap," *id.*, at 532. This disparity between Amy's achievement and her potential led the court to decide that she was not receiving a "free appropriate public education," which the court defined as "an opportunity to achieve [her] full potential commensurate with the opportunity provided to other children." *Id.*, at 534. According to the District Court, such a standard "requires that the potential of the handicapped child be measured and compared to his or her performance, and that the remaining differential or 'shortfall' be compared to the shortfall experienced by nonhandicapped children." *Ibid.* The District Court's definition arose from its assumption that the responsibility for "giv[ing] content to the requirement of an 'appropriate education'" had "been left entirely to the federal courts and the hearing officer." *Id.*, at 533.[8]

A divided panel of the United States Court of Appeals for the Second Circuit affirmed. The Court of Appeals "agree[d] with the [D]istrict [C]ourt's conclusions of law," and held that its "findings of fact [were] not clearly erroneous." 632 F. 2d 945, 947 (1980).

We granted certiorari to review the lower courts' interpretation of the Act. 454 U.S.— 1981. Such review requires us to consider two questions: What is meant by the Act's requirement of a "free appropriate public education?" And what is the role of state and federal courts in exercising the review granted by §1415 of the Act? We consider these questions separately.[9]

III

A

This is the first case in which this Court has been called upon to interpret any provision of the Act. As noted previously, the District Court and the Court of Appeals concluded that "[t]he Act itself does not define 'appropriate education,'" 483 F. Supp., at 533, but leaves "to the courts and the hearing officers" the responsibility of "giv[ing] content to the requirement of an appropriate education." *Ibid.* See also 632 F. 2d, at 947. Petitioners contend that the definition of the phrase "free appropriate public education" used by the courts below overlooks the definition of that phrase actually found in the Act. Respondents agree that the Act defines "free appropriate public education," but contend that the statutory definition is not "functional" and thus "offers judges no guidance in their consideration of controversies involving the 'identification, evaluation, or educational placement of the child or the provision of a free appropriate public education.' " Brief for Respondents 28. The United States, appearing as *amicus curiae* on behalf of the respondents, states that "[a]lthough the Act includes definitions of 'free appropriate public education' and other related terms, the statutory definitions do not adequately explain what is meant by 'appropriate.' " Brief for United States as *Amicus Curiae* 13.

We are loath to conclude that Congress failed to offer any assistance in defining the meaning of the principal substantive phrase used in the Act. It is beyond dispute that, contrary to the conclusions of the courts below, the Act does expressly define "free appropriate public education":

> "The term 'free appropriate public education' means *special education* and *related services* which (A) have been provided at public expense, under public supervision and direction, and without charge, (B) meet the standards of the State educational agency, (C) include an appropriate preschool, elementary, or secondary school education in the State involved, and (D) are provided in conformity with the individualized education program required under section 1414(a)(5) of this title." § 1401(18) (emphasis added).

"Special education," as referred to in this definition, means "specially designed instruction, at no cost to parents or guardians, to meet the unique needs of a handicapped child, including classroom instruction, instruction in physical education, home instruction, and instruction in hospitals and institutions." § 1401(16). "Related services" are defined as "transportation, and such developmental, corrective, and other supportive services ... as may be required to assist a handicapped child to benefit from special education." § 1401(17).[10]

Like many statutory definitions, this one tends toward the cryptic rather than the comprehensive, but that is scarcely a reason for abandoning the quest for legislative intent. Whether or not the definition is a "functional" one, as respondents contend it is not, it is the principal tool which Congress has given us for parsing the critical phrase of the Act. We think more must be made of it than either respondents or the United States seems willing to admit.

According to the definitions contained in the Act, a "free appropriate public education" consists of educational instruction specially designed to meet the unique needs of the handicapped child, supported by such services as are necessary to permit the child "to benefit" from the instruction. Almost as a checklist for adequacy under the Act, the definition also requires that such instruction and services be provided at public expense and under public supervision, meet the State's educational standards, approximate the grade levels used in the State's regular education, and comport with the child's IEP. Thus, if personalized instruction is being provided with sufficient supportive services to permit the child to benefit from the instruction, and the other items on the definitional checklist are satisfied, the child is receiving a "free appropriate public education" as defined by the Act.

Other portions of the statute also shed light upon congressional intent. Congress found that of the roughly eight million handicapped children in the United States at the time of enactment, one million were "excluded entirely from the public school system" and more than half were receiving an inappropriate education. Note to §1401. In addition, as mentioned in Part I, the Act requires States to extend educational services first to those children who are receiving no education and second to those children who are receiving an "inadequate education." § 1412(3). When these express statutory findings and priorities are read together with the Act's extensive procedural requirements and its definition of "free appropriate public education," the face of the statute evinces a congressional intent to bring previously excluded handicapped children into the public education systems of the States and to require the States to adopt *procedures* which would result in individualized consideration of and instruction for each child.

Noticeably absent from the language of the statute is any substantive standard prescribing the level of education to be accorded handicapped children. Certainly the language of the statute contains no requirement like the one imposed by the lower courts— that States maximize the potential of handicapped children "commensurate with the opportunity provided to other children." 483 F. Supp., at 534. That standard was expounded by the District Court without reference to the statutory definitions or even to the legislative history of the Act. Although we find the statutory definition of "free appropriate public education" to be helpful in our interpretation of the Act, there remains the question of whether the legislative history indicates a congressional intent that such education meet some additional substantive standard. For an answer, we turn to that history.[11]

B

(i). As suggested in Part I, federal support for education of the handicapped is a fairly recent development. Before passage of the Act some States had passed laws to improve the educational services afforded handicapped children,[12] but many of these children were excluded completely from any form of public education or were left to fend for themselves in classrooms designed for education of their nonhandicapped peers. The House Report begins by emphasizing this exclusion and misplacement, noting that millions of handicapped children "were either totally excluded from schools or [were] sitting idly in regular classrooms awaiting the time when they were old enough to 'drop out.'" H.R. Rep. No. 94-332, *supra,* at 2. See also S. Rep. No. 94-168, p. 8 (1975). One of the Act's two principal sponsors in the Senate urged its passage in similar terms:

> "While much progress has been made in the last few years, we can take no solace in that progress until all handicapped children are, in fact, receiving an education. The most recent statistics provided by the Bureau of Education for the Handicapped estimate that ... 1.75 million handicapped children do not receive any educational services, and 2.5 million handicapped children are not receiving an appropriate education." 121 Cong. Rec. 19486 (1975) (remarks of Sen. Williams).

This concern, stressed repeatedly throughout the legislative history,[13] confirms the impression conveyed by the language of the statute: By passing the Act, Congress sought primarily to make public education available to handicapped children. But in seeking to provide such access to public education, Congress did not impose upon the States any greater substantive educational standard than would be necessary to make such access meaningful. Indeed, Congress expressly "recognize[d] that in many instances the process of providing special education and related services to handicapped children is not guaranteed to produce any particular outcome." S. Rep. No. 94-168, *supra,* at 11. Thus, the intent of the Act was more to open the door of public education to handicapped children on appropriate terms than to guarantee any particular level of education once inside.

Both the House and the Senate reports attribute the impetus for the Act and its predecessors to two federal court judgments rendered in 1971 and 1972. As the Senate Report states, passage of the Act "followed a series of landmark court cases establishing in law the right to education for all handicapped children." ...

Mills and *PARC* both held that handicapped children must be given *access* to an adequate, publicly supported education. Neither case purports to require any particular substantive level of education.[15] Rather, like the language of the Act, the cases set forth extensive procedures to be followed in formulating personalized educational programs for handicapped children. See 348 F. Supp., at 878-883; 334 F. Supp., at 1258-1267.[16] The fact that both *PARC* and *Mills* are discussed at length in the legislative reports[17] suggests that the principles which they established are the principles which, to a significant extent, guided the drafters of the Act. Indeed, immediately after discussing these cases the Senate Report describes the 1974 statute as having "incorporated the major principles of the right to education cases." S. Rep. No. 94-168, *supra,* at 8. Those principles in turn became the bases of the Act, which itself was designed to effectuate the purposes of the 1974 statute. H.R. Rep. No. 94-332, *supra,* at 5.[18]

That the Act imposes no clear obligation upon recipient States beyond the requirement that handicapped children receive some form of specialized education is perhaps best demonstrated by the fact that Congress, in explaining the need for the Act, equated an "appropriate education" to the receipt of some specialized educational services. ...

It is evident from the legislative history that the characterization of handicapped children as "served" referred to children who were receiving some form of specialized educational services from the States, and that the characterization of children as "unserved" referred to those who were receiving no specialized educational services. ... By characterizing the 3.9 million handicapped children who were "served" as children who were "receiving an appropriate education," the Senate and House reports unmistakably disclose Congress' perception of the type of education required by the Act: an "appropriate education" is provided when personalized educational services are provided.[21]

(ii). Respondents contend that "the goal of the Act is to provide each handicapped child with an equal educational opportunity." Brief for Respondents 35. We think, however, that the requirement that a State provide specialized educational services to handicapped children generates no additional requirement that the services so provided be sufficient to maximize each child's potential "commensurate with the opportunity provided other children." Respondents and the United States correctly note that Congress sought "to provide assistance to the States in carrying out their responsibilities under ... the Constitution of the United States to provide equal protection of the laws." S. Rep. No. 94-168, *supra,* at 13.[22] But we do not think that such statements imply a congressional intent to achieve strict equality of opportunity or services.

The educational opportunities provided by our public school systems undoubtedly differ from student to student, depending upon a myriad of factors that might affect a particular student's ability to assimilate information presented in the classroom. The requirement that States provide "equal" educational opportunities would thus seem to present an entirely unworkable standard requiring impossible measurements and comparisons. Similarly, furnishing handicapped children with only such services as are available to nonhandicapped children would in all probability fall short of the statutory requirement of "free appropriate public education"; to require, on the other hand, the furnishing of every special service necessary to maximize each handicapped child's potential is, we think, further than Congress intended to go. Thus to speak in terms of "equal" services in one instance gives less than what is required by the Act and in another instance more. The theme of the Act is "free appropriate public education," a phrase which is too complex to be captured by the word "equal" whether one is speaking of opportunities or services.

The legislative conception of the requirements of equal protection was undoubtedly informed by the two district court decisions referred to above. But cases such as *Mills* and *PARC* held simply that handicapped children may not be excluded entirely from public education. ... The right of access to free public education enunciated by these cases is significantly different from any notion of absolute equality of opportunity regardless of capacity. To the extent that Congress might have looked further than these cases which are mentioned in the legislative history, at the time of enactment of the Act this Court had held at least twice that the Equal Protection Clause of the Fourteenth Amendment does not require States to expend equal financial resources on the education of each child. *San Antonio School District v. Rodriguez*, 411 U.S. 1 (1975); *McInnis v. Shapiro*, 293 F. Supp. 327 (ND Ill. 1968), *aff'd sub nom, McInnis v. Ogilvie*, 394 U.S. 322 (1969).

In explaining the need for federal legislation, the House Report noted that "no congressional legislation has required a precise guarantee for handicapped children, i.e. a basic floor of opportunity that would bring into compliance all school districts with the constitutional right of equal protection with respect to handicapped children." H.R. Rep. No. 94-332, *supra*, at 14. Assuming that the Act was designed to fill the need identified in the House Report—that is, to provide a "basic floor of opportunity" consistent with equal protection—neither the Act nor its history persuasively demonstrates that Congress thought that equal protection required anything more than equal access. Therefore, Congress' desire to provide specialized educational services, even in furtherance of "equality," cannot be read as imposing any particular substantive educational standard upon the States.

The District Court and the Court of Appeals thus erred when they held that the Act requires New York to maximize the potential of each handicapped child commensurate with the opportunity provided nonhandicapped children. Desirable though that goal might be, it is not the standard that Congress imposed upon States which receive funding under the Act. Rather, Congress sought primarily to identify and evaluate handicapped children, and to provide them with access to a free public education.

(iii). Implicit in the congressional purpose of providing access to a "free appropriate public education" is the requirement that the education to which access is provided be sufficient to confer some educational benefit upon the handicapped child. It would do little good for Congress to spend millions of dollars in providing access to a public education only to have the handicapped child receive no benefit from that education. The statutory definition of "free appropriate public education," in addition to requiring that States provide each child with "specially designed instruction," expressly requires the provision of "such ... supportive services ... as may be required to assist a handicapped child *to benefit* from special education." § 1401(17) (emphasis added). We therefore conclude that the "basic floor of opportunity" provided by the Act consists of access to specialized instruction and related services which are individually designed to provide educational benefit to the handicapped child.[23]

The determination of when handicapped children are receiving sufficient educational benefits to satisfy the requirements of the Act presents a more difficult problem. The Act requires participating States to educate a wide spectrum of handicapped children, from the marginally hearing-impaired to the profoundly retarded and palsied. It is clear that the benefits obtainable by children at one end of the spectrum will differ dramatically from those obtainable by children at the other end, with infinite variations in between. One child may have little difficulty competing successfully in an academic setting with nonhandicapped children while another child may encounter great difficulty in acquiring even the most basic of self-maintenance skills. We do not attempt today to establish any one test for determining the adequacy of educational benefits conferred upon all children covered by the Act. Because in this case we are presented with a handicapped child who is receiving substantial specialized instruction and related services, and who is performing above average in the regular classrooms of a public school system, we confine our analysis to that situation.

The Act requires participating States to educate handicapped children with nonhandicapped children whenever possible.[24] When that "mainstreaming"preference of the Act has been met and a child is being educated in the regular classrooms of a public school system, the system itself monitors the educational progress of the child. Regular examinations are administered, grades are awarded, and yearly advancement to higher grade levels is permitted for those children who attain an adequate knowledge of the course material. The grading and advancement system thus constitutes an important factor in determining educational benefit. Children who graduate from our public school systems are considered by our society to have been "educated" at least to the grade level they have completed, and access to an "education" for handicapped children is precisely what Congress sought to provide in the Act.[25]

C

When the language of the Act and its legislative history are considered together, the requirements imposed by Congress become tolerably clear. Insofar as a State is required to provide a handicapped child with a "free appropriate public education," we hold that it satisfies this requirement by providing personalized instruction with sufficient support services to permit the child to benefit educationally from that instruction. Such instruction and services must be provided at public expense, must meet the State's educational standards, must approximate the grade levels used in the State's regular education, and must comport with the child's IEP. In addition, the IEP, and therefore the personalized instruction, should be formulated in accordance with the requirements of the Act and, if the child is being educated in the regular classrooms of the public education system, should be reasonably calculated to enable the child to achieve passing marks and advance from grade to grade.[26]

D

In assuring that the requirements of the Act have been met, courts must be careful to avoid imposing their view of preferable educational methods upon the States.[29] The primary responsibility for formulating the education to be accorded a handicapped child, and for choosing the educational method most suitable to the child's needs, was left by the Act to state and local educational agencies in cooperation with the parents or guardian of the child. The Act expressly charges States with the responsibility of "acquiring and disseminating to teachers and administrators of programs for handicapped children significant information derived from educational research, demonstration, and similar projects and [of] adopting, where appropriate, promising educational practices and materials." Section 1413(a)(3). In the face of such a clear statutory directive, it seems highly unlikely that Congress intended courts to overturn a State's choice of appropriate educational theories in a proceeding conducted pursuant to § 1415(e)(2).[30]

We previously have cautioned that courts lack the "specialized knowledge and experience" necessary to resolve "persistent and difficult questions of educational policy." *San Antonio School District v. Rodriguez,* 411 U.S. 1, 42 (1973). We think that Congress shared that view when it passed the Act. As already demonstrated, Congress' intention was not that the Act displace the primacy of States in the field of education, but that States receive funds to assist them in extending their educational systems to the handicapped. Therefore, once a court determines that the requirements of the Act have been met, questions of methodology are for resolution by the States.

V

Entrusting a child's education to state and local agencies does not leave the child without protection. Congress sought to protect individual children by providing for parental involvement in the development of State plans and policies, *supra,* at 4-5 and n. 6, and in the formulation of the child's individual educational program. As the Senate Report states:

> "The Committee recognizes that in many instances the process of providing special education and related services to handicapped children is not guaranteed to produce any particular outcome. By changing the language [of the provision relating to individualized educational programs] to emphasize the process of parent and child involvement and to provide a written record of reasonable expectations, the Committee intends to clarify that such individualized planning conferences are a way to provide parent involvement and protection to assure that appropriate services are provided to a handicapped child." S. Rep. No. 94-168, *supra,* at 11-12. See also S. Conf. Rep. No. 94-445, p. 30 (1975); 45 CFR §121a.345 (1980).

As this very case demonstrates, parents and guardians will not lack ardor in seeking to ensure that handicapped children receive all of the benefits to which they are entitled by the Act.[31]

NOTES

4. Despite this preference for "mainstreaming" handicapped children—educating them with nonhandicapped children—Congress recognized that regular classrooms simply would not be a suitable setting for the education of many handicapped children. The Act expressly acknowledges that "the nature or severity of the handicap [may be] such that education in regular classes with the use

of supplementary aids and services cannot be achieved satisfactorily." § 1412(5). The Act thus provides for the education of some handicapped children in separate classes or institutional settings. See *ibid.*; § 1413(a)(4).

6. The requirements that parents be permitted to file complaints regarding their child's education, and be present when the child's IEP is formulated, represent only two examples of Congress' effort to maximize parental involvement in the education of each handicapped child. ...

15. The only substantive standard which can be implied from these cases comports with the standard implicit in the Act. *PARC* states that each child must receive "access to a free public program of education and training *appropriate to his learning capacities*," 334 F. Supp., at 1258, and that further state action is required when it appears that "the needs of the mentally retarded child are not being *adequately* served," *id.*, at 1266. (Emphasis added.) *Mills* also speaks in terms of "adequate" educational services, 348 F. Supp., at 878, and sets a realistic standard of providing *some* educational services to each child when every need cannot be met.

21. In seeking to read more into the Act than its language or legislative history will permit, the United States focuses upon the word "appropriate," arguing that "the statutory definitions do not adequately explain what [it means]." Brief for the United States as *Amicus Curiae* 13. Whatever Congress meant by an "appropriate" education, it is clear that it did not mean a potential-maximizing education.

The term as used in reference to educating the handicapped appears to have originated in the *PARC* decision, where the District Court required that handicapped children be provided with "education and training appropriate to [their] learning capacities." 334 F. Supp., at 1258. The word appears again in the *Mills* decision, the District Court at one point referring to the need for "an appropriate educational program," 348 F. Supp., at 879, and at another point speaking of a "suitable publicly-supported education," *id.*, at 878. Both cases also refer to the need for an "adequate" education. See 334 F. Supp., at 1266; 348 F. Supp., at 878.

The use of "appropriate" in the language of the Act, although by no means definitive, suggests that Congress used the word as much to describe the settings in which handicapped children should be educated as to prescribe the substantive content or supportive services of their education. For example, § 1412(5) requires that handicapped children be educated in classrooms with nonhandicapped children "to the maximum extent appropriate." Similarly, § 1401(19) provides that, "whenever appropriate," handicapped children should attend and participate in the meeting at which their IEP is drafted. In addition, the definition of "free appropriate public education" itself states that instruction given handicapped children should be at an "appropriate preschool, elementary, or secondary school" level. § 1401(18)(C). The Act's use of the word "appropriate" thus seems to reflect Congress' recognition that some settings simply are not suitable environments for the participation of some handicapped children. At the very least, these statutory uses of the word refute the contention that Congress used "appropriate" as a term of art which concisely expresses the standard found by the lower courts.

23. This view is supported by the congressional intention, frequently expressed in the legislative history, that handicapped children be enabled to achieve a reasonable degree of self sufficiency. After referring to statistics showing that many handicapped children were excluded from public education, the Senate Report states: "The long range implications of these statistics are that public agencies and taxpayers will spend billions of dollars over the lifetimes of these individuals to maintain such persons as dependents and in a minimally acceptable lifestyle. With proper education services, many would be able to become productive citizens, contributing to society instead of being forced to remain burdens. Others, through such services, would increase their independence, thus reducing their dependence on society." S. Rep. No. 94-168, *supra*, at 9. See also H.R. Rep. No. 94-332, *supra*,

at 11. Similarly, one of the principal Senate sponsors of the Act stated that "providing appropriate educational services now means that many of these individuals will be able to become a contributing part of our society, and they will not have to depend on subsistence payments from public funds." 121 Cong. Rec. 19492 (1975) (remarks of Sen. Williams). See also 121 Cong. Rec. 25541 (1975) (remarks of Rep. Harkin); 121 Cong. Rec. 37024-37025 (1975) (remarks of Rep. Brademas); 121 Cong. Rec. 37027 (1975) (remarks of Rep. Gude); 121 Cong. Rec. 37410 (1975) (remarks of Sen. Randolph); 121 Cong. Rec. 37416 (1975) (remarks of Sen. Williams).

The desire to provide handicapped children with an attainable degree of personal independence obviously anticipated that state educational programs would confer educational benefits upon such children. But at the same time, the goal of achieving some degree of self sufficiency in most cases is a good deal more modest than the potential-maximizing goal adopted by the lower courts.

Despite its frequent mention, we cannot conclude, as did the dissent in the Court of Appeals, that self sufficiency was itself the substantive standard which Congress imposed upon the States. Because many mildly handicapped children will achieve self sufficiency without state assistance while personal independence for the severely handicapped may be an unreachable goal, "self sufficiency" as a substantive standard is at once an inadequate protection and an overly demanding requirement. We thus view these references in the legislative history as evidence of Congress' intention that the services provided handicapped children be educationally beneficial, whatever the nature or severity of their handicap.

25. We do not hold today that every handicapped child who is advancing from grade to grade in a regular public school system is automatically receiving a "free appropriate public education." In this case, however, we find Amy's academic progress, when considered with the special services and professional consideration accorded by the Furnace Woods school administrators, to be dispositive.

29. In this case, for example, both the state hearing officer and the District Court were presented with evidence as to the best method for educating the deaf, a question long debated among scholars. See Large, Special Problems of the Deaf Under the Education for All Handicapped Children Act of 1975, 58 Washington U.L.Q. 213, 229 (1980). The District Court accepted the testimony of respondents' experts that there was "a trend supported by studies showing the greater degree of success of students brought up in deaf households using [the method of communication used by the Rowleys]." 483 F. Supp., at 535.

30. It is clear that Congress was aware of the States' traditional role in the formulation and execution of educational policy. "Historically, the States have had the primary responsibility for the education of children at the elementary and secondary level." 121 Cong. Rec. 19498 (1975) (remarks of Sen. Dole). See also *Epperson v. Arkansas*, 393 U.S. 97, 104 (1968) ("[b]y and large, public education in our Nation is committed to the control of state and local authorities").

31. In addition to providing for extensive parental involvement in the formulation of state and local policies, as well as the preparation of individual educational programs, the Act ensures that States will receive the advice of experts in the field of educating handicapped children. As a condition for receiving federal funds under the Act, States must create "an advisory panel, appointed by the Governor or any other official authorized under State law to make such appointments, composed of individuals involved in or concerned with the education of handicapped children, including handicapped individuals, teachers, parents or guardians of handicapped children, State and local education officials, and administrators of programs for handicapped children, which (A) advises the State educational agency of unmet needs within the State in the education of handicapped children, [and] (B) comments publicly on any rules or regulations proposed for issuance by the State regarding the education of handicapped children." § 1413(a)(12).

APPENDIX D

IRVING ISD V. TATRO

(excerpts from the majority opinion, in which all members of the Court joined and agreed that "related services" include clean intermittent catheterization)

IRVING INDEPENDENT SCHOOL DISTRICT
v.
TATRO ET UX, INDIVIDUALLY AND AS NEXT FRIENDS OF TATRO, A MINOR

Chief Justice Burger delivered the opinion of the Court.

We granted certiorari to determine whether the Education of the Handicapped Act or the Rehabilitation Act of 1973 requires a school district to provide a handicapped child with clean intermittent catheterization during school hours.

I

Amber Tatro is an 8-year-old girl born with a defect known as spina bifida. As a result, she suffers from orthopedic and speech impairments and a neurogenic bladder, which prevents her from emptying her bladder voluntarily. Consequently, she must be catheterized every three or four hours to avoid injury to her kidneys. In accordance with accepted medical practice, clean intermittent catheterization (CIC), a procedure involving the insertion of a catheter into the urethra to drain the bladder, has been prescribed. The procedure is a simple one that may be performed in a few minutes by a layperson with less than an hour's training. Amber's parents, babysitter, and teenage brother are all qualified to administer CIC, and Amber soon will be able to perform this procedure herself.

In 1979 petitioner Irving Independent School District agreed to provide special education for Amber, who was then three and one-half years old. In consultation with her parents, who are respondents here, petitioner developed an individualized education program for Amber under the requirements of the Education of the Handicapped Act, 84 Stat. 175, as amended significantly by the Education for All Handicapped Children Act of 1975, 89 Stat. 773, 20 U.S.C. §§ 1401(19), 1414(a)(5). The individualized education program provided that Amber would attend early childhood development classes and receive special services such as physical and occupational therapy. That program, however, made no provision for school personnel to administer CIC....

This case poses two separate issues. The first is whether the Education of the Handicapped Act requires petitioner to provide CIC services to Amber. ... States receiving funds under the Act are obliged to satisfy certain conditions. A primary condition is that the state implement a policy "that assures all handicapped children the right to a free appropriate public education." 20 U.S.C. § 1412(1). Each educational agency applying to a state for funding must provide assurances in turn that its program aims to provide "a free appropriate public education to all handicapped children." § 1414(a)(1)(C)(ii).

A "free appropriate public education" is explicitly defined as "special education and related services." § 1401(18).[5] The term "special education" means

> "specially designed instruction, at no cost to parents or guardians, to meet the unique needs of a handicapped child, including classroom instruction, instruction in physical education, home instruction, and instruction in hospitals and institutions." §1401(16).

"Related services" are defined as

> "transportation, and such developmental, corrective, and other *supportive services (including* speech pathology and audiology, psychological services, physical and occupational therapy, recreation, and *medical* and counseling *services, except that such medical services shall be for diagnostic and evaluation purposes only) as may be required to assist a handicapped child to benefit from special education,* and includes the early identification and assessment of handicapping conditions in children." §1401(17) (emphasis added).

The issue in this case is whether CIC is a "related service" that petitioner is obliged to provide to Amber. We must answer two questions: first, whether CIC is a "supportive servic[e] ... required to assist a handicapped child to benefit from special education; and second, whether CIC is excluded from this definition as a "medical servic[e]" serving purposes other than diagnosis or evaluation.

A

The Court of Appeals was clearly correct in holding that CIC is a "supportive servic[e] ... required to assist a handicapped child to benefit from special education."[6] It is clear on this record that, without having CIC services available during the school day, Amber cannot attend school and thereby "benefit from special education." CIC services therefore fall squarely within the definition of a "supportive service."[7]

As we have stated before, "Congress sought primarily to make public education available to handicapped children" and "to make such access meaningful." *Board of Education of Hendrick Hudson Central School District v. Rowley,* 458 U.S. 176, 192 (1982). A service that enables a handicapped child to remain at school during the day is an important means of providing the child with the meaningful access to education that Congress envisioned. The Act makes specific provision for services, like transportation, for example, that do no more than enable a child to be physically present in class, see 20 U.S.C. § 1401(17); and the Act specifically authorizes grants for schools to alter buildings and equipment to make them accessible to the handicapped, § 1406; see S. Rep. No. 94-168, p. 38 (1975); 121 Cong. Rec. 19483-19484 (1975) (remarks of Sen. Stafford). Services like CIC that permit a child to remain at school during the day are no less related to the effort to educate than are services that enable the child to reach, enter, or exit the school.

We hold that CIC services in this case qualify as a "supportive servic[e] ... required to assist a handicapped child to benefit from special education."[8]

B

We also agree with the Court of Appeals that provision of CIC is not a "medical servic[e]," which a school is required to provide only for purposes of diagnosis or evaluation. See 20 U.S.C. §1401(17). We begin with the regulations of the Department of Education, which are entitled to deference.[9] See, *e.g., Blum v. Bacon,* 457 U.S. 132, 141 (1982). The regulations define "related services" for handicapped children to include "school health services," 34 CFR §300.13(a) (1983), which are defined in turn as "services provided by a qualified school nurse or other qualified person," §300.13(b) (10). "Medical services" are defined as "services provided by a licensed physician." §300.13(b)(4).[10] Thus, the Secretary has determined that the services of a school nurse otherwise qualifying as a "related service are not subject to exclusion as a "medical service," but that the services of a physician are excludable as such.

This definition of "medical services" is a reasonable interpretation of congressional intent. Although Congress devoted little discussion to the "medical services" exclusion, the Secretary could reasonably have concluded that it was designed to spare schools from an obligation to provide a service that might well prove unduly expensive and beyond the range of their competence.[11] From this understanding of congressional purpose, the Secretary could reasonably have concluded that Congress intended to impose the obligation to provide school nursing services.

Congress plainly required schools to hire various specially trained personnel to help handicapped children, such as "trained occupational therapists, speech therapists, psychologists, social workers and other appropriately trained personnel." S. Rep. No. 94-168, *supra,* at 33. School nurses have long been a part of the educational system, and the Secretary could therefore reasonably conclude that school nursing services are not the sort of burden that Congress intended to exclude as a "medical service." By limiting the "medical services" exclusion to the services of a physician or hospital, both far more expensive, the Secretary has given a permissible construction to the provision.

Petitioner's contrary interpretation of the "medical services" exclusion is unconvincing. In petitioner's view, CIC is a "medical service," even though it may be provided by a nurse or trained layperson; that conclusion rests on its reading of Texas law that confines CIC to uses in accordance with a physician's prescription and under a physician's ultimate supervision. Aside from conflicting with the Secretary's reasonable interpretation of congressional intent, however, such a rule would be anomalous. Nurses in petitioner's school district are authorized to dispense oral medications and administer emergency injections in accordance with a physician's prescription. This kind of service for nonhandicapped children is difficult to distinguish from the provision of CIC to the handicapped.[12] It would be strange indeed if Congress, in attempting to extend special services to handicapped children, were unwilling to guarantee them services of a kind that are routinely provided to the nonhandicapped.

To keep in perspective the obligation to provide services that relate to both the health and educational needs of handicapped students, we note several limitations that should minimize the burden petitioner fears. First, to be entitled to related services, a child must be handicapped so as to require special education. See 20 U.S.C. § 1401(1); 34 CFR § 300.5 (1983). In the absence of a handicap that requires special education, the need for what otherwise might qualify as a related service does not create an obligation under the Act. See 34 CFR § 300.14, Comment (1) (1983).

Second, only those services necessary to aid a handicapped child to benefit from special education must be provided, regardless how easily a school nurse or layperson could furnish them. For example, if a particular medication or treatment may appropriately be administered to a handicapped child other than during the school day, a school is not required to provide nursing services to administer it.

Third, the regulations state that school nursing services must be provided only if they can be performed by a nurse or other qualifed person, not if they must be performed by a physician. See 34 CFR §§ 300.13(a), (b)(4), (b)(10) (1983). It bears mentioning that here not even the services of a nurse are required; as is conceded, a layperson with minimal training is qualified to provide CIC. See also *e.g., Department of Education of Hawaii v. Katherine D.,* 727 F. 2d 809 (CA9 1983).

Finally, we note that respondents are not asking petitioner to provide *equipment* that Amber needs for CIC. Tr. of Oral Arg. 18-19. They seek only the *services* of a qualified person at the school.

We conclude that provision of CIC to Amber is not subject to exclusion as a "medical service," and we affirm the Court of Appeals' holding that CIC is a "related service" under the Education of the Handicapped Act.[13]

NOTES

10. The regulations actually define only those "medical services" that *are* owed to handicapped children: "services provided by a licensed physician to determine a child's medically related handicapping condition which results in the child's need for special education and related services." 34 CFR § 300.13(b)(4) (1983). Presumably this means that "medical services" *not* owed under the statute are those "services by a licensed physician" that serve other purposes.

11. Children with serious medical needs are still entitled to an education. For example, the Act specifically includes instruction in hospitals and at home within the definition of "special education." See 20 U.S.C. §1401(16).

12. Petitioner attempts to distinguish the administration of prescription drugs from the administration of CIC on the grounds that Texas law expressly limits the liability of school personnel performing the former, see Tex. Educ. Code Ann. §21.914(c) (Supp. 1984), but not the latter. This distinction, however, bears no relation to whether CIC is a "related service." The introduction of handicapped children into a school creates numerous new possibilties for injury and liability. Many of these risks are more serious than that posed by CIC, which the courts below found is a safe procedure even when performed by a 9-year-old girl. Congress assumed that states receiving the generous grants under the Act were up to the job of managing these new risks. Whether petitioner decides to purchase more liability insurance or to persuade the state to extend the limitation on liability, the risk posed by CIC should not prove to be a large burden.

13. We need not address respondents' claim that CIC, in addition to being a "related service," is a "supplementary ai[d] and servic[e]" that petitioner must provide to enable Amber to attend classes with nonhandicapped students under the Act's "mainstreaming" directive. See 20 U.S.C. § 1412(5)(B). Respondents have not sought an order prohibiting petitioner from educating Amber with handicapped children alone. Indeed, any request for such an order might not present a live controversy. Amber's present individualized education program provides for regular public school classes with nonhandicapped children. And petitioner has admitted that it would be far more costly to pay for Amber's instruction and CIC services at a private school, or to arrange for home tutoring, than to provide CIC at the regular public school placement provided in her current individualized education program. Tr. of Oral Arg. 12.

APPENDIX E

EHA DEFINITIONS

(taken from implementing regulations)*

Reg. 300.5   Handicapped Children

(a) As used in this part, the term "handicapped children" means those children evaluated in accordance with Regs. 300.530-300.534 as being mentally retarded, hard of hearing, deaf, speech impaired, visually handicapped, seriously emotionally disturbed, orthopedically impaired, other health impaired, deaf-blind, multi-handicapped, or as having specific learning disabilities, who because of those impairments need special education and related services.

(b) The terms used in this definition are defined as follows:

(1) "Deaf" means a hearing impairment which is so severe that the child is impaired in processing linguistic information through hearing, with or without amplification, which adversely affects educational performance.

(2) "Deaf-blind" means concomitant hearing and visual impairments, the combination of which causes such severe communication and other developmental and educational problems that they cannot be accommodated in special education programs solely for deaf or blind children.

(3) "Hard of hearing" means a hearing impairment, whether permanent or fluctuating, which adversely affects a child's educational performance but which is not included under the definition of "deaf" in this section.

*Printed here out of sequence.

(4) "Mentally retarded" means significantly subaverage general intellectual functioning existing concurrently with deficits in adaptive behavior and manifested during the developmental period, which adversely affects a child's educational performance.

(5) "Multihandicapped" means concomitant impairments (such as mentally retarded-blind, mentally retarded-orthopedically impaired, etc.), the combination of which causes such severe educational problems that they cannot be accommodated in special education programs solely for one of the impairments. The term does not include deaf-blind children.

(6) "Orthopedically impaired" means a severe orthopedic impairment which adversely affects a child's educational performance. The term includes impairments caused by congenital anomaly (e.g., clubfoot, absence of some member, etc.), impairments caused by disease (e.g., poliomyelitis, bone tuberculosis, etc.), and impairments from other causes (e.g., cerebral palsy, amputations, and fractures or burns which cause contractures).

(7) "Other health impaired" means:

(i) having an autistic condition which is manifested by severe communication and other developmental and educational problems; or

(ii) having limited strength, vitality or alertness, due to chronic or acute health problems such as a heart condition, tuberculosis, rheumatic fever, nephritis, asthma, sickle cell anemia, hemophilia, epilepsy, lead poisoning, leukemia, or diabetes, which adversely affects a child's educational performance.

(8) "Seriously emotionally disturbed" is defined as follows:

(i) The term means a condition exhibiting one or more of the following characteristics over a long period of time and to a marked degree, which adversely affects educational performance:

(A) An inability to learn which cannot be explained by intellectual, sensory, or health factors;

(B) An inability to build or maintain satisfactory interpersonal relationships with peers and teachers;

(C) Inappropriate types of behavior or feelings under normal circumstances;

(D) A general pervasive mood of unhappiness or depression; or

(E) A tendency to develop physical symptoms or fears associated with personal or school problems.

(ii) The term includes children who are schizophrenic. The term does not include children who are socially maladjusted, unless it is determined that they are seriously emotionally disturbed.

(9) "Specific learning disability" means a disorder in one or more of the basic psychological processes involved in understanding or in using language, spoken or written, which may manifest itself in an imperfect ability to listen, think, speak, read, write, spell, or to do mathematical calculations. The term includes such conditions as perceptual handicaps, brain injury, minimal brain disfunction, dyslexia, and developmental aphasia. The term does not include children who have learning problems which are primarily the result

of visual, hearing, or motor handicaps, of mental retardation, of emotional disturbance, or of environmental, cultural, or economic disadvantage.

(10) "Speech impaired" means a communication disorder such as stuttering, impaired articulation, a language impairment, or a voice impairment, which adversely affects a child's educational performance.

(11) "Visually handicapped" means a visual impairment which, even with correction, adversely affects a child's educational performance. The term includes both partially seeing and blind children.

(20 U.S.C. 1401(1), (15))

[Subparagraph (b)(9) amended in 42 Fed. Reg. 65083 (Dec. 29, 1977).]

[Subparagraphs (b)(7) and (b)(8) amended in 46 Fed. Reg. 3865 (Jan. 16, 1981).]

Reg. 300.4   Free Appropriate Public Education

As used in this part, the term "free appropriate public education" means special education and related services which:

(a) Are provided at public expense, under public supervision and direction, and without charge.

(b) Meet the standards of the State educational agency, including the requirements of this part,

(c) Include preschool, elementary school, or secondary school education in the State involved, and

(d) Are provided in conformity with an individualized education program which meets the requirements under Regs. 300.340-300.349 of Subpart C.

(20 U.S.C. 1401(18))

Reg. 300.14   Special Education

(a)(1) As used in this part, the term "special education" means specially designed instruction, at no cost to the parent, to meet the unique needs of a handicapped child, including classroom instruction, instruction in physical education, home instruction, and instruction in hospitals and institutions.

(2) The term includes speech pathology, or any other related service, if the service consists of specially designed instruction, at no cost to the parents, to meet the unique needs of a handicapped child, and is considered "special education" rather than a "related service" under State standards.

(3) The term also includes vocational education if it consists of specially designed instruction, at no cost to the parents, to meet the unique needs of a handicapped child.

(b) The terms in this definition are defined as follows:

(1) "At no cost" means that all specially designed instruction is provided without charge, but does not preclude incidental fees which are normally charged to nonhandicapped students or their parents as a part of the regular education program.

(2) "Physical education" is defined as follows:

(i) The term means the development of:

(A) Physical and motor fitness;

(B) Fundamental motor skills and patterns; and

(C) Skills in aquatics, dance, and individual and group games and sports (including intramural and lifetime sports).

(ii) The term includes special physical education, adapted physical education, movement education, and motor development. (20 U.S.C. 1401(16))

(3) "Vocational education" means organized educational programs which are directly related to the preparation of individuals for paid or unpaid employment, or for additional preparation for a career requiring other than a baccalaureate or advanced degree. (20 U.S.C. 1401(16))

Comment. (1) The definition of "special education" is a particularly important one under these regulations, since a child is not handicapped unless he or she needs special education. (See the definition of "handicapped children" in section 300.5.) The definition of "related services" (section 300.13) also depends on this definition, since a related service must be necessary for a child to benefit from special education. Therefore, if a child does not need special education, there can be no "related services," and the child (because not "handicapped") is not covered under the Act.

(2) The above definition of vocational education is taken from the Vocational Education Act of 1963, as amended by Pub. L. 94-482. Under that Act, "vocational education" includes industrial arts and consumer and homemaking education programs.

Reg. 300.13   Related Services

(a) As used in this part, the term "related services" means transportation and such developmental, corrective, and other supportive services as are required to assist a handicapped child to benefit from special education, and includes speech pathology and audiology, psychological services, physical and occupational therapy, recreation, early identification and assessment of disabilities in children, counseling services, and medical services for diagnostic or evaluation purposes. The term also includes school health services, social work services in schools, and parent counseling and training.

(b) The terms used in this definition are defined as follows:

(1) "Audiology" includes:

(i) Identification of children with hearing loss;

(ii) Determination of the range, nature, and degree of hearing loss, including referral for medical or other professional attention for the habilitation of hearing;

(iii) Provision of habilitative activities, such as language habilitation, auditory training, speech reading (lipreading), hearing evaluation, and speech conservation;

(iv) Creation and administration of programs for prevention of hearing loss;

(v) Counseling and guidance of pupils, parents, and teachers regarding hearing loss; and

(vi) Determination of the child's need for group and individual amplification, selecting and fitting an appropriate aid, and evaluating the effectiveness of amplification.

(2) "Counseling services" means services provided by qualified social workers, psychologists, guidance counselors, or other qualified personnel.

(3) "Early identification" means the implementation of a formal plan for identifying a disability as early as possible in a child's life.

(4) "Medical services" means service provided by a licensed physician to determine a child's medically related handicapping condition which results in the child's need for special education and related services.

(5) "Occupational therapy" includes:

(i) Improving, developing or restoring functions impaired or lost through illness, injury, or deprivation;

(ii) Improving ability to perform tasks for independent functioning when functions are impaired or lost; and

(iii) Preventing, through early intervention, initial or further impairment or loss of function.

(6) "Parent counseling and training" means assisting parents in understanding the special needs of their child and providing parents with information about child development.

(7) "Physical therapy" means services provided by a qualified physical therapist.

(8) "Psychological services" include:

(i) Administering psychological and educational tests, and other assessment procedures;

(ii) Interpreting assessment results;

(iii) Obtaining, integrating, and interpreting information about child behavior and conditions relating to learning.

(iv) Consulting with other staff members in planning school programs to meet the special needs of children as indicated by psychological tests, interviews, and behavioral evaluations; and

(v) Planning and managing a program of psychological services, including psychological counseling for children and parents.

(9) "Recreation" includes:

(i) Assessment of leisure function;

(ii) Therapeutic recreation services;

(iii) Recreation programs in schools and community agencies; and

(iv) Leisure education.

(10) "School health services" means services provided by a qualified school nurse or other qualified person.

(11) "Social work services in schools" include:

(i) Preparing a social or developmental history on a handicapped child;

(ii) Group and individual counseling with the child and family;

(iii) Working with those problems in a child's living situation (home, school, and community) that affect the child's adjustment in school; and

(iv) Mobilizing school and community resources to enable the child to receive maximum benefit from his or her educational program.

(12) "Speech pathology" includes:

(i) Identification of children with speech or language disorders;

(ii) Diagnosis and appraisal of specific speech or language disorders;

(iii) Referral for medical or other professional attention necessary for the habilitation of speech or language disorders;

(iv) Provisions of speech and language services for the habilitation or prevention of communicative disorders; and

(v) Counseling and guidance of parents, children, and teachers regarding speech and language disorders.

(13) "Transportation" includes:

(i) Travel to and from school and between schools,

(ii) Travel in and around school buildings, and

(iii) Specialized equipment (such as special or adapted buses, lifts, and ramps), if required to provide special transportation for a handicapped child. (20 U.S.C. 1401(17))

Comment. With respect to related services, the Senate Report states:

The Committee bill provides a definition of "related services," making clear that all such related services may not be required for each individual child and that such term includes early identification and assessment of handicapping conditions and the provision of services to minimize the effects of such conditions. (Senate Report No. 94-168, p. 12 (1975)

The list of related services is not exhaustive and may include other developmental, corrective, or supportive services (such as artistic and cultural programs, and art, music, and dance therapy), if they are required to assist a handicapped child to benefit from special education.

There are certain kinds of services which might be provided by persons from varying professional backgrounds and with a variety of operational titles, depending upon requirements in individual States. For example, counseling services might be provided by social workers, psychologists, or guidance counselors; and psychological testing might be done by qualified psychological examiners, psychometrists, or psychologists, depending upon State standards.

Each related service defined under this part may include appropriate administrative and supervisory activities that are necessary for program planning, management, and evaluation.

Reg. 300.10   Parent

As used in this part, the term "parent" means a parent, a guardian, a person acting as a parent of a child, or a surrogate parent who has been appointed in accordance with Reg. 300.514. The term does not include the State if the child is a ward of the State.
(20 U.S.C. 1415)

Comment. The term "parent" is defined to include persons acting in the place of a parent, such as a grandmother or stepparent with whom a child lives, as well as persons who are legally responsible for a child's welfare.

Reg. 300.9   Native Language

As used in this part, the term "native language" has the meaning given that term by section 703(a)(2) of the Bilingual Education Act, which provides as follows:

> The term "native language," when used with reference to a person of limited English-speaking ability, means the language normally used by that person, or in the case of a child, the language normally used by the parents of the child.

(20 U.S.C. 880b-1(a)(2); 1401(21))

Comment. Section 602(21) of the Education of the Handicapped Act states that the term "native language" has the same meaning as the definition from the Bilingual Education Act. (The term is used in the prior notice and evaluation sections under Reg. 300.505(b)(2) and Reg. 300.532(a)(1) of Subpart E.) In using the term, the Act does not prevent the following means of communication:

(1) In all direct contact with a child (including evaluation of the child), communication would be in the language normally used by the child and not that of the parents, if there is a difference between the two.

(2) If a person is deaf or blind, or has no written language, the mode of communication would be that normally used by the person (such as sign language, braille, or oral communication).

GLOSSARY

affirmed (aff'd.)   a word that indicates in a citation to a case that a higher court has agreed with the result, and usually the reasoning, of a lower court and approved the judgment of the lower court. Sometimes a higher court can affirm part of a lower court's judgment and reverse part of it, depending on the nature of the judgment.

amicus curiae   a Latin term indicating an individual or organization that is neither plaintiff nor defendant in a civil case but, because of special expertise or interest, is allowed by a court to become involved in the case as a "friend of the court." The involvement usually consists of submitting a brief (written presentation) containing supporting legal arguments and special facts to the court.

appeal   the process whereby a court of appeals reviews the record of proceedings and judgment of a lower court to determine if errors of law or fact were made which might lead to a reversal or modification of the lower court's decision. If substantial errors are not found, the lower court's decision will be affirmed. If they are, its decision will be reversed or modified.

C.F.R.   an abbreviation for *Code of Federal Regulations,* a publication of the U.S. government that contains the regulations of the executive agencies of government (e.g., U.S. Department of Education) implementing laws (statutes) passed by Congress (e.g., P.L. 94-142).

cert. den.   an abbreviation that indicates in a citation to a case that a higher court (usually, the Supreme Court) has declined to order a lower court to send the case to it for review. By contrast, *cert. granted* means the higher court has ordered a lower court to send a case to it for review.

certiorari (cert.)   a Latin term that indicates in a citation to a case that an order from an appeals court (usually, the Supreme Court) to a lower court has been entered, either requiring or declining to require the lower court to send up a case for review. The right-to-education cases decided by the U.S. Supreme Court usually go to that court on a petition (request) for *certiorari* by one of the parties (and the Court sometimes grants the request and orders the lower court to send the case to it for review).

civil case   a lawsuit brought by one or more individuals to seek redress of some legal injury (or aspect of an injury) for which there are civil (non-criminal) remedies. In right-to-education cases, these remedies are based on the federal or state constitutions, federal or state statutes, or federal or state agency regulations, or a combination of federal and state constitutions, statutes and regulations. Right-to-education cases are always civil suits.

class action   a civil case brought on behalf of the plaintiffs who are named in the suit, as well as on behalf of all other persons similarly situated, to vindicate their legally protected interests. *Mills v. D.C. Board of Education* was brought on behalf of 12-year-old Peter Mills and six other school-age children who were named in the complaint, as well as all other exceptional children in the District. By contrast, *Board v. Rowley* was not a class action lawsuit because it was brought on behalf of only one person, who sued to protect only her rights, not the rights of other people.

competing equities   a term describing a situation in which two or more people or groups of people have rights or privileges that cannot be fully satisfied without infringing on the rights or privileges of each other. For example, children with disabilities have some rights to be integrated with nondisabled children, but nondisabled children also have rights to an education that is not disrupted by children with disabilities (see chapter 6). In such a case, the competing equities of both children must be weighed against each other and a decision made by a court or other policy maker as to which claims prevail. Another way of thinking about competing equities is to ask: Whose rights or privileges are to be reduced for the benefit of other people?

complaint   a legal document submitted to the court by plaintiffs, in which they inform the court and the defendants that they are bringing a lawsuit and set out the underlying reasons for which they sue and the relief they want.

concur   a term that indicates in a citation to a case that one court agrees with the judgment of another and follows the precedent of that court's decision.

consent agreement   an out-of-court agreement reached by the parties to a suit, which is formally approved by the court. In *Pennsylvania Association for Retarded Children v. Pennsylvania*, a court entered an order that it adopted pursuant to a consent agreement between plaintiffs and defendants.

constitutional right   a legal right based on provisions of the U.S. Constitution or a state constitution. Equal protection and due process of law are the federal constitutional rights most relevant to the right to education. The Fourteenth Amendment applies to state (and therefore, local) governments and guarantees the rights of due process and equal protection. (See chapters 2 through 8.)

damages   money awarded by a court to someone who has been injured (the plaintiff), which must be paid by the one who is responsible for the injury (the defendant).

de facto   a Latin term that means, literally, "by reason of the fact." Integration by race and disability now is required by law (*de jure* integration), but may not actually occur in some schools or among some students (*de facto* segregation).

defendant   the person against whom a lawsuit is brought for redress of a violation of one or more of a plaintiff's legally protected interests.

defense   a reason cited by a defendant why a lawsuit against him or her is without merit or why he or she is not responsible for the injury or violation of rights as alleged by the plaintiff.

de jure   a Latin term that means, literally, "by law." Segregation of the schools by race or disability was required by laws of some states; thus, *de jure* segregation was enforced. Present law requires de jure integration.

dicta   a Latin term describing language in a judicial opinion that is not essential to the disposition of the case or to the court's reasoning and that is regarded as gratuitous. *Dicta* are persuasive but not binding on other courts, whereas the court's holding and reasoning are.

discovery the process by which one party to a civil suit can find out about matters relevant to the case, including information about what evidence the other side has, what witnesses will be called, and so on. Discovery devices for obtaining information include depositions and interrogatories to obtain testimony, requests for documents or other tangibles, and requests for physical or mental examinations.

due process of law a right to have any law applied by the federal or state government reasonably and with sufficient safeguards, such as hearings and notice, to ensure that an individual is dealt with fairly. Due process is guaranteed under the Fifth and Fourteenth Amendments to the federal Constitution.

EHLR an abbreviation for the works of a commercial publisher that report the opinions and judgments of many of the special education cases decided by state and federal courts in reports cited as *Education for the Handicapped Law Reporter (EHLR)*. In this book, the citation is stated in this way: *EHLR* 552:104—indicating that the report begins at section 552 of *EHLR* and at page 104. The case name precedes the *EHLR* citation, and the abbreviation of the court and date of judgment are set out in parentheses after the page reference.

Eighth Amendment the Eighth Amendment to the federal Constitution guarantees that the federal government will not impose a cruel and unusual punishment upon conviction of a crime. The amendment does not forbid the use of corporal punishment on students. It is not a factor in right-to-education cases.

en banc a Latin term referring to a situation in which a court consisting of more than one member (such as the federal appeals courts) hears a case with all of its members present at the hearing and participating in the decision. Usually, federal courts of appeals are divided into panels (or groups) of judges; a panel hears a case and normally makes the judgment of the court by itself, without participation of the other members of the court. Sometimes, however, a case is so difficult or important that all members of the court hear the case and decide the outcome. The court then sits *en banc*—all together.

equal protection of law a right not to be discriminated against for any unjustifiable reason, such as because of race or handicap. Equal protection is guaranteed under the Fourteenth Amendment. (See chapters 2 and 3)

et seq. a Latin term that means "and following" (*et* means "and"; *seq.* is an abbreviation for *sequens*, which means "following"). The phrase always follows a noun (e.g., Vol. 20, United States Code, Sections 1401 *et seq.*—hence, "and the following sections").

ex rel. a Latin term that indicates a lawsuit is brought on behalf of one person by another (e.g., the attorney general of a state may sue on behalf of an individual; thus, the case is captioned *"State of Kansas, ex rel. Jane Doe, an incompetent, v. Superintendent, State Hospital"*). The lawsuit normally is one in which the state attorney general seeks to vindicate a legal position that is favorable to the state and its citizens on behalf of a person not able to bring a lawsuit directly.

expert witness a person called to testify because he or she has a recognized competence in an area. For example, experts in the *PARC* right-to-education case had doctoral degrees in the field of special education, were authors of numerous professional publications pertaining to exceptional children, and were consultants to advisory committees on education.

F. 2d an abbreviation, in a citation to a lawsuit's reported judgment and order, that indicates that the case was decided by a federal court of appeals and is reported in a certain volume of the reports of the federal courts of appeals (shown as "Cir." for Circuit Court(s) of Appeal(s)). The volume of the reports precedes the *F. 2d (Federal Report, 2d Series)* designation; the page at which the report begins follows the *F. 2d* designation; and the identity of the court and the date of the judgment are set out in parentheses after the page number. Thus, *Smuck v. Hobson,* 408 F. 2d 175 (D.C. Cir. 1969), shows that the appellate judgment (in the case involving school classification practices of the District of Columbia Board of Education) is reported at volume 408 of the *Federal Reports, 2d Series,* beginning at page 175, and is a decision of the federal court of appeals (D.C. Circuit Court of Appeals) for the District of Columbia in 1969.

F. Supp. an abbreviation, in a citation to a lawsuit's reported judgment and order, that indicates that the case was decided by a federal trial court (a "district" court) and is reported in a certain volume of the reports of the federal trial courts. The volume of the reports precedes the *F. Supp. (Federal Supplement)* designation; the page at which the report begins follows the *F. Supp.* designation; and the identity of the court and the date of the judgment are set out in parentheses after the page. Thus, in *PARC v. Commonwealth of Pennsylvania,* 343 F. Supp. 279 (E.D. Pa. 1972), the case is reported at volume 343 of the *Federal Supplement,* beginning at page 279, and is a decision of the federal district court for the Eastern District (section) of Pennsylvania in 1972.

Fed. Reg. an abbreviation for *Federal Register,* a daily publication of Congress that contains the text of new laws and regulations and comments by members of Congress on matters of public policy.

Fifth Amendment the amendment to the federal Constitution that guarantees that the rights of life, liberty, and property will not be taken from a citizen by the federal government without due process of law. Due process guarantees apply to state and local governments under the Fourteenth Amendment.

First Amendment the amendment to the federal Constitution that guarantees free speech, assembly, worship, and petition for redress of grievances.

Fourteenth Amendment the amendment to the federal Constitution that applies to the states (not the federal government, which is bound by the first 10 amendments) and guarantees the rights of due process and equal protection to the citizens of each state.

in re a Latin term in a captioned title of a case that indicates "in the matter of" and always is followed by the name of a party to a lawsuit (e.g., *In Re: John Doe, a minor*—here, the caption/title to the lawsuit reads "in the matter of John Doe, a minor/child").

infra a Latin word in a citation to a case that indicates that the same case is referred to in a later part of the same article, chapter, book, judicial opinion, or other writing (e.g., the court may refer to the *Rowley* case, *infra,* meaning later, or, literally, within, its opinion).

injunctive relief a remedy granted by the court forbidding or requiring some action by the defendant. Injunctive relief includes temporary restraining orders and preliminary and final injunctions. The difference among these types of relief is that they are issued for varying lengths of time, at various stages of the litigation process, and on the basis of varying degrees of proof.

judgment an order by a court after a verdict has been reached. The judgment declares the relief to be granted.

on remand a reference in a citation to a case that indicates that a lower court has entered a judgment, for at least a second time, when it received the case from a higher court with a judgment and order to act in a particular way (e.g., the court's initial judgment is appealed, the appeals court enters a judgment to reverse in part and affirm in part and directs the lower court to change its original order, and the lower court then does so when the case is "on remand" to it from the higher court).

parens patriae a Latin term that means, literally, "father of the country," and that refers nowadays to the doctrine that a state may act in a paternalistic way on behalf of its citizens, especially those who are children or who are mentally disabled and therefore less effective than other people in protecting themselves. The *parens patriae* doctrine justifies compulsory education, which is regarded as beneficial to children and the state alike but, because of its benefit to children, can be required for their own good.

per curiam a Latin term in a citation to a case that refers to the judgment of a court entered "by the court" (rather than by a judge who writes the opinion for the court). *Per curiam* cases normally do not have opinions of the judges, only the court's disposition of the case (e.g., affirmed, petition denied, etc.).

P.L. an abbreviation for "Public Law," referring to a statute passed by Congress as a public law. Every public law has a number that follows the P.L. designation—thus, P.L. 94-142 refers to Public Law 142 of the 94th Congress.

plaintiff a person who brings a suit to redress a violation of one or more of his or her legal rights.

precedent a decision by a judge or court that serves as a rule or guide to support other judges in deciding future cases involving similar or analogous legal questions. In the early right-to-education cases, courts cited some famous education decisions as precedents, including *Brown v. Board of Education,* outlawing segregated schools, and *Hobson v. Hansen,* outlawing the track system in the District of Columbia. Just as *PARC* and *Mills* were cited as precedent by other courts for finding a constitutional right to education, so *Rowley* is now cited on various legal issues (see chapter 5).

private action a case brought on behalf of one or more individuals to vindicate violation of their own legally protected interests. As distinguished from a class action, where the relief applies to all persons similarly situated or within the class represented by the plaintiffs (e.g., *PARC*), any relief granted in private action applies only to those plaintiffs actually before the court (e.g., *Rowley*).

procedural right a right that relates to the process of enforcing substantive rights or to obtaining relief, such as the right to a hearing, the right to present evidence in one's defense, and the right to counsel.

quid pro quo a Latin term that literally means "something for something" and indicates an exchange of money and/or goods (e.g., a school district provides inservice training in exchange for—as a *quid pro quo* for—state aid to defray expenses).

relief a remedy for some legal wrong. Relief is requested by a plaintiff, to be granted by a court, against a defendant.

reversed (rev'd.) a word that indicates in a citation to a case that a higher court has overturned the result, and usually the reasoning, of a lower court and entered (or ordered the lower court to enter) a different judgment. Sometimes a higher court can reverse part of a lower court's judgment and affirm part of it, depending on the nature of the judgment.

settlement an out-of-court agreement among parties to a suit, which resolves some or all of the issues involved in a case.

statutory right   a right based on a statute or law passed by a unit of federal, state, or local governments (see chapter 1).

sub nom.   a Latin abbreviation in a citation to a case that indicates the case was decided by another court under a different name (*sub* meaning "under," and *nom.* being an abbreviation for the Latin word *nomine,* meaning "name").

substantive right   a right such as the right to an education, usually granted by statutes and constitutions.

supra   a Latin word in a citation to a case that indicates that the same case has been referred to in an earlier part of the same article, chapter, book, judicial opinion, or other writing. It means the opposite of *infra.*

U.S.   an abbreviation, in a citation to a decision of the U.S. Supreme Court, that indicates that a judgment of that Court is reported at a certain volume of the *United States Reports,* which contain only the judgments and other orders of the U.S. Supreme Court. The volume number precedes the *U.S.* designation, the page number follows it, and the date of judgment is set out in parentheses after the page reference.

U.S.C. (also U.S.C.A.)   an abbreviation for *United States Code,* an official publication of the United States government (or *United States Code Annotated,* a commercial publication) that contains the codified acts of Congress.

U.S.L.W.   a commercial publication that reports the judgments of various courts in *United States Law Week.* The volume of *USLW* precedes the USLW designation, and the page of the report follows it, with the identity of the court and date of judgment set out in parentheses after the page number.

vacated   an abbreviation that indicates in a citation to a case that a higher court has set aside the judgment of a lower court.

verdict   a decision by a judge or jury in favor of one side or the other in a case.

TABLE OF CASES

CASE INDEX

INDEX